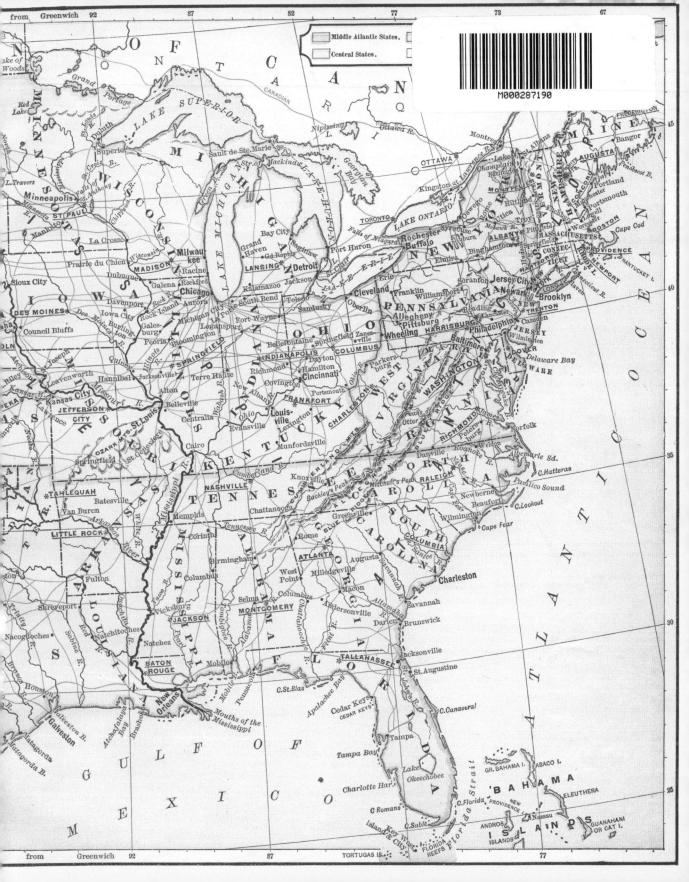

THE CURIOUS
BARTENDER'S
WHISKEY
ROAD TRIP

THE CURIOUS

BARTENDER'S

WHISKEY

ROAD TRIP

*A coast to coast tour of the most exciting
whiskey distilleries in the US, from
small-scale craft operations to the
behemoths of bourbon*

TRISTAN STEPHENSON

WITH PHOTOGRAPHY BY ADDIE CHINN

RYLAND PETERS & SMALL
LONDON • NEW YORK

Designers Leslie Harrington and Paul Stradling
Editor Nathan Joyce
Head of Production Patricia Harrington
Picture Manager Christina Borsi
Art Director Leslie Harrington
Editorial Director Julia Charles
Publisher Cindy Richards
Prop Stylist Sarianne Plaisant
Indexer Stephen Blake

First published in 2019 by
Ryland Peters & Small
20–21 Jockey's Fields
London WC1R 4BW
and
341 E 116th St
New York NY 10029

www.rylandpeters.com

10 9 8 7 6 5 4 3 2 1

ISBN: 978-1-78879-159-5

A CIP record for this book is available from
the British Library.

US Library of Congress CIP data has been
applied for.

Printed in China

CONTENTS

INTRODUCTION

This book is a journal of whiskey discovery, touring over 500 years of history and 10,000 miles of road. Each chapter marks another stage of the physical tour that myself and crack photographer Addie Chinn embarked upon, but also of whiskey's cultural journey in America: its conception, development, commercialization, and perfection. You will see how whiskey is made, learn how it is consumed, come to appreciate the craftspeople that make it, and learn a little more about the history of the United States into the bargain.

America is in the midst of a whiskey renaissance, and there may never be a better time to experience this spirit. Whiskey is a comestible embodiment of the history of the United States. In the uncertain era that we live in, its rich heritage offers a link to the past, and to simpler times. Here we encounter forgotten stories of innovation and ingenuity from the pre-Prohibition era, the Civil War, and the Revolutionary War. These historical events—and

many others—have whiskey running through them. By retelling them, we can enrich the experience of enjoying and assessing whiskey. They speak of the golden era, of frontiers, explorers, settlers, cowboys, and the Old West.

In some distilleries, these themes are combined with ecological initiatives, such as local sourcing, and environmental pursuits like carbon-neutral production and smart waste management. Other producers employ novel production methods or utilize cutting-edge flavor science.

It's for all of the above reasons that American whiskey is the fastest-growing spirit category in the world right now. It is a multifaceted drink that appeals to a wide range of consumers for very different reasons, whether it's stirred down in a cocktail or served up in a shot glass, from dive bar to hotel bar, from farmer's market to stock market.

Every journey has a first step. We take ours in Richmond, Virginia.

ROAD TRIP MAP

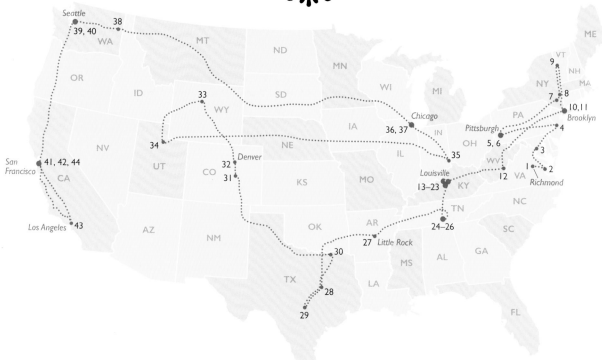

THE DISTILLERIES

1 Reservoir
Richmond, VA

2 Copper Fox
Williamsburg, VA

3 George Washington's
Distillery
Mount Vernon, VA

4 Dad's Hat
Mountain Laurel Spirits
Bristol, PA

5 Wigle
Pittsburgh, PA

6 Liberty Pole
Mingo Creek Craft
Distillers
Washington, PA

7 Tuthilltown
Gardiner, NY

8 Hillrock
Ancram, NY

9 WhistlePig
Shoreham, VT

10 New York
Distilling Company
Brooklyn, NY

11 Kings County
Brooklyn, NY

12 Smooth Ambler
Lewisburg, WV

13 Heaven Hill
Louisville, KY

14 Jim Beam
Clermont, KY

15 Woodford Reserve
Versailles, KY

16 Four Roses
Lawrenceburg, KY

17 Buffalo Trace
Frankfort, KY

18 Wild Turkey
Lawrenceburg, KY

19 Willett
Bardstown, KY

20 Barton 1792
Bardstown, KY

21 Maker's Mark
Loretto, KY

22 Brown–Forman
Louisville, KY

23 Michter's
Louisville, KY

24 Prichard's
Kelso, TN

25 Jack Daniel's
Lynchburg, TN

26 George Dickel
Tullahoma, TN

27 Rock Town
Little Rock, AR

28 Balcones
Waco, TX

29 Garrison Brothers
Hye, TX

30 Ironroot Republic
Denison, TX

31 Distillery 291
Colorado Springs, CO

32 Leopold Bros.
Denver, CO

33 Wyoming Whiskey
Kirby, WY

34 High West
Wanship, UT

35 MGP
Lawrenceburg, IN

36 Koval
Chicago, IL

37 FEW
Evanston, IL

38 Dry Fly
Spokane, WA

39 Copperworks
Seattle, WA

40 Westland
Seattle, WA

41 Hotaling & Co.
San Francisco, CA

42 St. George
Alameda, CA

43 Lost Spirits
Los Angeles, CA

44 Endless West
San Francisco, CA

The route we're driving will see us through the doors of 44 distilleries and offer a fleeting glimpse of numerous more. The distilleries we have chosen to visit were selected both because they make tasty whiskey and because they celebrate the diversity of whiskey. That could mean they're ultra modern, staunchly traditional, emphasize a particular part of the whiskey-making process, or represent some other important aspect of the category.

There are, of course, many distilleries that we won't be visiting, but to attempt to see every whiskey maker in the US would be a never-ending task, since new operations materialize on an almost weekly basis. The journey follows a roughly east to west trajectory, which matches the east to west evolutionary story of the nation itself. It also means we're visiting more traditionally motivated operations to begin with and more modern and progressive distilleries towards the end. Buckle up and grab a glass!

ROUTE MAP DETAIL—KENTUCKY

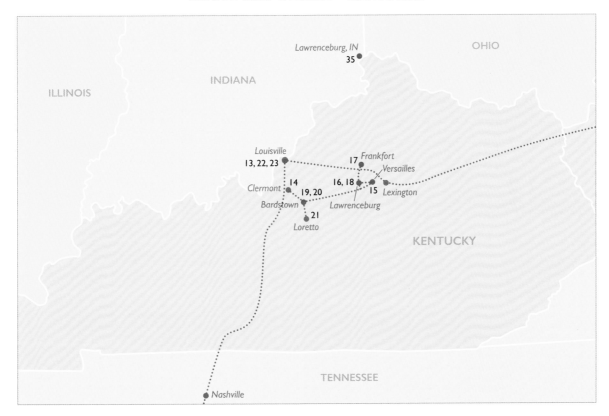

PROLOGUE: RESERVOIR

THE SPIRIT OF DISCOVERY

"In wine there is wisdom, in beer there is Freedom,
and in water there is bacteria."

BENJAMIN FRANKLIN (1706–90), POLYMATH AND FOUNDING FATHER

Richmond, Virginia, is 90 minutes south of Washington, DC. It sits on the James River, which begins at the Appalachian Mountains and flows east, down to the Chesapeake Bay, and out into the Atlantic Ocean. About 20 miles downriver from Richmond is Jamestown. Like the river, Jamestown was named after King James I, who acceded to the English throne in 1603. In 1607, Jamestown became the first English-speaking settlement in America and, if the historian William Kelso is to be believed, "where the British Empire began."

At the time, Jamestown was little more than a bug-infested swamp with a few timber cabins and a small fort. Colonists were instructed to build on land that wasn't occupied by indigenous people to avoid conflict—not that it stopped local tribes from attacking. The plan was to farm the swamp land. Unsurprisingly, many colonists starved to death. Others resorted to eating horses, cats, rats, and mice.

Ten years later, things had started to improve. Explorers like John Smith (of Pocahontas fame) ventured further up the James River and established new settlements, including Berkeley, about 10 miles southeast of where Richmond is today. Although nobody could claim to own the land where Berkeley was established (least of all the British upper classes), it was sold by the Virginia Company in London to a group of investors. A year later, on December 4, 1619, 38 settlers arrived in Berkeley aboard the *Margaret*.

No sooner had they rowed to shore than Captain Woodlief instructed his men kneel and pray: "We ordaine [sic] that this day of our ships arrival, at the place assigned for plantacon [sic], in the land of Virginia, shall be yearly and perpetually kept holy as a day of Thanksgiving to Almighty God." And that's how Thanksgiving began.

In March of 1620, one of the Berkeley investors, a cleric named George Thorpe, arrived at Berkeley and relieved Captain Woodlief of his managerial duties. Colonization was primarily a commercial venture (and secondarily a religious one), and Thorpe was there to grow stuff (mulberry, grapes, tobacco), find stuff (gold, iron) and report back to London everything he learned of the strange New World.

Thorpe's strategy seemed sound enough: build a rapport with the Powhatan tribes, then leverage the relationship to trade items of interest. As part of this endeavor he built a "university" that masqueraded as a cultural institution to educate the natives about European life, but was in fact intended to indoctrinate them into the Christian faith. He also built a house for the Powhatan chief (the father of Pocahontas) in the English style.

It was during the course of his dealings with the indigenous population that Thorpe was introduced to corn. They had been growing corn in Virginia for centuries and, just like the indigenous people of Mexico (where corn originates from), it was a

principal component of their diet. Most of the early English colonists disliked corn fervently, viewing it as a pale imitation of the barley and oats of the British Isles. But Thorpe was interested in the potential of this exotic crop. He assigned some land at Berkeley to growing corn and developed an appreciation for the food and drink that corn could produce—primarily the alcoholic kind.

Beer was as popular then as it is today, and to the colonists it offered a small taste of home. But beer was also one of the most difficult things to transport from England, since it spoiled quickly on long voyages. Thorpe had knowledge of winemaking so didn't waste any time brewing beer from corn. In one letter, dated December 19, 1620, he wrote: "we have found a way to make so good [a] drinke of Indian corne and I confess I have most times refused to drinke good strong Englishe beare and chosen to drinke that."

Having acquired a taste for corn beer (which by the way is dreadful no matter how you make it) Thorpe didn't stop there. French brandy and domestically produced grain spirits were popular in Britain, and they proved especially suited to the colonies since they packed down smaller (i.e. more alcoholic content per barrel) and instead of spoiling, they actually improved with age. The *Margaret* carried "15 gallons of aqua vitae" in its hold and resupplies brought more. Aqua Vitae was a catch-all term used to describe any drink of spirit strength that had been made through a process of distillation. It translates to "water of life," and got its name from European alchemists believing that liquids which "flame up when set on fire" could hold the secret to eternal life.

With a steady supply of corn beer and the basic knowledge of distillation, it was just a matter of time before colonists began to make their own spirits. At some point in 1621, Thorpe built a small distillery at Berkeley, next to a corn plantation. No physical trace of its existence remains, only vague references to a "copper still" in old records from the time. If these are to be believed, it's quite likely that Thorpe was the first person to make whiskey in North America.

Of course, it wouldn't have been known as whiskey back then, and it wouldn't have had much in common with the expertly crafted, oak-matured spirits that we enjoy today. In the early 17th century, spirits were in a state of flux, serving as both a form of medicine and as a social lubricant. But whatever the intended use, there was strong demand for spirits from toiling colonists: the least they could expect was a little alcohol-induced escapism.

The awful taste and horrific hangovers that these spirits induced did nothing to detract the attention of the indigenous people. Spirits were traded for food and fur by the Berkeley colony and in many future colonies for years to come. In some, yet-to-be-established frontiers, developing an alcohol trade that ultimately led to dependency on the part of the indigenous population became a fundamental tactic in their exploitation. This, however, was a strategy that failed to win over the Powhatans.

By 1622 the relationship between Berkeley and the Powhatans, on the surface at least, seemed friendly enough. Tribesmen could freely wander into the colony to trade and even assist with the activities that took place there, like milling and brewing. This amicable relationship was all a ruse, however, conceived by a Powhatan chieftain with a zero-tolerance policy to foreigners encroaching on Powhatan land.

On March 22, 1622, a group of Powhatans wandered into Berkeley, grabbed weapons and began slaughtering the workers. It was the beginning of a coordinated attack that resulted in the death of 350 colonists—around a quarter of English-speaking Virginians. Thorpe's "special relationship" with the chieftain awarded him special treatment—he was one of the first to be killed and his body viciously mutilated. This became known as the Indian Massacre of 1622 (although this event is also referred to as the Powhatan Uprising of 1622 by some historians) and it put a stop to the settlement of Berkeley, the annual celebration of Thanksgiving there, and America's first distillery.

The Tidewater region saw sporadic colonial settlements over the 100 years that followed the Massacre/Uprising, but ongoing wars with the indigenous tribes curtailed the development of any major settlements. In 1742, Richmond was chartered as a town and managed by the House of Burgesses, a legislative body modeled after the English Parliament. Richmond became a center of activity prior to and during the Revolutionary War. Patrick Henry's famous speech "Give Me Liberty or Give Me Death" was delivered at Richmond's St. John's Church and was said to have inspired the House of Burgesses to pass a resolution to deliver Virginia troops to the Revolutionary War in 1775. The rest, as they say, is history.

❦❦❦

As we have already learned, Virginia is ground-zero for whiskey-making in the US and it's where the first English-speaking colonies were established. Richmond is also home to a whiskey distillery called Reservoir.

Reservoir was founded in 2008, which is not very old compared to Thorpe's distillery, or even America's longest-serving distilleries (in Kentucky). But when compared to the hundreds of "craft" distilleries in America today, Reservoir is older than most. In 2000, there were no distilleries in Virginia; by 2008 there were half a dozen. Now there are over 50.

Reservoir uses three distinct types of cereal/grain to make their whiskey: wheat, rye, and corn. Although it's not a legal requirement for these styles of whiskey, the "wheat whiskey" at Reservoir is made only from wheat, the "rye whiskey" is made only from rye, and the "bourbon whiskey" is made only from corn (see pages 61–62 to learn what differentiates a bourbon whiskey from a "corn whiskey").

Of greater importance than a name or legal classification is the flavor that these cereals impart. Wheat is known for its soft, sweet, and fresh flavor; rye is renowned for its nutty, spicy, and dry characteristics; and corn tends to be oily and light.

The corn and wheat at Reservoir are both sourced from a farm in Charles City which is, coincidentally, just minutes from the Berkeley Plantation where George Thorpe made his corn spirit. The rye comes from a farm in New Kent, on the York River, 10 miles north of Charles City and about 20 miles from Reservoir.

ABOVE Fermentation is the only stage of the whiskey-making process where alcohol is made. Shown here are three of Reservoir's 400-gallon fermenters.

Once the grains arrive at the distillery, they are milled to a coarse powder known as "grist" and then cooked (or "mashed") with water in a 400-gallon kettle. This breaks the starch molecules in the cereal down to simple sugars.

Sugar is essential for the next stage of production: fermentation. Reservoir has six 400-gallon fermenters, which hold the mash and yeast (complete with all the spent grain) for up to 11 days while fermentation takes place. The action of the yeast turns sugar into alcohol, resulting in a beer of 5–10% alcohol by volume (ABV), depending on which cereal they are fermenting.

The next stage is distillation, where the beer is pumped over to a large kettle called a "pot still". A still is an essential piece of equipment in all distilleries, and the pot still is the most basic and traditional of all still types. The design has remained largely unchanged since the time of George Thorpe.

The still is heated both by steam and alcohol in the mixture, the latter boiling at 78.3°C/172.94°F. The resulting vapor rises up to the top ("head") of the still, then down into the condenser. As the vapor cools, it turns back into a liquid, only now it's crystal clear and with a higher alcohol concentration.

A single distillation in a pot still isn't sufficient to make a spirit however, as water vapor always sneaks its way into the condenser too (hot water still produces steam at 78.3°C/172.94°F). So Reservoir, like most distilleries that use pot stills to make whiskey, distill twice. In fact they have two pots stills for this very reason.

The first distillation conducts a "stripping run" and captures all of the alcohol in the beer but strips out around 70% of the water. The result is a "low wine" of around 25% ABV. The second distillation takes place in a smaller pot (because there is less liquid to distill) and increases alcoholic strength up to 70–80% ABV. The taste and aroma of the spirit will change during the course of the distillation process. The hand of the distiller, who decides how aggressively the still is run and which section of the spirit to collect (and which to discard), will determine the final flavor of the whiskey.

But it's not whiskey yet!

To be legally classed as "whiskey" in the US, the spirit must be matured in an oak barrel. For the most basic classification of "whiskey," there is no minimum time that the spirit needs to be aged for, and even a quick swirl around an oak bucket is satisfactory from the legislators' perspective (if not the whiskey connoisseurs). The rules for whiskey labeled as bourbon, rye, wheat, or malt are a little more specific and ask that the spirit be aged in "charred new oak containers." In layman's terms, this means a barrel that has not been used before, that is made of oak, and that has been charred by an open flame on the inside.

There are no restrictions on the size of the barrel, and in Reservoir's case they regularly use four different sizes: 5, 10, 25, and 52 (the most common across the industry) gallons. However, barrel size can have a profound effect on the rate at which the spirit matures. Other factors like temperature, humidity, the strength of the spirit in the barrel, the type of wood the barrel is made from and the intensity of the char will also play their part. We'll explore them in more detail in later chapters.

When resting in a barrel, the spirit quickly begins to take on color and flavor from the wood. After a few weeks it may resemble the color of straw, but if given enough time it may turn amber, then red, then as dark as mahogany. The color of the spirit can sometimes give us some clues about how the whiskey will taste. It can also mislead.

When the spirit is deemed to have reached optimal maturity, it is dumped out of the barrel and made ready for bottling. In most instances the whiskey (it can be called whiskey now) will be blended with other barrels to create a harmonious, balanced expression. Sometimes the whiskey may be bottled as a "single barrel" expression, which is exactly what it sounds like.

The whiskey will usually be "proofed down" prior to bottling, which means adding water until the desired alcoholic strength is reached. Water is sometimes added before the whiskey goes into the barrel too, since alcoholic strength impacts the palette of flavors that are extracted from the wood (and the color). On occasion we will encounter whiskeys bottled at "barrel proof" (no water added) but 40% (80 proof) is the industry standard and also the minimum bottling strength. Reservoir bottle most of their whiskeys at 50% (100 proof). Besides the obvious fact that there's more alcohol in a 100-proof bottle than an 80 proof, the spirit will also taste a little different. Higher concentrations of alcohol tend to make for a spicier, dryer whiskey and a flavor that lingers for longer.

At every stage of the whiskey-making process there are decisions to be made that impact the next stage of production and shape the finished product.

TOP LEFT Racks containing smaller-than-industry-standard 10-gallon barrels.
TOP RIGHT A fairly standard pot still, which connects to a copper condenser.

BOTTOM Reservoir is a modest but accomplished operation that just so happens to be in the heartlands of American whiskey making.

ABOVE Well, at least it comes with a warning... **RIGHT** Bungs for the bung hole. Mallets for banging the bung in the bung hole.

OPPOSITE Their biggest sellers are wheat, rye, and bourbon whiskeys, but Reservoir also makes interesting special releases.

No two distilleries are the same. But if you were to average out all of the small distilleries in America today into one balanced representation of what a "craft" distillery looks like... it would look a lot like Reservoir: a hands-on approach where very little is left to chance and authenticity is prized above all else.

We drain our glasses and get on our way. Heading east out of Richmond we travel down the James River, towards the Chesapeake Bay Area.

RESERVOIR WHEAT (50% ABV)

Typically light, as is the reputation of this cereal. The aroma has a touch of tobacco, hazelnut, and orange marmalade. The taste is slightly sweet, with barbecued fruits followed by cracked cocoa, and more of that nuttiness. There's the sensation of something like aniseed at the tail end. This is a light, accessible whiskey: good if you're at the first stop of a road trip which will see you taste upwards of 300 whiskeys.

RESERVOIR BOURBON (50% ABV)

This 100% corn bourbon has an immediate aroma of vinyl/rubber flooring accompanied by just a touch of smoke. This whiskey is sweet and fragrant on the palate, with a toasted pecan flavor and a little honey through the finish.

RESERVOIR RYE (50% ABV)

Dark cherry, a touch of walnut, and polished furniture on the nose. It's big, juicy, and dry on the palate. It feels peppered and rich with a really nice balance between cereal and cask. Shisha and leather come through on the finish.

❧

ROAD TRIP PLAYLIST

"Coming to America" – Neil Diamond

"America" – Simon & Garfunkel

"Virginia Plain" – Roxy Music

RESERVOIR

WHEAT WHISKEY
750 ML. 50% ALC./VOL.(100 PROOF)
YEAR 18 BATCH 6 BOTTLE 24

COPPER FOX

SCOTTISH BUT NOT SCOTCH

*"A good gulp of hot whisky at bedtime—it's not very scientific,
but it helps."*

ALEXANDER FLEMING (1881–1955), SCOTTISH MICROBIOLOGIST

After an hour of driving, we arrive in Williamsburg—the capital of the Virginia Colony from 1699 to 1780. The Colonial center of Williamsburg is a bit like a live action role-play game, where actors in period costume depict daily colonial life. As fun as that sounds, though, we have serious work to do here and it involves drinking whiskey.

We're here to visit the Copper Fox distillery, which was established here in 2014, but serves as the younger sibling to the original Copper Fox distillery located in the north of the state. Copper Fox produces a range of whiskeys with special focus on "single malt." The proprietor of Copper Fox, Rick Wasmund, is a little a bit of a Caledophile (the unofficial term for someone obsessed with Scotland) and given where he's chosen to set up his distillery… well, that kind of makes sense.

The first Scottish communities in America were established in the 1680s, and Virginia served as the hub of early Scottish commercial activity in the colonies. In 1707, the Act of Union was signed, merging Scotland with England (and Wales and Ireland) to form the United Kingdom of Great Britain. At that time, Virginia grew mostly tobacco, and trading vessels that traversed the Atlantic swapped Scottish workers and indentured servants for parcels of Virginian tobacco destined for Glasgow. In fact, Glasgow traded almost all of Britain's tobacco, and in Virginia's port towns, like

Norfolk, which is on the opposite side of the James River from Williamsburg, were transformed into Scottish municipalities.

Scottish migration continued to ramp up in the early 1700s, first during the failed Irish harvest of 1717, then again after the Jacobite rising of 1745. More came following the dismantling of the Highland clan structure, and then another load after the Highland Clearances. In 1700, Scots accounted for 3% of the 250,000 inhabitants of the English American Colonies. By 1750, Scots comprised 7% of the population and there were as many Scots then as there had been total inhabitants in 1700. Some anthropologists believe that there are more descendants of Highland clans living in America today than there are in Scotland.

Then there were the Scots-Irish, who had been sent to Ireland by James I to spread Protestantism. The Scots-Irish hated Britain. Come to think of it, they didn't much like authority of any kind. When they arrived in America, they lived as they pleased, claiming farmland, building cabins, and rearing cattle. Some of them made whisky, too.

Not that we should be surprised. The Scottish and Irish had been distilling aqua vitae for centuries, and it would take more than the mere crossing of an ocean to eradicate the memory of the craft.

The earliest reference to the production of aqua vitae in Scotland comes from the Royal Exchequer

Rolls of 1494, which lists the sale of 500 kg of malt to one Friar John Corr, "wherewith to make aqua vitae." Interestingly, this boozy purchase order was to be delivered to none other than King James IV of Scotland (later King James I of England and Scotland). The story goes that James (aged 21) had been asserting his royal authority on the Hebridean island of Islay the previous year, and at some time or other got a taste for the spirit made there. In fact, the order he placed in 1494 would be enough to manufacture over 1,200 bottles of whisky by today's standards!

By 1600, whisky-making had become a common farm practice in Scotland and the first commercial distilleries were starting to show up. The early part of that century saw a linguistic transition in Scotland too, away from Latin aqua vitae and on to the Gaelic "uisge beatha." This term would later be shortened to "whisky," the first written references of which occurred in 1715 ("whiskie") and 1735 ("whisky"). As for when whisky gained an 'e' as per the American spelling… well, that's a story for later.

Thanks to favorable growing conditions (i.e. cold and wet), barley has remained the favored base material for Scotch whisky for half a millennium. Although, technically speaking, it's "malted barley" that's used in most Scottish distilleries. A malted cereal is a cereal that has been germinated by first soaking it in water and then drying it out. The process simulates the same steps that occur in nature when a cereal detects seasonal changes and decides it's time to become a plant. Moistening the grain causes hormones in the embryo (the "brain" of the grain) to trigger the release of enzymes that self-destruct cell walls and proteins, and ready the grain for breaking down starch stored in the endosperm (the "muscle") into simple sugars.

If things continue this way, the seed sprouts a rootlet and begins to grow—great for the plant but not so good for the whisky maker. When a distiller, brewer, or malt house malts a cereal, the aim is to halt the process and kill the endosperm before the seed consumes too much sugar. If done correctly, what you're left with is an enzyme-rich store of accessible energy that can be extracted through cooking.

If we hopped in a time machine and traveled back two centuries, we would quickly learn that most distilleries and breweries malted their cereals on-site. These operations built floors or entire structures (malt houses) dedicated to sprouting, drying, and roasting grain. Malting was a highly laborious process however, requiring regular human interaction and a lot of space. The technological changes during the Industrial Revolution changed all this, and most booze makers began buying their malt from centralized malt houses from the middle of the 19th century onwards. Today, in Scotland, there are just eight distilleries that malt their own barley in the traditional manner (and only one of them malts their entire requirement).

The last malting floor in the US closed down when Prohibition took effect, in 1920.

And then Rick Wasmund came along.

It was April of 2000 when Rick took a trip to Scotland to visit a few whisky distilleries. Well, one thing led to another, and he ended up spending six weeks there as an intern at the famed Bowmore distillery on Islay.

It was while working at Bowmore that he learned about the whisky-making process. But what really struck a chord with Rick was how Bowmore went to the effort of malting and drying their barley in kilns using peat smoke, and the flavors that this process imparted into the whisky. Peat bogs are formed when plant roots, moss, heather, and other vegetation decompose in an acidic environment without drainage. The vegetation only part-decomposes, because it's always wet, and over hundreds and thousands of years of crushing gravity, it forms a loose organic mass that, if dried, can be burned. Peat produces a lot of smoke when it burns and it's that smoke that imparts itself into the barley grain and characterizes some of the famous brands of whisky from Scotland. Like it or loathe it, there's something primal about the intoxicating aroma of smoke, and smoky whiskeys continue to have a strong following among aficionados.

Inspired by his time at Bowmore, Rick set about building a distillery in Virginia where he would craft his own, Virginian take on single malt whisky. The

ABOVE A distillery that malts its own barley is still a very rare occurrence, in both the United States and in Scotland. **RIGHT** Suffice it to say that Copper Fox is an American whiskey distillery that looks to Scotland for a great deal of its inspiration.

first Copper Fox distillery was converted from an old apple-packing factory and it got its license in 2005. It's still operational today, located in Sperryville, which is adjacent to Virginia's stunning Shenandoah National Park.

The simplest way make smoky whiskey in the US is to ship already-smoked malted barley over from the UK. For a startup distillery, this would be the easiest and lowest risk option, since it requires very little upfront capital, very little space for storage, and you can guarantee a consistent product. So, Rick didn't do that. Instead, he used Virginian barley.

Barley was a slow-starter in Virginia, on account of the fact that early colonists found it didn't take readily to eastern American soil. That's why many looked to the corn and rye grown by the indigenous people instead. Lucky for us, agriculture has moved on a fair bit since then, and it's now possible to grow barley that will flourish in certain parts of the state. Copper Fox manages to source all of its grain from a single farmer, who grows a specific variety (suited to the Virginian climate) developed by Virginia Tech's barley breeding program.

Of course, the barley grain is the easy part. There's still the "malt" part of "malted barley" to deal with.

Rick could have approached a commercial malting house to take care of this, but there weren't any in the US at the time with smoking capabilities. So that really only left one option.

And so it was that Rick Wasmund built the first floor malting in America since Prohibition. Malting one's own cereals is not something for the hobbyist distiller. But once you've felt the strain of raking warm malt and tasted the product of all that labor… cutting corners no longer becomes a viable option.

The malt house is the first stage of making any whiskey at Copper Fox and it goes like this: the grain is dumped into tanks where it is hydrated with water for a couple of days until the grains swell to around 45% moisture content. The water is then drained and the grains are spread out on a malting floor for up to a week. At this stage they become exothermic and require regular turning with a rake or shiel (a flat wooden shovel) every few hours to ensure sufficient airflow over the grains to avoid mold growth. Once a preferred starch-to-enzyme ratio is achieved, the "green malt" is transferred to a kiln oven and gently cooked to halt the germination process.

ABOVE The spirit that evaporates out of a barrel through the course of maturation is called the "angels' share." **LEFT** These little stills are not dissimilar to the equipment used by many distillers in the 18th century. At Copper Fox, they are used for test runs.

But what to burn in the kiln? Sure enough, there are peat bogs in Virginia too, but by this point Rick was basically creating a whole new category of American whiskey, so could choose to take a more American approach to smoking. Perhaps he was inspired by the barbecue culture of the neighboring Carolina states, because he picked fruit woods as the fuel for his smoke.

"It was such a good idea, but no one else was doing it," he says, shaking his head.

Whether it's apple, cherry, pecan, or peach, just like the fruits of these plants, fruit woods are imbued with a unique array of aromatic compounds and smoke-producing carbohydrates. And just like a pit master tailors the type of wood to the cut of meat, Rick has been able to finely tune the smoke aroma that is imparted into his whiskeys through experimentation. For Copper Fox's core single-malt bottlings, the malt is dried using a 60:40 ratio of apple wood and cherry wood, smoked in a Weber grill. The smoke passes up from the low-ceilinged kiln room, through a perforated floor, then intermingles with the barley grains, drying and flavoring them simultaneously.

"People ask if I have ever tried smoking fish or meat…" says Rick, "and the answer is I tried to smoke fish but it kept ripping the rolling paper because it was wet."

Rick is quick to crack a joke and there's a dryness to his humor that feels more Scottish than it does American. Perhaps that playful quality is the source of his experimental streak. Or perhaps he can afford to be playful given the success Copper Fox has had and the regard that he is held in. Either way, this is a distillery that has taken risks—and it's paid off.

In the early days of the distillery, the plan was to make the barrels out of fruit woods too, creating a marriage between smoke and timber, set to a backdrop of whiskey. However, the expense and the fact they don't hold liquid particularly well made this idea a non-starter. Undeterred, a solution eventually presented itself: suspend the wood in the spirit rather than the spirit in the wood. The casks (nearly all of them 53-gallon) are sourced from bourbon producers so have already been filled once, and each barrel has a cloth bag suspended in it, which is filled with applewood chips. "For our American Single Malt, we chip the whiskey for about 18 months, then remove the chips and let the spirit mature until we need to bottle it—generally another six to 12 months," Rick tells me.

In Scotland, almost all of the whisky is matured in used oak barrels, the vast majority of which are procured from bourbon distilleries in Kentucky. At the risk of doubling down on my analogies, a used barrel is much like a used tea bag—it loses some of its potency after the first steeping. If you think that sounds bad, remember that some of the most prized teas in the world are considered at their best after the second or third steep.

"There's something that happens once a barrel is kind of played-out," Rick says. "You're still getting 'something', and it's that something which gives some of our whiskeys that Scotch aroma."

You'll remember from the previous chapter that American whiskeys labeled as malt (as well as rye, bourbon, and wheat) must be aged in "new oak containers." From a legislative point of view, this places Rick's malt whiskeys in a peculiar territory. They can't legally be classed as "Malt Whiskey" because he's not aged them in new oak.

What they should be called is "American Single Malt Whiskey" but no such categorization currently exists. That hasn't stopped Rick from proudly declaring just that on the label though. While there is no law defining what "American Single Malt Whiskey" means, there also isn't a law prohibiting its use. And Rick's aren't the only whiskeys using it. That's why the American Single Malt Whiskey Commission has been set up. With over 100 member distilleries, the collective goal of this organization is to accelerate the establishment and definition of this new category of spirits.

After all that chat about malt whiskey, the first whiskey Rick serves us is actually a rye. Not just any rye though: "Sassy Rye" is made from 100% malted rye grown in Virginia. Like barley, rye can be malted so that the grain's sweet resources are made available to distillers. Malted rye is quite uncommon however, and rye that has been floor-malted at the distillery—like this—is practically unheard of anywhere in the world. The rye undergoes the same process as Copper Fox's barley does during malting, but during the kiln-drying stage, it's sassafras wood that's used as the source of smoke.

On the subject of rye, Copper Fox also makes an "Original Rye," built from two parts un-malted rye and one part floor-malted barley. The inclusion of Copper Fox's own floor-malted barley in the recipe makes this rye the only rye in America with a smoked malt component in its recipe. Except, that is, for another one of their products, made from the same rye/malt spirit matured for a further two years in "port-style barrels" sourced from nearby Rappahannock Cellars winery.

Of the four single malt expressions that Copper Fox currently bottles, three are made from the aforementioned base of cherrywood and applewood smoked malt. They are the previously discussed "American Single Malt," plus a single malt matured in port-style barrels, and a single malt aged in ex-apple brandy barrels. Then there's the "Peachwood American Single Malt," which is made from a base of floor-malted barley smoked over—you guessed it—peachwood, matured with peachwood chips.

I think we're getting the hang of this now.

There's one more product made here that's especially interesting to me. It's not a whiskey that falls under the Copper Fox brand; instead it's labeled under the Belle Grove 1797 brand, named after one of the largest Virginian plantations in the 18th century. It was also the birthplace of the fourth president and "Father of the Constitution," James Madison, and they made whiskey there. The Belle Grove recipe comprises 51% corn, 25% unsmoked malted barley, and 24% oats.

"We're trying to reproduce what was happening in the 18th century," Rick tells me. "The recipe would have changed depending on the harvest so this is representative of what they were growing on the plantation at that time."

We could stay for hours at Copper Fox, consuming the elemental forces of fire and wood that shape the character of their whiskeys. There's another elemental force at play as we head to the car: rain. We buckle up and get on our way to the next stage of our journey, which will take us towards the nation's capital and towards the home of its namesake.

APPRECIATING A GLASS OF WHISKEY

The Japanese author Haruki Murakami was known to say "Whiskey, like a beautiful woman, demands appreciation. You gaze first, then it's time to drink." But you can only tell so much about a spirit from looking at it.

Color can sometimes be an indication of how long a whiskey has been matured (un-aged spirits are naturally crystal-clear) but it's easy to be fooled since some whiskeys are legally permitted to have color added to them. Even when a spirit hasn't been colored by anything other than a barrel, you'd be wise not to take too much notice as there are a whole host of factors that can influence color extraction and its relationship with time in the cask.

Cloudiness is not something you would normally expect to see in a premium spirit, but it does happen sometimes with whiskeys that haven't been filtered. A process called "chill-filtering" is used by most producers to remove the compounds that cause haziness, but some distillers (like Rick Wasmund) prefer not to filter too much, believing that it can negatively impact the flavor. It's usually best to ignore the "legs" of the spirit too. I was taught that the regularity of the vertical lines that form in the inside of the glass shortly after swirling the spirit are a sign of quality but it turns out that closely scrutinizing them is actually a sign that you're an idiot. They're caused by the tendency of alcohol to evaporate quickly from the side of the glass, leaving the watery components of the spirit (which tends to be 40–60%) to stick together, then fall down the glass in little streams. Slower forming legs mean a higher strength spirit—that's about it.

Assessing the aroma of the whiskey is where the real fun begins. I always suggest doing this with the same level of caution that an untrusting cat would demonstrate if you glued a live mouse to the floor.

Show some respect for the spirit and approach it with caution. Most of the time you can detect all the aromas in a glass without being in the glass. If your nose becomes numb or feels "burnt," move back for a little while. Sometimes sniffing your hand or wrist can help to reset this sensation.

Use your nose to detect familiar aromas. More often than not, it's the detection that's the easy part and the assigning of a description that's much harder. Try to categorize the aroma you're smelling: is it a fruit? Is it a stone fruit or berry? Dried or fresh? This is the method that I use and it helps me refine my tasting notes.

When drinking the whiskey, give it a little time to move around your palate before swallowing (a colleague advises that whiskey should be held on the tongue for one second for every year of maturation). When you swallow, be sure to breathe out through your nose, sending the aromatic components of the spirit up, past your nasal receptors.

Think about how the spirit feels in the mouth: is it thin or watery? Oily or full bodied? Is it spicy, and if so, what sort kind spice? Pepper or chili? Then think about the taste sensation (which will actually be a combination of taste senses and aroma): how does it compare to the smell? How are the aromas interpreted now that the tongue and mouth get to have their say?

Finally, think about the "finish:" how long does the flavor last? Where is the taste and feel of the spirit most felt? Does it leave you desperate for more or desperately reaching for the spittoon?

If you're beginning to think that all this detailed evaluation might take some of the joy out of drinking spirits, don't worry! If you've successfully made it to adulthood, you're already adept at analyzing the food and drink you put in your body. Learning to appreciate and objectively assess a spirit is just a case of applying some methodology to your judgment and building your taste vocabulary. As a whiskey writer, it's important to have the ability to do this so that I can articulate the differences between one spirit and another. But as someone who genuinely enjoys drinking spirits—I'm this person too—it's by no means essential. The most important question any of us can ask of the drinks in our glasses is this: do I like it?

AMERICAN SINGLE MALT (43% ABV)

Subtle smoke with notes of anise and jerk spices on the nose. The taste has sweet smoke, rounded with tropical fruits and freshly laundered linen. It's soft and supple through the finish.

RYE (45% ABV)

Root beer, old leather, pineapple, and baking spice on the nose. The taste is almost effervescent, feeling bright and fruity. Smoke is soft but definitely present. The finish dries up with a light tickle of spice.

PORT-STYLE BARREL FINISH SINGLE MALT (50% ABV)

Christmas pudding spice, red grape juice, charred red pepper, and a touch of cinnamon on the nose. On the palate, there's tannin, and juicy grape bubblegum; it's dry, elegant, and flavorsome. It would be a great match for cheese.

PORT STYLE BARREL FINISH RYE (50% ABV)

All the desserts—Neapolitan ice cream, red berry cheesecake, and orange sorbet. Less port cask flavor than the malt—it feels tighter and more woody. There's prickly wood spice on the finish.

"SASSY" RYE (45% ABV)

Tropical and fragrant: mango, apricot, and ginger on the nose. It's tight and fresh on the palate with subtle smoke, like burnt leaves. It remains light and elegant through the finish.

ROAD TRIP PLAYLIST

"Virginia in the Rain" – Dave Matthews Band

"Copperhead Road" – Steve Earle

"I'm Gonna Be" – The Proclaimers

GEORGE WASHINGTON'S DISTILLERY

REVOLUTIONARY SPIRIT

"Freedom an' whisky gang thegither!"

ROBERT BURNS (1759–96), SCOTTISH POET

The penultimate line of Robert Burns' *The Author's Earnest Cry and Prayer* was intended to inspire patriotism amongst Scottish parliamentarians during a time when whiskey was being heavily taxed. It was written in 1786, however, just three years after the American Revolutionary War ended, so could just as easily have applied to the United States.

Civil unrest in the Thirteen Colonies began in the 1760s, marked by a number of political and philosophical differences that created tension between the New Worlders and London. The colonists' primary grievances was that of "taxation without representation," which was exacerbated by the Stamp Act, which required that many printed materials in the colonies be produced on embossed, revenue-stamped paper produced in London. This escalated into boycotts, culminating, in 1773, with the Sons of Liberty famously throwing chests of tea into Boston Harbor.

Lesser known, but equally important was the Sugar Act of 1764, which followed the Molasses Act of 1733. Both levied heavy taxes on sugar and molasses imported from foreign (non-British) colonies in the Caribbean, forcing colonists to buy their molasses from the more expensive British plantations. In New England, in particular, this was a big problem, since rum was the primary spirit made there, and molasses was the main ingredient. Thanks to protests organized by various soon-to-be Founding Fathers, like Samuel Adams, Benjamin Franklin and George Washington, both the Stamp Act and Sugar Act were repealed in 1766. After that, the wheels of insurrection began to gather pace.

It began with skirmishes in Massachusetts, in 1775, but soon spread into other areas, and by the next summer it had become a civil war. France got involved and on October 19, 1781, they assisted the Continental Army in forcing the surrender of General Cornwallis in Yorktown, Virginia.

It was George Washington that led the Continental Army to victory in Yorktown, having been appointed the role of Commander-in-Chief since 1775. Besides being an expert tactician and popular leader, Washington was also a farmer and, later, a distiller; his Mount Vernon distillery would become one of the biggest whiskey distilleries of the era. And crucially, for our tale, he made whiskey, not rum.

The transition from rum to whiskey didn't take place overnight, but the turning point was during the midst of the war, on August 29, 1777. On that date, John Adams, who in 1797 would become the nation's second president, wrote a letter to his wife, Abigail, in which he remarks on the availability and prices of

PREVIOUS PAGES Although this millstone is centuries old, the one used in the gristmill today is practically identical.

various goods: "As to sugar, molasses, rum etc. we must leave them off. Whiskey is used here instead of rum, and I don't see but it is just as good. Of this the wheat and rye countries can easily distill enough for the use of the country."

This, then, was the moment that whiskey became the spirit of America.

Present-day Mount Vernon is technically part of Virginia, but it's easily engulfed by the southern sprawl of Washington, DC. Back in the 18th century, it was simply a large chunk of agricultural land on the banks of the Potomac River. It had been in the Washington family since the time of John Washington, George's English-born great-grandfather, who acquired a small plot of land there in 1674.

George Washington inherited the estate in the 1750s (along with six slaves) when it comprised 2,100 acres. By the end of the war, his estate had ballooned to five farms, encompassing 8,000 acres. A gristmill was added in 1771 which was significant, since up until that point the Washingtons had, like most Virginian planters, focused mainly on growing tobacco. Tobacco was a valuable crop, but farming it was unsustainable and a fantastically efficient way of destroying soil. So the estate turned its gaze to grain, and particularly to rye and wheat. Cereals proved to be a far more successful endeavor, and by the 1780s the mill was exporting flour to Portugal, Spain, and the Caribbean.

The Revolution marked a turning point in whiskey's domestic fortunes. With sovereign status, the US could begin shedding all the trappings of British rule and turn its attention to being… well, American. And there were few things that spoke of being British quite like rum.

By that point, Washington was a hero of the Revolutionary War, and in 1784 he resigned his commission and returned to Mount Vernon. He was 52 years old, struggling with a tumor on his thigh and dental problems that had plagued him most of his life. It must have seemed the perfect opportunity to retire to his estate and live out a peaceful existence, running his farms in the newly independent United States that he had fought for.

ABOVE The first modern barrel of whiskey produced at Mount Vernon is signed by the biggest names in whiskey. **OPPOSITE** With no air conditioning and lots of hot liquids, it gets rather steamy at Mount Vernon.

But his retirement plan would have to be put on hold. There was a Constitution to write and someone needed to run the country. For the latter, Washington was everybody's favorite pick.

As it goes, he was elected as president not once but twice and didn't get a chance to return to Mount Vernon until 1796. He was 64 years old and feeling every year of it, so he hired a farm manager to assist him with running the huge estate. That man was James Anderson, a former whiskey merchant and mill manager from Scotland. And ever the canny Scotsman, it was Anderson who convinced Washington of the expansive potential market for whiskey.

Besides the fact that people liked to drink and whiskey fulfilled that need, making whiskey added value to cereals. In addition to this, spirits were much more cost- effective to transport than grain and not susceptible to spoilage. A distillery also gave a miller or farmer options if they had surplus grain or needed to navigate a slump in the market value of cereals.

But Washington was cautious not to overextend. He furnished Anderson with two small pot stills to play with, temporarily housed in the estate cooperage. Anderson made 600 gallons of spirit in 1797 and sold all of it. With Washington satisfied that there was a demand for whiskey, the pair began construction of a dedicated distillery building in October of that year.

ABOVE Vaporizing alcohol with a wood-burning furnace—what could possibly go wrong?

The first spirits ran off the new distillery in March 1798 and production totaled 4,500 gallons.

In 1799 Washington wrote to his nephew, "Two hundred gallons of Whiskey will be ready this day for your call, and the sooner it is taken the better, as the demand for this article (in these parts) is brisk." This was to be the year of Washington's death, when the output of the distillery doubled to nearly 11,000 gallons of whiskey, generating $7,674 in revenue. To put that into context, the average Virginian distillery made 650 gallons a year at that time—and there were over 3,000 of them at the turn of the 19th century. Washington died perhaps owning the largest and hardest-working distillery in the country. It would have been an incredible legacy were it not overshadowed by a generally exceptional life.

Besides the distillery and gristmill, there was also a miller's cottage, garden and orchard, cooperage, a malt house, hog and cattle sheds, plus a wharf that sent flour and whiskey along the river. The day-to-day operations were overseen by James Anderson and his son John, along with six enslaved workers (Hanson, Peter, Nat, Daniel, James, and Timothy). One of the benefits of the proprietor being the first US President is that detailed historical records are available, giving us an insight into how whiskey making was undertaken on this kind of scale, as well as clues as to how other distilleries may have gone about their work.

Anderson grew wheat, rye, oats, corn, and barley on the estate. But his mill could chew through up to 8,000 pounds of cereal a day, so he bought-in cereals to keep its appetite assuaged. The mill also ground cereals for other farms, who paid for the service with an eighth of their load. It was common for larger mills to take these payment parcels of grain, which would be mixed together and allocated for whiskey making. Corn, which was a staple part of the workers' diet, was also often sent for distilling, since, at the time, it had a lower value than the other grains.

The mill itself was powered by a 16-ft water wheel, turned by a millrace (think miniature canal) that was fed from a millpond two miles away. The wheel turned gears, which moved the top millstone, hovering barely an inch above the stationary, bottom millstone. Grain was fed in through a hole in the top stone, and was ground and crushed by the two stones as it worked its way towards the edge of the stone and down a small hole. Once ground up, the cereals were packaged as flour, or (of much greater interest) transported from the mill to the still house.

Once they arrived in the distillery, the cereals were mashed with boiling water from a 210-gallon wood-fired copper pan. The mashing was done in 120-gallon open-top barrels. Corn and rye were mashed first, then malted barley was added later. The cooking process extracted the starches from the cereals, utilizing the enzymes present in malted barley to thin the liquid and convert the starches into sugar. Washington's distillery operated in a time before electric pumps, so at all stages of production, the various liquids were ladled by hand between vessels. Anderson removed one of these laborious stages of the process by fermenting in the same barrels that he mashed in. The downside of doing this is that the hot mash would need to stirred (or "rowed") with large paddles to cool it down before pitching yeast. Once the yeast was added, fermentation ensued and, over the course of a few days, converted the sugar in the mixture into alcohol.

Now an alcoholic beer, the liquid was ladled into the brick-jacketed base of one of the five copper pot stills, whose capacities ranged from 90–135 gallons. This was a common size for stills of this era, as anything larger than 150 gallons would be difficult to transport by cart. The head of the still (the top part that transports the spirit vapor into the condenser) was then fitted on top, and the fire underneath the pan was lit. The distillation process would be carried out once, then repeated, to bring the spirit up to a strength of around 70% ABV. Occasionally they would distill a third or fourth time to produce a cleaner, higher-grade (higher-priced) style of whiskey. The spirit was stored in barrels for transport, but not intentionally matured. Nothing was wasted. Leftover stillage (see page 136) and slops from fermentation were fed to Washington's livestock, which in turn fertilized the fields that grew the cereal.

Who knows how big the distillery may have become if Washington had lived to his 80s? George Washington's nephew inherited the estate in 1802, but was unable to support the upkeep. The distillery fell into disrepair and burned down in 1814.

As interesting a historical story Mount Vernon is for whiskey geeks, it would have remained just that—a story—were it not for the events that have taken place over the past 20 years. In 1999, Mount Vernon commenced a long-term archaeology and research program that was partly funded by a $2.1 million grant from the Distilled Spirits Council of the United States. Their ultimate goal? Document the history and technology of Washington's distilling enterprise and rebuild the distillery to its 18th-century spec.

Walking around the grounds of Mount Vernon today, visitors are transported back to a bygone era of squat, stone buildings and manual labor. The mill and distillery were carefully restored between 2004 and 2007. The new mill at Mount Vernon was designed in the 1970s by the English millwright Derek Ogden. Everything is 18th-century accurate. Besides the stones that actually do the grinding work, the entire mill, including the 16-ft wheel, is built from wood. Big, heavy-looking chunks of wood.

The distillery began production runs in 2009. Steve Bashore is the modern-day James Anderson here, with the appropriate job title of "Director of Historic Trades." He was a traditional miller—a trade he has practiced for a quarter of a century. Now he leads a team of costumed historic interpreters, who bring the story of Washington's gristmill and distillery to life.

Steve shows us around the mill first. Wheat is ground on French burr stones made from freshwater quartz. Corn and other cereals are milled on granite. Furrows are cut into the stones and the individual pattern dictates the consistency of the cut, along with a compound lever that can raise and lower the upper stone to control how coarse or fine the cut is. "There's more mathematics to it than just that," Steve says, "such as the entry angle off the spindle of the master furrow which controls how long the grain remains sandwiched between the two stones."

I'm blown away by the craftsmanship it must have taken to design and build a machine like this. Although the technology has moved on and these mills have been superseded by modern roller and hammer mills, the engineering in this mill seems—to this wide-eyed traveler—far more impressive than a clever box with lights and buttons.

But what really makes it special? Is it that I'm able to stand in front of one of only a handful of water-powered gristmills in North America? Or is it that it serves as testament to the countless mills that are not here anymore, belonging, instead, to a time when gristmills were not a novelty, but a central component of distilleries and, indeed, civilization?

In Washington's day, most of the distillery's grain requirements were grown on the estate. But since most of that land has been developed now, Steve instead sources rye and corn from a farm in Tidewater, close to where Reservoir and Copper Fox get theirs from. Steve uses a combination of these grains at a ratio of 2:1, along with a little malted barley to make the distillery's flagship rye whiskey. When making bourbon whiskey, he sources a type of corn from the best-known of all the bourbon-producing states, Kentucky, which in Washington's day would have still been a part of Virginia.

Almost every stage of production is done in the same, arduous fashion as it was over 200 years ago.

ABOVE The mill at Mount Vernon uses the same system—designed by inventor Oliver Evans (1755–1819)—that featured in the distillery during Washington's era.

Seven distillers, most of whom are tour guides at the Mount Vernon estate, chop wood to fuel boilers that heat water from the adjacent pond. There's no electricity in the still house, save for a single pump which speeds the cooling of the mash. You have to cool a mash before you add yeast to it, otherwise the yeast will die as soon as it goes in there. Leaving the mash to cool overnight would be the obvious option but that takes up space and increases the risk of bacterial infection. "Anderson may have used ice from the estate to cool mash quickly," says Steve.

Even the five wood-fired copper stills are manufactured to the same spec and size as Anderson's originals. Per square-footage, Mount Vernon Gristmill and Distillery probably has more workers than any other distillery in America. One of the workers I speak to, Tony, runs another gristmill in Pennsylvania, just south of Philadelphia.

The mill produces grist and flour for various products sold out of the distillery gift shop and drinks on the menu in the Mount Vernon Inn. Over a five-week period that runs from late October to late November, 20,000 lbs of ground cereal goes to the distillery, to produce just 1,200–1,500 proof gallons of spirit. Such a short window of operation is reflective of the way things were hundreds of years ago, when grains needed to be used before they spoiled. Little wonder that a bottle of Mount Vernon whiskey is so expensive then!

The distillery bottles three expressions, all made from the same rye mash bill. Perhaps the most exciting bottling is also, thankfully, the cheapest. George Washington's Rye Whiskey is un-aged and therefore faithfully representative of the whiskey Washington was making in 1799. A 375-ml bottle will set you back $98. If you've a little more money to

ABOVE This is the manner in which fermentation was once conducted across every distillery in the United States: in a barrel

spend, there's a 2-year-old priced at $188 and a 4-year-old at $225. To be frank, the price is mostly linked to scarcity and, of course, exclusivity of the liquid. The aged expressions are typically released in the summer months and sell quickly.

Oh, and there's another catch: the only place you can buy a bottle is at Mount Vernon!

2 YEAR OLD RYE (43% ABV)

Meadowsweet, plum wine, and apricot jam on the nose. Dry and vanilla notes on the palate. Nutty caramel and plenty of wood spice to finish.

4 YEAR OLD RYE (43% ABV)

Dark honey, hay, and orange cordial on the nose, and soft on alcohol. The palate feels like a candy shop, rounded out with spiced marmalade and apricot compote. It's softly sweet through the finish.

ROAD TRIP PLAYLIST

"American Pie" – Don McLean

"All Right Now" – Free

"Revolution" – The Beatles

CHERRY BOUNCE À LA MARTHA WASHINGTON

500 g/18 oz caster/granulated sugar
1 kg/2¼ lbs ripe cherries, de-stoned
700 ml/24 oz Mount Vernon Rye Whiskey
1 cinnamon stick, bashed
5 whole cloves, bashed
1 whole nutmeg, bashed

Take approximately half the sugar and mix well with the fruit. Place the mixture in a clean cheesecloth and sit over a bowl overnight. In the morning, twist the cheesecloth to extract as much juice as possible. Mix it with the whiskey, the rest of the sugar, and the spices, and infuse for a couple of weeks.

Enjoy straight, chilled, or over ice. Cherry Bounce also makes a fantastic modifier for other cocktails, such as an Old Fashioned.

Because the quality of the whiskey that farmers and millers produced was inconsistent at best (and consistently terrible at worst) it was very common to flavor whiskeys with whatever herbs, fruits and spices were available. Cherry was one of the most popular infusions of the time and this drink became known as a Cherry Bounce.

This was also one of only a handful of recipes that was used by the Washington family. We know this, because a recipe for "Excellent Cherry Bounce" was discovered among the papers of the [first] First Lady, Martha Washington. This infusion was known to be a favorite of General Washington's, so much so that he packed a "canteen" of it, along with Madeira and port, for a trip west across the Allegheny mountains in September 1784. Here's the recipe:

"Extract the juice of 20 pounds well ripend Morrella cherrys. Add to this 10 quarts of old french brandy and sweeten it with White sugar to your taste.

To 5 gallons of this mixture add one ounce of spice such as cinnamon, cloves and nutmegs of each an Equal quantity slightly bruis'd and a pint and half of cherry kirnels that have been gently broken in a mortar. After the liquor has fermented let it stand close-stoped for a month or six weeks then bottle it, remembering to put a lump of Loaf Sugar into each bottle."

In her recipe, Martha uses aged French brandy, but this was a luxury that most Americans at that time could not afford (the same can also be said for the spices and the "White sugar"). I've adapted the recipe to use whiskey instead of brandy, and scaled down the quantities a bit since five gallons is excessive (for most people). Although they do taste great, I don't use the cherry kernels in my recipe either, since they are now known to contain amygdalin, which breaks down into hydrogen cyanide when ingested. The fact that some fruit stones are carcinogenic was not known when the recipe was penned.

DAD'S HAT

RYE-DRAM

*"Rye whiskey makes the sun set faster
Makes the spirit more willing..."*

FROM THE SONG "RYE WHISKEY" BY PUNCH BROTHERS

Driving north out of the most famous of General Washington's namesakes, Washington, DC, we immediately drop into the state of Maryland, skirt past Baltimore, briefly touch the northern tip of Delaware, then cross the border into Pennsylvania. The cities in the so-called Northeast megalopolis (which runs from DC up to Boston) are so tightly packed together that you never really escape the urban sprawl, but it's no surprise that the area, with its navigable rivers and natural harbors, initially attracted settlers. In time, heavy industry would spread throughout the region, with rivers such as the Hudson and Delaware being transformed into vital shipping lanes.

By the 1750s, the English colonial territory was bigger than England itself, extending from the Eastern seaboard all the way to the Appalachian mountains. That's a lot of farmland. Each colony produced a bit of everything, but over time they began focusing on the crops that grew best since these would deliver the biggest economic advantage. Virginia and Maryland had their tobacco, South Carolina grew rice and indigo, and North Carolina centered on cotton.

In Pennsylvania and New York, cereals were the main focus. Wheat was the most widely-grown crop but barley, oats and rye also featured. Rye gained some popularity in Pennsylvania particularly, partly due to favorable growing conditions that the land offered and the crop's resistance to disease. Another important factor was culture.

Germans poured on to American shores from the early 18th century onwards, spurred by political, economic, and religious dissatisfactions in their homeland. Rye was their cereal. Philadelphia became the largest city and busiest port in British America, second in scale only to London in the British Empire. Philadelphia was where the Declaration of Independence was written and signed (in 1776) and where the early draft of the Constitution was drawn up, (which was also presented in German.) When the war ended, Philadelphia was the most populated city in the nation, and first-generation Germans and descendants of earlier German settlers made up about one-third of the total population of Pennsylvania.

German settlers seemed to have an almost supernatural knowledge of the land and how to farm it. Additionally, their loyalty to the republic set them in good stead to develop the western frontiers.

On the meadows outside of Philadelphia, and further west, towards the Susquehanna River, in the counties of Berks, Dauphin, and Lancaster, rye was grown as a winter crop, sown in November, mostly upon sandy ground or on land which had been used to grow wheat in the previous summer. After harvesting,

PREVIOUS PAGES Philadelphia was founded by William Penn, the Englishman who lends his name to Pennsylvania.

ABOVE This picture captures literally everything you could hope to see when visiting Herman at Dad's Hat distillery: whiskey, barrels, and *the* hat.

TOP RIGHT The glass cylinder contains a hydrometer that is used to check the strength of the spirit as it leaves the still. **ABOVE** Not my ideal method of consumption, but it'll do.

in the spring, farmers would load it on to their Conestoga wagons (a large German wagon of stout proportions drawn by four or five horses) and head to market in Philadelphia. The first American railroads weren't constructed until the early 19th century, so wagon or boat were the only options. The Conestoga were capable of transporting heavier loads than any other form of land transportation at that time. They also doubled up as accommodation and kitchen for the thrifty traveling farmer.

The markets weren't charmed by the rye that these farmers brought. Wheat was much more desirable but not as easy to grow. This often meant that some of the rye harvest was kept back for personal consumption, but this suited the German farmer just fine, since they could bake their pumpernickel and bauernbrot and experience a taste of home. And—of course—they made booze.

Documentation of German-made rye-based spirits (they called them "rye-dram") in Pennsylvania go as far back as the 1760s. Farmers would convert excess grains or fruits into spirit to make transportation easier, but also as a means of preserving the value of the base material. As with the Scots, this was a practice that had been going on in Germany for a couple of centuries already, but with fruits more than cereals.

In the latter part of the 1700s, hundreds of distilleries popped up in Pennsylvania, all of them operated by farmers. A typical Pennsylvanian farm at that time might have comprised a hundred acres with a few small barns constructed from logs and a still house built from stone. Access to a water source was essential and there would be a fireplace and telltale chimney. These buildings became essential production spaces, particularly for those in more remote areas who had limited access to markets.

In 1788, a traveler (who identifies himself literally as "A. Traveller") writes in the *Pennsylvania Gazette* that, "In the neighborhood of Pittsburg almost every other farm has a still-house on it. All the rye made in those parts is distilled in to whisky."

In the western part of Pennsylvania, whiskey served as a form of currency when cash was hard to come by.

Entire plantations were sometimes sold in exchange for whiskey. A. Traveller also offers some insight into how drinking culture had embedded itself in farm life:

"I was surprised to find some German farmers infected with the pernicious custom of using whisky in their families. Every morning a dram was handed round to each man, woman and child in the house, and so much have some of them become attached to it, that they mix it with cucumbers for their breakfast."

In addition to family breakfasts, harvest laborers and farmhands expected a noontime dram of whiskey, too. While the New England Colonies of Massachusetts, Rhode Island and Connecticut imported molasses from the British Caribbean to make rum, German-descended farmers in Pennsylvania were developing an extensive cottage industry producing the first truly American spirit.

Of course, the story of rye doesn't end there and we shall return to it shortly, but first it's time to drink some authentic Pennsylvanian Rye.

❧❧❧ ❧❧❧ ❧❧❧

Mountain Laurel Spirits was established in 2010, located in the northern Philadelphia suburb of Bristol. Housed in a massive former textile mill only a few blocks from the Delaware river, the distillery was founded by college buddies John Cooper and Herman Mihalich. Given that they make a rye whiskey called Dad's Hat, fittingly, Herman greets us on arrival, wearing a hat belonging to—that's right —his dad. At this point I'm unsure as to whether or not I should acknowledge that he's wearing a stetson that's almost identical to the one pictured on every bottle of whiskey he sells. A few seconds pass and I come to the conclusion that he's probably already aware of it.

I choose instead to wax lyrical about his product, which was, when I first tried it in 2014, probably the best rye whiskey I had ever tasted. But looking back on it I think I had lowered my guard. Sometimes packaging that might be construed as… gimmicky… can function as an apology for poor-quality liquid. And when I saw the hat thing I kind of assumed this was one of those. I was wrong.

There's a good reason for the hat, too. Herman's granddad came to the US from Croatia in 1905 and opened a speakeasy just outside Pittsburgh in the 1920s. The bar was licensed after Prohibition and Herman's dad ran it as the family business (while wearing his hat) throughout Herman's childhood.

In spite of the massive building, the Dad's Hat distillery only occupies a small area and also includes a tasting area, bar and gift store. There's a mash cooker, fermenters, and a still squeezed in there, as well as a selection of barrels. Herman tells us he's got loads of storage space upstairs with more barrels in it, and plenty of space to expand if needed.

Any product labeled as "rye whiskey" must, by law, contain a minimum of 51% rye in its mash bill. The remaining portion of the recipe can be made up from any other cereal, but its usually malted barley and occasionally corn that's used.

In the past, malted cereal would be an essential component of any mash bill because un-malted cereals don't have the enzymes that are necessary to convert starch into sugar during the cooking stage. Without sugar you can't make any alcohol.

Any cereal can be malted, but when distilleries refer to "malt" they are almost always referring to malted barley. Barley is favored over other malted cereals because it has higher concentrations of enzymes, and that means you need less malt in your mash, so you can devote more space to other cereals, such as rye.

Distillers are also permitted to add concentrated enzymes to their mash, which of course wasn't an option back in the 1700s. Adding enzymes gives the distiller the freedom to mash 100% un-malted cereal and eliminates the need to use malted barley. You might remember Reservoir (see page 13) used 100% rye, 100% corn, and 100% wheat in their mashes, with no malted cereal at all. These whiskey thoroughbreds are only possible through the use of enzymes during cooking. Even Steve Bashore, at Mount Vernon, permits himself some historical leniency and adds a little enzyme to his cooks, despite using malted barley in his recipe. Herman is of the same mind: "The rye we make is the pure

43

Pennsylvanian style," says Herman. "Our mash is 80% rye and 20% malted barley. That amount of barley is sufficient to convert the starch, but we throw some enzymes in there too."

Adding enzymes in there to support the malt is what Herman calls a "belt and braces" approach to whiskey making. It's basically an insurance policy, removing any doubt that the proper conversion of starch into sugar will occur. And that's particularly important when you're making a high-rye mash, because without the necessary enzymes your cook will transform into a viscous, claggy mess. Rye contains a high concentration of a starch called ß-glucan, which thickens the mash into an oatmeal consistency when it gets heated. This causes more foaming during fermentation and it can bake on to the insides of the still.

Now, some purists view 100% rye whiskey as the true representation of traditional rye whiskey—a pedigree breed whose bloodline is untainted by the DNA of lesser cereals. They believe that malted barley has no place in proper rye and that the rye should either be malted itself, or enzymes used to facilitate conversion. They're entitled to their opinions of course, but historically, rye whiskey was always made with other malted cereals, because it would be impossible to make it without. The classic Pennsylvanian style that Herman mentions is thought to be about 80% rye, which is about as high as you can go while leaving enough space for the malted barley to work the conversion.

Herman works with a rye farmer called Nevada Mease who operates Meadow Brook Farm in the Lehigh Valley, about 50 miles north of Philadelphia.

"We found Nevada produces the best rye because he leaves it in the field longer. Riper berries produce a black pepper-like, nutty flavor. Underripe berries give a green jalapeño note, and a grassiness that's something like a Sauvignon Blanc—that's not the flavor we want."

Herman runs a fairly long fermentation here, and allows 1,050 gallons of mash five to seven days to ferment. Besides making alcohol, fermentation also produces heat, which, if left unchecked, can actually kill the yeast and stall the ferment. At this distillery the five fermenters are equipped with automatic chillers to stop things from getting too hot. Long fermentations also tend to produce fruitier spirits. When Herman was developing the recipe for his whiskey he worked with a microbiologist at Michigan State University (MSU) to select a yeast producing a particularly fruity beer so as to create aromas of apricot and pineapple in the ferment. During distillation, these aromas will be encouraged to travel up the still and incorporate themselves into the spirit.

During his time at MSU, Herman ran trial distillations on a still manufactured by the German still-maker Christian Carl. He later discovered that the US sales representative for Carl lived only 20 minutes from his distillery (what did I say about Germans in Pennsylvania?!), so he chose to buy a 2,000-liter (530-gallon) model from them. This meant that all the test runs that he had conducted at MSU could easily be transitioned to his Philadelphia distillery, avoiding potentially dramatic changes in flavor and style that come with changing equipment.

The condensers that cool the spirit vapor and convert it back into a liquid use a lot of water. Mountain Laurel have a neat trick up their sleeves though, sending the water used to cool the condensers straight to the mash cooker for use in the next cook.

We've already established that rye whiskey must be made from a minimum of 51% rye and matured in new oak barrels that have been charred on the inside. There is no minimum aging requirement. However, a whiskey labeled as "straight rye" (this is actually applicable to all "straight" whiskeys) must follow additional rules, and be aged for a minimum of two years, have no added coloring or flavoring, and be the product of one state. If your powers of deduction are strong, you may conclude correctly that rye whiskey without the "straight" denomination is permitted to be colored and flavored and can be a blend of rye whiskeys from distilleries in more than one state.

Straight rye must include an age statement on the bottle if the youngest spirit in the bottle is under 4 years old. If the whiskey is over 4 years in age, a

ABOVE Yours truly (wearing my own hat) chatting to Herman Mihalich (wearing his dad's hat).

number on the bottle is optional but if there is one it'll be referencing the youngest whiskey, not the average age or the oldest.

Finally, there's the rather antiquated (but cherished by many) classification of "bottled in bond", which follows the same rules as straight rye but must be bottled at 50% ABV/100 proof and contain a blend of whiskeys that are all the same age (i.e. whiskey that was distilled in the same year). In the old days, this was a way to protect the consumer from brands that were merely bottling up whiskey from other distilleries and blending or adulterating that whiskey.

Herman bottles all three of the above sub-categories (rye, straight rye, and bonded rye) as well as two further rye expressions that are finished in port and vermouth casks for a few months. For the standard rye bottling, Herman matures in 15-gallon casks, which speed up some of the effects of maturation and allow him to bottle a product that's barely a year old. This is a strategy that many young distilleries adopt as it gets bottled product on the shelf quickly and brings cash into the business.

For his "straight" and "bottled in bond" expressions, he needs larger, 53-gallon barrels to avoid swamping the spirit with oak character. Large barrels cost about the same as small ones, so while these whiskeys will take longer to mature (and there is a cost associated with storing them) the cost of materials per gallon of liquid will be lower.

Herman leads us over to a rack that holds about two-dozen barrels and quickly gets in among them, pulling out bungs and handing out samples directly from the cask.

"People love to get excited about single barrel bottles," he says (in response to my excitement), "but for me it's the vatting of the liquids that make the best product."

"Vatting" is a term that's sometimes used to describe a blend or mixture of many barrels of whiskey. At Dad's Hat, it's also describing a process. Dad's Hat Pennsylvania Rye is bottled from a literal vat of whiskey that never gets emptied.

As soon as the level on the vat drops below halfway, it's time to feed it with more of those 15-gallon barrels of mature whiskey. The vat is made of steel, so no further maturation will take place, but by mixing and never emptying, a level of consistency between batches is ensured, plus Herman and team can credibly claim that every bottle of Pennsylvania Rye contains whiskey from every 15-gallon cask they've ever filled.

Herman uses a tapered copper tube to draw samples out of the barrel. The first is from one of the 15-gallon casks. This whiskey is coming directly from the barrel and hasn't be "cut" with water, so sits at around 120 proof. The liquid sloshes with energy as it drops into the tasting glass, with a color of red burgundy.

"Rye should be young and vibrant," Herman says, "and should smack you in the face a little bit."

We sip and talk. Then we move on to another barrel. Then another. "When we taste our barrels," he says "we find they tend to fall in to one of four categories: spicy, floral or grassy, fruity or malty, and woody. We don't want any one of these flavors to pop out more than the rest in our vatting."

For the port and vermouth expressions, Herman is finishing his 12-month old rye whiskey for three to six months in port casks and vermouth casks from Quady Winery, who are based in California. Port casks (okay, not technically a port cask because the wine isn't made in Portugal) are quite common fixtures in whiskey distilleries but a vermouth cask is a new one on me. But when you consider how great whiskey and vermouth pair together in a Manhattan, it feels like a perfect match.

The afternoon quickly descends into misty, whiskey-fueled debate around such topics as authenticity, legislation, and hats. Our planned two-hour visit ends after four hours, but only because the distillery is closing for the day and Herman has invited us out for dinner.

PENNSYLVANIA RYE (45% ABV)

Juicy cherry and toasted nuts on the nose, with a distinct bready, cereal note. Taste remains true to the cereal, cherry becoming dried, with the barrel playing a supporting role, amplifying toasted notes without contributing too much caramel. A touch of tobacco on the finish.

RIGHT For every whiskey we tasted on this trip, we drove, on average, 31 miles.

STRAIGHT RYE (47.5% ABV)

Stewed stone fruit aromas are the most noticeable aroma, with Mirabelle and sweet plum tart. On the palate, the whiskey is full-bodied, juicy, and concentrated with chili-spiced-fruit-and-nut-chocolate-bar and dark wood spiciness. The finish is dry and tacky, demanding another sip.

BOTTLED IN BOND (50% ABV)

More nutty and caramel on the nose, with less fruit and more wood spice. Flavor is very chocolate-y, with bread crust, basil nut, and cacao nib. Cinnamon-spiced mole sauce continues through to the finish.

ROAD TRIP PLAYLIST

"Maybe Tomorrow" – Terry Bush

"Rye Whiskey" – Punch Brothers

"Streets of Philadelphia" – Bruce Springsteen

OLD FASHIONED

60 ml/2 oz Dad's Hat Pennsylvania Rye
10 ml/2 teaspoons brown sugar syrup
10 ml/2 teaspoons water
a dash of Angostura Bitters

Add all of the ingredients to an old fashioned glass filled with cubed ice. Stir well for a minute or two.
Garnish with a twist of orange, or a cherry, or both.

The earliest reference to the term "cock-tail" comes from London, in 1798, but we're left guessing as to what the drink comprised. A few years later, in May 1806, Harry Croswell, the editor of *The Balance and Columbian Repositor* in Hudson, New York, tells us:

"Cock-tail is a stimulating liquor, composed of spirits of any kind, sugar, water, and bitters."

If you know your drinks you'll recognize that this is essentially a recipe for an Old Fashioned (where the water component is obtained through the melting of the ice). That's because, at the time, the drink we know as an Old Fashioned would simply have been called a "whiskey cock-tail," since, by definition, that's what it is. Flash forward 50 years, and cocktails had advanced in both their abundance and complexity, with many drinks being modified with fruit juices and fancy, imported liquors. By that point, drinks like those consumed by your grandparents—like the whiskey cocktail—seemed kind of quaint and, well… old-fashioned.

Some people like to use granulated sugar in this drink for reasons of authenticity, but it can become a little frustrating trying to get it to dissolve in a cold alcoholic drink, so I opt for syrup. Some bartenders insist on muddling fruit (cherry, orange… even pineapple!) in their Old Fashioned glasses. I wholly admonish this approach—it ruins the appearance and doesn't benefit the flavor. The Old Fashioned is a perfectly simple, reassuringly strong drink, not a fruit salad. If you like fruit, eat it for breakfast.

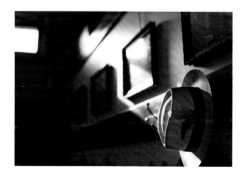

WIGLE

THEY'RE RYE-OTING ON THE STREETS!

*"I thought it safest to use good words and good drink,
rather than balls and powder."*

HUGH HENRY BRACKENRIDGE (1748–1816), AUTHOR AND LAWYER

The next morning, we're nursing hard-earned hangovers, but manage to bundle ourselves into the car and hit the road. Instead of exiting Philly on Interstate 95 (I-95), which would take us north, to New York, we jump on I-76, heading west. We're not done with Pennsylvania yet, and while this slight detour (around 10 hours driving) makes little sense geographically, it makes perfect sense from the perspective of the narrative! In other words: Pennsylvania has more history to explore and more whiskey to consume.

The problem with overthrowing a colonial ruler is that once the job is done someone needs to run the country. You also need to manage the debt that's been racked up through the war effort—$24 million in state government debt and a further $54 million in borrowed cash. Following the Revolutionary War, the responsibility of sorting it all out and turning the nation into a profitable business fell on first Secretary of the Treasury, Alexander Hamilton.

His first move was to consolidate the state and national debts into one big pool that could be funded by the federal government. He then used federal clout to impose duties on all imported products, simultaneously claiming precious tax dollars and stimulating domestic economic growth. But the books still didn't balance, so Hamilton passed the first tax levied by the national government on the domestic product. And that product? Whiskey.

Since whiskey was considered a non-essential item and arguably a luxury, Hamilton saw whiskey as the least objectionable tax that the government could levy. It also gained him support from social reformers, who hoped that a "sin tax" would raise public awareness of the harmful effects of alcohol.

The tax on whiskey was federally imposed and therefore collectable everywhere. And like all taxes, it wasn't popular. But it was particularly hated in the West.

Distilleries in eastern, urban areas were taxed—as they are today—based on the amount of spirit they produced. This figure could be closely monitored by the tax man, who would visit and record the goings-on. But on the frontier, to the west of Pennsylvania, where no tax man would be seen dead (though that was potentially the fate that waited for them there) tax was usually estimated, and distilleries were taxed based on the size of their stills and an assumed 4-months production. Very few distilleries produced for that much of the year though (and some for as little as a week) so in those parts, small producers were being taxed for whiskey they never even made. For many, this tax was reminiscent of the colonial era. The Revolutionary War was fought on the principle that there should be "no taxation without representation" and many of the producers in the west of Virginia and Pennsylvania, who were culturally and geographically quite far removed from Philadelphia—and who had

themselves fought in the Revolutionary War—believed that history was repeating itself.

The tax was also payable in cash, which favored bigger distilleries in the developed East, because they were routinely paid in cash. Smaller distilleries, on the western frontiers, of which there were perhaps a couple of orders of magnitude more, existed amongst a barter economy, which meant trading whiskey for other goods or services.

And if you couldn't pay the tax or didn't register your still? Well then you needed to ride a wagon 300 miles to appear in court in Philadelphia.

Many small-scale distillers believed that Hamilton deliberately designed the tax to ruin them and promote big business. Whatever the case, they were left with only two options: shut up shop or stick it to the man and go down fighting. Most chose the latter.

Right from the start, collection of the tax in the West was thwarted. Most distillers simply refused to pay it, but some took it a step further, harassing tax collectors and chasing them out of town. Those that were seen to house or feed traveling tax men were threatened too.

Opposition to the tax was particularly prevalent in four southwestern counties near Pittsburgh: Allegheny, Fayette, Westmoreland and Washington. On September 11, 1791, a recently appointed tax collector named Robert Johnson was tarred and feathered by a gang in Washington County. Then a man was sent to serve court warrants to Johnson's attackers and was whipped, tarred, and feathered too. In Pittsburgh, a semi-militant group known as the Mingo Creek Association organized a militia and issued demands to the government to abolish the tax. The Mingo Creek Association actually modeled their actions on the protests of the American Revolution, encouraging the raising of liberty poles in town centers and on roads, as a symbol of the individual's right to freedom and prosperity.

In the summer of 1794, federal marshal David Lenox began the process of serving writs to 60

distillers in western Pennsylvania who had not paid the tax. He enlisted the help of local wealthy landowner and tax collector, John Neville. The pair attempted to extract unpaid taxes from a man named William Miller, and in retaliation Neville's house was besieged by 700 rebels the following day. As the Governor of Pennsylvania, Thomas Mifflin, wrote, "bodies of armed men attacked the house." Neville escaped, which was fortunate, because the mob set fire to the entire estate.

Back in Philadelphia, President Washington was facing up to the reality of the rising insurrection in the West. The handling of the rebellion would be the first real test of the Federal Government to see if it could enforce laws across the nation. Washington issued a two-pronged attack: first by sending commissioners to negotiate with the rebels, and second, "with the deepest regret," raising a militia of 12,000 men (a huge force for that time) to protect the commissioners and assist with suppressing the uprising. In September of 1794, Washington accompanied the militia west—the first and only time a sitting President has led troops in the field.

When the mob got wise to Washington's imminent arrival they took the decision to strike first. Wealthy landowner David Bradford, along with several other men, attacked a mail carrier and discovered three letters from Pittsburgh expressing disapproval of the attack on Neville's property. Bradford used the letters as an excuse to encourage attacks, inciting 7,000 men to rally in the West of Pittsburgh, which was little more than a village at that time.

The response from Pittsburgh was to send barrels of whiskey to quell the temper of the mob as the founder of the *Pittsburgh Gazette*, Hugh Henry Brackenridge, recounted in his 1795 book, *Incidents of the Insurrection in the Western Parts of Pennsylvania*: "I thought it safest to use good words and good drink, rather than balls and powder. It cost me four barrels of old whiskey that day, and I would rather spare that than a quart of blood."

Washington's show of might had the desired effect. Some rebels were arrested but most of them fled, with up to 2,000 escaping to the Allegheny mountains.

OPPOSITE This pot still can be configured to make high-strength spirits for vodka and gin, as well as whiskey.

Nearly all those that were arrested were acquitted due to a lack of evidence, but two men—John Mitchell and Philip Wigle—were sentenced to hang.

Even in the aftermath of the Whiskey Rebellion, taxes in the West went largely uncollected. The events had far-reaching repercussions however, as they divided the population and expedited the formation of political parties. In 1802, the whiskey tax was repealed after Thomas Jefferson's Republican Party came to power.

As tough as it was on small producers, the tax signified the beginning of whiskey's slow transition away from agriculture startup venture and into the commercial, industrialized era. The eradication of the whiskey's cottage industry would certainly have had a negative impact on marketplace variety and perhaps availability. But the larger distilleries would unquestionably have produced consistently better quality spirits than "mom and pop" in their cabin. It's interesting to see that the farm distillery is not an entirely forgotten enterprise, though. We will be visiting a few of them later in our journey.

For now though, we're in Pittsburgh, right in the heartlands of the Whiskey Rebellion. Fort Pitt was built here in the 1750s, on the point where the Allegheny and Monongahela rivers meet to become the Ohio River. The three rivers made the site ideal for a settlement, both as a trading route, and for defense. In the 19th century, Pittsburgh experienced huge population growth, fueled by the most productive coal mines in the country and the iron and steel industries which they supported. Then the Great Depression came along, marking the beginning of a long period of industrial decline in "Iron City."

The Pittsburgh metropolitan area has half a dozen or so distilleries today, but we're here to visit the biggest and oldest of them. The Wigle distillery is located in Pittsburgh's Strip District, not far from the banks of the Allegheny. This area is full of old warehouses, some of which date back to the early 19th century, when they operated as mills and factories, benefiting from close proximity to the river. Now, it's a trendy area and many of the buildings have been converted into restaurants and, yes, a distillery.

If you've been paying attention you'll recognize that the Wigle brand is named after Philip Wigle, hero of the Whiskey Rebellion (depending on which side you're on). The story goes that Wigle was one of the first to throw a punch during the uprising, triggering a chain reaction that inspired numerous others to take up arms. That's why he was afforded special treatment by the courts and sentenced to hang (he was actually later pardoned by George Washington).

Entering the distillery door, we're first greeted by the distillery shop and tasting room, which is decorated with images of Philip Wigle and historical trivia from the time of the Rebellion. But this isn't some gloomy museum—it's a bright and airy bar space, filled with dozens of bottles for interested folk to sample.

"We make tons of stuff," the head of product development, Michael Foglia, tells me.

He's not exaggerating. The distillery has released around 50 bottlings in the past seven years, and around two-thirds of those were whiskey. This is a distillery that's excited to be making whiskey and that isn't at all afraid to try things out and see if they work.

Aside from the great range of bottles, it's the bottles themselves that are the first point of interest. Wigle branding is somewhat reminiscent of Google, and each product label is characterized with a bright color scheme or vivid pattern. The overall impression—controversially—is one of an accessible, family-friendly whiskey. (That said, earlier iterations of their branding included a long noose on the label that affixed itself to the wonky 'g' in "Wigle"—a reference to Philip Wigle's narrowly escaped fate.)

"We want to invite in as much fun as possible," Michael tells me.

I'm all for it. If whiskey is to succeed in the next 20 years, it needs to challenge convention and appeal to more than just spirits geeks, good ol' boys, and dive bar drunks. The entire Wigle ethos seems to be built around building and nurturing a community of whiskey advocates in Pittsburgh.

This is why Wigle's founders, the Meyer family, devoted two years of hard work to lobbying the state government to change the laws so that they could sell product directly to consumers from their tasting

room. It's also why Wigle has gone on to host an annual "Tar & Feather" party, where whiskey lovers can gather, drink whiskey, and remember the Whiskey Rebellion (I'm told nobody is actually tarred or feathered, which is actually a little disappointing).

As far as their own history goes, the distillery was built in 2011 and the first products were launched in 2012. In the beginning, they made ends meet by selling gin, along with un-aged rye and wheat whiskeys, while laying down whiskey in cask for future releases. Seven years on, the operation is sitting on 2,000 barrels of maturing stock. In that time, they've expanded the operation to include bottle shops, a barrel house restaurant and cider brewery. And it's thanks in part to the many types of whiskey they make here that Wigle has been the most awarded whiskey distillery in the US by the American Craft Spirits Association for four straight years!

Unsurprisingly, the biggest product here is rye.

The Wigle rye mash comprises 68% rye, 20% malted barley and 12% wheat. The cereals are loaded into a mill by hand (using buckets) then sent to the 3,600-liter (950-gallon) mash cooker. The grains are

TOP This is one of Wigle's aging facilities, located a short drive away, over the Allegheny River.
ABOVE Philip Wigle was, like many Pennsylvanian whiskey makers, German, so probably pronounced it *vee-gel*.

cooked at 180°F (82.2°C) and like all the whiskeys made here, enzymes are used to aid conversion. It's in one of two 3,600-liter (950-gallon) fermenters or a bigger, 6,200-liter (1,650-gallon) fermenter that the alcohol gets made, in a ferment that tends to lasts around four days. The same yeast is used for all whiskeys, with the exception of Wigle Malt, which has its own specific strain.

Wigle has two German stills: "Carl," which has a 400-gallon capacity, and "Carol," with a 530-gallon capacity. Both stills are able to perform the first stripping distillation, but only Carl is used for the finishing run. Hot water from the condensers is recycled directly to the mash cooker for the next cook. The spirit is cut from still strength of around 70% down to 59% for barrel entry. The main distillery has only a handful of casks, which are either filled or emptied, ready for bottling. Wigle has two warehouses on the north side of the Allegheny.

After rye, bourbon is the second best-selling bottle on the roster, and besides their standard mash of 70% corn, 15% wheat and 15% malted barley, Wigle also makes a bourbon to the same recipe but using an heirloom corn variety sourced from Weatherbury Farms in Washington, Pennsylvania. The variety is called Wapsie Valley and it looks like normal yellow corn that's been tie-dyed red.

"Although we're expected to make great rye, demand was telling us to make a bourbon too and this was the best corn we could find," says Michael. "It has a higher protein count, so makes less alcohol, but it gives our whiskey a great, earthy flavor."

Wigle also produce a few mashes of malt whiskey every year, as well as wheat whiskeys. At this point, Michael starts listing other mashes the distillery has experimented with. A lot of the distillery team has come from a brewing background, so tinkering at the mashing stage of production makes sense.

"Our approach is informed by what we see around us in craft brewing," Michael says.

There's experimentation in warehousing going on here as well. Wigle bottle a bourbon finished in Madeira casks and a rye finished in port casks. Then there's a malted rye/malted barley whiskey, aged in

Mexican mezcal casks called "Oaxaca Rye" and another whiskey, using the same mash, aged in ex-Laphroaig casks called "Kilted Rye."

When you consider they also produce half a dozen flavored whiskeys, plus rums, gins, vodka, absinthe, liqueurs, and bitters, it's no wonder they lobbied so hard for a tasting room!

PENNSYLVANIA RYE (42% ABV)

Pleasing aromas of walnut whip, salted pecan, and caramelized peanut on the nose. This is a nutty rye for sure. Dry and slightly spicy tasting, with a dry but relatively light finish. A slightly tacky mouthfeel.

OAXACA RYE (40% ABV)

The nose is eerily soft on this spirit, like it's hiding a secret it's not ready to reveal yet. There's a baked, cakey note to it, and perhaps a suggestion of smoked almond. The taste is also not as boisterous as the name suggests (seemingly the mezcal and rye have canceled each other out) as soft smokiness toys with the fruitier aspects of the rye.

SINGLE-BARREL STRAIGHT BOURBON (50% ABV)

Bright and inviting on the nose, with a nice orange marmalade note that pairs with light corn syrup and buttered toast (it smells like breakfast pancakes). There's some gentle spice there too: mace and ground ginger. It's hotter and dryer than the nose suggests, but it's big and satisfying too. There's a surprisingly pronounced cereal note to finish. A great whiskey.

ROAD TRIP PLAYLIST

"Reelin' In The Years" — Steely Dan

"Rebellion" — Arcade Fire

"Fortunate Son" — Creedence Clearwater Revival

COLD RYE FLIP

50 ml/1⅔ oz Wigle Port Rye
10 ml/2 teaspoons water
15 ml/½ oz gomme
1 whole egg

Add all of the ingredients to a cocktail shaker filled with ice. Shake really well for 10 seconds, then strain into a chilled coupe (cocktail) glass. To garnish, grate a little nutmeg on top.

These days the "Flip" family of mixed drinks usually consist of spirit, egg, sugar and spices. Generally, this drink is "thrown" or shaken into a chilled alcoholic custard that's not dissimilar to egg-nog. Modern flips are nearly always served cold but 200 years ago they tended to be warm, and were served as an essential cold weather pick-me-up.

Go back even further however, and you'll see a back bar with considerably fewer eggs on their spec sheet and rather more beer. The original flip, popularized in colonial taverns, consisted of a large bowl filled with sugar (or molasses), beer, spices, and rum. The barkeep would plunge a red-hot loggerhead (also known as a "hottle" or "flip dog") into the mixture and watch it seethe and foam. The drink, which took on a mousse-like texture and subtle bitterness from the burning sugar, was then dispensed into handled mugs for consumption.

By the 1870s, the flip had misplaced the beer and evolved into a drink containing egg which, when shaken, achieved a similarly frothy texture to the original but without all the health and safety issues associated with swinging a hot poker around a bar room. Jerry Thomas' 1887 *How to Mix Drinks* lists quite a few flip recipes, including one for a Cold Whiskey Flip that uses either bourbon or rye.

LIBERTY POLE

MONONGAHELA, THE WHISKEY THAT HISTORY FORGOT

"That drove the spigot out of him!" cried Stubb. "'Tis July's immortal Fourth; all fountains must run wine today! Would now, it were old Orleans whiskey, or old Ohio, or unspeakable old Monongahela! Then, Tashtego, lad, I'd have ye hold a canakin to the jet, and we'd drink round it! Yea, verily, hearts alive, we'd brew choice punch in the spread of his spout-hole there, and from that live punch-bowl quaff the living stuff."

FROM *MOBY DICK*, BY HERMAN MELVILLE (1819–91)

In the 1800s, dozens of distilleries perched on the Monongahela River's "falling banks" (the Lenape Unami language translation of *monongahela*), harnessing its water to turn mills and cool stills. This river was also a vital trading route for Pennsylvanian rye whiskey, as it fed into the Ohio River, which fed into the Mississippi, and the Mississippi dropped down to New Orleans, from where whiskey could be transported anywhere. As such, "Old Ohio" and "Monongahela Rye" featured on whiskey packaging and in advertising throughout the 19th century, becoming an indicator of quality, much as Kentucky would later become famous for its bourbon.

Tracing the path of the Monongahela, we drive through the small Pittsburgh suburb of Large, which took its name from the Large family who established a farm there in 1796. Jonathan Large built a distillery there shortly after the Whiskey Rebellion. They bottled a "Pure Monongahela Rye," which was known nationally by 1900. The Large Distillery was later sold to The National Distillery Company, who retired the Large label but bottled the whiskey produced there as Old Overholt.

We stop for a time at Belle Vernon, where I-70 crosses the river. It's here that the Gibson distillery

once resided, which was a 40-acre site once comprised a distillery, eight bonded warehouses, a four-story malt house, a drying kiln, a gristmill, a saw mill, two carpenter shops, a blacksmith shop, an ice house, and a cooper's shop. At its peak, in the late 1880s, Gibson was filling 150 barrels of whiskey a day and was the biggest rye distillery in America.

A few more miles downriver and east of here is West Bethany, in Westmoreland County, which was the location of the second biggest distillery of that time, The Samuel Dillinger Distillery (aka Ruffsdale Distillery). Dillinger was of German descent, and did all those things that German farmers in Pennsylvania liked to do, such as driving his Conestoga wagon with a team of six horses across the Allegheny mountains, shifting merchandise between the cities of Pittsburgh and Baltimore. Although their advertising stated that the distillery was founded in 1834, it was actually in the 1850s when Dillinger purchased a custom gristmill and built his distillery.

Westmoreland County was also home to the most famous brand of Pennsylvanian rye and the oldest

PREVIOUS PAGES The Monongahela river area housed the biggest and best distilleries during the early 19th century.

continually maintained whiskey brand in America: Old Overholt. Its story deserves some special attention, and since we're cruising through suburban Pittsburgh, there's no better time like the present.

It begins with the *Mary Hope*, which sailed from Gravesend, England, arriving in Philadelphia on September 23, 1710. On board were Marcus and Elizabeth Oberholzer and their five children, who originated from the village of Oberholtz, near Zurich, Switzerland. Also aboard the *Mary Hope*—which has a solid claim for being the most momentous chapter in American whiskey history—was a German man called Jacob Boehm (more on him and his descendants on page 125—Jim Beam). Soon after reaching America, the Overholtzers settled on a 500-acre tract on the west bank of the Schuylkill River in Pennsylvania. Following the Revolutionary War, the family began to fragment, and one faction, the Oberholds, led by Henry Oberhold, moved west of the Allegheny mountains, along what is now the Lincoln Highway, to West Overton.

It was Henry's sons (Marcus' grandsons), Abraham and Christian, who established the "Old Farm" distillery in 1810, which eventually led to the establishment of Old Overholt Rye Whiskey.

Abraham took on the day-to-day running of the distillery, which was producing about a barrel of whiskey a week in the 1820s. Although it began as a farm operation, it wasn't long before the distillery had outgrown itself and graduated into a commercial enterprise. In 1832, Abraham built a new stone still house and expanded capacity tenfold. He also added a gristmill and made a fair bit of cash contract milling for other farms. In 1854, Abraham's sons, Jacob and Henry, joined forces with their cousin Henry O. Overholt (the fourth generation of the family, in case you're struggling to keep up) and built a new distillery at Broad Ford. The A. Overholt & Co. Whiskey Company made "Old Monongahela" whiskey out of this modern facility.

Back in West Overton, Abraham's operation continued to grow, and in 1859 he demolished the old mill and still room, replacing it with a massive brick building, six stories high and 100-ft long. This distillery was capable of making 860 gallons of whiskey a day—one of the largest capacity distilleries of the era—and today it's a whiskey museum. The same year his new distillery opened, Jacob, his son, died and Abraham bought his shares in the Broad Ford operation. Between the two distilleries, Abraham had become a major player in the whiskey world.

Abraham died in 1870, and the distilleries changed hands a few times, passing from one incompetent family member to another until they finally ended up in the hands of one of Abraham's grandchildren, Henry Clay Frick. Frick was about as far from incompetent as any man can be, a self-made millionaire who had amassed a fortune manufacturing coke (the fuel made from coal), which he supplied to his friend Andrew Carnegie's steel business. Carnegie would become one of the richest men in history, and Frick one of the richest men in America. Frick's fortune enabled him to finance things like the construction of the Pennsylvania Railroad, but it also allowed him to buy his granddad's quaint old whiskey distilleries. The A. Overholt operation may have been a sentimental acquisition for Frick, but the man knew how to run a business. He recruited his friend, banker Andrew Mellon, in as one-third owner, while selling another third to one Charles W. Mauck, who got two-thirds of the profit in exchange for running the business. In 1888 they changed the name of the whiskey to "Old Overholt" and stuck an illustration of a scowling Abraham Overholt on the bottle so there was little doubt about who the name was referencing.

The next 30 years were a boom time for Pennsylvanian rye, and in particular Old Overholt. Rather poetically, Frick died on the eve of Prohibition, in December 1919. The company passed to Andrew Mellon, ending 109 years of family ownership. Old Overholt was one of a select bunch of distilleries that was granted a license to produce medicinal whiskey during Prohibition (more on this later), and so remained in more or less continuous operation.

The period following Prohibition was less kind to Old Overholt, as the business changed hands a couple of times while the popularity of rye whiskey tanked. By the 1960s, Old Overholt was the only nationally distributed brand of rye whiskey. In 1987, the James B. Beam Distilling Company bought the struggling brand and moved production to its Kentucky distillery, where it is still produced today. This, for me anyway, is a rather satisfying end to the tale, given that Marcus Oberholzer and Jacob Boehm stepped on to American soil at exactly the same hour, on September 23, 1710.

However, the rehoming of Old Overholt in Kentucky also spelled the end of Old Monongahela Rye—an entire category of whiskey ceased to exist.

⁂ ⁂ ⁂

We bid farewell to the Monongahela and continue on I-70 and head west, skirting under Mingo Creek park, the place that gave its name to the rebellion militia that raised liberty poles. This road will take you all the way to Utah if you let it. Our next stop is only a few miles away though.

The city of Washington, Pennsylvania is sometimes called Little Washington to distinguish it from DC. That'll be a point of contention for the locals I expect, since both the Pennsylvanian city and county of Washington were named in 1781, a full ten years before the nation's capital adopted the name. There's no contesting the fact that it's "little," though.

Washington is home to the Bradford House museum, former home of David Bradford, who was the leader of the rebellion there. It is a National Historical Landmark and open to the public for tours. Right behind the house is Mingo Creek Distillery, makers of Liberty Pole Spirits.

Like Wigle, Liberty Pole lean heavily on the history of Pennsylvanian rye. But unlike Wigle, history penetrates through the entire distillery experience, the spirits they make, and the packaging they're dressed in. The distillery and tasting room are modeled on an 18th-century residence and feel like the kind of place one might plan insurrections or discuss who's sheltering tax men and how best to deal with them. On the wall there's a portrait of the greatest tax man of them all, Alexander Hamilton. Although…

"The portrait is upside down as a symbol of disrespect," co-owner Jim Hough says, "but we always tell people that even though we honor the rebels, we still dutifully pay our taxes every quarter."

Co-owner (and wife of Jim) Ellen Hough tends the distillery bar on this occasion, dispensing both whiskey and historical trivia in generous measures. The Liberty Pole bottles feature a spirited-looking heroine beside a pole dressed in colored cloths. The labels have a faux-aged feel to them, so you'd never know the distillery was founded in June 2016.

Such is the knowledge of Jim and Ellen, I could imagine folks with no interest in whiskey visiting this distillery just for the history lesson. Business is good here, and the Houghs have just completed an equipment upgrade, which has doubled their capacity. They make four types of whiskey here: bourbon, peated bourbon, rye, and corn.

If it wasn't obvious already, bourbon whiskey is not limited to the state of Kentucky. It can be made anywhere in the US. Bourbon whiskey must be made from a mash bill comprising a minimum 51% corn and bottled at least 80 proof (40% ABV). It is not permitted to be distilled to more than 160 proof (80% ABV) and must be aged in a new oak containers, entering the barrel at no more than 125 proof (62.25% ABV). All of these rules are intended to ensure that every product labeled bourbon reaches certain quality standards and that it conforms to recognized flavor norms. The more specific the rules, the better the quality control, but also the greater the suppression of creativity and innovation.

"Straight" bourbon follows the same rules as bourbon, except it must be aged for a minimum of two years. "Bottled in Bond" bourbon is the same as any other whiskey, in that it must be bottled at 50% ABV, must be at least four years old, and must contain all the same age spirit in the bottle.

For bourbon, it's things like the majority corn mash bill, distillation strength, the use of new charred casks and limits on fill strength that define the flavor of the product. The corn ensures a sweet, buttery flavor; the distillation limit prevents the flavor being stripped out; the charred barrel filtered out unpleasant notes and adds plenty of oak flavor; the fill strength ensures that a particular set of flavor compounds are extracted from the oak. But as long as you play within those parameters, anything goes. Until the recent craft distillery revolution, bourbon distilleries had been either ignorant or uninterested in new flavor-making opportunities that were available to them. But now we're seeing a wealth of new whiskeys hitting the market that intend on pushing the rules to the limits.

As any good lawyer would tell you, if you want to find a legal loophole it's usually best to focus on what the contract doesn't cover. The law where bourbon is concerned is short and to the point, leaving a number of creative options available. We've seen one of these options leveraged at Wigle (see page 54); now, at Liberty Pole, we have ourselves a heated bourbon.

The bourbon here is made from a mash of 57% corn, 18% wheat, and 25% malted barley. Peated bourbon also uses 59% corn but the rest of the mash is peated malt. The rye is 61% rye, 13% wheat, 13% malted rye, and 13% malted barley. Corn whiskey is made from 80% corn and 20% malt.

Corn, rye, and wheat are sourced from a farm in Westmoreland County, which grow 25 acres of rye and corn exclusively for Liberty Pole. The corn is of particular interest, as it's an heirloom variety called "bloody butcher." Like most non-GMO varieties, it's a low-yield crop but the pay-off comes in the bold flavor and oily texture it imparts in the whiskey.

Most of the barrels here are 30 gallons in size, but like most distilleries that are using small casks, the plan is to transition over to larger casks in time.

"Our hope, now that the new system is up and running," says Jim, "will be to put at least two 53-gallon barrels away each week while continuing to fill 30 gallon barrels for the next few years."

Ironically, the whiskey that interests me the most in the Liberty Pole range is the one that has barely seen the inside of a barrel. Of all the whiskeys on the market that claim to reproduce a 200-year-old style of rye, Bassett Town Whiskey is probably one of the more authentic. The name comes from the proposed name for the town, which appeared on early deeds but was scrubbed out in favor of Washington. The whiskey is the same mash bill as their aged rye, and while this isn't what you would call a classic formula, it does illustrate the probable randomness of the mash bills

that would have built the whiskeys of early 1800s. Its appearance is almost like water, despite being aged, as Jim puts it, "only about as long as it takes to get it over the mountain on the back of a strong horse."

BASSETT TOWN RYE (40% ABV)

Green and fresh on the nose, with some notes of blackcurrant and warm hay. There's some soft citrus aromas too, probably as a result of the wheat component. The taste is spicy but not what you would call "hot." There's a toasted, malty finish.

RYE WHISKEY (46% ABV)

Aromas of caramel and hazelnut, and even a touch of tobacco on the nose. It's sweet on the palate, with lots of honey and butterscotch, which gives way to rye spice, a touch of fennel seed, and a slight citric quality. A good entry-level rye.

BOURBON (46% ABV)

Aroma is big and ripe, with banana bread and baking spices. On repeat visits it reminds me of gooey banana baked in foil. Barrel-char dryness comes through on the finish. A balanced and fragrant bourbon.

PEATED BOURBON (46% ABV)

The smoke is sooty, and reminds me of the smell of new carpet! Smoke is less apparent on the taste, which reintroduces some of the plantain/banana notes that were present on the bourbon.

ROAD TRIP PLAYLIST

"Whiskey River" — Willie Nelson

"Other Side" — Josh Ritter

"Ohio" — Crosby, Stills, Nash & Young

OPPOSITE ABOVE "Little" Washington might be little but it's certainly big on American history (and whiskey). **OPPOSITE BELOW** And if there's a heroine, there must be a villain too—shame on you, Mr. Hamilton!

LIBERTY POLE: MONONGAHELA, THE WHISKEY THAT HISTORY FORGOT

CUCUMBER SPRITZ

35 ml/I ¼ oz Bassett Town Rye Whiskey

35 ml/I ¼ oz cucumber juice

5 ml/I teaspoon gomme

soda water, to top up

Add all of the ingredients to a highball glass filled with ice.
Stir well and garnish with a cucumber ribbon.

Inspired by the musings of A. Traveller (see page 42), I was intrigued to discover what cucumber and whiskey mixed together actually tastes like. Unfortunately I had very little to go on as far as a recipe was concerned, as all A. Traveler tells us is that this concoction was served for breakfast… and to children. It brings to mind a bowl of grated cucumber mush, steeped in still-strength booze. Perhaps the cucumber component was steeped/preserved in the whiskey (like a pickle), meaning that this delicacy could be served year-round (yay!).

I used a juice extractor to blitz a whole cucumber into a pulp-free, green-colored water. I peel the cucumber before juicing, which gives the juice a cleaner, less vegetal flavor. When mixed with Liberty Poll's Basset Town Whiskey, the flavors worked surprisingly well together, but were improved dramatically with a little bit of fizz and some sugar.

And thus, the Cucumber Spritz was born. Perfect for long afternoons in the sun or, indeed, family breakfasts (for those members of the family that are old enough to drink).

TUTHILLTOWN

WATER OF LIFE

"We call it aqua vitae, and this name is remarkably suitable, since it really is the water of immortality. It prolongs life, clears away ill-humors, strengthens the heart, and maintains youth."

ARNALDUS DE VILLA NOVA, (C.1240–1311), PHYSICIAN

So far, the narrative of our journey has concerned itself with the pioneering whiskey makers of the colonial era and the nascent United States. We've learned that even in the most hellish environments (or perhaps especially in those environments) people will find a way to make booze because of the freedom from hardship that it offers. And we've learned that those same people will fight to protect their right to make alcohol. So with the motivation established, let's explore the key ingredients that are required to make whiskey. Over the next three chapters we will visit three whiskey distilleries in the north east of the country, each producing a unique brand of spirit, and each with a special connection to the ingredients that make whiskey: water, cereal, and wood.

We're traveling first to the town of Gardiner, in New York's beautiful Hudson Valley. This place is the home of the Tuthilltown Distillery, producer of the Hudson brand of American whiskey, which has been one of the greatest success stories of the modern era.

Now, if this book was written before 2004, this would be the moment when I hit you with the incredible revelation that the gristmill at Tuthilltown is the oldest continually running mill in the state of New York. Unfortunately it was decommissioned the following year.

The original mill was built in 1788, by Selah Tuthill, when he was just 18 years old. The location

was chosen because it was on the Albany Post Road, which was the main mail route from New York City to Albany (tracing the original Wickquasgeck Trail, carved into the brush of Manhattan by Native American inhabitants). The other reason for the location is it sits on the banks of the Shawangunk Kill, a 50-mile- (80-km-) long stream that flows northward through Orange, Sullivan, and Ulster counties. It is a tributary to the Wallkill, which is itself a tributary to the Hudson.

One thing that every distillery in this book has in common, no matter how different they may appear to do things, is that they all have a dependable water source. Water is the single most important resource for a booze-making operation. You can always find a way to transport grains and barrels to a distillery, but even today, a distillery without a reliable water supply is destined to fail. Perhaps it's no coincidence that the state that produces the most whiskey (Kentucky) has more miles of navigable water than any other state in the union.

I have a well-respected whiskey book in my library that devotes a number of pages to the significance of water sourcing for the making of whiskey. It stresses how many whiskeys around the world owe much of their character to water filtered through "granite mountains" and "sandstone stacks", or water sourced from "ancient lakes." In another book I own,

The Malt Whisky File, which is concerned with Scottish single malt whisky, the author lists the water source for each distillery along with a short H_2O biography.

The whiskey marketeers of the late-20th century loved nothing more than to emphasize the importance of water to the quality of their product. And most of us greedily lapped it up, believing that water imparted some intangible, supernatural quality to a whiskey that was elemental to the uniqueness of the distillery. Indeed, we will soon find ourselves in Kentucky, where a great deal of emphasis is still placed on the "limestone filtered" water. We'll discuss specifics of that in due course.

Around a decade ago I was speaking to my friend Stuart Howe, one of the world's most accomplished brewers, on the subject of water in brewing. He told me that he could add and remove minerals from his water so as to emulate naturally occurring water from anywhere in the world. I was rather taken aback by this unholy claim, having been led to believe that good quality, natural water was the backbone of any great brewing or distilling operation. But the more I investigated the more I found that you would be hard pushed to find any distilleries that don't tamper with their water a little. Even those that use water fresh from a spring still need to pass it through a mesh filter. Those that get their water from the municipal supply might filter for hardness, chlorine, and microorganisms, for example.

Of course, 250 years ago a good water source was probably the defining factor when deciding where to locate a distillery. Not only because the operation needed water for cooking cereals and cooling stills, but also because it would almost certainly be vital to a gristmill, which requires water for turning the mill and grinding the grains.

In the first of these examples, water serves as a substrate in which the sugars of the cooked cereal can dissolve into in preparation for fermentation. The precise mineral content, total dissolved solids, and pH of the water will have some impact on what gets extracted from the grain, and how the fermentation process plays out. But unless the water is contaminated or has an excessively high pH, it shouldn't hinder the beer-making process that much.

From a flavor standpoint, the most important water in the whiskey is the water that goes in the bottle to proof down the whiskey to the correct strength, as this water will be present in every glass. Does the hardness or mineral content of this water matter? Since it's unlikely to make up more than 10% of a bottle, my answer is "probably not, but don't rule it out." What's absolutely of great importance is the water you use to make your ice, which, once melted, could make up to 50% of your glass.

For folk living in the 18th century, microbiology, mineralogy and hydrogeology were not subjects discussed around the colonial kitchen table. That said, water was held in high esteem by many for its therapeutic properties, but the average distiller or miller in colonial New York would have spent very little time thinking about its quality.

The Hudson Valley was once home to around 1,000 distilleries, almost of them harnessing the power of New York's rivers, streams and ponds. The industrial era put an end to many of them, when cereals started being sourced from massive farms, and steam (then electric) mills were invented. Distilleries consolidated, grew in size, and the memory of the tiny farm distilleries that populated the land slowly began to fade. The few traditional distilleries that remained by the time Prohibition came about were the last survivors of a dying dynasty.

Following Prohibition, the Hudson Valley remained "dry" for 85 years, but the first trickle of change occurred when a new distillery opened its doors in 2005. It was the first in New York state since Prohibition and one of the first half-dozen new, small distilleries across the nation. Today there are dozens of distilleries in the Hudson Valley, which has become such a hotbed of whiskey production that some producers are suggesting that an entirely new category of whiskey is being made here, and that it deserves legal recognition just like bourbon. But what of that first distillery? The one that started it all?

Tuthilltown Distillery shouldn't actually exist. When Ralph Erenzo bought the property in 2001, his plan was to turn it into a ranch for rock climbers who climb the nearby Shawagunk Mountains. Ralph had himself been climbing the gunks for 55 years. He was going to call the B&B "Bunks in the Gunks." Difficult neighbors scuppered the plans though, and over the next three years, under substantial financial duress, Ralph began selling off parts of the property to pay lawyers and engineers.

Another option was urgently needed. Well, it turned out that the old Tuthilltown site had a few hidden treasures lurking amongst its various buildings, including that old gristmill dating back to 1788. Before Ralph bought the place, the mill was still in every day operation milling kosher flour for Jewish bakeries. Ralph considered recommissioning the mill, but it was difficult to see the business opportunity in a mill that takes four hours to produce five pounds of flour.

And then Brian Lee got involved. Brian was working for ESPN at the time as an on-site technical consultant, and being a man with a passion for making things (including Windsor back chairs and kayaks) he was attracted by the opportunity of creating wooden components for the mill. With his options dwindling, Ralph was only too happy to let Brian have a crack at it. But within 48 hours of arriving at Tuthilltown, Brian declared, "This isn't an opportunity; it's a death sentence."

A new plan was required.

So Ralph approached the zoning commission and asked them outright, "what can I do with this property?" Their response made him start to consider the possibility of starting a winery, but given that there are three within a two-mile radius and over 100 in the Hudson valley, he decided against it.

The idea of making alcohol was something that seemed to fit, however. And this was when Ralph discovered a piece of New York legislation that would change everything. Prior to 2000, if you wanted to open a distillery of any kind in New York, you needed to find $65,000 for the license. But in 2000 a new category of "farm distillery licenses" was created, which cost just $1,500. You could apply for one of these licenses on the proviso that you

ABOVE The tasting room and "country store" at Tuthilltown is modeled on colonial American architecture.

produced less than 35,000 gallons (132,000 liters) of liquid each year.

This possibility of distilling spirits caught a hold of Ralph and he began experimental apple brandy brews, distilling them on top of his kitchen stove in a kettle. And with the help of Brian Lee, Ralph managed to get a distilling license and in 2003 opened New York state's first distillery since 1919. (I suspect the neighbors wished they'd kept quiet about the B&B!)

It took a couple of years to get there, mind you. Ralph and Brian spent months learning the intricacies of fermentation and distillation and when they took delivery of their distilling equipment they plumbed and welded it all together themselves. The first product off the stills was an apple vodka, made from reject apples collected from nearby orchards.

Besides the physical building of the distillery, Ralph also had a challenge ahead of him on the marketing side of things too. "In the beginning, I had to explain that, 'Yes, you can make bourbon in New York.'"

Early feedback of his startup bourbon operation ranged from curious amusement to outright dissent. Besides being the first legal whiskey made in New York, this was the first bourbon whiskey ever made in New York. Innovation in any market can go one of two ways: either there's no demand for what you're selling and the product fails, or it catches on and you become the instigator of a whole new category. Ralph is rather fond of the word "gumption," which he describes as "the ability to see there is a need for

TOP Newly coopered bourbon barrels waiting to be filled with spirit. They'll return to this room when the spirit is ready to be dumped.
ABOVE Tuthilltown is home to a huge cat called "Bourbon" (there's another called "Rye" that we didn't get to meet.)

something and to have the temerity to believe that you can do something about it."

In 2005, Tuthilltown released their first product: Hudson Baby Bourbon. "Baby" because it was aged in 3-gallon barrels for less than a year. Producing a mature product in a short space of time was key to get the business off the ground, and small barrels, which were quite unconventional at the time, were a big part of this. Ralph also explored even less conventional strategies too, such as blasting Led Zeppelin into the warehouse in attempts to use sonic waves to speed up maturation. While this was surely

an excellent way to piss off a neighbor who had already made it clear they didn't want you there, I question the effectiveness. Tuthilltown thinks sound waves can reduce maturation time by up to 10%, but as a growing business it became impractical for them to play music in every warehouse so "rock-turation" has ceased in Gardiner.

Only 132 bottles were produced in that first batch of Baby Bourbon, and they were all bought by one bar in Red Hook, Brooklyn. Ralph was no doubt thrilled to sell his entire stock list in one transaction, but who knows how much that little collection would be worth today?

Sourcing great, local cereals was top of the list for Ralph right from the start, and they managed to find a local farm that was serving up heirloom varietals of corn that date back to Native American times. This commitment to cereals continued when, in 2009, the distillery harvested the first batch of rye grown on its own farm, and it's some of that stuff that you'll be tasting in the current rye bottlings.

As we tour the distillery I note all the usual indicators of an operation that cannot keep up with demand. Small whiskey-making artifacts from the early days of the operation are still dotted around the place, meaning you can clearly visualize the various stages of expansion along the way. There's a 900-gallon mash cooker that's actually a re-purposed pasta cooker. One of the stills is a recycled mash cooker that was bought on Craigslist.

Meanwhile, there's evidence everywhere of new buildings coming up and old ones being modified. Distillation is currently undertaken in two pairs of pot stills: the larger ones have a 750-gallon capacity and the smaller ones 450 gallons. New, larger stills are arriving imminently from renowned still maker Christian Carl, and a new still house is being built to accommodate them.

The current eight 3,000-gallon fermenters will be joined by a further 28 of them. In order to house all of the whiskey these pieces of equipment will make, Tuthilltown plans to add 37 rick houses by the beginning of 2020. That sounds like a lot (because it is), but consider that there are only seven warehouses currently here in early 2019. So that's a 500% increase in a year!

When the solar panels outside the still house were installed a few years ago, they catered for all of the distillery's power requirements. Now they barely manage half.

Needless to say, Tuthilltown is running with the pedal to the metal, working 24 hours a day, seven days a week. As of early 2019, the record production of un-aged whiskey in a single day is 612 gallons. By the beginning of 2020, I suspect that number will seem rather paltry.

We join Ralph for a glass of whiskey on the tasting room porch. A wedding party wanders past, heading for the 220-year old gristmill which has been converted into a restaurant. I remind Ralph that the first occasion we met was in 2010, during the UK launch of Hudson Whiskey, which was held in one of my London bars. It was that same year that Tuthilltown Spirits sold the Hudson Whiskey brand to William Grant & Sons, who, amongst other products, own the most famous brand of single malt whisky in the world: Glenfiddich.

In 2017, William Grant & Sons went one step further and bought the entire distillery. There were cries of "sell out!" and "you're not craft!" emerging from the comments sections of various online articles. There can be little doubt that these deals made Ralph a fair bit of money and expedited the global reach of Hudson beyond the potential of an independent operator. But, the partnership with William Grant & Sons also helped to increase consumer awareness of "craft" distilled spirits and encourage people to seek out whiskeys made outside of Kentucky and Tennessee. Even more than that, the deal with William Grant & Sons established confidence in potential venture capitalists seeking a clear exit strategy when looking to fund small whiskey operations. By selling Tuthilltown, it's likely that Ralph will indirectly help to finance a bunch of new distilleries and fulfill the dreams of hundreds of spirits entrepreneurs.

FOUR GRAIN (46% ABV)

Get beyond the typical new-oak vanilla/wood notes and there's an herbal note here, like an herb scone with lashings of butter, or thyme-scented cornbread. The taste loses some of the more subtle top-notes, however, revealing licorice, treacle, and spiced fudge.

MANHATTAN RYE (46% ABV)

Bags of fruit here on the nose, with sour cherry, strawberry, dried mango, and a hint of licorice. There's a darkness too though: black pepper, cayenne, and hot coals. On the palate there's a peppery olive-oil taste, which is reflected in the glossy, furniture polish mouthfeel, too. The finish is dominated by char and a spiced, cracked, nutty linger.

SINGLE MALT (46% ABV)

Like a harvest festival, this whiskey is all cereals, oak, and warm autumn fruits. Poached pear, pine nut, pine cone, and some delicate florals that would be better at home in Scotland than New York. The palate is all wood upfront, leading into leather and vanilla, then finally revealing just a touch of soft tropical fruit and finishing on the dry side of things.

HUDSON MAPLE CASK (46% ABV)

Wood, and more wood. The maple syrup is clear and present, but the double maturation has imparted a huge oak influence, with cigar box, oak flooring, and dusty old planks of wood. On the palate there's little change, with tannic and bitter notes (with oak influence) coming through, but fortunately some sweetness partly balances it out, like chewing on 20 cocktail sticks with only a blob of maple syrup for lubrication.

ROAD TRIP PLAYLIST

"Whisky & Water" – Chris Norman

"Born To Run" – Bruce Springsteen

"Streams of Whiskey" – The Pogues

BOURBON & BRANCH

40 ml/1⅓ oz Hudson Four Grain
120 ml/4 oz mineral water

Add the ingredients to a highball glass filled with ice and stir well for a minute.

This was the favored drink of legendary imbibers J.R. Ewing (From the TV series *Dallas*) and James Bond, who enjoyed more than one of them in the novel *Diamonds Are Forever*:

"[Bond] spent an hour drinking the drink that Leiter had told him was fashionable in racing circles — Bourbon and branch water. Bond guessed that in fact the water was from the tap behind the bar, but Leiter had said that real Bourbon drinkers insist on having their whiskey in the traditional style, with water from high up in the branch of the local river where it will be purest."

The idea is that the water from higher up the river is purer than the stuff further down.

The drink shares many parallels with the Japanese whisky serve known as a Mizuwari, which is simply whisky stirred with ice and water in a tall glass.

I know—it sounds too simple to be complex, delicious, or even interesting. Surely all the nuances are drowned by all that water? Well, no. Lowering the strength of a spirit actually has the effect of heightening the aromatics, not diminishing them. This is because alcohol and aroma molecules are similarly sized, and so both vie for attention in ardent spirits. This is why whiskey blenders—the people responsible for what goes in a bottle—will often dilute cask samples to around 20% ABV for nosing.

Fair enough—but what about the taste? Isn't it a little… watery?

Not in my experience.

The chilling of the liquid actually increases the perceived viscosity and creates body and weight. A generous sip whipped around my mouth hammers home tropical fruits like pineapple and lychee, then slipping away like a fruity little serpent. The other surprising thing was the sweetness—oh, the sweetness!—despite having had no sugar added at all. I put much of that down to the gloopiness of the liquid post-chilling. Since then, I often heavily dilute whiskey to see what effect it has on the flavor of the dram. You see, alcohol, whilst accentuating some flavors, does a very good job of masking others. Take it out of the equation (almost) and you have the chance to experience whiskey in a whole new light.

Once water becomes 75% of your drink, things like the pH, mineral content, and TDS (Total Dissolved Solids) begin to have a big impact on flavor perception. Mineral salts are very much like table salt, so can accentuate certain characteristics, as well as provide a harder, chalkier texture. Soft water, with a lower TDS, tends to feel sweeter as it slinks about your mouth, and water with a particularly high pH (alkaline) or low pH (acid) can give a boost to spicy flavors and smoke.

HILLROCK

SEEDS OF CHANGE

"In all things of nature there is something of the marvelous."

ARISTOTLE (384–322 BC), GREEK PHILOSOPHER

In the early colonial period of America, the Hudson Valley was the breadbasket of the nation and New York produced around a half the entire crop of barley and rye. Wheat, however, was the most popular crop, and made fortunes for many notable New Yorkers (including Philip Schuyler [1744–1804], US Senator and father-in-law of Alexander Hamilton). The Hudson Valley had been an agricultural hub since the British took occupation from the Dutch in the late 17th century. Wealthy landowners built manor houses and rented their land to subsistent tenants who could just about make a living by selling their milled cereals at local markets.

In the 1800s, despite growing industrial change, many cereals were still grown around the New York region, processed by small community mills. Then production moved towards large-scale commercial facilities, and as production changed, manufacturing moved into the urban center of New York City. Farmers in the Hudson Valley began to focus on providing food for the emerging urban areas, while the old practices of food self-sufficiency made way for the sale of cash crops, such as grapes and apples. Cereal farming and flour production began to migrate westward towards the prairies of Kansas and North Dakota with increasingly larger conglomerates running both farming and milling. A myth was born that good wheat could not thrive in the Northeast.

Today, the Hudson Valley is still home to many farms that rear livestock or grow vegetables, lettuces, berries and—the big one—apples. Cereals make up only a fraction of the farming economy, but the seeds of change are beginning too sprout. New initiatives are aiming to transition cereal production away from large-scale agro-ecological farming to smaller-scale operations that promote non-GMO and organic cereals. The rise of farmer's markets and artisan bakeries over the past 30 years has increased demand for heirloom cereal varieties, building confidence in these crops among the farming community. Then came the brewing industry, closely followed by whiskey.

It's late fall in the Hudson Valley as we leave Gardiner. This means the summer crops have already been harvested and the winter ones recently sowed. In this climate, rye and corn can enjoy a mutually beneficial relationship that plays over the course of the year. Corn is a warm weather crop that flourishes in the summer months. Rye is then planted in the fall as a cover crop, for its ability to restore nitrogen to the soil that the corn drew out. Before the cold weather and frost sets in, rye's roots grow down quickly, anchoring loose soil and decreasing top soil loss due to run off and snow melt. When it snows, the rye transitions into a kind of hibernation, waiting for the snow to melt in the spring, then growing to full maturity by May.

Heading east out of Gardiner, we cross the Hudson

PREVIOUS PAGES Heading back to New York, we take the scenic route through the Hudson Valley.

at Poughkeepsie and head north. We pass by Hyde Park, birthplace of Franklin D. Roosevelt, the president that all who read this book should be thankful for, since he was instrumental in repealing Prohibition in 1933. We join the Taconic State Parkway heading north. This road was originally imagined by FDR, as a way to providing access to existing and planned state parks in the region. Its winding, hilly route was designed to offer scenic vistas of the Hudson Highlands, Catskills, and Taconic regions.

Hillrock Farm dates back to 1806 and similarly to Mount Vernon, belonged to a revolutionary war captain who later became a grain merchant.

The long driveway at Hillrock is quite a spectacle in itself. The farmhouse sits on top of a small hill, while the distillery buildings are clustered together at the bottom. To our right is a field that has been recently sewn with something (we find out it was a winter rye crop) and to our left is rolling green pasture. It's as beautiful an entrance to a distillery as I have ever seen.

The reverie quickly ends when we pull into the drive and are met with the tragic news that Dave Pickerell, the master distiller at Hillrock, passed away unexpectedly just the day before. It comes as quite a shock to us, but the sense of loss is palpable amongst the team here. Dave was an industry legend, having served as master distiller at Maker's Mark for 14 years before setting up a consulting firm called Oak View that aided over 100 small distilleries. Besides his work at Hillrock, Dave also served as master distiller at WhistlePig Distillery in Vermont (see page 84) and consulted with Metallica on their "Blackened American Whiskey", a whiskey that's matured in the presence of low-frequency sound waves. A chemical engineer by trade, Dave is considered by many to be the "founding father" of craft distilling in the US. In fact, it's possible that no one has made more of an influential contribution to the modern American whiskey industry than Dave.

If you were a new distillery intent on making great tasting whiskey with very few corners cut, Dave was your man. That's why the owner of Hillrock, Jeff

Baker asked him to come on board. Jeff comes from a farming background and was one of the early advocates of grass-fed beef, serving up his own herd of Black Angus beef in his Saratoga Springs restaurant. He made his money as a real estate investment banker in New York City, and his wife, Cathy, with whom he co-owns the business, also works in real estate, in the City. This allowed them to buy the Hillrock farm in 1999. The original plan was a farm-to-table type operation, but when Jeff discovered the original merchant had been a grain merchant, he began thinking about what products could be made from local cereals.

Flash forward to 2014, and Hillrock have harvested approximately 170 tons of organic barley, rye, and corn, all of it grown on the estate itself or on nearby leased farmland. In doing so, they became the first whiskey distillery in the modern era to take complete control of production from seed to glass, meticulously creating a working model that pays testament to an industry that formerly dominated the Hudson landscape.

Dylan Strang is our tour guide for the day. He's one of the distillers here, but what quickly becomes apparent is that being a distiller at Hillrock also requires an understanding of plant breeding, biology and pathology, traditional agricultural systems, and soil science (not to mention malting, brewing, distilling, and maturing).

"We use a few different varieties of rye—Brasetto and Danko—plus around three types of barley," says Dylan. "We basically have complete control over the cereals that we use."

Most ryes grown in the Northeast are cover-crop varieties and have small seeds with a high bran-to-starch ratio, making them a poor choice for baking, malting, and distilling, but Danko has large blue-green berries with a good flavor balance between bread-y and spicy. For this reason, it's a favorite among beer makers and distillers.

It turns out new varieties of rye and barley are constantly being developed as farmers look to maximize yield. Considerations like the stature of the crop come into play, because shorter crops are easier

ABOVE The mist gently rolls over New York's colorful Hudson valley during a typically picturesque fall morning.

to harvest. Uniformity of maturity is also important, as well as a high falling number, which is a measurement of how susceptible the cereal is to premature germination. Of course, it also needs to taste good too.

"We just used a barley called 'Synergy' for our last harvest," he says, "Cornell University ran trials of it and we took it on based on their findings."

Harvesting has to take place at the right time, when the moisture content of the grains has dropped to around 16%. Any higher and the cereal becomes susceptible to spoilage once it's cut. Once harvested, the cereals are transferred straight to drying bins, which circulate air and reduce the moisture content of the cereal down to around 12%. At this point the grains are stable enough to be stored for long periods.

"We make about two or three trips to the farm every week," says Dylan. "The distillery team drive down there with small grain silos on a trailer and collect our requirements."

Hillrock makes three types of whiskey: bourbon, rye, and single malt. The bourbon mash bill could very nearly be classified as a rye seeing as it's made of 51% corn and 49% rye. Since there's no malt component, Hillrock use enzymes for conversion. Enzymes are also needed for their rye mash, comprising 100% rye. The single malt they make is made from 100% malted barley, all of it malted onsite.

Although there are now about a dozen distilleries in the US that have a floor malting, Hillrock was the first to build a dedicated malting house to aid with the endeavor. And it's here, perhaps more than anywhere, that the malting floor feels most at home. After all, a malt floor is an essential link between the farm and the still house, and in a place that prides itself on making "farm to glass" whiskey, outsourcing it simply wasn't an option.

One thing that is outsourced however, is the peat that Hillrock uses. New York does have some peat bogs, but in this instance, Dave Pickerell knew that quality was paramount and decided to look elsewhere.

"We want to make our single malt as authentically Scottish as possible," says Dylan. "So we import our peat from Scotland and use that to dry the barley."

We climb the wooden staircase to the top of the malting house. These structures are usually built with gravity in mind and Hillrock's is no exception. The cereal is transported up to the top floor via a grain elevator where it undergoes the first stage, steeping. From then onwards it only needs to be

TOP RIGHT There is something Zen about the raking of barley on a malt floor. The hatch in the middle is used to push the barley downstairs, into the kiln.

ABOVE The mash cooker (to the left) and pot still (to the right) at Hillrock. The smaller copper vessel at the bottom is for collecting the spirit.

TOP LEFT Malted barley resting on the grated floor of the kiln room. Smoke or heat is pumped up, from below, through the malt.

ABOVE Hillrock is the first distillery in history to mature their bourbon in a multi-barrel "solera" system.

dropped down (on to the floor for germination, through to the kiln for drying, and over to the mill) for each subsequent stage.

The malting floor here is one of the smallest I've ever seen. It's also the most beautiful I've ever seen. The room is light and airy and the Georgian windows offer views of the farm and distillery buildings, while pendant light fittings and painted walls complete the picture. It could just as easily be a dining room in a really nice house, if it weren't for the fact that someone had dumped a ton of cereal on the floor. That ton of cereal is enough for four mashes, or 120 gallons of whiskey (just over two barrels).

"We can control the temperature and humidity of this room," says Dylan, "which is essential so that we can malt all year around."

To the side of he room is the steeping tank, which is a raised, stainless steel cylinder. Here, the cereal is immersed in water for a couple of days until it reaches a moisture content of around 40% (up from 12%), then the water is drained off and the malt undergoes an "air-rest" period, where air is pumped through and the malt absorbs the surface water, increasing its hydration level to 46%.

The moist cereals are then dumped onto the floor and spread out for the germination process to take hold. This takes around five days at Hillrock, during which time the floor will be raked twice a day. This is to break up any heat patches and to ensure that all of the barley has adequate airflow.

"We might rake a little more towards the end of the process," says Dylan as he adeptly demonstrates how to use their custom-made rake. "That's because the malt is starting to generate more energy and heat, and we don't want mold to form. You know when it's nearly done because there's a cucumber smell in the room and the cereal has sprouted little rootlets."

At that stage the "green malt" is sent for drying, which halts the germination process. They open up a hatch and sweep the malt down in to the kiln room below. The kiln floor is a metal screen with a small room below containing a grill. The peat is burned on this grill for six hours a day, for a total of three days. After three days, they start circulating warm air at 122°F for eight hours, which is sufficient heat to kill the enzymes and halt germination. The next day, the kiln is ventilated and blasted with hot air at 160°F for four or five hours. This gives the malt a little color and a slightly roasted characteristic.

All of the brewing and distilling equipment here is made by the Kentucky based still-maker, Vendome, which we'll discuss in later chapters.

The distillery uses a different yeast for each of the three whiskeys. The beer typically tops out at 6% ABV and one 250-gallon batch will be converted into 30 gallons of 65–70% ABV spirit after distillation. The particular design of the still at Hillrock allows the distiller to produce spirit in a single run, rather than two. One notable point of difference at this distillery occurs during the production of single malt. Unlike most of the distilleries this book, Hillrock mash their malted barley in the same way as is common in Scotland. This means filtering the sweet liquid (known as "wort") from the spent barley grains prior to fermentation, rather than pumping the whole soupy mess over to the fermenters and then on to the still. This results on a fruitier spirit, which is more reminiscent of Scotch.

In the warehouse, Hillrock have a "solera" system for maturing their bourbon, a technique borrowed from the Spanish sherry industry. It's basically an interactive process of blending younger spirits with older ones while they mature, transferring them from one cask to another. It's sometimes useful to imagine a solera system like stories in a warehouse, whereby the oldest spirits are on the bottom floor and the youngest on the top. When it's time to bottle, spirit is taken from the barrels on the bottom floor, which are topped up by the barrels on the next floor up. They, in turn, are topped up by the floor above them. Un-aged spirit is introduced on the top floor. Crucially though, no casks are ever entirely emptied, so remnants of spirits as old as the system itself will turn up in every bottle.

Hillrock operates a four-tier system and all of their warehousing is on the farm. Oloroso sherry casks are the final stage of the system, from which their bourbon is bottled. The third tier, which comprises

141 casks, holds the oldest whiskey, which is six years and older. The second tier, another 141 casks, contains adolescent whiskey of around four to six years old. And finally there's the first tier, the nursery whiskey, which holds spirit aged zero to four years old. They never take more than 10–15 gallons from a barrel, and when they do the barrel is topped up from the next tier down. The nursery tier is topped up with un-aged whiskey at 62.5% ABV.

Besides being an effective way of blending and maturing whiskey, this strategy is also a neat workaround for the legal requirement that bourbon be aged in new, charred oak barrels. "We're never emptying the barrel," says Dylan, "so they can't be classed as 'used.'"

In reality, they do still retire barrels once their potency is diminished. Every two or three years, the contents of the nursery barrels are briefly vatted, then re-filled into new charred barrels.

Leaving the cooperage, I've had just about all I can take without drinking some whiskey. The entire Hillrock experience is so uniquely perfect that it's almost unbelievable. It's hard not to be won over by the whole thing. And the whiskey itself? Well, it ain't cheap. But suffice to say that all that hard work hasn't gone to waste.

BOURBON (41.3% ABV)

Plenty of toffee and vanilla on the nose, but it's supported by dried fruits and some exotic florals. The palate opens up with some of that rye spice and more

LEFT Attention to detail at Hillrock extends to every stage of production, from cereals right through to cask treatments.

toffee, then vanilla orchids, walnuts, cinnamon toast, and golden raisins. The finish is long and smooth with notes of butterscotch.

SINGLE MALT (45% ABV)

Smoke comes through like an old campfire, joined by pig sweat, manure, golden raisins, grilled vegetables, and burnt green wood. The taste has concentrated rum and raisin, heather honey, and overripe plum. Soft smoke drifts in, with fruity tobacco. Totally delicious.

RYE (45% ABV)

Like the best birthday party ever: cherry bubble gum, Dr Pepper, and vanilla ice cream. The taste is sweet and spicy, packed with nutty characteristics and hot fruit syrup. A touch of chipotle chile comes through on the finish. Absolutely delicious.

DOUBLE CASK RYE FINISHED IN SAUTERNES CASK (45% ABV)

The nose is very fruity, with fresh grape juice, soft pineapple, and banana toffee. There's a subtle green tea note there too. On the palate the wood takes hold. This whiskey is concentrated with fruit becoming dried and spicy. The lingering taste is white pepper and bitter almond.

DOUBLE CASK RYE FINISHED IN PORT CASK (45% ABV)

The aroma here is of baked plum, prune juice, and dates soaked in brandy. On the palate there's raspberry soda, nutmeg, ginger, and a touch of hibiscus. Strawberry and black pepper come through on the palate. Outrageously tasty.

ROAD TRIP PLAYLIST

"Whiskey Man" – The Who

"Broadway" – The Goo Goo Dolls

"I Wanna Rock" – Twisted Sister

JOHN COLLINS

40 ml/1⅓ oz Hillrock Bourbon
20 ml/⅔ fl oz fresh lemon juice
10 ml/2 teaspoons gomme
chilled soda, as needed

Fill a tall glass with ice, add the first three ingredients and stir briefly. Top up with soda and stir gently.
Garnish with a slice of orange and a cherry.

You'll note that the recipe for this drink is basically a compacted version of the Whiskey Punch (see page 109)—and there's a good reason for that. The Collins family of cocktails is based on the same formula as punches, but they are intended for individual consumption rather than sharing. This was the natural evolution of things when mixed drinks moved away from banqueting rooms and onto bar tops.

What's interesting here though, is that the drink known as the John Collins didn't evolve directly from the Whiskey Punch. Instead, it took a detour, via a gin-based punch that originated in London, England.

The Limmer's Punch was created in the 1830s at the London Hotel with the same name. Comprising gin, lemon juice, lemon peel, sugar, soda water, and capillaire (a kind of syrup aromatized with orange flower water), it was a huge hit and one of a great number of punch recipes hidden up the tailored sleeves of the bar's manager. His name was John Collins. When American cocktail culture began to pick up pace in the mid-1800s, it was the reliable large serves, like the Limmer's Punch, that got the single-serve treatment. And what better name for this sweet and sour fizzy delight than the name of its creator, John Collins?

Now, the most popular gin in America at that time was Holland's Gin (aka genever), which originated from the Netherlands. Tastes began to change towards the end of the century however, towards a sweeter style of gin from England called Old Tom. So the name of the drink changed to accommodate it, from John Collins to Tom Collins.

With Holland's Gin becoming increasingly scarce and some time passing since anyone had ordered a John Collins, the moniker melted away like the final ice cube of a long-finished drink. On the plus side, this freed up the name to be recycled, and for the Whiskey Punch to be reincarnated into a new form. And so it was, that some bright spark substituted whiskey for gin in a Collins and assigned it a completely unoriginal name that had previously belonged to one of the nation's most beloved drinks: John Collins.

WHISTLEPIG

HOGS AND LOGS

"The tallest oak tree was once an acorn that any pig could have swallowed."

ARTHUR SCHOPENHAUER (1788–1860), GERMAN PHILOSOPHER

The number of "craft distilleries" (which is defined by the Craft Spirits Association of America as a distillery producing no more than 750,000 proof gallons of spirit a year) fluctuates enormously from state to state. There is a pattern to it though—the numbers loosely correlate to the population of the given state. California, Texas, and New York rank in the top four by population and by number of small distilleries.

And then there are states like Vermont. Only Wyoming has a smaller population than Vermont. And Vermont is the sixth smallest state by landmass. You can fit 70 Vermonts into Alaska and 30 into Texas. Yet Vermont has twice as many distilleries as Alaska. There's 23 of them by the last count, which works out to be one craft distillery for every 27,000 people.

This fact is made all the more interesting because Vermont is not an obvious place to make whiskey. Indeed, the entire New England region (with the exception of Boston) has never really been one for whiskey-making in general. Without the large expanses of rich farmland or a mild climate, generations of exasperated New England farmers turned away from cereals and instead focused on logging, ship building, and fishing.

But we're now witnessing an unprecedented growth in distilling activity in Vermont, seeded by small producers wishing to celebrate the agricultural produce of the state and nurtured by the Distiller Spirits Council of Vermont. Perhaps the most prominent of these operations is WhistlePig, a brand that has grown from strength to strength and achieved a strong following domestically and abroad.

Raj Bhakta acquired the 500-acre farm that WhistlePig calls home in 2007. It was bad timing however, as the world was in the midst of a financial downturn. Monetizing the estate required out-of-the-box thinking: "I triangulated my love of America and whiskey with the farm, and came up with the idea of a luxury American whiskey," says Raj.

The concept of terroir was important to the WhistlePig story right from the start. This was a difficult dram for many to digest, since in the first few years of the business, all of the whiskey WhistlePig was bottling came not from the farm itself but was sourced from contract distilleries in Alberta and Indiana. Fortunately, they were great whiskeys, but some people felt they were getting a different product to the one the story was telling. The reason behind all the smoke and mirrors was an economic one—WhistlePig needed to sell a whiskey to finance making their whiskey. "If you're going to be serious about the whiskey business, you need years. You can put out a two year old whiskey, but it's only going to be a two year old whiskey," Raj tells me.

So Raj brought Dave Pickerell (considered the founder of craft distilling in the US) on board, who happened to have recently gained access to a large

LEFT Sunrise over WhistlePig Farm, which is covered in snow for around a third of the year.

consignment of 10 year old Canadian rye whiskey. Dave had been looking for someone to bottle the whiskey (which he thought was fantastic), but every American producer he approached turned their noses up at it on the basis that it was Canadian. Raj wasn't phased by it at all, and even less so when he tasted it.

"We were very happy to talk about where the whiskey came from," Raj tells me, "...and we sincerely believed that it was the best f***ing whiskey in the world."

For Raj and Dave, it didn't matter where the whiskey came from but it had to be the best, and that would have to do until they were ready to bottle whiskey from the farm— however long that took.

What came next was a back and forth between WhistlePig and the TTB (Tax and Trade Bureau), which couldn't decide whether the product (which had matured for two years in the US) was American or Canadian. The back label went through a number of iterations to reflect the changing attitudes of the TTB, and the whiskey mafia pounced with vigor.

Meanwhile, back on the farm, plans were underway to build the distillery. Like Hillrock (see page 77), they proposed to grow rye, but like absolutely nobody else at the time, WhistlePig were also managing their own oak too. It's one thing waiting for your whiskey to mature in barrel, but it's another thing waiting for your oak trees to actually mature to make your barrels.

The whiskey barrel is perhaps the most important component of any distillery. It contributes the majority of flavor in any aged spirit, and most of the flavor in older expressions. And as we will discover, good wood (and management of the cellar) is as important to a whiskey operation as the right mash bill or an adept distiller.

Because barrels are used almost exclusively for maturing spirits and wine these days, it's easy to forget that (a) they were once used to store other things, whether it was whale oil, nails, eels, dead bodies, or booze and (b) barrels were the carrier of choice for moving said things from one place to another. Until the forklift truck and palette arrived, barrels were containers that supported economic growth.

The simple design is obvious but ingenious. Forcing the barrel staves (the individual wood strips) together means that each one supports each other, and oak being oak means they're unlikely to snap or splinter, even when they fall from a height. Maneuverability is also key, and whiskey barrels have the perfect balance of being big enough to store quite a lot of stuff, with a shape that bows out in the middle allowing you to move it around. This means a single person can roll a cask around, rock it back and forward to stand it back up, and pivot easily on a single edge to change direction or maneuver in to a space—even when the weight exceeds 300 lbs.

Oak is the best and most common wood for barrel construction. It's also a legal requirement for many types of whiskey, including bourbon.

There are two main varieties of oak used for aging whiskey, white oak (*Quercus alba*), and red oak (*Quercus robur* or *Quercus petraea*) although we will encounter others on our journey. White oak is grown widely across America, and red oak is from Europe (though America imports around ¼ of all European oak and Europe their fair share of American). American oak has a paler bark than European, but there's little difference between the color of the cut wood.

Red oak grows slowly, twists and turns, and only reaches maturation after 150 years. The resulting whiskey is more tannic (a trait of the slow growth), peppery, and spicy with, rather fittingly, flavors of red-colored things like cherries, grapes, red apples, and tea. White oak grows much faster, accelerating along to maturation in only 60–80 years. The result is a more "obvious" wood influence, with plenty of vanilla and associated white things, like banana, white chocolate, buttermilk, and custard.

After felling, the wood is first dried off the tree for up to a year, in log form. Next it is sliced into quarters, like batons of a carrot, then cut down to stave billets that follow the grain of the wood. Bourbon barrels are usually cut with a slightly curved saw that traces the curvature of the barrel along the width of the stave. European cuts are normally straight and the wood is later trimmed to form flush joints between staves. Naturally, there is significant wastage from the tree, comprising bits of wood too small to be made into staves, but some coopers use the waste to fuel the fires used for toasting or charring later.

Only the inner 80% of the log, known as the heartwood, is used, since the outer sapwood, which sits directly behind the bark, is too porous. Most staves made from American oak that's destined for American whiskey maturation are traditionally kiln-dried for about 30 days at this stage. This takes its moisture level down from 50% to 12%, at which point the wood is ready to be coopered into a cask. Oak that will be used by the Sherry industry in Europe on the other hand, is yard-dried in stages for a further 9 months to 3 years. Yard-dried wood is becoming increasingly common in the US now, however.

What's the difference you may ask? Well, if we had asked 20 years ago the answer may have been "nothing". But kiln-drying is quite an aggressive process, and recent studies suggest that the kiln-dried wood skips an important stage of fungal growth that assists in the conversion and liberation of flavorsome compounds in the wood. Yard-dried wood plays host to a succession of traveling microscopic fungi during its seasoning period, which "acupuncture" hydrogen peroxide into the surface of the wood, softening and relaxing the harder structure and allowing better penetration from the spirit. The fungi, along with rainfall, are also thought to assist in the removal of tannins, even leaving behind a visible tea-stain of tannin on the ground where the wood has been.

Staves are born straight, so to form the familiar barrel shape they must be trimmed down and bent into submission. The stave is cut so that it tapers in at either end, a necessary step to form the bulge in the barrel. A 53-gallon "bourbon cask" is constructed from roughly 30 finished staves, which are placed in hoops, then heated by steam and forced together mechanically. A European 65-gallon "wine butt" needs approximately 50 staves.

The circular barrel ends are made from shorter stave cuts that are drilled out and pinned together with dowel rods to form a square. They are then sawed into a circle and sent on for toasting or charring along with the barrel shell.

Toasting and charring are not interchangeable terms, even though they might sound the same. Charring is an all-out flamethrower assault in the interior surfaces of the barrel, as ruthless licks of heat blast the wood for up to a minute, causing the surface to bubble and crack as it catches fire.

When a cask is toasted, heat is applied more gently, sometimes through convection rather than direct flame, and over a longer period of time—from five to 20 minutes. The difference between charring and toasting is somewhat analogous to the difference between barbecuing a sausage quickly, or baking it slowly. Visually, there is a similar contrast too.

Charred barrels look as if they have (barely) survived a pirate ship battle, with blackened scabs and brittle blisters. A light char is the color of graphite and a heavy char a black as coal. These char levels are graded by cooperages from one to four, four being the heaviest and one the lightest. The color of the internal surfaces of a toasted cask on the other hand can range from vanilla fudge through to dark coffee. The toast level is controlled during the process and categorized as either light, medium, medium+, or dark.

Whether by toasting or charring, the heat treatment of these casks is a critical step in the influence of flavor in whiskey. Grilling the barrel like this achieves three primary functions—the degradation of wood polymers into flavorsome compounds, the destruction of unpleasant resinous compounds in the wood, and in the case of charring, the forming of a thin layer of active carbon. I would also propose that the char or toast assists in fusing the spirit to the wood by absorbing the liquid and holding it close to the adjacent wood surface—kind of like pressing a wet sponge against your skin.

Barrels intended for the bourbon industry are legally required to be charred, but in most cases they are toasted as well. Things have gotten rather technical in this realm in recent years. For example, the Independent Stave Company, which makes barrels for many American whiskey producers, offers a computer-controlled barrel profiling service where its customers can request specific flavors and the cask is charred to a unique heat curve—kind of like roasting coffee to liberate a distinct aroma.

Independent Stave is actually the company that coopers WhistlePig's barrels. Every year, WhistlePig fells enough oak trees to make 10,000 casks. Some of these trees are located on the estate and others are located in nearby sustainable forests. Some of the

TOP LEFT WhistlePig's copper pot stills were manufactured in Kentucky by Vendome Copper & Brass.
MIDDLE "Grain to glass" means the managing of whiskey production all the way from the cereal to the label.
LEFT The clue was in the name: there are pigs living on WhistlePig Farm.

casks are sold to breweries, or used to mature their sourced whiskeys.

Vermont oak tends to grow outwards as well as upwards, meaning there's less straight timber to work with, so you can only expect to get a couple of barrels out of each tree. On account of the temperature in Vermont, the oak trees here have a shorter growing season than those farther south, which produces a tighter grain in the wood. This makes for a barrel that imparts more flavor more quickly.

"We're getting a lot more of the structural, mouthfeel components that you might normally associate with longer maturation," says master blender Pete Lynch. "And creamy lactone notes too. The distillate has a nice citrus note that is being amplified by the barrel, and that's resulting in burnt orange flavors and notes of maple syrup."

Pete concedes that it's still early days though. Their oldest spirits at the time of writing are three and a half years old, and in the cool climate of Vermont that's still quite young. Tighter wood grain may help speed up maturation, but freezing cold winters will certainly slow it down.

Distillery equipment at WhistlePig includes a 900-gallon mash cooker and five 900-gallon fermenters into which the mash is fed. The two stills here are copper pots with special heads containing trays that increase the strength of the spirit vapor as it passes up the still. This means a sufficient strength of spirit can be achieved in a single distillation pass.

WhistlePig 15 Year is finished in Vermont oak barrels for one to three years, and all of the new whiskey made at the distillery goes into them too. The first of these estate-distilled whiskeys can be found in the FarmStock Rye series. FarmStock is WhistlePig's annual experimental release, which is now in its third year. In it's present form, it's a blend of sourced whiskeys and whiskeys made on the farm, the latter component now taking up an increasingly large percentage of the blend. When it was first released in 2017, Farmstock contained just 20% WhistlePig spirit aged for one year. The most recent release was 52% WhistlePig spirit aged for 3 years. You can see where this is going, and the hope is that soon,

Farmstock will entirely comprise, well, farm stock. Though that's not necessarily the destiny of all WhistlePig products. Having released 15 Year and 18 Year expressions over the past few years, we will be waiting a while for these spirits to be supplanted by home-grown offerings.

And even when, in 2034, WhistlePig are sitting on 18-year-old stocks of Vermont rye, will it taste the same as what they're bottling now? "No. We'd be foolish to think that we can recreate the whiskeys we source on the farm." Pete tells me.

STRAIGHT RYE 10 YEAR OLD (50% ABV)

There's a fresh, green herbal quality to this whiskey, like peppermint and cardamom. This gives way to a little rye nuttiness, with almond butter and croissant. The taste is a great balance of bittersweet chocolate, vanilla caramel, and baking spices, softening to stewed cherry and oak.

FARMSTOCK RYE CROP NO.001 (43% ABV)

Cocoa butter and Nutella on the nose, with cinnamon cotton candy and a little of that rye gluey-ness. It's light and juicy on the palate, showing some of the youthfulness of the WP spirit. Pistachio nut and toffee are joined by a green, bitter herbal quality.

THE BOSS HOG 2018 14 YEAR OLD (CALVADOS CASK FINISH) (57.9% ABV)

All the fall fruits, with apple and pear marrying nicely with rich barrel spices and dark fruits from the rye. The taste is big and thick, striking a balance between pain and pleasure; it reminds me of making cherry jam and tasting it before it's had a chance to cool properly! Tobacco and more, deeper wood spices arise through the finish.

ROAD TRIP PLAYLIST

"Going Up the Country" – Canned Heat

"Whiskey, Whiskey, Whiskey" – John Mayer

"Maggie's Farm" – Bob Dylan

BENTON'S OLD-FASHIONED

50 ml/1¾ oz Bacon-infused WhistlePig Farmstock (see below)
10 ml/2 teaspoons WhistlePig Maple Syrup

Add the ingredients to a mixing beaker filled with cubed ice. Stir for a minute, then strain into an ice-filled rocks glass. Garnish with a fresh cherry.

BACON-INFUSED WHISTLEPIG FARMSTOCK (ONE BOTTLE)

50 g/1¾ oz bacon fat (see below)
700 ml/24 oz WhistlePig Farmstock

Heat the bacon fat over a low heat until it melts. Combine the molten fat and bourbon in a glass Mason jar and shake well. Infuse for four hours, then place the container in the freezer for two hours. Remove the solid fat (which should have floated to the top) and fine-strain the whiskey through a cheesecloth before bottling.

I first became aware of this drink from a colleague who had visited New York City in 2008. He came back raving about a mad old-fashioned style drink that was flavored with bacon. Bacon?!
"How do you flavor a drink with bacon?!" I asked.
"You wash the whiskey in bacon fat!" he replied.

Needless to say, bacon and bourbon are an inspired combination—a rare affinity of flavors. When we think about the best maple-cured bacon, slightly crispy and slightly sweet, it's a bourbon-esque flavor we're imagining. Equally, when we consider what makes a great whiskey, it's often something smoky, sweet, and concentrated in flavor that we envisage.

So the issue was never whether the two ingredients would pair well, it was more a case of how you go about integrating bacon into whiskey without it being a weird, boozy, meat smoothie.

The cocktail was invented by renowned East Coast bartender Don Lee, while he was working at PDT in the East Village, New York. It gained international recognition and opened doors to a whole new family of flavors in mixed drinks.

Fat-washing works on fairly simple principles: melt the fat (if necessary), mix it with your spirit, then chill it so that the fat solidifies and can be removed. Some of the flavors in the fat will dissolve into the spirit, imparting flavor without imparting fat.

This is an apt drink to enjoy with WhistlePig since it also contains maple syrup, and Vermont produces over 5% of the global supply. WhistlePig actually bottles its own maple syrup from maple trees on the farm, so when you combine this with its Farmstock whiskey (and bacon from their own pigs) you have yourself a complex cocktail with hyper-local credentials.

NEW YORK DISTILLING COMPANY

EMPIRE STATE OF RYE

"Half a cup of rock and rye
Farewell to you old southern sky
I'm on my way"

FROM THE SONG "MISSISSIPPI HALF-STEP UPTOWN TOODELOO" BY GRATEFUL DEAD

Leaving Vermont, we're going back to New York, only this time it's the Big Apple itself that's our destination. As we drive past Albany again, we cross the Hudson and join Route 9, heading south. This slight detour takes us on a more scenic tour of upstate New York which, in fall, is every shade of yellow, orange and brown imaginable. It also takes us through the village of Kinderhook, around 10 miles south of Albany. This was the birthplace of Martin Van Buren, the eighth president of the United States.

Uniquely, Van Buren was the first US president born neither as a British subject, nor of British ancestry. He was also the first and only president to be born in a distillery.

His father, Abraham Van Buren had been a Patriot during the American Revolution, but his real trade was farming (and owning the Kinderhook Tavern.) Being both a farmer and retailer of alcohol, we can be absolutely certain that Abraham also made spirits, manufactured from leftover portions of his grain crop.

The earliest record of distillation in New York comes from settlers on Staten Island (which was a Dutch Colony at the time), in 1640. The instigator of this craft-distilling trend was William Kieft, the 3rd Director General of the Dutch West Indies Company.

He also owned a tavern, which was the only place you could buy his creations, or indeed any spirits at all, as Kieft deviously outlawed the production and sale of any liquor not made by him. Goods produced at Kieft's distillery included brandy and a crude whiskey made from the leftover dregs of beer. Being of Dutch origin, Kit probably flavored his whiskey with juniper and other botanicals, in the style of the Dutch spirit genever.

The Dutch influence, especially in Brooklyn, meant that by 1740 genever was one of the most popular spirits, and available in taverns throughout the City of New York and beyond. By the time Augustus Lucas put his New York distillery up for sale in *The Boston News-Letter*, on August 7, 1704, it was a substantial operation, with a still house measuring 50ft by 22ft complete with two good copper stills, one measuring 140 gallons.

When Alexander Hamilton levied the taxes on whiskey that resulted in the Whiskey Rebellion, unlike the aggrieved Pennsylvanians, the New Yorkers grudgingly agreed to pay the tax, but only on the proviso that imported genever was taxed more heavily. By 1810, New York state was home to over 400 working breweries comprising the largest brewing industry in the nation. By 1825, the state had more than 1,000 distilleries.

Genever remained a popular tipple right up until Prohibition, thanks to folks of Dutch ancestry in the Hudson Valley and Catskills. The drink makes an appearance in Washington Irving's *Rip Van Winkle*, which tells the tale of a man who falls asleep in the Catskill Mountains and wakes up 20 years later, having missed the American Revolutionary War (1775–1783). While nine-pin bowling with dwarfs in the mountains, the title character "quaffed liquor… which he found had much the flavor of excellent Hollands."

As distilling migrated into urban areas, which became more densely populated, the scale of the operations increased exponentially. In the 1840s, Brooklyn had become a center for ship-building and other manufacturing as businesses moved out of Manhattan, and new distilleries—some of the biggest around—flared up to fuel the thirsty masses. Soon, there were dozens of distilleries producing millions of gallons of whiskey annually, but it would all change. We'll explore what happened in the next chapter.

Leaving Kinderhook, we drive south for about an hour, until we cross back over the Hudson at Kingston. Kingston became New York's first state capital in the summer of 1777 before being burned to the ground by the British in October that year. A few miles to the south of Kingston, on the banks of the Wallkill, is Coppersea Distillery. This is another operation that celebrates the farm-to-glass ways of yesteryear, growing their own rye and corn and floor-malting their barley requirements. Their bourbon, Excelsior, uses all those farm grown grains, but also takes advantage of local oak. Coppersea partnered with US Barrel to craft barrels made of Hudson Valley oak for a bourbon that is truly 100% New York.

It's late afternoon by the time we arrive in Brooklyn. As of 2019, there are at least 20 distilleries in Brooklyn alone, which by my reckoning makes it the most densely packed urban-distilling environment in the world. Such is the audacity of growth in New York distilling in recent years, that it's difficult to keep track of how many distilleries there are in the state. It's likely, however, that by 2020 there will be more distilleries making whiskey in New York than in Scotland.

As far as distilleries in New York City go, The New York Distilling Company (NDC) was the first modern distillery to gain a license. It has, therefore established the yardstick by which all other distilleries measure themselves. There's a sense of community amongst the distillers of Brooklyn too, and that can also be attributed to the early authors of the modern whiskey category.

NDC is located in the Williamsburg area of Brooklyn, right next to the Brooklyn-Queens Expressway. About a fifth of the distillery is taken up by a cocktail bar called Shanty. This is a particularly welcome sight for two weary travellers, so we enthusiastically preface our tour of the distillery by ordering a Manhattan cocktail. I first visited Shanty while on vacation with my wife in 2012, just a few days after the bar had opened its doors. It was a novel experience to walk into a distillery bar, since NDC was the first distillery to have a bar attached to it. Not just the first in New York—the first in the United States.

With our blood softly warmed by the untameable heat of the icy drink, we take a wander through the 5,000-sq. ft warehouse that makes NDC products. The story of the distillery starts with Tom Potter, the co-founder of Brooklyn Brewery and one of the patriarchs of the East Coast craft brewing fraternity. Potter sold most of his shares in Brooklyn Brewery by 2004, planning a gentle retirement process with the proceeds. But the craft-distilling scene was gathering pace and after visiting a handful of distilleries on the west coast he hatched a scheme to open his own in New York. Potter and his son Bill teamed up with Allen Katz, a renowned bartender and spirits educator, who would go on to become master distiller and frontman of the NDC.

Allen actually comes from Baltimore, Maryland, which goes some way towards explaining his fascination with rye whiskey. He grew up tending bar, and enjoyed sharing a Manhattan or two with

ABOVE Williamsburg is now full of hipster bars, but it once contained 11 breweries on a 12-block stretch.

his grandmother. These would often be made with Pikesville Rye, one of few surviving ryes of the 1990s. The Manhattans he was enjoying were of course true to the original formula, which called for rye whiskey, not bourbon. When he discovered that the state of Maryland was concealing a rich but sadly forgotten heritage in respect to rye, the wheels were set in motion.

Just like its Pennsylvanian cousin, Maryland rye pre-dates bourbon in its popularity. In Jedidiah Morse's *The American Universal Geography*, which was published in 1805, he tells us that, "Rye whiskey is manufactured in great quantities in [Maryland]. From some single distilleries 12,000 gallons are produced a year. In Frederick county alone there are 80 grist-mills." This trend continued for at least the next 100 years. One report from 1874 concerning the commercial activities of Baltimore tells us that, "Maryland whiskey… has, for years past, gained an enviable reputation and is in extensive demand throughout the South, also in the Eastern and New England states." It goes on to describe a whiskey "made out of pure rye" and that

"a considerable increase of trade may be reasonably anticipated in the future."

That prediction was correct. By 1911, Maryland was home to 44 distilleries, producing a combined total of 5.6 million gallons of whiskey in that year — an all-time record for the "Free" state. By the end of World War II, though, there were no distilleries left in Maryland.

As for what defined the Maryland rye style, it was basically a softer, sweeter version of what was being made in Pennsylvania. At least that's what most people agree. One thing that most distillers agree upon, however, is that Maryland rye tended to have a lower proportion of rye in the mash bill and more corn or malted barley. Some historians suggest that it might have been sweetened with sugar or caramel and that might be where the softening of the spice came from. Others believe that Maryland never really had a style, or that the style shifted so much over the years (due in part to trading of product with Pennsylvanian distillers) that it was a category in name only.

That, of course, doesn't stop us from using the Maryland classification to describe certain styles of

rye whiskey. For what it's worth, I consider the Maryland style to be some kind of mid-point between Pennsylvanian Rye and bourbon, or rye and malt whiskey. There are brands on the market that already fit this description though: Pikesville Rye and Rittenhouse Rye being two of them (which we'll encounter very shortly).

However, one way to guarantee you're making a Maryland rye is to make a rye whiskey in Maryland. And fortunately for whiskey lovers, there is a rye revival going on there too. The state now has 20 whiskey distilleries, most of them producing their own unique take on the Maryland style. At Sagamore Spirits, for example, this means blending together aged spirits from two distinct mash bills: one comprising 95% rye, the other 52% rye. Blending post-maturation allows them to hone in on the exact balance of sweetness and spice that they're after. Baltimore Spirits Co. make their Epoch Rye using 70% rye and 30% malted rye. Other distillers are running mash bills of just rye and malted barley.

Allen has also been one of the key figures in establishing the "Empire Rye" category of whiskey. This currently unregulated classification was established in 2015 by six New York distilleries: The New York Distilling Company, Kings County Distillery, Tuthilltown Spirits, Coppersea Distilling, Finger Lakes Distillery and Black Button Distillery.

"We were interested in rye whiskey for its American heritage," says Allen, "but also from an agricultural standpoint. Rye was a significant grain for New York state."

The classification also fits in to the wider movement towards the sourcing of local, sustainable products—an approach to food and drink that has been especially celebrated in the Empire State. These days,

TOP LEFT Williamsburg developed a reputation for gang crime in the 1960s, but is currently experiencing a period of renaissance.
MIDDLE Like many startup whiskey distilleries, New York Distilling Company has a still that's versatile enough to make gin and other spirits too.
LEFT The German still manufacturer, Christian Carl, has done rather well from the craft distilling revolution.

people want to know who is growing their food, who is harvesting it and, perhaps most importantly, when it is at its tastiest.

The so-called "Farm Distillery License" that helped Ralph Lorenzo get his Gardiner operation off the ground has been beneficial to the state for more than just its low cost. It has reminded New Yorkers that distilling was (and still can be) a farm-originated practice, and re-established a bond between the two industries in ways that could never have been imagined 20 years ago.

So what is Empire Rye?

Well, it's a rye whiskey that has to be made in New York state (that much ought to be obvious!) Like straight whiskey, it must be aged for a minimum of two years and be distilled to no more than 160 proof. Unlike straight whiskey, the maximum barrel entry strength is 115 proof (as opposed to the 125 proof of straight whiskeys). The real deal clincher is that Empire Rye must be made from a mash comprising at least 75% New York-grown rye.

"Our effort at New York Distilling Company—among other distilleries—is to build on the tradition of rye," says Allen, "but to introduce ryes with a more substantial rye presence in the mash bill."

NDC gets its rye from the Pedersen Family Farms in the Finger Lakes region of upstate New York. In the distillery itself, production is overseen by Bill Potter, son of Tom Potter. In spite of the age of the distillery, NDC is modestly sized and very much a hands-on operation. Cereals arrive pre-ground and are loaded in to the mash cooker from 55lb bags, 32 bags at a time, for a 1,750-lb mash. After cooking, fermentation of the rye mash (up to an alcoholic strength of 5%) takes around four days. Double distillation is done in a 1,000-liter Christian Carl copper pot-still. All maturation at NDC is done in 53-gallon American oak barrels and it's been that way since day one.

That loyalty to larger casks, and the benefits that bigger barrels can offer with regard to a balanced maturation character, meant that waiting for NDC's first rye whiskey to be released seemed to take an eternity. While other distilleries were popping out mahogany-colored spirits from tiny casks in under a year, NDC were patiently waiting for time to do all the hard work. During those expectant years, Allen released a teaser product called Mister Katz's Rock & Rye—a nod to the famous pre-Prohibition drink "Rock & Rye," which was essentially a pre-mixed bottled cocktail created by adding spiced rock candy syrup to rye whiskey (among other things).

The medicinal effects of Rock & Rye were so immediate and so powerful that by the time Prohibition came into effect, it had migrated from the bar to the pharmacy. Bottled versions made by Charles Jacquin et Cie (in production since 1884, the only pre-Prohibition survivor), Tolu, Arrow, Koch's, and Rocko-Ryo were often patented as "alcoholic medicinal preparations." A recipe for Rock & Rye even appears in *The Savoy Cocktail Book* (1930), which simply called for dosing whiskey with rock candy and lemon. Celebrated in popular culture, Rock & Rye was mentioned by none other than Sheriff Pat Garrett as the libation of choice for his pals as they chased Billy The Kid across the rugged Western landscape.

Mister Katz's Rock & Rye is a blend of the distillery's young rye whiskey with rock candy sugar, sour cherries, cinnamon, and citrus. I've included my own recipe for Rock & Rye on page 99.

Finally released in 2015, NDC's Ragtime Rye has a mash bill comprising 72% New York rye, 16% corn, and 12% malted barley, matured for two to three years. Now, the most astute amongst you will recognise that the Ragtime mash bill is short by 3% for qualification as an "Empire Rye." What a blunder! But there's a good reason for this. Barrels of Ragtime had already been maturing years before the Empire classification was first imagined. However, Katz and team have more recently released a bottled in bond version of Ragtime. It's aged for four years, bottled at 100 proof and made from a mash of 75% New York rye, 13% corn, and 12% malted barley. This is their first bottling that meets the Empire Rye requirement.

Other expressions in the Ragtime family include single barrel releases, as well as Ragtime finished in Applejack barrels. New York is the second biggest apple-producing state, but the inspiration for this product came from George Washington, who liked to make apple brandy alongside his rye whiskey.

With the tour complete and night having fallen, it feels improper not to bookend our visit with another Manhattan. And another…

RAGTIME RYE (45.2% ABV)

Honeycomb, muscovado sugar, burnished teal, and a little nutmeg on the nose, and perhaps some damson? It's bone-dry on the palate, belying the sweet smells. More of that dried stone fruit follows, with almond kernel and bitter oak notes.

RAGTIME RYE BOTTLED IN BOND (50% ABV)

It's big and zippy on the nose, with hints of raspberry and cracked cacao that soften to more barrel characteristics of crème brûlée and pimento on repeat visits. There's a deep, rich cherry note to the flavor (like the kernels from the standard bottling have developed into fruit) followed by a long, bittersweet finish.

NDC THAT BOUTIQUEY WHISKEY COMPANY 2 YEAR OLD (50% ABV)

Chocolate fudge brownie, sweet plum pudding, and floral notes on the nose. It's bold and juicy on the palate, with baked fall fruits, pistachio, black pepper, and bitter chocolate.

ROAD TRIP PLAYLIST

"Empire State of Mind" — Alicia Keys

"Red Eyes" — War on Drugs

"Where the Streets Have No Name" — U2

TOP New York City is home to a growing number of distilleries, many situated in Brooklyn.
ABOVE The beer industry took off in Brooklyn in the mid-19th century thanks to its skilled German immigrants.

ROCK & RYE

50 ml/1⅔ oz Ragtime Rye
Spiced Rock Candy Syrup (see below)

Take a rocks glass and fill it with ice. Pour in the rye whiskey and follow it up with 5–20 ml (1–4 teaspoons) of syrup, depending on how sweet you want it.

SPICED ROCK CANDY SYRUP

630 g/22 oz fine granulated sugar
1 can Dr Pepper
30 ml/1 oz rye whiskey
1 cinnamon stick
1 star anise

Add all the ingredients to a zip-lock bag and seal, ensuring as much of the air is removed as possible. Place the bag in a water bath (or a pan of water) and maintain a temperature of 50°C/122°F for five hours.

Strain the liquor while it's still warm and store in a wide-necked jar in the cupboard.

When Rock & Rye was first imagined, it was the job of the imbiber to mix the two components together according to their taste. It was only much later, when branded versions of the cocktail became available in pharmacies, that the drink came pre-made.

My recipe harks back to the original serve, so simply requires you to make an infused rock candy syrup and serve it alongside a bottle of Ragtime Rye. The ratio in which you mix the two together will depend on how sweet and spiced you want the cocktail to taste.

Rock candy syrup, by the way, is nothing more than an exceptionally sweet sugar syrup. Where normally I would advise mixing (by weight) 1.5 parts sugar to 1 part water, with rock candy syrup you can increase the ratio to 2.2 parts sugar to 1 part water. I know—it doesn't seem like that much sugar can fit into so little water, but trust me, it does.

My recipe for rock candy syrup is so devilishly simple that you'll be screaming "cheat!" at the book. But once you try it, you'll appreciate its deliciousness and perhaps never mix rye whiskey with anything else ever again. I do add a splash of rye whiskey to it, which helps to preserve the syrup for months.

Spiced Rock Candy Syrup makes approximately one liter, enough for 100 serves.

KINGS COUNTY

THE RETURN OF THE KING

"Civilization begins with distillation."

WILLIAM FAULKNER (1897–1962), AUTHOR

eaving Williamsburg the next morning, we take one of our shortest trips between two distilleries. Just three miles away, heading west towards the Brooklyn Bridge, is Kings County Distillery, located in the old paymaster building in the Brooklyn Navy Yard. It's a historic location for very obvious reasons, but what's less apparent is the Navy Yard's connection to the history of whiskey.

You'll remember that Pennsylvania fought a Whiskey Rebellion in the early 19th century that came about due to taxation on spirits. And 60 years later, New York had its own whiskey-fueled battle with the federal government, also brought about by taxation, which became known as the Whiskey Wars.

As we've already learned, the early 19th century saw New York's distilleries graduate far beyond charming little farm operations, into industrial powerhouses of spirits production. Whiskey had become big business, so the government did what governments do best and started taxing it.

The Bureau of Internal Revenue (the precursor to the IRS) reinstated a tax on whiskey in 1862, which was the first time whiskey had been taxed since 1817. The cash was desperately needed to fund the Union side of the Civil War effort, and then even more cash was needed afterwards to rebuild the nation. Initially,

it levied a 20-cent tax per 100-proof gallon, then between 1865–8 it was raised to $2 per 100-proof gallon, which is roughly equivalent to twice the tax on spirits today.

Having enjoyed 50 years of duty-free distilling, the distillers were no more inclined to pay the tax than those that came before them. The industry quickly devolved as the desperate distillers took their operations off-grid and underground. The reality was that the government was just as desperate as the whiskey makers. If it didn't generate revenue quickly it would soon go bankrupt, but if the whiskey tax was successful, it could provide over 20% of government revenue. The stakes were high at both ends.

This fact the distilleries of this era were much larger should have made them hard to conceal, but a bustling metropolis offers an array of secluded spots to a well-motivated distiller, including one located in an old chapel on Manhattan's East Broadway.

The problem for revenue collectors wasn't only finding the distilleries, but in convincing the distillers to pay up and avoiding getting beaten to death. By 1869, illicit distilling in New York had become so widespread, and the gangs associated with it so violent, that cops and revenue collectors needed military backup. Early "battles" in 1869 saw hundreds of army veterans and artillerymen engage in knife and fist fights in alleys, weeding out illegal stills and smashing barrels of aging whiskey in the streets. In one afternoon in December 1869, stills of sufficient

PREVIOUS PAGES Walking along the wooden planks of the iconic Brooklyn Bridge (and risking death by straddling the cycle lane).

size to produce 250 barrels of whiskey a day were destroyed – equivalent to $5,000 in taxes every day.

Nowhere in New York was the tax so flagrantly ignored than in Brooklyn's Fifth Ward, or Vinegar Hill. In the 1860s, this was a rough, overcrowded neighborhood with a predominantly Irish population, manufacturing whiskey as well as their native potato spirit, poitín. *The New York Times* would later recall the days of the Whiskey Wars in an 1894 article:

"The peasantry of the Wickford (sic) Mountains were never firmer in their sympathy with the makers of 'potheen' than were these denizens of ancient 'Irishtown.' The wary intruder who passed that way had good reason to avoid suspicion of being a spy. The least intimation that he was inquisitively included would bring a rabble at his heels and insure him a cracked crown if not more grievous injuries."

On the morning of November 2, 1870, battalions under the command of Col. John L. Broome arrived by boat at the Brooklyn Navy Yard. Guided by the revenue assessors, they marched through the narrow streets armed with muskets, axes, and crowbars. They raided basements and backstreets, getting pelted with stones and lumps of coal on the way.

Just like the modern "war on drugs," the government was fighting to regain control over a product that was financing gangs and criminals, who employed tactics reminiscent of the mob and cartel. Bribery ensued, paving the way for decades of political corruption.

All of this spelled bad news for the New York whiskey industry, starting with a marked decay in distilling standards. The timing wasn't ideal, as operations in the West were increasing capacity, improving quality, and benefitting from becoming increasingly easy to transport. By the time Prohibition arrived in 1920, New York's economy had evolved and most of the distilleries had already packed up.

※※※ ※※※ ※※※

Now, back in the modern era, we have distilleries popping up like Kings County, who aim not only to make delicious whiskey, but to shine a light on the rich history of whiskey-making in New York. Colin Spoelman and David Haskell founded their operation in 2009, when they were still distilling on five 24-liter (6.5-gallon) stainless steel stills out of a studio space in Bushwick. Housed in a 325-sq. ft. space, they reckon it was the smallest commercial distillery in the country at that time. Demand was good though, and they were distilling 16 hours a day, seven days a week.

Things have grown up a little since then.

The Navy Yard approached Colin and David back in 2010, and in 2012, the distillery moved to the Paymaster building which was originally the bank of the Brooklyn Navy Yard.

"Many people don't realize that New York was outputting more than Kentucky in the early 19th century," says Kings County Production Manager, Ryan Ciuchta. "It's nice to have these historical links that legitimize all the startups that we're seeing now."

As distillery upgrades go, to them this must have felt like a big one. The Paymaster building is expansive, with the distillery itself taking up most of the ground floor space, with a shop, tasting room, and small warehouse up top.

Colin is from Kentucky (the eastern/coal mining part, not the glitzy horse racing/bourbon part) so at first glance, his distillery location in New York appears to be a bit of a betrayal to his home state. But as we have already learned, New York whiskey pre-dates Kentucky spirits (by at least 100 years) so Colin is probably exactly where he needs to be. As a published author, he knows his stuff when it comes to whiskey history and its present-day boom. His status as an ambassador for the whiskey renaissance has allowed him to travel a fair bit, and it was while he was on his travels the I first met him, at the World Whisky Forum in England.

I was giving a seminar on whiskey flavor and how we should be talking to consumers about taste and styles. Colin was talking about the growth of craft distilling in the US, and particularly in New York, where he reminded the hundred or so delegates (that were mostly from the Scotch Whisky industry) that there are now more whiskey distilleries in New York State than in Scotland. With that bombshell dropped,

Colin proceeded to show a bunch of pictures of his distillery in Brooklyn, eliciting nervous glances from the Scots in the audience, since Colin's distillery looks like a Single Malt Whisky distillery.

"It's not that we're starting a new industry," he said. "We're reviving an old one."

The five 440-gallon fermenters at Kings County are atypical for an American whiskey distillery – but not for a Scottish single malt distillery – as they're made from oak, by the same company that makes many of the water towers that populate the New York skyline. The stills here are, for the time being, Scottish too, made by Forsyth's coppersmiths in Speyside.

We have encountered pot stills at every distillery we've visited so far. We have already established that principles of a pot still are quite straightforward: heat the liquid, evaporate the alcohol, and collect something stronger than what you started with.

A pot still does not create flavor; it selects it. Based on the shape and design of the still, as well as the hand of the distiller, the distillation process determines which aromatic and tactile components find their way up the neck of the still and down into the condenser.

Pot stills are most often constructed entirely from copper, which is used because of its high thermal conductivity, malleability, and catalytic properties. Generally speaking, a still comprises four sections: the base, where the liquid goes; the head, where the vapor travels up; the lyne arm (the pipe the vapor travels along to reach the condenser); and the condenser, where the vapor is converted back into a liquid.

Pot stills can look like ugly steel tanks with a couple of gauges adorning the outside, or beautiful teardrop-shaped works of art (Kings County's stills are the latter). The shape, size, and height of the still have parts to play in all of this. The higher the still, the harder the spirit vapor has to work to reach the top, and the less likely it is to make it over. In squat little stills, the heavier, oilier, and more dense flavor compounds make it over the top since they have less distance to cover.

In addition to this, tall stills give a spirit more opportunity for interaction with copper. Copper has a purifying effect on a distilled spirit and a greater degree of "conversation" removes sulphurous flavors, which in turn heightens the delicate fruit and floral aromatics. This is especially so in small stills, since there is a greater surface area of copper in comparison to the volume of liquid than there would be in a large still. Of course the effects of size vary based on how much liquid is put in the still, too.

Different still shapes encourage a varying degree of "reflux" in the system. Reflux in a still is similar to reflux in a stomach, but in this instance, it's spirit vapor that moves up and down rather than stomach acid. A short still can produce spirit that is reminiscent of a tall still by bulging out and pinching in at certain stages up the neck of the still, by giving the vapors a clear run, or teasing them into crevices and overhangs that lead back down to the bottom.

Back at Kings County, I'm looking at two of the smallest stills that Forsyths have ever made: 264 gallons and 172 gallons. They're both teardrop-shaped and generally conform to classic Scottish pot-still dimensions. The larger still performs the first "stripping" run, increasing the strength of the beer from 3–5% up to around 25% alcohol over a 3–4 hour run. By that point there's only around 40 gallons of liquid, which is ready to be distilled a second time.

Unlike the first distillation, which was allowed to go about its merry way, the second distillation must be carefully monitored by the distiller so that the correct volume, strength, and quality of spirit is collected. This is a process that is common to all pot-still distillations.

The first trickles of liquid that come through the spirits safe are known as "foreshots". These account for approximately 1% of the entire distillation run and comprise hard-hitting compounds with very low boiling points (hence why they arrive first). These liquids are toxic so must be discarded.

Next comes the "heads," containing some ethanol (drinkable alcohol) and variable amounts of aldehydes and esters (fruity and floral aromas) and methanol (ethanol's evil sister). Small amounts of these chemicals can be desirable in the finished product, so

STRIPPING STILL
STILL NO 1
264 GALLON CAP

it's up to the distiller to decide when is the right time to stop collecting the heads and when to start collecting the "hearts," which is known as a "cut." The heart of the spirit is basically all the good stuff, and comprises ethanol, water, and lots of fruity, grassy, and nutty aromas that were created during the process of fermentation.

As time goes on, the strength of the spirit the distiller collects will begin to diminish, from a starting place of perhaps 80% alcohol to (eventually) 0% alcohol. The types of alcohol that distill over will change during this time too, from clean-tasting

ethanol to heavy, smelly compounds like amyl alcohol and isobutyl alcohols (known collectively as "fusel oils") along with increasing amounts of water. The distiller must make their second hearts cut at this point, with the aim of capturing a balanced expression of the spirit. If they get greedy and extend the collection of their heart, they will be punished with a lower-strength spirit with very heavy, buttery, diesel-like, and solvent-like aromas. If they collect a smaller heart, the spirit will be stronger and taste lighter and more delicate… but they'll have a lot less of it.

Most distilleries that use pot stills (Kings County included) tend to run the spirits still until all of the alcohol has been collected. These "feints" or "tails" are married with the heads and mixed together with the low wines from the first distillation, ready for the second distillation… and so the cycle continues.

Now, you might be wonder why a distiller would want to mix their dirty leftover food in to what promised to be a delicious new meal? Well, since this is a practice that was originated by the canny Scottish, it won't surprise you too much to learn that it's a strategy developed for economic success. Although the heads and tails contain plenty of undesirable components, they also contain a fair bit of ethanol too. By recycling them the distiller gets another go at recovering that alcohol (as well as some of those sought-after fruity and floral aromas) and increasing their yield. And, of course, more alcohol means more money.

Those of you paying attention here may have noticed a slight mathematical issue with this. If the foreshots and feints from every spirits run are mixed in with the low wines for the next, surely there would be a concentration of "colorful" compounds building up in the feints receiver over time? Well, yes, and this is the reason why many feints receivers are periodically stripped of the dangerously alluring alien sludge that accumulates on the walls. If you're lucky you may even find lumps of copper in there too, which is interesting since the seemingly clear spirit is obviously transporting a significant amount of solid matter over at either the start or the end of the run.

Kings County Bourbon is made from 75% corn and 25% malted barley. The Single Malt is made from a combination of un-peated and medium-peated malt, and their Peated Bourbon involves a straight swap-out of un-peated for peated malt in the bourbon mash bill. No enzymes are used for these products. They're also making an increasing amount of rye here too—production has doubled every year for the past year.

The distillery is in the midst of another significant expansion, however, which includes a new 1,350-gallon still made by Vendome, four 4,000-gallon fermenters, and maxi-versions of pretty much every other vessel, pipe, tank, and valve that's needed to make a bottle of whiskey.

That goes for the barrels too.

The distillery is holding around 4,000 barrels but less than 10% of them are full-size 53 gallon "bourbon barrels." This is set to change as the smaller five and ten-gallon barrels are phased out.

"We'll be holding primarily 15 and 53 gallon barrels by the end of 2019," says Ryan.

The 53-gallon casks are earmarked to be the new flagship product once they reach maturity, which is expected to be at around seven years old.

For bourbon and single malt, the spirit is proofed down to 58% before going to the barrel. The rye spirit goes in to the barrel at 55%, in accordance with the proposed Empire Rye category that we discussed in the previous chapter.

Kings County definitely belongs in the "one to watch" column on any distillery data sheet. There's a sense that things are being done the right way here, with a strong commitment to technical details while keeping an eye on the past too. I look forward to seeing how their products develop.

BOURBON (45% ABV)

On the nose there's a slight sooty barrel char note, backed up by burnt banana, and an extremely strong oak aroma. So nothing out of the ordinary for a bourbon. Sweetness dissipates quite quickly in the taste, leaving a nice, dry finish. Black pepper tingles in the finish.

BOTTLED IN BOND BOURBON (50% ABV)

The nose is more restrained, but the extra maturation brings about leather and soft fruit. There's the sensation of a banana and strawberry smoothie that's been blended so long it cooked, and turned into a weird fruity soup. Dryness kicks in hard on the palate—bitter almond, tannin, and red fruits. Lovely.

PEATED BOURBON (45% ABV)

On the nose there's a subtle campfire smoke, burnt marshmallow, and green sappy smoke too. Really well balanced on the palate, like a peated Scotch in a very active cask (which is what it is, basically). Dries out a lot on the finish… with a linger of apricot.

STRAIGHT RYE (51% ABV)

Slightly gluey on the nose. Then comes a menthol, eucalyptus, caraway, and funky Brazil nut. Juicy and concentrated on the palate, with a touch of cardamom and rye bread. This is a challenging rye, but definitely one for the lovers of the style.

SINGLE MALT 3 YEAR OLD (47% ABV)

The nose is delicate with notes of orange zest and subtle smoke. It's creamy, and honeyed on the palate… light but with a great integration of peat smoke. Difficult to distinguish from Scotch malt, but then… so it should be.

ROAD TRIP PLAYLIST

"Nancy Whiskey" – Shane MacGowan

"Whiskey In The Jar" – Thin Lizzy

"King of the Road" – The Proclaimers

WHISKEY PUNCH

240 ml/8 oz Kings County Peated Bourbon
120 ml/4 oz lemon juice
60 ml/2 oz sugar syrup
500 ml/17 oz cold, unsweetened tea
5 dashes Angostura bitters

(makes enough for six servings)

Mix all of the ingredients and store in a bottle in the fridge until you're ready to serve.
Pour over cubed ice into a rocks glass and garnish with a strip of orange.

Recipes for punch go back as far as the 17th century. They were the original sharing cocktail before cocktails were a thing. The word "punch" is thought to derive from the Hindi word for five ("panche") in reference to the holy "quintinity" of ingredients that coalesce to make a punch: spirit, citrus, sugar, spice, and water. Punch houses became common in India during the time of the British East India Company – hence the use of the Hindi word.

Whiskey punches were extremely popular in Ireland during the 18th century, which meant they were also popular in American cities with strong Irish representation, such as Boston and New York. Punches were not the kind of drinks you might see in your local tavern though; rather, they were intended for polite company and refined society. That's why there's scant historical reference to mixing American whiskey into punches during this period, because homegrown whiskey was still considered a drink for peasant farmers and people of disrepute. Mixing American whiskey into a punch would have been like combining fresh salad leaves with lard.

Fortunately, we don't have to go far to find good whiskey these days, and the Kings County range offer plenty of options for a mixologist. You can adapt your punch recipe to include different types of tea, fruit juices, spices, and herbs. I'm keeping my recipe simple, but I suggest using it like a template rather than canon.

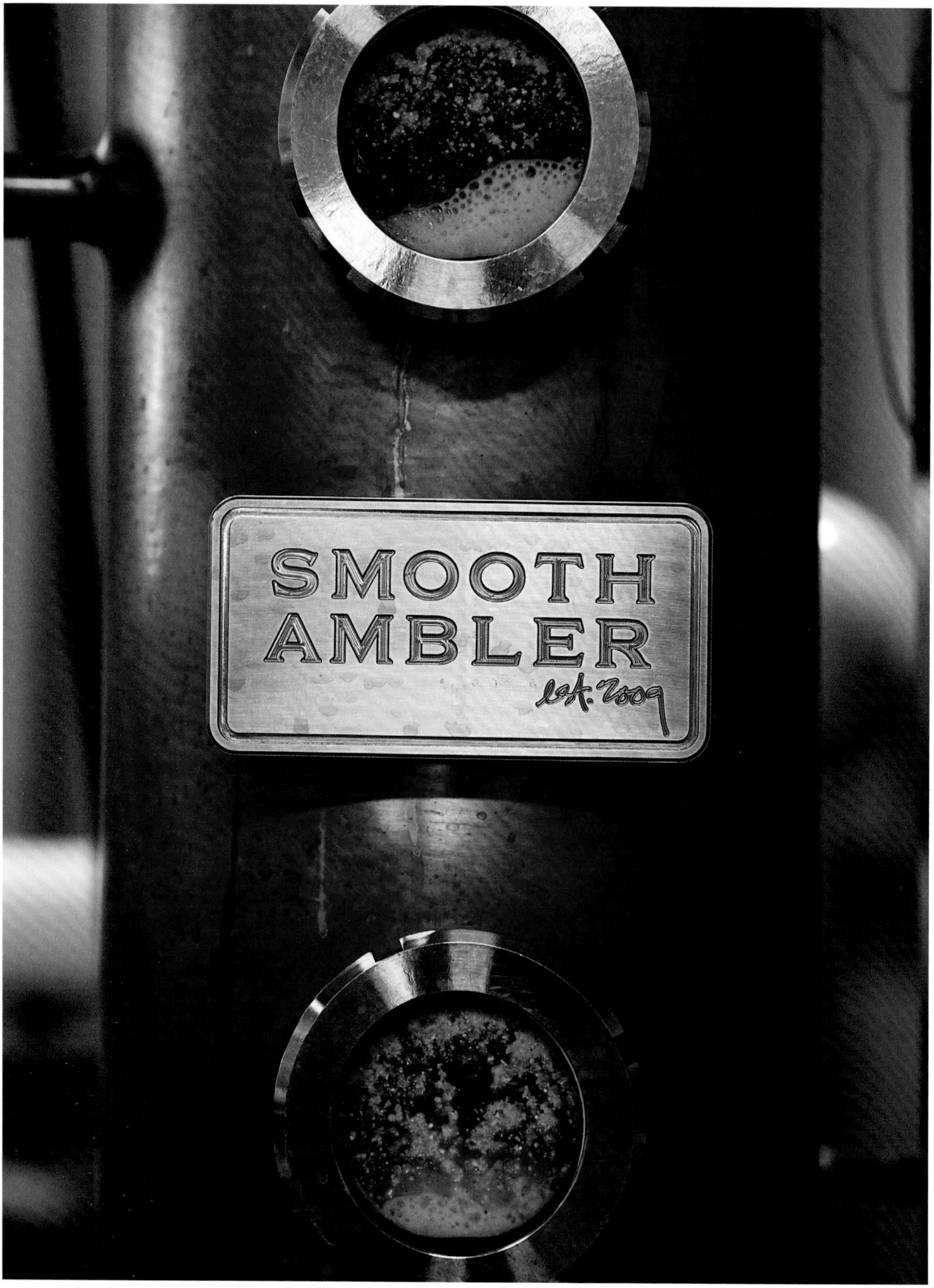
SMOOTH
AMBLER
est. 2009

SMOOTH AMBLER

TAKING A LONG AMBLE

"Tell me what brand of whiskey that Grant drinks. I would like to send a barrel of it to my other generals."

ABRAHAM LINCOLN (1809–65), 16TH PRESIDENT OF THE UNITED STATES

Contrary to popular belief, bourbon can be made anywhere in the US, not just in the state of Kentucky. If you had told this to someone 20 years ago they might have pointed out to you that all of the bourbon distilleries (with one or two exceptions) were located in Kentucky. Nowadays, there are ten times as many bourbon distilleries outside of Kentucky than there are inside, so the case is already made. That said, Kentucky is still home to the biggest bourbon distilleries and accounts for more than nine out of every ten barrels filled.

We're on our way to Kentucky, but there's a fair bit of country to cover to get there.

In 1776, the Virginia legislature reorganized the western section of its land and called it Kentucky County. Within Kentucky, the counties of Fayette, Lincoln, and Jefferson were established in 1780. Then came Nelson, Mercer, and Bourbon, in 1786. Bourbon County encompassed a huge swathe of land, almost a third of the landmass of present-day Kentucky. Little wonder then that it was named after the Royal house of King Louis XVI of France, who was a powerful ally of George Washington during the Revolutionary War.

As a sign of gratitude to Louis— mostly for supplying weapons—he got a big chunk of America as a namesake. The debt must have been quickly forgotten however, as Bourbon County rapidly shrunk, reduced to less than 10% of its previous size

by 1792. But on June 1 of that same year, Kentucky became the 15th State.

Bourbon was invented in Kentucky. Probably.

To define where and when anything was invented, you have to first classify exactly what that thing is, and then attempt to establish when and where it got its name.

However, it is extremely likely that barrel-aged corn whiskey was being made before bourbon got its name. And that whiskey, produced in a similar way to bourbon, pre-dates American Independence, the existence of Bourbon County, and Kentucky itself. It's also possible the people referred to another spirit as "bourbon" before the spirit resembled anything like what we would consider to be bourbon today. In fact, one thing we can be sure of is that the methods and recipes used to make bourbon have continued to evolve over the past 200 years (less so in the past 50 years), re-establishing the identity of the product.

In later chapters we will explore some of the facts that surround bourbon's embryonic years, how this particular style of whiskey known as bourbon gained its reputation, and we'll discuss the changes in method that followed thereafter.

We'll do all of this once we get to Kentucky. But we have one important stop to make before we get there.

Backtracking the route we took north, from Philadelphia to New York, we head west to Harrisburg, Pennsylvania, then drop down to

Gettysburg, the site of the battle that turned the tide of the American Civil War, and where Abraham Lincoln delivered his famous 1863 Address. If Lincoln were alive today, he would probably drink Knob Creek bourbon. It's a whiskey produced by Jim Beam, but it's named after Lincoln's childhood home and where he said his "earliest recollection" came from.

After Gettysburg we join I-81, heading south. This highway runs parallel to the Appalachians range, through Shenandoah National Park. It's there where we'll traverse the Appalachian mountains and cross the West Virginia state line. They call it the "Mountain State" and a quick glance at a map will tell you why. West Virginia is dominated by the Appalachian mountain range and over 75% of the state is covered in forest.

Besides being geographically quite different to the (mostly) low-lying topography of Virginia, the culture here is quite different too. Virginia had its wealthy tobacco planters (like Washington and Jefferson) and became a political hub for the aristocracy. West Virginia on the other hand was frontier land, where subsistence farmers, coal miners, and frontiersmen settled through the 18th century. The University state athletics mascots tell you everything you need to know: Virginia has the Cavaliers, a mounted swordsman with flashy crossed sabers. West Virginia has the Mountaineers, which is usually a bearded guy in a buckskin suit with a rifle and a coonskin hat.

John Little has some of that resourceful, straight-shootin' mentality about him (but sadly no buckskin suit, alas). He's the co-founder and master distiller at Smooth Ambler Spirits in Lewisburg, West Virginia. Nestled into the foothills of the Appalachians, Greenbrier County is the kind of place where people would rather not work at all, but when they do work they work hard. Making whiskey incentivizes the downtime, and making good whiskey does so even more.

This distillery was founded in 2010 by John Little and his father in law, TAG Galyean (he goes by a capitalized first name), in 2010. The plan was to celebrate the natural beauty of the area, its clean air and water, in a spirit that speaks of place. Like WhistlePig (see page 81), they spent the first few years bottling whiskey sourced from other distilleries under their Old Scout brand while their own spirit matured. Also, like WhistlePig, they managed to source some really great liquid, and it's those spirits that have fueled growth.

The plan, of course, is to become less reliant on other distilleries, but such is the success of Old Scout that the only way Smooth Ambler can meet future demand is to keep upgrading the distillery.

"We started in 2010 and we've expanded about five different times," says John. One of the more recent expansions shifted production from 80 barrels a month to 300 barrels a month. Then, in late 2016, Smooth Ambler sold a majority stake to drinks giant Pernod Ricard.

The current still house used to contain the entire operation, from grain store to mashing, fermentation, distillation, barreling, and bottling. Now the operation stretches out in every direction from the still house, encompassing multiple buildings. Smooth Ambler started with a single 175-gallon still, but now the mashing and distillation equipment runs 24 hours a day, seven days a week.

The appetite of the distillery has had further knock-on effects too.

"As we've grown," says John, "we've exceeded the capability of our local farms."

Couple that with a tragic farming accident involving their long-time local partner, and Smooth Ambler now have to supplement their grain supply with product from the Midwest. All the cereals they buy in are non-GMO.

To summarize in three words how this operation runs, I'd go for: clean, hi-tech, meticulous. The name Smooth Ambler might give an impression of some endearingly backwoods, hillbilly-run operation, but believe me—these guys are not messing about.

The distillery runs four main mash bills: a wheated bourbon (71% corn, 21% wheat, and 8% malted barley), a mid-rye bourbon (71% corn, 21% rye, and 8% malted barley), a high-rye bourbon (52% corn, 40% rye, and 8% malted barley), and a rye (88% rye and 12% malted barley).

Mashing is all controlled electronically, wherein the programmed recipe pulls in water, corn, wheat, and malt. Enzymes are added too, which help to reduce the viscosity of the mash.

"We cook our corn at 200°F," says John, "we tried it at a boil but didn't like the flavor and didn't notice any difference in yield by dropping the temperature."

The mash cooker has an 800-gallon capacity, which matches the size of the fermenters. Once the mashing is done, more cold water is added to help cool the mash down to 75°F, ready for yeast to be pitched. There are 22 open-top fermenters in this distillery, which will soon increase to 27 to keep up with the 5 mashes the distillery is completing every day. Mashing at such a furious rate simply wouldn't be possible without the automated systems that John has installed. This will probably be the last distillery upgrade that takes place with the current scale of equipment, though.

"We'll need to move up to 5,000-gallon mash cookers and fermenters next," says John. "But we're a couple of years off that yet."

The fermenter room is no less technical. Each fermenter is electronically controlled and records temperature, pH, and timings into a database that can be referenced up to ten years in to the future. Besides ensuring consistency, the ability to monitor anomalies and translate them to the taste of future whiskeys could be a powerful tool if you wanted to recreate something that tastes particularly delicious.

"Fermentation is where the flavor is made," says John. "Yeast is where it's at, man."

Besides the important role of creating alcohol, fermentation has an important role in making flavor in un-aged whiskey (distillation only selects the flavor), so really sets the starting point for a future bottled whiskey.

Fermentation begins with the metabolic process known as glycolysis, where yeast converts one glucose (sugar) molecule into two pyruvate molecules. Pyruvate is a form of "free energy" that can be used to create other energy-providing compounds, and this is exactly the same process that takes place in the human body to convert glucose into a usable energy

TOP Clean air and clean water make West Virginia a paradise for distillers.
ABOVE A telltale giveaway for any bourbon distillery is when you see inexplicable turrets rising above the roof.

currency. The pyruvate has three carbon atoms which, during the fermentation of bread, the yeast then combines with oxygen to make CO_2 and voila: your bread proves.

In the case of fermenting sugary liquids, such as mash or wort, the liquid doesn't have access to much oxygen—a layer of CO_2 sits on top of the brew, and

oxygen can't penetrate down through the liquid—so the process is anaerobic. In this instance, the pyruvate can't combine all its carbon with oxygen (to create CO_2) so it instead produces molecules of ethanol, methanol, and other types of alcohol.

It is of course the ethanol that gives the fermented liquid its alcoholic strength, but it is the other alcohols, along with the development of aldehydes and esters, which are the true designators of flavor. Aldehydes are made when alcohol becomes oxidized, and are therefore more likely to occur later on in fermentation. An example of an aromatic aldehyde is benzaldehyde, which has a cherry-like aroma.

Esters are mostly made by cellular processes within the yeast. The reactions are complex, beginning with fatty acids reacting with other organic molecules, which in turn interact with enzymes that finally combine with alcohol to produce an ester. Some examples of esters produced during fermentation are ethyl butyrate (providing a tropical fruit flavor), iso-amyl acetate (candy), and isobutyl acetate (raspberry and strawberry).

The variety and quantity of these compounds is dictated by a whole number of factors that include the mineral content and pH of the mash, the pitching

LEFT Smooth Ambler uses a column still to make whiskey... we'll discuss how they work in the coming chapters
BELOW LEFT Rows of fermentation tanks, each being monitored using state-of-the-art equipment.
BELOW RIGHT Peering inside a fermenter, we can see (and smell) the yeast doing its thing.

rate (i.e. the amount of yeast going into the fermenter), the concentration of sugar, the length and temperature of fermentation, and the type of yeast utilized.

Fermentation produces CO_2 as a by-product, which manifests itself as bubbles on top. Depending on how complete the fermentation is, the bubbles may be large, light, and airy, or small, brief, and furious. At some stages of fermentation, the yeast is so active that the liquid appears to be aerated or moving through some kind of pump.

The friction caused by this movement is one of the reasons why fermentation is exothermic. In some southern states this can sometimes be problematic as, when things get too hot, the yeast cells are in danger of dying. Distilleries will often combat this problem by installing coils or veins of cooling water in their fermentation tanks.

"We just went though a big yeast trial," says John. "It's part of a wider experiment we've been doing to try and control fusel oils during distillation. We've looked at everything from Brix levels, how thick the mash is, fermentation temperatures, pH."

During the course of their experiments, they encountered yeast varieties that did seem to limit fusel oil production and produce a cleaner spirit. However, this shifted the style of the spirit away from what they considered to be quintessentially "Smooth Ambler" whiskey.

"It turns out the yeast we've been using all along is the best yeast for us," says John.

As we walk down towards the barrel store, John sweeps some gravel off the pristine tarmac with his boot. I realize he's been doing this kind of thing ever since we started the tour—wiping down a surface, cleaning up garbage, polishing out a smear. He's a perfectionist and I give him a look of sympathy. "I've seen ten things I want to fix," he says.

Smooth Ambler is a surgically clean operation, because the team is instructed to keep it that way, and because John Little is multitasking in every room he walks into.

All whiskeys go into new 53-gallon American oak barrels with a heavy char (#4 on the scale of 1–4).

The distillery has eight buildings onsite, storing 8,000 barrels. They also have stocks in Indiana to the tune of 11,000 barrels.

Smooth Ambler bottle a range of whiskeys (and only whiskeys), some of which are sourced and others made at the distillery. Contradiction is a blend of two bourbon mash bills (one with rye one with wheat) aged between 4 and 11 years. The Old Scout range includes a few expressions, including American Whiskey (a blend of nine-year old-bourbon and five-year-old bourbon aged in re-charred barrels), Single Barrel (a high rye bourbon), and Single Barrel Select (a low-rye bourbon from Tennessee).

All of these products will eventually transition over to the West Virginia distillery once the whiskey has reached maturity. For the time being, the only product available that is entirely made at the distillery is Big Level, a bourbon made from their wheated mash bill.

Smooth Ambler products are currently available in 35 states, plus UK, France, Hungary, and Australia.

OLD SCOUT (49.5% ABV)

Delicate but boozy on the nose with blueberry muffin, vanilla custard, and light coconut aromas. The taste is initially savory but then rounds off with sourdough bread coated in hot jelly and butter. There's spice through the finish, which feels like white pepper and wasabi.

CONTRADICTION BOURBON 46% (ABV)

An initial wave of banana cake (spiced with mace and pimento) gives way to hard toffee and sweet cornbread. There are spicy/savory notes on the palate, with buttered sweetcorn and a dry, coffee finish.

ROAD TRIP PLAYLIST

"Highway Patrolman" – Bruce Springsteen

"Carry on Wayward Son" – Kansas

"One Mint Julep" – Louis Prima

MINT JULEP

50 ml/1⅔ oz Old Scout Bourbon
10 ml/2 teaspoons sugar syrup
12 mint leaves

Add all the ingredients to a julep tin or rocks glass and churn well with crushed ice.
Add more crushed ice as necessary and garnish with a couple of sprigs of
slapped mint (to release the aroma).

The word julep derives from the Persian word "gulab", meaning rosewater. In the 18th century, juleps became a popular type of medicinal cordial, intended to treat stomach complaints. All types of herbs and spices were infused into them, along with sugar and sometimes alcohol. What differentiates a julep from other sorts of medicinal infusions is that all of the ingredients were soluble and the resulting liquid transparent. Through my research, I discovered a 1791 book, published in Edinburgh, Scotland, called *Domestic Medicine* that included a recipe for a "Musk Julep" that called for spirit, musk, cinnamon, and peppermint water. It was designed to get rid of hiccups.

Over in the US, however, juleps were beginning to find a fanbase as a morning pick-me-up. The mint julep was first referenced in print in 1803 by British traveler John Davis, who mentioned a beverage he drank at a Virginia plantation. Davis described the drink as "a dram of spirituous liquor that has mint steeped in it, taken by Virginians of a morning."

Julep is synonymous with the Kentucky Derby, the annual thoroughbred horse race held in Louisville, Kentucky. Over the course of the Kentucky Derby weekend, the Churchill Downs race track make an estimated 120,000 mint juleps for spectators. The Derby Museum reports that the mint julep became Churchill Downs' signature drink in 1938, the year they began serving it in souvenir glasses for 75 cents.

Like many of the most enduring drinks, the julep is a drink that requires patience and preparation. But in the picking of mint, preparing of the ice, and the slow stirring of bourbon we find a ritual that builds anticipation amongst the lucky recipient. A julep that's simply handed to you five seconds after placing the order will never taste as good as the one you had to wait for. Also, like nearly all of the best drinks, the julep is fiendishly simple: whiskey, mint, sugar, ice. That's it! And being so simple means it's wide open to customization too. Making crushed ice out of sweet tea is one of my favorite modifications of this cocktail.

A julep is traditionally served in a julep tin with a julep strainer placed on top. This drink pre-dates the modern use of straws in cocktails, and while the crushed ice holds the mint in place, you still need something to stop the crushed ice from falling all over your face.

HEAVEN HILL

HEAVEN ON EARTH

*"If I cannot drink bourbon and smoke cigars in heaven
then I shall not go."*

MARK TWAIN (1835–1910), AUTHOR

The next stage of our journey finally takes us to the state that has the most enduring association with whiskey. The state that produces more whiskey than any other, has the largest whiskey distillery, the oldest continually operating whiskey distillery, and the oldest distiller. Take a bow, Kentucky.

Now, there are a handful of individuals who are regularly credited with "inventing" bourbon, but it's extremely unlikely that any one individual was the sole originator. Bourbon probably came about as a result of a concerted movement towards a certain way of doing things, rather than an individual gospel. Nonetheless, we will explore all of the major candidates across the following chapters.

And we'll start with candidate number one, the Reverend Elijah Craig, who lends his name to a whiskey produced by Heaven Hill Distillers. Craig was from Virginia, where he had begun preaching as a "Separate Baptist" (an early form of evangelism) in the 1760s. Baptists of the "Great Awakening" were persecuted in 18th century Virginia, since it still conformed to the rules of the Church of England. Craig was jailed on more than one occasion for preaching "schismatic doctrines," but nevertheless, he attracted a substantial following, who literally followed him—all 500 hundred of them—to Kentucky County in 1786.

Craig and his congregation built a town called Lebanon, which was later renamed Georgetown. He got busy building mills and founding the Rittenhouse Academy (now sharing its name with a rye whiskey made at Heaven Hill), which became Georgetown College. Legend has it that one of the Greek revival columns of Giddings Hall at Georgetown College hides a keg of whiskey belonging to Elijah Craig.

Craig managed 1000 acres of land, a gristmill, and a fulling mill (used for thickening and cleaning cloth), and like anyone else with an industrious streak, he made whiskey. Craig is credited with instigating the practice of charring the inside of a whiskey barrel. The legend describes how Craig wanted to store his whiskey in oak casks that had previously held fish (other reports state that it was nails) so he aggressively charred the inside to remove the fishy flavor. Whether it was Craig or not who came up with this plan, I'd say that the man or woman who did first char a cask was attempting to overcome a similar problem.

Craig wasn't even the only preacher/distiller of that time. In 1787 a Baptist minister by the name of James Garrard was indicted for retailing whiskey without a license. Another Baptist evangelist, John Shackelford, received 36 gallons of whiskey as payment for preaching in 1798.

Craig is the most famous of these bourbon Baptists and the only one to get his name on a bottle along with the tagline, "The Father of Bourbon," a tenuous claim deriving from a passage in *The History of Kentucky*, published 66 years after Craig's death. This was a time

ABOVE Their Bernheim distillery in Louisville makes dozens of whiskey brands and sells spirit to bottlers all over the US.

when the temperance movement was on the rise and historically minded distillers leapt at the chance to link the origins of whiskey with a man of faith.

The Elijah Craig trademark was first registered in 1960 by Commonwealth Distillers, who also owned the T.W. Samuels brand. Heaven Hill acquired it in 1976, and it seems that it was never an active brand until the whiskey's first release in 1986, as the bourbon market neared its nadir. The Barrel Proof Elijah Craig was named *Whisky Advocate* magazine's "Whisky of the Year" in 2017.

Another entry to our "who invented bourbon?" showdown is Evan Williams. This man, who also has his name on a bottle of bourbon produced by Heaven Hill Distillers (the second biggest selling bourbon brand in the world no less) was born in Wales in 1755 and moved to Kentucky in the 1780s. Like Craig, he didn't mess around, and had finished constructing his distillery in Louisville by 1783. It was located right on the banks of the Ohio River, on the east side of what is now Louisville's 5th Street.

The story that was recounted in *The Centenary of Kentucky*, a book published in 1892 by the Filson Club (now the Filson Historical Society), tells us that the locals weren't fans of Williams' operation. In the book, they declare his spirit "very bad whisky" and eventually forced him to close the operation down after he had repeatedly polluted the harbor with waste stillage (the irony will become clear shortly).

Unfortunately some of the timings don't quite add up here. Bourbon historian Michael Veach discovered that Williams' passage from London to Philadelphia was on board a ship named *Pigoe* that sailed May 1, 1784—a year *after* he was alleged to have opened his distillery in Louisville.

Nevertheless, many people have latched on to the idea that Williams' operation was the first commercial whiskey distillery in Kentucky, not least of all Heaven Hill Brands (for obvious reasons) but also the State of Kentucky, which erected a plaque detailing his escapades. If Louisville was the birthplace of bourbon, the Williams distillery would have to be one of the earliest, since Louisville wasn't settled until 1778, and in 1784 had the appearance of a small frontier town where all the inhabitants lived in forts to protect themselves from attacks by Native Americans.

Williams held several civic leadership positions, including serving as one of Louisville's seven elected city trustees. According to legend, he would bring a bottle of his whiskey (which it turns out nobody liked all that much) to the Board of Trustee Meetings. He was also a stonemason, and oversaw construction of the first jail and courthouse in Jefferson County. In 1797, he was elected Louisville's first wharf master (there's that irony). Williams died in 1810.

So steeped in history (or mythology depending on which way you care to look at it) are the products produced by Heaven Hill Brands, that it's surprising their own history dates back a mere 88 years. "The Old Heavenhill Spring distillery" was founded by the Shapira brothers in Bardstown, in 1935. It was a venture that would have seemed every bit a risky move just two years after Prohibition. What was even riskier was the complete lack of history that this brand new distillery could offer. So they did what any savvy business operator would do: they made one up. The long-dead farmer/distiller William Heavenhill was central to this, a man born in 1783 in the middle of an attack by Native Americans. He was a rugged-looking salt-of-the-earth kind of guy, plus he had a great name. The strategy worked, and set a precedent for fictional backstories that are still played out by new brands to this day.

The Evan Williams brand was introduced in 1957 and the 1990s saw the acquisition of Cabin Still Bourbon, J. W. Dant Bourbon and Old Fitzgerald Bourbon, as well as the introduction of Henry McKenna Bottled In Bond Single Barrel Bourbon, an 18-year-old expression of Elijah Craig and Evan Williams Barrel Vintage.

On November 7, 1996, the distillery was almost completely destroyed by a colossal blaze. The fire started in an maturing warehouse and spread to other buildings and vehicles. In total, 90,000 barrels of flammable bourbon ignited, creating a "river of fire". Following the fire, Heaven Hill acquired the

Bernheim distillery in Louisville and it's this facility that makes all of their products today (totaling at least 35 different expressions of whiskey!). Heaven Hill Brands are the US's largest independent distiller of spirits and the second biggest bourbon producer after Beam Suntory, which owns Jim Beam.

Since the Heaven Hill Springs distillery is now used only for warehousing and includes a visitor's center, all the hard work is done by the Bernheim distillery, which is located on West Breckinridge St., in Louisville. This site dates back to 1881, but has been rebuilt and remodeled a couple of times since then.

The most recent of those upgrades took place in 2017 and cost $25,000,000. It added four new fermenters and a new still, making it the largest bourbon distillery in the US. "That increased capacity by about a third," says Josh Hafer, their communications manager. "We can now fill 400,000 barrels of whiskey a year."

It's no surprise to find that Bernheim is every bit a factory. It's best to forget any notion you have about bluegrass hills and copper stills you've seen on "Bourbon Trail" advertising when you come to Bernheim. This is an unembellished, urban, whiskey-making machine that devours an entire truck of cereal every hour of every day, 365 days a year.

The distillery makes bourbons with two different mash bills, one of them with rye (78% corn, 12% rye, 12% malted barley) and the other one wheated (68%

RIGHT The Shapira brothers ceremonially filling the first barrel of whiskey at Heaven Hill's original distillery in Bardstown in 1935.

TOP The fiery gate of hell that is the mash cooker at Heaven Hill. You really don't want to fall in there.

LEFT In 2017, Heaven Hill underwent a $25 million upgrade. To be fair, with the distillery gobbling up an entire truckload of cereal an hour, you can't blame their equipment for looking fairly well used by then.

ABOVE The enormous grain silos at Heaven Hill, which make a truck look like a child's toy.

corn, 20% wheat, 12% malted barley). The latter is
used only for Old Fitzgerald and Larceny brands,
plus the occasional special release. They also run a rye
mash for the Rittenhouse and Pikesville (51% rye,
35% corn and 14% malted barley) a wheat whiskey
mash (51% wheat, 37% corn, 12% malted barley),
which is used to make Bernheim Straight, and a corn
whiskey mash (90% corn, 10% malted barley) used
to make the Mellow Corn brand.

Josh leads us through the enormous production space
of the facility, past a 14,000-gallon mash cooker and
to the doorway of the fermentation room. He grabs the
door handle, then turns back and fixes me with a
stare. "Prepare to see the largest fermenters you have
ever seen in your life," he says. I respond by telling him
I've visited over 300 distilleries and I'm not so easily
impressed. But as we walk into the room I quickly
begin to appreciate his point. These fermenters are
more like medium-sized buildings than somewhere you
might brew a beer. Each one of them is big enough to
house some of the distilleries in this book. At 124,000
gallons each, they are probably the largest fermenters
in the world used to make whiskey. Oh, and there are
17 of them! Each fermenter holds six mashes, and four
fermenters are filled every day. Over a period of 4–6
days (depending on where the weekend sits) a strong
beer of roughly 7% ABV is produced... do that math
and you'll discover that Heaven Hill are making a
quarter of a million gallons of pure alcohol a week.

The still house is no less impressive, containing
three massive beer-stripping columns, each of them 6
feet in diameter and five stories high. Larger whiskey
distilleries, and particularly ones in Kentucky and
Tennessee, tend to use a beer-stripping column in
place of double-pot distillation because they're more
efficient and can be run continuously. Unlike batch-
distilling in pots, in this kind of setup the column
completes the first distillation, then a connected pot
does the second.

The beer is pumped in near the top of the column,
and steam is pumped up from the bottom. Inside,
there are lots of "one-way" perforated trays, which
allow the steam to rise up through the still. The beer
spreads across each tray and flows down special

ABOVE The fermenters at the Bernheim distillery are
so large that it's all but impossible to photograph them
(a curious bartender inserted for scale.)

apertures like a waterfall on to the tray below. The
steam coming up through the column vaporizes the
alcohol from the beer, which then rises up to the top
of the column, while leaving the water and grain
solids to keep flowing down to the bottom.

When the vaporized alcohol reaches the top of the
still, it is further purified (or rectified) through
extended copper contact. Instead of trays in this
section, there are perforated plates with mushroom-
like caps on top of them. In a sense, these "bubble
caps" perform hundreds of minute distillations,
extending copper contact time and cleaning the spirit
of undesirable components. That includes the "heads"
and "tails" that a distiller would normally need to cut
from a pot-distillation run, which either fall down to
the bottom of the still with the water, or rise up and
out the top. It's for this reason that there are no spirit
cuts in larger whiskey distilleries.

The alcohol vapor exits the beer-stripping column near the top and will be in the vicinity of 60% ABV. It's then common for the spirit to undergo a second distillation that's used to raise the proof of the spirit a little higher. This is done here in two types of continuous pot still: a "doubler" or a "thumper." This final stage can be undertaken in a pot because there are no longer any solids to worry about. The waste product of the doubler/thumper is only water.

In a doubler, the vapor off the column still is condensed back into liquid and this is run through the pot still to increase the strength. The thumper works in much the same way as a doubler, except the sprit enters as vapor and the pot contains water. As the spirit vapor enters the thumper and meets the water, an exothermic reaction takes place, causing the alcohol vapors to flash off through the top of the still. The knocking noise generated by this reaction is where it gets its name from.

The doubler is likely named as such, because in the past it would have been paired with another pot instead of a column and therefore "doubled" the strength of the spirit. Thumpers and doublers are not required by law, and you can in fact use any number and combination of pots and columns you wish, so long as you don't distill over 160 proof.

The spirit comes off the still (a thumper in this case) at 159.5 proof, just under the maximum-permitted strength for bourbon whiskey. It's then transported down to Bardstown, then diluted to 125 proof before entering the cask, the maximum-permitted strength for filling barrels. Speaking of barrels, Heaven Hill have enough warehouse space to hold over 1.3 million barrels of bourbon. That little cache accounts for one quarter of all the bourbon in the US.

BERNHEIM ORIGINAL STRAIGHT WHEAT (45% ABV)

Like a fruit loaf that's been baked over oak chips, it has a nice aromatic balance of spice, oak and sweet vanilla aromas. The taste is very sweet, with a fruity brioche thing going on that is backed up by candy and menthol. The finish is hot butter on toast.

EVAN WILLIAMS SINGLE BARREL 2010 (43.3% ABV)

Lots of barrel aromas on this one, with oak, vanilla and cinnamon dominating on the nose. The taste is soft and supple, allowing some dried fruits and shisha incense to drift through. Then comes the spicy finish, where a dry tobacco note lingers around for a while.

ELIJAH CRAIG SMALL BATCH (47% ABV)

Wafts of toasted hazelnut and with caramel sauce, held together by a shortcrust pastry base. Vanilla barrel char enters the fray on further sniffs. The taste is dry and nutty, with notes of coconut and dark fruits coming through. Dry and peppery on the finish.

PIKESVILLE STRAIGHT RYE (55% ABV)

Charred oak, burnt cocoa, and crispy creme brûlée rule the aroma of this whiskey, but there's a sense of something fruity or herbal there too, like caraway or anise. The taste also presented some aromatic spice: clove, mace, and fennel seed, but it's the heat that draws the attention. Nutty and bright to finish.

MELLOW CORN (50% ABV)

Young and sweet like freshly popped corn, the nose here is all about vanilla, butter and just a hint of barbecue plantain. The taste brings about more sweet, young oak flavors with a green banana note and sweetcorn juice finish.

RITTENHOUSE BOTTLED IN BOND (50% ABV)

Model airplane solvent, chocolate-coated raisins and hot varnish. Taste is initially brown bread and black pepper, dissolving into vanilla and oak tannin. The finish is dry but shades of nut butter and caramel trickle through.

ROAD TRIP PLAYLIST

"Take Me Home, Country Roads" – John Denver

"Son of a Preacher Man" – Dusty Springfield

WHISKEY SOUR

50 ml/1⅔ oz Pikesville Straight Rye
25 ml/1 oz lemon juice
12.5 ml/½ oz gomme
½ an egg white

Shake all the ingredients with ice, then strain into another vessel. Discard the ice, pour the liquid back into the shaker, then "dry" shake the cocktail. This second shaking helps to aerate the drink. Take a chilled sherry glass or small wine glass and pour the cocktail in. No ice. Garnish with a strip of lemon and a cherry.

Any spirit can "soured" by shaking it with ice and 50% lemon or lime juice and 25% sugar syrup. But American whiskey—and particularly bourbon—performs especially well with the sour treatment.

The drink's origins date back to the world's first complete cocktail book, Jerry Thomas' *How to Mix Drinks*, published in 1862. Sours really have their origins in punches—of which they are a single-serve variant—and as we know already know, they date back at least another 150 years.

For me, the texture of a sour is an important element of the cocktail, and also one way in which it should differ from a punch. Sours are traditionally shaken with egg white, which creates a mousse-like texture to the drink and leaves a nice, foamy head on top. More recently, bartenders have sought out alternative protein sources, such as aquafaba (the water from a can of chickpeas—though any bean water will do), or isolated protein powder. If you wish, you can leave out the protein altogether.

JIM BEAM

FOLLOW THE WILDERNESS ROAD

"By Whiskey grog he lost his breath,
Who would not die so sweet a death."

PART OF THE EPITAPH OF TOM JOHNSON, KENTUCKIAN POET

Leaving Louisville, we head south for 30 minutes, to Clermont in Bullitt County.

Where Baptists like Elijah Craig came to Kentucky to escape persecution, others were attracted by commercial opportunity and adventure. The frontier was a dangerous place, but politicians like Thomas Jefferson realized the necessity of enticing normal people there in order to build a rural economy. The 1776 Corn Patch and Cabin Rights Act gifted settlers with 400 acres of wasteland in Kentucky County providing they built a cabin and planted a patch of corn before January 1, 1778. As you might expect, this piece of legislation generated a substantial influx of migrant farmers. The term "wasteland" might give the impression that these plots of land were barren dust bowls where wild dogs fought for scraps, but Kentucky was largely a beautiful savannah of mixed grasslands interspersed with enormous oak trees. No wonder the Iroquois called it the "great meadow."

In fact, the naming of Kentucky was and still remains a point of contention. The Cherokee translation is "dark and bloody ground" while the Wyandotte tribe interpret it as "the land of tomorrow," and the Shawnee translation is "head of the river."

Access to Kentucky's verdant panorama wasn't as easy as just boarding a train, or even hopping aboard a wagon, though. There was the inconvenience of the Appalachian Mountains to deal with, which run along the western boundaries of the states of Virginia and North Carolina, parallel to the eastern seaboard, forming a natural border with Kentucky and Tennessee. Crossing a mountain range by foot or on horseback is one thing, but creating a passage that can accommodate a steady stream of wagons is something else entirely. Expeditions led by Joseph Martin and Daniel Boone, in 1769 and 1775 respectively, helped to remedy this by widening the existing trail at the Cumberland Gap, allowing passage to the western frontiers.

One of the settlers that crossed the Gap in 1788 was a second-generation American of German descent, called Jacob Boehm. Like many others at that time, Jacob was searching for a nice spot to hunker down and build a life, so he took the brave decision to head west, crossing the Shenandoah Valley of Virginia, then through the Cumberland Gap on the Wilderness Road.

The Wilderness Road was just as daunting as it sounds. Robbers and criminals were common, as were wolves and panthers, but the greatest threats came from the Shawnee tribe who, unlike the Cherokees, had not ceded their right to the Kentucky land.

The road forked after the Gap. The southern section went in the direction of Nashville, Tennessee via the Cumberland River. The northern fork split into two parts: the eastern spur towards the Bluegrass region of Kentucky, to Boonesborough near

Lexington. The western spur ran all the way to the Falls of the Ohio near Louisville.

The Boehms took the western spur.

Although the Road was only 250 miles long, the trip took 5 months to complete. Finally, in 1789, Jacob and Mary Boehm, along with their two young children, settled in Hardin Creek, located in modern day Washington County.

The Beams were representative of the broader mood among Americans at that time. Independence, the birth of democracy, and the promise of liberty stirred up a powerful sense of individualism and rugged conviction there in the late 18th century. They had crossed an ocean to get there (or were the descendants of someone who had) so why worry about walking into the wilderness for half a year? Doggedness trickled down into their basic standard of living, which tended to involve a limited diet (mostly corn and corn- fed animals) and permanent inebriation. When Frances Trollope visited the US, researching her 1832 book *Domestic Manners of the Americans*, she noted that, "the luxury of whiskey is more appreciated by the men than all the green delicacies from the garden."

At that time, most Americans on the western fringes consumed alcohol consistently through the day. They made what liquor they could and they greedily drank what liquor they made. Whiskey cost next to nothing to produce, was made in abundance, and had secured its place as a patriotic drink of the working class. It was also emblematic of the struggle for liberty and independence. Drunkenness and pride in being drunk is a powerful combination of ingredients in any cocktail.

It's estimated that a quarter of a million migrants passed through the Gap before 1810 (Today, the Cumberland Gap is a national park, which sits on the tristate line between Virginia, Kentucky, and Tennessee, and sees approximately 18,000 cars daily.) And while the early 1800s witnessed the rise of larger distilleries in the urban centers of Boston, New York, and Baltimore, by 1810, the Ohio River valley was producing over half of all the whiskey in the nation.

The population of Kentucky tripled between 1810 and 1830 and the number of American distilleries increased too, rising from an estimated 14,000 in 1810 to 20,000 in 1830. That's around seven times the number of distilleries in America today, compressed into approximately one-third of the land.

Like his contemporaries, Jacob Boehm quickly set about establishing a farm, rearing livestock and growing corn, which inevitably lead to distilling. Not one to renounce his patriotism, he also changed his name, from Boehm to the more American-sounding "Beam."

Whiskey production became quite lucrative for the Beam family, and by 1810 they owned no less than 800 acres of prime Kentucky farmland. Jake's son David Beam took over the farm in 1820, then his son David M. Beam in 1853. David M. had more ambition than most and in the 1860s he built a new distillery in Nelson county to take advantage of the railroad. He also incorporated a continuous still into the design. Also around that time, David M. brought his 16-year-old son James into the family business, but most people know him better as Jim. Jim took over running the distillery in 1892 and brought his own son Jeremiah "Jere" Beam into the business. Jim's only other offspring, Margaret, married a man by the name of Frederick "Booker" Noe, and it's his grandson Fred Noe who stands as the seventh-generation Beam distiller today.

Back in 1920, Prohibition shut the Beam operation down and Jim Beam turned his hand to fruit farming. However, when it was repealed in 1933 he went back to Kentucky and purchased the old Murphy Barber Distillery at Clermont, and for the first time began producing bourbon under the Jim Beam brand name. The business wasn't sustainable though — there were simply too many family members needing a cut of the profits — so factions began splintering off and new distilleries were established. Jim's nephew, Earl, went on to set up Heaven Hill in 1934, which has had a Beam running its stills ever since. The first distiller at Maker's Mark was a Beam, too, and there are countless Beam descendants today continuing the family tradition.

The present-day Beam distillery is a monster. It is so big that a standard tour involves a walk around a fully-functioning micro-distillery because the real distillery is simply too large for the average human brain to process. This distillery-in-miniature is overseen by Jim Beam's great grandson and namesake, Jim Beam Noe.

The Clermont distillery pumps out about a gallon of whiskey every single second, which is enough to fill almost half a million barrels a year. Despite the size, there is some self-sufficiency here, and a good proportion of the product is bottled on site. The rest is bottled at another plant in Frankfort, which also handles distribution.

Amazingly, considering the number of products that the distillery outputs, there are just three main mash bills used at Jim Beam: the standard bourbon mash (75% corn, 13% rye, 12% malted barley); a high-rye bourbon mash (63% corn, 27% rye, 10% malted barley); and a rye mash bill, which is undisclosed, but likely to be a shade over 50% rye, 10% malted barley, and corn taking up the balance.

The rye mash bill is used to make Jim Beam Rye, Knob Creek Rye, Old Overholt, Little Book and (r?)I only. The high rye bourbon mash is used for Old Grand-Dad and Basil Hayden's only. Everything else (Jim Beam White Label, Booker's, Baker's, Knob Creek, Old Crow, Old Taylor and a few more) is made using the standard bourbon recipe.

The high-rye bourbon brands have some interesting origin stories, such as the one involving Meredith Basil Hayden Sr.

Hayden Sr. was another Baptist distiller, who led a group of 25 Catholic families from Maryland into what is now Nelson County, Kentucky (near Bardstown) in 1785. The tale goes that he was known to use a larger amount of rye in his mash just as corn whiskeys were becoming popular. Later, Hayden's grandson Raymond B. Hayden founded a distillery in Nelson County and named his label "Old Grand-Dad" in honor of his grandfather. The image on the Old Grand-Dad bottle is supposed to be Basil Hayden Sr.

When Beam Industries introduced their "small batch" collection (comprising Baker's, Booker's, Knob Creek, and Basil Hayden's) in 1992, the company differentiated Basil Hayden's from the rest, noting that it used a mash similar to that originally utilized by Hayden in 1792.

Of the other "small batch" whiskeys (by the way, the term "small batch" has no legal definition) there is Knob Creek; Baker's (a high-strength 7-year-old); and the most revered of them all: Booker's.

It was Booker Noe who was responsible for launching Jim Beam's "small batch" collection and, indeed coining the term "small batch." The releases were in response to the launch of Blanton's (which is made at Buffalo Trace), the first "single barrel" expression of bourbon. In 1987, Jim Beam's master distiller, Booker Noe, introduced Booker's uncut, unfiltered cask strength bourbon to friends and family, and then went on to release it to the public in 1992. The idea of "small batch" was Booker Noe's creation, and delineated by specially selected casks of older whiskeys.

Baker's is one of the younger "small batch" releases at seven years old. It is named after Baker Beam, the grand-nephew of Jim Beam and cousin to Booker Noe, a former distiller at Jim Beam. Baker's supposedly uses a different yeast strain than the others.

So, to production: after cereals are ground on a hammer mill they're mashed, then sent to one of 19 45,000-gallon fermenters. Using an original yeast strain from 1935, the ferment lasts four to five days. The beer is pumped into a column still, which strips the alcohol up to a strength of 120 proof, and is then increased to 135 proof after passing through the doubler. This is a relatively low distillation strength for a bourbon whiskey (well below the legal maximum of 160 proof), which means more of the flavor of the raw materials are preserved and less water needs adding prior to the spirit going in the cask.

All whiskeys go into new charred American oak casks. The total number of barrels currently in Jim Beam warehouses has now exceeded the 2 million mark (approximately one-third of all the whiskey in the state of Kentucky). All these casks are secured in warehouses up to nine stories high (or 27 barrels in height) which are among the biggest in the industry.

Jim Beam White Label is aged for three to five years and Jim Beam Rye for a similar period. Jim Beam Black is a slightly older version of White, bottled at 43% ABV. Jim Beam Double Oak is first aged in newly charred American White Oak barrels, then, just to get the point across, it's poured into another freshly charred white oak barrel to mature for a second time. Jim Beam also bottles a bonded expression as well as single barrel examples.

It's worth dedicating the final word to the second Jim Beam distillery, known as the Booker Noe Plant. Located in Boston, Kentucky, about 10 miles south along I-65 from the Clermont distillery, this distillery was once called the Churchill Distillery and dates back to the early 20th century. Jim Beam purchased the 450-acre site in 1960. The site is not publicly accessible and it's not common knowledge exactly which products get made here, but the thought is that it's mostly Jim Beam White Label. And it needs to be, because it is by far the No. 1 selling bourbon brand in the world.

There are many distilleries in this book that make multiple brands out of one distillery (Jim Beam make around 70 expressions in total!), but Jim Beam is the only bourbon brand that make the same expression out of more than one distillery.

WHITE LABEL (40% ABV)

Sweet and boozy on the nose and reminiscent of sugared donut with crème anglaise filling. Light on the palate, it lacks heat and grip and feels slightly greasy. The finish is sweet and slippery.

RYE (45% ABV)

Rye delivers a little more cereal character in this expression. There's shortbread and bran flakes, then more of that new-cask custard oozing through. The palate is less sweet tasting, but lacks proper depth. It's dry and slightly peppery on the finish.

DOUBLE OAK (43% ABV)

Lots of barrel aromas here: burnt banana fudge, Honey Smacks, and plenty of vanilla caramel. The taste is of buttered corn on the cob and sesame oil.

This whiskey delivers a little spice, but fails to overcome the sweetness of the two casks.

KNOB CREEK CASK SAMPLE

Art room aroma involving lead pencil, poster paints, and wet clay. Then comes the wood, rippling with intensity. There's a touch of cherry here too, with vanilla fondant. Concentrated spice holds the center of the tongue, meaning this whiskey is initially dry, but lingers into sugary coffee and nut shells.

BOOKER'S (63% ABV)

Hard to ignore the alcohol on this one. Once quieted, there's sponge cake, warm golden raisins, caramel, and banana. Syrupy and intense on the palate, with controlled and well- dispersed heat; macadamia brownie, violet, coconut, and sweet tomato linger.

JIM BEAM SIGNATURE 12 YEARS (43% ABV)

Vibrant on the nose: pistachio ice cream and big vanilla, bursting with fresh cherries and blueberries, drifting into perfumed nutty musk. Surprisingly light and clean on the palate, like hot stones, with anise and a gentle mint coolness. The finish is old dry wood and stewed damsons.

JIM BEAM SIGNATURE SIX GRAINS (44.5% ABV)

Sour cream and buttermilk on the nose, then there's a distinct musty plastic note that reminds me of an old action figure I had as a child. It's hot on the palate, with spiced molasses cake, brown sauce, chewy apricot, and dates.

ROAD TRIP PLAYLIST

"Thunder Road" – Bruce Springsteen

"Running Down a Dream" – Tom Petty

"Green Onions" – Booker T. & the M.G.'s

WHISKEY DAISY

50 ml/1⅔ oz Basil Hayden's
20 ml/⅔ oz lemon juice
10 ml/2 teaspoons water
10 ml/2 teaspoons sugar syrup
5 ml/1 teaspoon yellow Chartreuse

Shake all of the ingredients with cubed ice then strain into a chilled cocktail glass.
Garnish with some raspberries on a cocktail stick.

The Daisy was once a well-known family of cocktails that rivaled "sours" and "fizzes" for cocktail list inches. One of the first examples was published in the 1876 second edition of Jerry Thomas's *The Bartender's Guide or How To Mix Drinks: The Bon-Vivant's Companion.*

The drink was made from a base of brandy and rum, sweetened with Curaçao and soured with lemon juice. Modifying spirits with citrus and fancy imported liqueurs was a very popular strategy in the mid-to-late 19th century, as it gave an exotic feel to the American cocktail. The Daisy was based loosely on a much earlier drink called a Brandy Crusta, and became the precursor to the family of drinks that are now sometimes referred to as New Orleans Sours, which include the Margarita and Cosmopolitan.

Harry Johnson's 1888 *The Bartender's Manual* published the earliest recipe for a Whiskey Daisy that I could find. It calls for:

½ table-spoonful sugar;
2 or 3 dashes lemon juice;
1 dash of lime juice;
1 squirt of Syphon Selters, dissolve with the lemon and lime juice;
¾ of the glass filled with fine shaved ice
1 wine glass of good Whiskey
½ pony glass Chartreuse (yellow)

It's also one of a select few drinks in the book that is accompanied by an illustration. The picture shows a crystal glass that you might serve sherry or wine in, filled with crushed ice and accompanied by a spoon (which was presumably used to stop the ice from falling into your face) and fresh raspberries.

Harry comments, "This drink is very palatable and will taste good to most anybody." And who can argue with that?

FOLLOWING PAGES The gently rolling fields of Kentucky at sunrise in the fall paints a pretty picture.

WOODFORD RESERVE

THE EAGLE-EYED CROW

*"I have never in my life seen a Kentuckian who didn't have
a gun, a pack of cards, and a jug of whiskey."*

ANDREW JACKSON (1767–1845), 7TH PRESIDENT OF THE UNITED STATES

Arriving at the Woodford Reserve distillery, near Frankfort, it's as if you've driven into Scotland. The landscape of Woodford county is that little bit more undulating than the rest of Kentucky. Many of the Woodford Reserve buildings are made from limestone, in the style of traditional Scottish farmhouses. And this 500-acre site feels like an oasis of serenity compared to the more industrial feel of other Kentucky distilleries. Inside, the five, striking red, cypress-wood fermenters are reminiscent of the Scotch whisky "washback." There are even three copper pot stills that would look just as comfortable in the still house of Auchentoshan or Glenmorangie.

This distillery was only remodeled 25 years ago, but its arguably the oldest operational distillery in Kentucky (but like most distilleries in America, it hasn't remained in continuous operation). There's some loose historical precedent for all the Scottishness too, and we'll get to that shortly.

Elijah Pepper was born in Fauquier County, Virginia, in 1775. He married Sarah O'Bannon in 1794 and moved to Kentucky some time later. In 1812, he built a cabin on the modern-day site of Woodford Reserve distillery. The specifics of the location, not far from the town of Versailles, were no doubt influenced by the Glen's Creek river, and the spring that emerges from the riverbank, now known as the Pepper Spring.

Their cabin was quickly followed by a water-powered gristmill and whiskey distillery. This was a strange time to start making whiskey, though. James Madison reinstated a whiskey tax between 1814 and 1817 to help pay for the War of 1812, in which, among other things, the British burned down the White House. Perhaps Pepper had deeper pockets that most? Well, if he didn't, then he certainly did by the time he died in 1831. Census records from the previous year show Elijah owned 350 acres of land, 25 slaves, 22 horses, and over 100 pigs and sheep. An inventory taken at the time of his death shows a distillery with six small copper kettle stills, 74 mashing barrels, and 41 barrels of aging whiskey.

Following Elijah's death, his wife, Sarah Pepper, ran the distillery and farm for a period of around seven years. Then she sold the operation to eldest son, Oscar.

Oscar bought out his brothers and sisters too, and gave the distillery its first real name, which was (deservingly so) "the Oscar Pepper Distillery." With no family members left to help, Pepper turned to a master distiller, Scotsman Dr. James Christopher Crow, who began employment there in 1833. Under the watch of Crow and Pepper the distillery grew, and the 1840s saw the construction of many of the limestone buildings that still exist today. Neither Pepper nor Crow invented bourbon whiskey, but between them they probably contributed more than anyone to the process of making whiskey in Kentucky, laying the foundations for the product that we know as bourbon today.

Distilling equipment had improved considerably in the years preceding the Pepper distillery and all the way through Crow's employment there. The first American steam-powered stills appeared in New York in 1810, and in the first 15 years of the 19th century, over 100 patents were filed in connection to the distilling business, amounting to 5% of all US patent grants. Then came the earliest versions of the continuous still, which were conceived in the 1820s and perfected by Irishman Aeneas Coffey in 1831. This industrial innovation massively increased the potential throughput of a distillery while proportionately reducing the required labor.

However, much of the innovation that took place at the Oscar Pepper Distillery wasn't of an obvious nature, but in the meticulous measuring and recording of details. It's James Crow we have to thanks for pieces of sanitary advice, such as "always keep sheep and livestock at least 200 yards from the fermentation vats." Crow also insisted that no more than 2.5 gallons of whiskey should be produced from a bushel of grain, suggesting that yield was the enemy of quality at the Oscar Pepper Distillery

As Chris Morris, Woodford Reserve's master distiller puts it, "Crow didn't invent anything… but he perfected everything."

Crow was probably the first American distiller to keep detailed records of temperatures during fermentation and distillation. He also used a hydrometer to check the spirit's strength as it came off the still, and even recorded the pH of the water and the fermentation to ensure his yeast was happy.

It's difficult to have a conversation in Kentucky without somebody bringing up the state's famous limestone water. The limestone karst structure, which is an enormous underground drainage system, forms a horseshoe shape in the west of the state; a large pocket also centers around the Frankfort/Lexington Bluegrass region in the north. It comprises sinkholes and caves, which serve as an infusion system for the water. The Shawnees believed that these underground caves were entrances to the underworld. On the surface, much of the state's beautiful scenery, particularly the horse farms of the

Inner Bluegrass, is the result of development of karst landscape. Underground, the water that filters through this limestone structure deposits calcium and magnesium carbonates as well as iron.

There's another term you can use to describe mineral-rich water: "hard water". If you've ever lived in a hard water area, you'll be familiar with the limescale deposits that accumulate on faucets and in boilers. Hard water might not be the nicest water to drink, but minerals like calcium and magnesium are popular among yeast cells.

Applying a scientific method to each stage of production also allowed James Crow to perfect the "sour mash" process too, which is now practiced by most of the distilleries in Kentucky. Whereas "sweet mash" is made by cooking cereals with water and fermenting them into a beer, in a sour mash, a proportion of the water is actually leftover waste water from distillation (known variously as "stillage", "pot ale", or "backset"). This is an effective strategy for a few reasons: first, it means you need less water since you're constantly recycling your waste water; second, the acidic stillage lowers the pH of the naturally alkaline limestone water, serving as a better breeding ground for yeast while limiting the potential of bacterial infection; and finally, recycling old stillage provides a greater consistency of flavor between batches.

One of the earliest recordings of a sour mash whiskey comes from 1818, in Casey County, Kentucky. The recipe is attributed to Catherine Carpenter, a cattle farmer on the Kentucky frontier. She was twice widowed and had nine children to raise, turning to whiskey making to help support her large family. It wasn't uncommon for women to make whiskey and during the war against the British in 1812, women were issued licenses to distill in Kentucky. Things went well for the Carpenters, and by the time Catherine died in 1848, she was a well-to-do lady who owned around 1,000 acres and 20 slaves. Catherine's "Receipt for Distilling by a Sour Mash" goes as follows:

"Put into the mash tub six busheles [sic] of very hot slop then put in one bushel of corn meal ground pretty course. Stir well then sprinkle a little meal over the mash let it stand 5 days, that is 3 full days betwist the day you mash and the day you cool off—on the fifth day put in 3 gallons of warm water then one gallon of rye meal and one gallon of malt work it well into the mash and stir 3 quarters of an hour then fill the tub half full of lukewarm water. Stir it well and with a fine sieve or otherwise break all of the lumps fine then let stand for three hours then fill up the tub with lukewarm water."

Assuming she used the industry standard barrel of that time (48 gallons) as a mash tub, she would have used about 15% backset to sour her mash. Crow was thought to favor up to 50% of his mash as backset. Recipes from contemporary distilleries vary enormously, from 10% up to 50%, which is more than enough to affect the final flavor of the distillate.

In the 1850s, the Oscar Pepper Distillery was making around 4,000 gallons of whiskey a year. As a pat on the back for Dr. Crow's contribution, Oscar Pepper named a whiskey after him "Old Crow" and gifted him a house on the property. James Crow died in 1856, but the Old Crow brand was just getting started. It would go on to be one of the biggest and most hotly contested labels in all of bourbon, regularly invoking James Crow's heritage, including ads that showed him delivering whiskey to the statesman Henry Clay.

When Oscar died in 1865 (aged 56), his estate was split between his seven children who were, amazingly, all between the ages of seven and fifteen! As the guardian of both the children and their inheritance, Oscar's wife, Nannie, had her hands full. She leased the distillery to Gaines, Berry & Co. of Frankfort. This deal increased the availability of "Old Crow" (they renamed the distillery to reflect this) and increased the fortune of The Frankfort company. Gaines, Berry & Co. invested the proceeds into the nearby "Hermitage" distillery, which was run by one of the firm's partners, the legendary Colonel E. H. Taylor. We'll explore Taylor's story in more detail later, but his considerable influence transmitted into the Pepper story too, and we'll touch upon that part right now.

Notwithstanding some considerable fuss, James Pepper (the eldest of the Pepper children) gained control of the distillery from his mother in 1872. He was possibly egged on by Col. Taylor, who parted company from Gaines, Berry & Co. at the same time and worked with James to update the distillery. Unfortunately for Pepper and Taylor, Gaines, Berry & Co. retained the "Old Crow" brand name (first trademarked in 1882) even though it was Pepper's distillery that was still producing it.

The 1870s saw the start of the Long Depression causing Pepper and Taylor to both suffer large financial losses. Pepper filed for bankruptcy in 1877, and The Old Oscar Pepper Distillery was bought by Leopold Labrot and James Graham in 1878. Graham became the plant manager and Labrot was responsible for wholesale and retail sales. They produced Old Oscar Pepper Whiskey as their only brand.

James Pepper went on to open another distillery (which we'll discuss later) but had second thoughts about ceding the Old Oscar Pepper name to Labrot & Graham, unsuccessfully suing them for infringing on his trademark. Despite the deaths of Graham (1900) and Labrot (1911) the distillery continued to grow and was remodeled. Many structures still in place today, like the three chimneys marked "L", "&", and "G", were built during this pre-Prohibition period but the advent of Prohibition in Kentucky led to the distillery's closure in 1918.

The Labrot & Graham Company resurfaced after Prohibition, however, and the distillery reopened in 1935. Then the facility was sold to Brown-Forman (whose story will be told later) in 1940 for $75,000, but was mothballed and remained idle for over 50 years. In the 1990s, Brown-Forman refurbished the site and brought the distillery back to operation, installed three pot stills, and introduced the Woodford Reserve brand in 1996.

All of the whiskey made at Woodford Reserve is made using Pepper Spring water. The Woodford engineers have gone to great lengths to ensure it does not surface before reaching the distillery, which is a trick that neatly avoids what would normally be a legally required purification process. Instead, it is simply particle-filtered, then sent to the mash cooker. "We attribute the floral aromatics of Woodford to the Pepper Spring water," says Chris. I'd say the triple-distillation and high-rye mash-bill (70% corn, 18% rye, 12% malted barley) have a lot to answer for too.

And speaking of mashing, Woodford grind their cereals finer than any other distillery in Kentucky, into an almost flour-like consistency. Why? Well, that would be a requirement of their triple pot-distillation process. American whiskeys are almost always fermented and distilled without filtration; this means the liquid entering the still is more like a thin oatmeal than a milky tea. Column stills handle the beer solids quite well by ejecting them out of their base once all the alcohol has been extracted. But during a pot-still cook, the solids are free to burn onto the sides of the still and cause all sorts of havoc. To mitigate this problem, Woodford mill their cereals finer and also perform a caustic wash every day (after every fourth run) on the beer still, to remove all the cooked-on crud. The beer-still has a specially designed conical bottom that helps remove the spent beer solids as well.

Both the "beer still" and "high wines" still conduct a single run before the 55% liquid is sent to the spirit still and concentrated up to 79%—just under the legal limit. The white whiskey is cut back down to 55% for maturation. Chris Morris argues that the spirit requires less added water after maturation because of its low fill-strength, "it means the liquid in a bottle of Woodford Reserve has had 14% more contact with wood than had it been filled at 63%."

Either way, nearly half the volume of the cask is lost during the seven-year average aging period. Most of the barrels here are, of course, new American oak, but Woodford also experiment with cask finishes. Chris was responsible for creating the world's first bourbon finished in Chardonnay and Pinot Noir barrels. He's also credited with developing the world's first maple barrel; a difficult feat, but made easier when you work for a company that owns its own cooperage.

Truth be told, much of the meticulous production process here is negated by the fact that Woodford Reserve is a blend of whiskeys from the Woodford Reserve Distillery near Frankfort and Old Forester distillery (which we will visit later) in Shively, on the outskirts of Louisville. This is not something that's publicly talked about all that much, but it is something that most of the whiskey industry has become wise to over the years. Woodford is beautifully quaint and very popular among tourists. But beauty is not usually conducive to production and there's simply no way that three modest pot stills could produce all the whiskey going in to Woodford Reserve bottles.

WOODFORD WHITE DOG

Heavy and round with golden raisins, plums, cherry stone and something not dissimilar to a mincemeat pie. There's a residual, fusel oil note there too and a "green" zing of youthfulness. On the palate it's hot and more than a little sulphury, which is no doubt the backbone of what is to come during maturation.

WOODFORD RESERVE CASK SAMPLE FILLED 07/11, DUMPED 03/14

Initially on the nose there's buttered brown toast and pecan nuts. This leads in to some cereal aromas, finally picking up lychee, rose hip, and other red fruits. On the palate there is less in the way of complexity, with a streak of pepper and some vague glue-like notes. The finish is surprisingly long, slip-sliding away into a pit of wood toast and resin.

WOODFORD RESERVE DISTILLER'S SELECT (43.2% ABV)

Surprisingly citrus at first, with toffee coming through, like lemon bon bons. It smells syrupy, sweet, and stewed. The taste is refined and defined, with more lemon and a herbal note that gets washed away by oak spice and some drowning burbles of rye fruit. The finish is citrus and wood.

WOODFORD CLASSIC MALT EX-BOURBON CASK (45.2% ABV)

The nose is bakewell tart, monkey nuts, and dusty, with a touch of toasted almonds. There's cereal on the palate, with a smear of dry cherry in the finish with even a hint of "craisins". It's lacking a little in the finish and is perhaps guilty of being a bit too young.

WOODFORD STRAIGHT MALT NEW CASK (45.2% ABV)

The first impression is a slap in the face of coconut ice cream, with a big vanilla hit… it's all about the cask. There's plenty of residual sugar too. The traces of malt have been crushed by the big wooden container.

WOODFORD RYE NEW CASK (46.2% ABV)

Treacle tart and warm sand greet the nose on this fruity-smelling whiskey. This follows in to banana sugar, dry cacao, nutmeg, and rotten wood, with a slight herbaceous note. On the palate it's full and juicy, with a hint of mint that's trounced by fruit-shaped bits of wood. The finish plays out to fruity tobacco.

ROAD TRIP PLAYLIST

"Moonshiner" — Bob Dylan

"Jockey Full of Bourbon" — Tom Waits

"Milk and Honey" — John Lennon

CLARIFIED MILK PUNCH

250 ml/8½ oz Woodford Reserve
125 ml/4¼ oz strained lemon juice
70 ml/2⅓ oz honey
400 ml/13½ oz unsweetened black tea
180 ml/6 oz whole milk

Combine the first four ingredients into a wide-mouthed Mason jar or similar plastic container. Add the milk to a saucepan and bring to a boil, then mix the hot milk with the rest of the punch ingredients in the jar. It will look like a total mess but don't worry. Put the jar in the fridge overnight, then filter the liquid through a cheesecloth. Repeat the chilling and filtering for better clarification. Store your milk punch (the recipe will make approximately 1 liter/quart) in the fridge for up to six months.

Whiskey, tea, fresh citrus juice, and warm milk—it sounds like a wacky afternoon tea. But this is one of those drinks that sounds disgusting on paper, and turns out to be delicious in the glass. It's all down to the curdling of the milk (I'm not helping matters here, am I?), which removes all the dairy solids and leaves only a clear, vaguely sweet water. That, in concert with whiskey, tea, and citrus turns out to be something delicious.

The drink is British in origin, dating back to the 1600s and was probably made using brandy. But one of the great things about milk punches is their versatility—you can use virtually any spirit, any tea, mix up the fruit juice, and add spices if you so wish.

Because of its shelf stability, it was popular as a bottled drink. Queen Victoria issued a royal warrant in 1838 to the company of Nathaniel Whisson as "purveyors of milk punch to Her Majesty."

FOUR ROSES

BETWEEN TWO ORIGINATORS

*"I would enjoy having some Kentucky bourbon
with Mitch McConnell."*

BARACK OBAMA (1961–), 44TH PRESIDENT OF THE UNITED STATES

Four Roses distillery is only a 30-minute drive from Woodford Reserve. We drive through Versailles and head west on the Bluegrass Parkway, towards Bardstown. The distillery sits on the 150-mile long Salt River, which feeds into the Ohio River just south of Louisville. The river got its name from the animal salt lick (where animals go to lick essential minerals) just south of Shepherdsville, near where the river joins the Ohio. Located in Bullitt County, "Bullitt Lick" became the first commercial salt producer in the state of Kentucky. Salt played a critical role in frontier life for curing meats, and many great names in whiskey, like Booker Noe (see page 129), were legendary ham curers.

The story of how Four Roses Distillery got its name is a little more complicated.

Let's start with the version of the story that Four Roses likes to promote. This is a romantic story centering around the company's founder, Paul Jones, Jr. and the love of his life. Her name has been lost somewhere along the way, which to my mind puts the whole story into question, but bourbon could do with a little romance so let's go along with it.

Jones was born in 1840 in Lynchburg, Virginia to a very affluent family. In 1860, Atlanta was holding its annual grand ball, where the young, eligible men like Paul Jones, Jr. were expected to (a) be seen and (b) woo a nice Southern belle. As was the custom at the time, he sent a suitable Southern belle (who he'd not yet met) a marriage proposal in writing by personal carrier. In upper society they used a Victorian tradition called "flower language" to communicate. In the letter, he wrote, "when you show up at the ball, if you are wearing a corsage that has three roses I will consider it a rejection of my proposal. But if you wear a corsage with four roses it will clearly state your intention to accept my proposal of marriage." After an agonizing wait, she showed up wearing four red roses.

If this story is true, something must have gone wrong not long after because Jones remained a bachelor for his entire life.

Jones fought as a Confederate lieutenant in the Civil War along with his brother, and was called in by General Robert E. Lee to defend the city of Atlanta in 1864. His brother died in the Battle of Atlanta and when the south finally surrendered in 1865, Jones (according to one account) "returned home to find his home in ruins and the family destitute. His family's wealth, which before the war had been considerable, had been invested in Confederate bonds and was gone."

Jones and his father relocated to Virginia where Jones worked as a salesman under distiller Rufus Rose (who turns out to be a more plausible source for the name of the Four Roses distillery). Rose was from Connecticut and a pharmacist by trade. He relocated to Atlanta around 1867, when he started a whiskey-producing enterprise he called "House of Rose." He built a large distillery on Stillhouse Road in the nearby town of Vinings and established a retail store to sell his whiskey in downtown Atlanta. Among the products Rufus Rose made and sold was Rose's Atlanta Spirit Rye, Rose's Mountain Dew, Blue Ridge Whiskey, New Sweet Mash, Old Reserve Stock ,and Special Old Corn.

Things went well for Rose, but they were going well for Jones too. By the 1880s Paul Jones, Jr. had established a sizable liquor-distribution business thanks in part to the volume of liquor that Rufus Rose's distillery was making. Georgia had other plans though, as it began experimenting with temperance and, in 1884, the state legislature passed a temporary law banning the sale of alcohol. Paul Jones saw the writing on the wall and relocated back to Louisville.

Rufus Rose stuck it out for a while but when Georgia went dry in 1907, R.M. Rose Distillers were forced to relocate to Chattanooga, Tennessee. Rufus remained in Atlanta while his son, Randolph followed the operation to Tennessee. Rufus was still involved in the business, however, and in about 1906, according to accounts, he came up with the special blend that he called "Four Roses."

Meanwhile, Paul Jones Jr. had been busy, buying himself a distillery. In the mid-1800s, John Graves Mattingly of Marion County built several distilleries. One of them was built in 1845 in Louisville and named J.G. Mattingly & Sons. The other was called the Marion County Distillery, which was built in 1866. We'll explore it later.

The J.G. Mattingly Distillery, located between High and Rudd Avenues and 39th and 40th Streets, had fallen upon hard times. In September 1889, the distillery ceased operation and went up for auction. Jones bought it for $125,000 – equivalent to about $3 million today. The deal included a mill and fermenting house, a boiler house, a distillery spirits building, and a cattle barn. The property also held five warehouses, all of them brick with slate or metal roofs. The distillery went on to become one of the most productive operations of the late 19th century, producing whiskey under the brand names Paul Jones,

Jones Four Star, Old Cabinet, Old Cabinet Rye, Small Grain, West End, and Swastika (in the pre-Nazi days the swastika had very different connotations and the motif is found in some traditional Native American art).

Paul Jones Jr. died in 1905, which was around the same time that a fire destroyed the J.G. Mattingly still house. With no children, the business went to his nephew, Lavelle Jones. Meanwhile, R.M. Rose wasn't fairing much better, as Tennessee enacted statewide Prohibition in 1910. Possibly in frustration, Randolph Rose sold the Four Roses brand name to the Jones family.

Two years into Prohibition, the Paul Jones Company purchased the Frankfort Distilling Company and its Old Prentice Distillery. This distillery had been built in 1910, on the banks of the Salt River, featuring Spanish mission-style architecture rarely seen in Kentucky. It's now listed on the National Registry of Historic Places.

Although like all other distilleries it was rendered non-operational during Prohibition, it was one of six distilleries granted permits to sell their existing stocks of bourbon for medicinal purposes. The Frankfort distillery is one of the only examples of a distillery that stayed afloat during Prohibition, accounting for roughly one in every five bottles of whiskey sold in the US at the time.

That said, by 1928, stocks of pre-Prohibition whiskey had dwindled and the company contracted the Louisville-based A. Ph. Stitzel distillery to supply them with spirits. When Prohibition was repealed in 1933, Frankfort Distilleries Inc. took over the old Stitzel plant and built another distillery in Shively.

Lavelle Jones died in 1941, and in 1943, the Frankfort Distilling Company sold all of its liquor interests to Seagram's. By that point, Four Roses had become the biggest bourbon brand in America.

So it was a little surprising when Seagram's took the decision, two years later, to focus on export markets, like Japan and Europe, and bottle a re-hashed, blended version of Four Roses for US stores. Seagram's was a Canadian company, so blends and blending came naturally to them, but by all accounts the liquid was pretty bad, a combination of aged and up to 66% un-aged spirits from Seagram's Lawrenceburg, Indiana (now MGP) and Maryland distilleries. It took a few years, but consumer faith plummeted in the US, as Seagram's attempted to dupe them with identical packaging to the old bourbon, but with the word "bourbon" quietly removed. It would appear that Seagram's intuition was to snow-plow their newly acquired bourbon out of the marketplace to make way for their '7 Crown' and 'VO' Canadian whiskeys – cannibalization, in effect.

In the latter part of the 20th century, production was overseen by Charles L. Beam (a grandnephew of Jim Beam). During Beam's tenure, Four Roses introduced Benchmark Bourbon in 1969 and Eagle Rare in 1975. Charles Beam retired in 1982 and both brands were sold to the Sazerac Company in 1989 and are today made at their Buffalo Trace Distillery.

Four Roses Straight Bourbon continued to be produced for export, but true to the Canadian way, it was blended from five distilleries located in Athertonville, Fairfield, Louisville, and Cynthiana, along with the Four Roses distillery in Lawrenceburg. All five Seagram's bourbon distilleries used the same yeast culture at the time, known simply as "V". Slowly they got mothballed, but each of their unique styles were re-imagined in Lawrenceburg by introducing new yeast strains into the mix.

Jim Rutledge served as Four Roses master distiller for 20 years beginning in 1995, finally handing over the reins to Brent Elliot in 2015. I met Jim a few times during his posting and can recall some of the conversations we had.

Jim didn't draw any direct comparisons between the old whiskeys of the closed distilleries and the whiskey produced at Four Roses today.

"It's the water they used that characterized the product," he said. "Instead we use yeast to create a diverse stock of Bourbon that can be blended to our unique flavor profile."

The distillery uses five proprietary yeast strains each coded by the letters "K", "O", "Q", "F", and the original "V". The "Q" yeast, for example, is known to produce a floral spirit with notes of

magnolia and rose. The "F" yeast, on the other hand, makes a minty, herbal-smelling spirit.

At Four Roses Distillery, the team runs a different yeast strain each week, which helps to prevent cross-contamination of each of the strains. Yeast is pitched into one of the distillery's 27 fermenters at exactly 67°F, and fermentation lasts around 4 days.

In addition to the yeast, Four Roses use two separate mash bills: "B", which has 35% rye, and "E", which features 20% rye. This means that ten unique white whiskeys are produced, each of them different before and after they're dropped into wood. Four Roses Yellow label is a blend of all ten yeast and mash combinations, Small Batch is a blend of only the "S" and "K" yeasts with both mashes, and Single Barrel is always selected from the "B" mash and "V" yeast.

The distillery has just finished a $55-million expansion program that has seen two new buildings added, new fermenters, and a new column and doubler still. This has doubled potential production capacity from 4 million to 8 million proof gallons, or enough to fill more than 130,000 barrels a year.

Four Roses mature and bottle their products in Cox's Creek—around 50 miles from the distillery. These warehouses are unusual for Kentucky, since they cling low to the ground like military bunkers waging a war with gravity. Casks are racked only one-tier high, which explains the enormous footprint of the warehouse and the relative consistency of maturation between any two barrels,

"We only get a five degree temperature fluctuation between the top and the bottom of the rack," says master distiller Brent Elliot, "It's nothing compared to the six-tier houses that other producers use."

I can recall a conversation I once had with Jim Rutledge in the office of the Four Roses distillery. During the course of our meeting, he casually informed me that he had already made the best bourbon any of us are likely to taste. The only problem was it had all been sold already, and even he only has half a bottle left.

The story started back in 1995, just after he had been appointed master distiller. By way of seeking employee approval, he decided to give the staff a couple of weeks off over the festive season. The distillery operation was winding down and for one reason or another a sample of "V" yeast was left in the propagator too long and begun to mutate. A lab technician beckoned Jim over to the microscope and what he saw was the Arnold Schwarzenegger of yeast cultures, which had mutated into virile little hunks. The mash fermented, producing a one-of-a-kind fruity beer, and the resulting white whiskey was the best Jim had ever tasted—in his own words, "Everything the mutated culture touched turned to gold." Unfortunately, by that point, the super-yeast in question had been disposed of and to this day remains extinct.

The white dog was put to cask, and Jim recognized early on that this was a bourbon that would require more time than most to reach its full maturity. But eventually it did: 18 years later—an unusually long time for a bourbon. The mutated "V" culture whiskey was blended with two 13-year-old whiskeys and bottled as the 2013 Limited Edition Small Batch 125th Anniversary. In absurdly small volumes, Four Roses created a special selection bottling of the 18 year-old casks only.

As Jim recounted the story to me, he thoughtfully gazed out of his office window at the custard-yellow mission-style buildings that populate the distillery, then he said "If I'd have kept a sample of that yeast, right now I'd be making the best bourbon anyone has ever tasted, every day."

FOUR ROSES "YELLOW LABEL" (40% ABV)
A continental breakfast of a bourbon; marmalade, honey, fresh citrus and pain au chocolat… all served on a charred oak table. The taste is of hot and sweet oak, leaving a finish of sugar and spice.

FOUR ROSES SMALL BATCH (45% ABV)
There's a good feeling of wood on the nose here, but it quickly subsides, giving way to honeysuckle and jasmine. There's a subtle hint of orange oil too, giving an almost sherried characteristic accompanied by white chocolate sauce. On the palate it's dryer than I

would have expected with flavors of green peppercorn, peach, and burnt milk. The finish is short, drying, and moreish.

FOUR ROSES SINGLE BARREL (50% ABV)
The aroma here is softer, eclipsed somewhat by a good blast of alcohol. There's some saddle leather and warm oak on the nose though, followed up by some spiced dark fruit compote. Heavy in the mouth, with a lot of spice, which trounces all over any fruit notion. Refreshingly non-vanilla-like, but hot, spicy, and heavy with it.

FOUR ROSES SINGLE BARREL 2013 "V" YEAST 18-YEAR-OLD (57.3% ABV)
Silky smooth butterscotch, cotton candy, and buckets of ripe fruit like cherry, plum, and red grapes on the nose. It's impossibly chewy and fat on the tongue, releasing a hot jet of wood resin, dates, prunes, and dried apricot. The finish is long, warm, and peppered with spice and fruit.

ROAD TRIP PLAYLIST

"Walk of Life" – Dire Straits

"Kiss from a Rose" – Seal

"I am the Resurrection" – The Stone Roses

OPPOSITE Four Roses is architecturally very different from all of Kentucky's other distilleries, and the use of multiple yeast strains is also a departure from the norm.

WHISKEY SQUIRT

30 ml/I oz Four Roses "Yellow Label" Bourbon
30 ml/I oz Georgia peach purée
I5 ml/½ oz sugar syrup
soda water

Shake the first three ingredients with cubed ice then strain into a small chilled highball glass.
Top up with soda and drink quickly!

Since Four Roses originates from Georgia (and Georgia has very few distilleries itself), this seems like the ideal opportunity to make a cocktail using Georgia's best loved fruit: the peach.

Georgia's nickname is "The Peach State" on account of its reputation for producing the highest quality fruit. In terms of quantity, though, California is by far the biggest producer of peaches in the US, followed by South Carolina, and then Georgia. The Georgia/South Carolina rivalry in this area is actually a bone of contention. In 2018 the Georgia Department of Agriculture proclaimed that Georgia was the superior producer with sweeter fruits. The South Carolina Department of Agriculture shot back with the classic, "Bless your heart."

Peach and whiskey do have some historical connection. One of the more popular flavors of bitters during the first Golden Age of Cocktails was peach bitters. These, however, were infused with the flavor of the stone (which gives an almond-like flavor) more than the fruit itself.

The "Squirt" family of cocktails is detailed in David A. Embury's *The Fine Art of Mixing Drinks* (1948). He describes them as "a very sweet drink made of spiritous liquor in combination with fresh fruit or fruit syrups and charged with water" and references the Whiskey Squirt as a "typical example" of the style. For each spirit he recommends a specific fruit or combination of fruit, and for whiskey it's peach. My recipe is an adaptation of Embury's original.

BUFFALO TRACE

THE STAGG, THE BUFFALO, AND THE TAYLOR

"He drank it, slowly, not feeling the fire at all holding himself upright by holding to the bureau. The whiskey went down his throat cold as molasses without taste. [...] The whiskey began to burn in him and he began to shake his head slowly from side to side, while thinking became one with the slow, hot coiling and recoiling of his entrails: 'I got to get out of here.'"

FROM *LIGHT IN AUGUST* BY WILLIAM FAULKNER

Northern Kentucky was, in centuries past, known for the buffalo fording the Kentucky River (a tributary of the Ohio) and beating a path inland in search of nutrient-rich salt licks. This migration pattern was the beginning of old "Buffalo Trace".

Driving into Buffalo Trace feels a little bit like you're entering a post-apocalyptic fortress, cobbled together over a century or so in an effort to make it secure and self-sufficient from invading packs of zombies. Parts of the original Old Fire Copper (O.F.C.) distillery, which dates back to 1777, still remain, but newer buildings have been constructed too, made from limestone, wood-fired clay bricks, timber, steel, and marble. Its name has changed over the years too: O.F.C., George T. Stagg, Old Taylor, Schenley, Ancient Age, Leestown, and finally, Buffalo Trace. The whole place is like a patchwork quilt of mismatched walls and roofs, workplace to a dedicated community of over 300 souls, and a distillery operation like no other.

The complex story of this operation begins with a complex man, who would go on to become one of the biggest names in bourbon whiskey and one of the most prolific distillery owners of his day. Born in 1830, Edmund Taylor, later bestowed the honorific

title "Colonel," was orphaned at a young age and brought up by his uncles Edmund and Zachary Taylor. Edmund Sr. was a banker and Zachary would become the 12th President of the United States.

And so it was that Edmund Taylor followed in both of their footsteps and became both a banker and a politician. He traded in cotton, working with both Union and Confederate sides during the Civil War, reputedly tolerated because of strong political contacts in the North and South.

After the war, Taylor became increasingly interested in whiskey and toured a bunch of distilleries in Europe to better understand the practice. Upon his return to the US in 1867, he became a partner in a whiskey wholesale business out of Louisville with W.A. Gaines and Hiram Berry, called Gaines, Berry & Co. You might remember from a previous chapter, that this company briefly operated the Oscar Pepper Distillery (where the present-day Woodford Reserve distillery is located) and founded The Hermitage Distillery (named after President Andrew Jackson's estate) at Glenn's Creek. You'll also remember that Taylor was a partner in this business but jumped ship to work with his adopted son, James Pepper.

Shortly after parting company from Gaines, Berry & Co., Taylor bought the Leestown Distillery, a few miles north, in Frankfort. This is the distillery that – after numerous name changes – would become known as Buffalo Trace. Taylor completely renovated the site, installing all-copper stills and innovative steam-heated warehouses that controlled the temperatures during whiskey ageing. This distillery was named Old Fire Copper Distillery (some accounts call it "Old Fashioned Copper") or O.F.C.

Unfortunately, Edmund Taylor fell into financial difficulties during the downturn of 1873. Enter George T. Stagg, who recognized Taylor's financial plight as an opportunity.

Stagg's company, Gregory and Stagg, paid off Taylor's loans and gained control of the Colonel's two distilleries (O.F.C. and another operation called Carlisle). Stagg saw the value of Taylor as an ambassador for Kentucky bourbon and so employed him as distillery manager for a time. Stagg then established the E. H. Taylor Jr. Company in 1879, appointing himself president and majority shareholder and Taylor as vice president. The pair soon clashed over quality and corner-cutting, however, and in 1886, Taylor left O.F.C. and was able to set up another distillery, which he named The Old Taylor Distillery.

Taylor's new distillery was architecturally quite different to the other distilleries of the time and modeled on a German Rhenish castle. Taylor didn't just want to make great bourbon—he wanted to share the process with the masses. The distillery became a tourist attraction and was so successful at it that in 1917, he was awarded "The Degree of Master of Hospitality" by the American Association of the Collegiate Registrars.

George Stagg had something to say about all this though, since he was still producing Taylor-branded whiskey and was convinced he owned the rights to Taylor's name (which was still held in high regard). A legal battle ensued that ended in the Kentucky Supreme Court. The result was a fair compromise: both Taylor and Stagg were permitted to use "Taylor" on their bottles.

Wanting to differentiate the "genuine" Old Taylor whiskey from what he believed to be an imitation, Taylor printed an illustration of his face and signature on every bottle. Old Taylor bourbon was one of the first products to assign a face to a brand, and such was the popularity of the whiskey that Taylor became one of the most recognized faces in the US.

Taylor's contribution to bourbon history didn't end there. Spurred on by the heavy taxes that had previously bankrupted his business, Taylor began looking for a better system to tax whiskey. Aided in no small way by his powerful political connections, including Secretary of the Treasury John Carlisle (for whom Taylor had named a distillery) and another whiskey man and friend Ezra Brooks, in 1897 Congress pushed through the "Bottled in Bond Act," a law that still stands today.

Although the Bottled-in-Bond Act was aimed at creating a standard of quality in bourbon whiskey, the system also was connected to the tax laws, providing the key incentive for distilleries to participate. The new system worked by allowing distilleries to delay payment of the excise tax on stored whiskey until the aging process was complete and the whiskey transferred for sale.

By the time Taylor died, in 1923, he was a national celebrity (despite Prohibition having closed his distillery). His death was announced on the radio across the nation: "Mr. Taylor's name was known around the globe, for he had given it to 'Old Taylor' whiskey, made in his distillery, pronounced by expert distillers the finest plant of its kind in the world."

At one time over 1,000 people worked at this distillery and they even had an onsite cooperage, fire department, and hospital. The scale is still visible today and besides the mostly-typical spirit-making equipment, Buffalo possesses one-of-a-kind legacy machinery for processing distillery by-products. Every ounce of spent mash passes through evaporators, presses, mills, and roasters, and gets processed into animal feed for dogs, shrimp, catfish, and cattle. One simple operational effect of this is that corn, wheat, barley, and rye are deposited by a truck through a hatch, then 25 yards down the road the same truck collects animal feed that's ready to be sold back to farmers. Many ultra-modern distilleries do the same trick, but not with antique machinery. There's a huge workshop on the grounds that fabricates replacement parts for much of this equipment. Freddie, our tour guide, who is the third generation in his family to work at Buffalo, tells us that the price they sell the feed for is almost the same as what they pay for incoming cereals.

Freddie's grandfather worked at the distillery from 1912 until 1964 and his son (Freddie's father), James "Jimmy" Johnson, handled every barrel of whiskey in the distillery from when operations commenced after Prohibition until he retired over 40 years later. Jimmy was welcomed back to the distillery in 2008 to roll the six millionth barrel of whiskey since the end of Prohibition. The cask stands on its own in the smallest bonded warehouse in Kentucky. Jimmy passed away in 2011 at the age of 94. In 2013 another legend was lost in the form of the long-time master distiller, Elmer T. Lee who worked there from 1949 until 1985. Elmer was responsible for introducing the Blanton's range (named after Colonel Albert B. Blanton, another former distiller) and the man behind the Weller and Pappy Van Winkle range.

"Honor tradition, embrace change" is the distillery motto, and it's hard to argue that they don't live up to it. Harlen Wheatley, the master distiller, can monitor and control the old column still from anywhere in the world by using computer software and a phone app. The spent beer from the still is run through a heat exchanger, which provides 100% of the energy needed to heat the one-of-a-kind doubler. Most of the water requirements—1.5 million gallons a day to be exact—comes straight from the Kentucky River, which winds around the cluster of distillery buildings.

The distillery runs five different mash-bills to facilitate its 40+ product list, including Kentucky whiskey, wheated bourbon, high-rye bourbon, and straight rye. You'll recognize some popular brands amongst these, most notably W. L. Weller, Sazerac Rye, Blanton's, Eagle Rare, and Pappy Van Winkle—sanity is at least preserved in the consistent use of the same yeast strain. No setback is used.

Sazerac Rye is modeled on the 19th-century whiskey that was used to make the Sazerac cocktail, though the earliest iteration of that drink was actually thought to be made with a brandy from Sazerac de Forge et Fils. Buffalo Trace distillery is actually owned by the Sazerac Company today, who also own the trademark on the term "Sazerac," meaning you can't bottle or market a product with "Sazerac" in the name without getting a knock on the door from a lawyer.

The linguistic stacking of Sazerac as a brand, cocktail, and company has always amused me, and it culminated recently when I was on a camping trip with my friend Jon, who has a dog called Sazerac. It occurred to me that if I passed his dog a Sazerac cocktail using Sazerac Rye (made by the Sazerac Company) I could have legitimately said to her "It's a Sazerac Sazerac Sazerac, Sazerac.")

The distillery produces over 80 different labels of whiskey and supplies wholesale whiskey to independent bottlers and supermarkets. The master blender for all this lot is Drew Mayville, a man with an easy smile and a twinkle in his eye, like there's a joke and he's still deciding whether or not to let you in on it. "The real fun…is experimenting with warehouse conditions," he tells me.

We've seen how complex the interactions between cask and spirit are. But if you thought you'd wrapped your head around the science of maturation, there's more to contend with: warehousing is another dark art of the whiskey coterie.

Now, I wouldn't berate anyone for scoffing at the concept of a large, utilitarian building being a major force for flavor-making in their favorite whiskey, as very few producers draw attention to their warehouses. It's what's in them—the barrels—that tend to receive all the attention. Meanwhile, the ricks, walls, and roof of the warehouse secure the cache of casks and protect them from the elements.

Most of the warehouses in Kentucky are truly immense. Many are nine stories high, stacked three racks/ricks high on each story for a total height of 27 barrels vertically and a grand total of 20,000 barrels or roughly 4 million liters of spirit.

Traditionally, barrels are moved by an elevator/hoist system and trundled into position along the ricks. Care must be taken to ensure the bung is on top of the barrel when it rolls in to its resting position. Some modern warehouses stand their barrels upright on pallets and use forklift trucks to move them around.

"The materials, the height of the rick, and the position of the warehouse in relation to the sun and environmental elements—all of these things affect the product," Drew tells me.

Warehouses that are made of more conductive materials, like steel, are going to heat and cool quicker than those made from a less conductive material, like brick or stone. To that end, Blanton's, which was the first-ever single-barrel bourbon when it was released in 1984, is matured in steel warehouses. Eagle Rare is bottled from casks aged in warehouses constructed from various materials, including brick. These whiskeys are distilled from the same mash bill, so it's fair to say that the construction of the warehouses they are matured in is what distinguishes them.

But even inside a single warehouse the temperature from floor to ceiling can differ by over 10°C /18°F— like having your whiskeys at the top mature in Florida and the bottom in New York. That's why whiskey-makers have traditionally used the hotter, upper floors of a rick house to mature spirits that they want to be most affected by the wood in a relatively short time. Whiskeys intended for extended maturation are generally stored on lower, cooler levels. Additionally, whiskey maturing closer to the walls of the warehouse (or closer to the south-facing wall) tend to feel the effects of the barrel more quickly just as barrels in what Booker Noe (see page 129) called the "Center Cut" stay more constant, varying just a little bit.

OPPOSITE TOP LEFT Buffalo Trace was named a National Historic Landmark by the National Park Service in 2013.
OPPOSITE TOP RIGHT This is one of a handful of distilleries that processes all their waste stillage into animal feed.
OPPOSITE ABOVE RIGHT An experimental peated malt, filled in 2012, but it may be years until it sees the light of day.
OPPOSITE BOTTOM Buffalo Trace is more like a town than a whiskey operation. It'd be quite agreeable to get lost here.

These temperature shifts in different sections of the warehouse also cause variations in evaporative losses. But it doesn't end there…

As a rule, water molecules are more inclined to vacate a barrel than alcohol molecules, because they're smaller and can pass through the wood more easily. The air at the top of a warehouse is drier than the bottom, so while the volume of whiskey is constantly decreasing, the whiskey strength in high-altitude casks is rising. At the bottom of the warehouse, where the air can be quite humid, water leaves the barrel slower as it tries to equilibrate with its surroundings. In this instance, the volume of spirit also decreases (albeit at a slower rate than the barrels near the top) but the strength of the whiskey decreases over time. So although the legal maximum fill strength of a bourbon barrel is 62.5% ABV, it's not uncommon for whiskeys in very dry sections of a warehouse to top 70% ABV by the time they're dumped.

If you like bold whiskeys that are hot enough to melt your tongue, it's worth seeking out barrel-proof bottlings from dry sections of the warehouse. These whiskeys will have a higher proof than usual and therefore contain less water, meaning less dilution and a greater concentration of flavor-giving molecules.

When a warehouse was destroyed by a tornado and the surviving bourbon tasted delicious, they came up with an idea. They built a new warehouse ("X"), which essentially mimics the conditions of post-tornado carnage, with temperature, humidity, and airflow carefully controlled (and natural light supplied). "We're still learning" Drew tells me, pausing for a moment to widen his grin a little, "and we haven't made our best whiskey yet."

Even in the modern era of whiskey, it's quite rare to see a distillery take a proactive approach to warehousing. Granted, most successful producers observe the natural shifts in quality and style that different warehouses offer and blend their whiskeys appropriately, or bottle some as special releases that sometimes list the warehouse number and floor level to build in a little provenance to the product. But a distillery that designs warehouses to actively mess around with the spirit? Not so much.

There's a good reason for that though: warehousing is complicated enough already.

Buffalo Trace installed temperature sensors in their warehouses in 2017 to track the shift between day and night and from floor to floor. They had, of course, taken routine temperature measurements in the past, but always-on digital sensors were able to track the more subtle shifts in temperature and hopefully shine some light on how they affect the final product. A reading taken over nine days in August 2017 recorded readings on the first, third, and fifth floors of Warehouses "T" and "U." Warehouse "U" had lower temperatures than warehouse "T," but a higher temperature on the fifth story. "The warehouses were built to be twins," says Wheatley, "so they are very similar. However, since they are so large, the sheer location—east versus west, etc.—creates variations in the atmosphere."

BUFFALO TRACE WHITE DOG (62.5% ABV)

On the nose, it's apricot and cornmeal, with a touch of mustard seed coming through at the back. On the palate it's oily, but not greasy with a smattering of cut grass and the warm smell of hay.

BUFFALO TRACE RICE MASH 9 YEARS OLD (45% ABV)

Presents nothing too out of the ordinary on the first sniff: cocoa butter, vanilla, and butterscotch are all present and correct. However, a second dip uncovers a floral note that's not normally present. On the palate there's a serious amount of sweetness and a cleanness that I would normally associate with sake. Besides that, typical Buffalo flavors prevail.

BUFFALO TRACE WHEATED BOURBON 10 YEARS OLD (45% ABV)

Possesses much more brown flour, anise, and peppery notes on the nose. At first it feels like an altogether more savory affair, but the wheat sweetness soon kicks in. Very full on the palate, with intense heat (but I like it), and lip-smacking sweet/dry balance. There's a residual linger of brown sugar accompanied by dates, crème caramel, nutmeg, and vanilla.

EAGLE RARE 17 YEARS OLD (45% ABV)

There's a (pleasantly) large amount of sweetcorn on the nose, accompanied by exploding dark cherries and the aroma of the paint thinner shelf in my garage (I have a whole shelf for it). A brilliantly complex taste builds up into a rich spice mixture with some solid wood tannins to structure the whole thing. It's full-bodied too, with a long and sleepy crème brûlée finish.

GEORGE T. STAGG 2013 (64.1% ABV)

Nutty and corny, less sickly sweet, but still some coconut suncream and hot sand on the nose. Plenty of sugar on the palate though; it's thick, syrupy, and massively concentrated, crescendo-ing in to jalapeño as fruit attempts to gain traction but is vaporized in the maelstrom.

WILLIAM LARUE WELLER 2013 (68.1% ABV)

Airfix glue on the nose and that seems like all, but there's an effeminate, musky note in the background, like warm, blonde hair. Fruit comes through eventually in the form of blueberry ice cream. On the palate, the second sip (first is a dud and used only to overcome the alcohol) is creamy vanilla sponge leading into tempered spice. Back to the nose and there's white chocolate now. More pepper on the palate… easing away gently.

BUFFALO TRACE EXPERIMENTAL COLLECTION 19 YEAR OLD (45% ABV)

Thick beeswax polish and remnants of pipe tobacco and glossy maple wood on the nose. The taste is not as sweet as expected; there's a dryness here from flint and old wood. Finish is disappointingly short lived.

ROAD TRIP PLAYLIST

"Bourbon in Kentucky" – Dierks Bentley

SAZERAC

10 ml/2 teaspoons French Absinthe
I white sugar cube
5 dashes Peychaud's Bitters
50 ml/I⅔ oz Sazerac Rye

Grab two old fashioned glasses. Fill one with crushed ice and add the Absinthe. Stir.

In the other glass, crush the sugar cube with the bitters until dissolved, then add the whiskey, some cubed ice, and stir for 30 seconds. Chuck away the contents of the Absinthe glass, making sure you remove all fragments of the ice. This might seem wasteful, but believe me, the Absinthe will be entirely noticeable in the final drink.

Finally, strain the mixture into the empty Absinthe-washed glass. Garnish with a little twist of lemon.
No ice in the glass.

You can mix the ingredients in a standard mixing beaker, of course, but the original ritual
used two identical glasses.

It's the 1850s in New Orleans and a gent named Sewell E. Taylor begins importing Sazerac de Forge et Fils Cognac to New Orleans, Louisiana. Coincidentally, or not, at around the same time the Sazerac House bar opens in New Orleans, and they begin selling the Sazerac cocktail. The drink contained Sazerac de Forge et Fils Cognac and Absinthe, which at that time, across the Atlantic, was doing a great job of increasing France's artistic creativity and alcoholism. The drink was also rumored to use bitters produced at a local pharmacy owned by a local druggist called Antoine Peychaud. Peychaud's Bitters remain an essential requirement for any great Sazerac.

There is some historical reference to suggest that Peychaud served his own version of the drink from a French egg-cup called a coquitier. It's this egg-cup

that has led some people to believe that the word "cocktail" originally derived from Peychaud's Sazerac serving.

Despite the Sazerac being invented in the mid 19th century, its first appearance in a cocktail book wasn't until Bill Boothby's *The World's Drinks and how to mix 'em* (1908 edition). The recipe was apparently given to Bill by Thomas H. Handy, a later proprietor of the Sazerac House in New Orleans. Interestingly, the directions listed it with "good whiskey" instead of Cognac. This omission of Cognac is almost certainly due to the outbreak of the *phylloxera* bug in the late 19th century, which caused nothing short of a complete collapse of the French wine industry. Wine and Cognac became largely unavailable, so Bill "Cocktail" Boothby replaced the Cognac with whiskey in his book.

WILD TURKEY

FROM FATHER TO SON SINCE 1954

"You have got to give a man a good reason to vote with you. Don't try to force him. A man can take a little bourbon without getting drunk, but if you hold his mouth open and pour in a quart, he's going to get sick on it."

LYNDON B. JOHNSON (1908–73), 36TH PRESIDENT OF THE UNITED STATES

Heading north from Four Roses it's only a short drive to Lawrenceburg, past the rolling grass hills, shady trees, and white picket fences of Anderson County. Wild Turkey is just on the outskirts of the town.

Of the four distilleries in the Kentucky River cluster, Wild Turkey sits more or less in the center. At first appearance, it looks much the same as any of the other established Kentucky distilleries: a large plot of land filled with grain silos, a big still house, and large, silver-colored warehouses full of copious amounts of whiskey.

However, the visitor's center, museum, and shop at Wild Turkey is an altogether different kind of installation. Don't get me wrong, it's still large, and the architecture of the structure is modeled on the classic red barns that dot the landscape across many southern states, but about half of its construction is glass, giving it an extremely modern appearance. Complete with a whiskey museum and extensive gift shop, this, perhaps, is the future of whiskey marketing in Kentucky.

But before we delve into the modern practices of this distillery, let's first explore the history of distilling in this little area (because there's plenty of it!). It begins with the Rippey siblings (James, Jon, and Eliza), who emigrated to the US from Northern Ireland in 1830. Entering via Philadelphia, they immediately headed west and ended up in the newly established village of Lawrenceburg, Kentucky—population: 300.

James Rippey opened a mercantile store there and counted among his customers the many small farmers and distillery owners of Anderson County (who were probably supplying him with whiskey to sell, too). When he solicited the help of a local sign-writer to paint his name above the door of his store, the artist ran out of room and shortened the spelling of his name to "Ripy." In 1839, James made it official and went before a Bourbon County court, renounced his British citizenship, and became the American "James Ripy".

Some 20 years later, James had acquired a distillery in Steamville, a couple of miles out of Lawrenceburg, on the banks of the Kentucky River. This distillery was thought to date back to around 1850. By this point, James had sired two sons, the eldest, James P. Ripy, became a distiller after he married into the family that owned Bond & Lilliard Whiskey. The younger son, Thomas Beebe "T.B." Ripy, was born in 1847. Sometime around 1858, the distillery passed to T.B., who became the sole owner of the Cliff Springs Distillery at the tender age of 21.

Such was the influence of the growing Ripy business, that around 1868, T.B. renamed the area around the distillery Tyrone, presumably as a tribute to the county of Northern Ireland where the family came from. Tyrone became a bustling town of over 1,000 residents, but these days it constitutes little more than a few houses.

James Ripy died in 1872, aged 61. It was around this time that the business coined the slogan "From father to son since 1831" to market its products. The distillery was proving to be successful, and a year after his father's death, T.B. tore down some of the original Cliff Springs buildings and replaced them with sturdier brick, stone, and iron-clad structures. Like any distillery of that time, there was also a cattle barn. As a result of the improvements, the mashing capacity of the distillery was increased to around 15 tons of cereal a day.

T.B. built and acquired several more distilleries in his time, including another in Tyrone, called Clover Bottom, the Old Joe distillery (rumored to be one of the oldest distilleries in Anderson County, dating back to 1818), and the Belle Anderson Distillery in nearby Midway, Woodford County. When the state of Kentucky had to select one whiskey to feature at its exhibits at the 1893 Chicago World's Fair, it was Old Ripy whiskey that was chosen from a pool of over 400 brands.

T.B. and Sally Ripy had ten children and used a great deal of their wealth to build a massive mansion in Lawrenceburg. Completed in 1888, the property is now used as a location for film and TV, being marketed as "a work of art that is also a definitive piece of American history, representing the people who lived and defined the American Dream."

T.B. Ripy died on June 30, 1902, three years after selling his distilling interests in Tyrone. His sons Ezra, Ernest, Forest, and Robert (who were quite possibly a little annoyed by their father's decision to sell everything and then die) opened [yet] another distillery near Tyrone called "Ripy Brothers," and it was this distillery that would go on to become the Wild Turkey Distillery.

Prohibition closed the Ripy Brothers distillery for a while, but in 1935, Ernest Ripy set about rebuilding it. The operation went on to produce over 20 brands for various independent bottlers. One of their customers was Thomas McCarthy, who worked for Austin Nichols & Co., a grocery wholesaler based in New York. Apparently Nichols was a keen sportsman, who liked to hunt wild turkeys on his South Carolina estate. McCarthy liked to impress his friends by bringing the best bourbons with him on these hunting trips, which slowly developed a reputation for being "that wild turkey whiskey."

The Wild Turkey brand was launched in 1940 but was actually made from bourbon distilled at several different Kentucky plants. The biggest supplier was Ripy Bros., though. And as a result of that, together with the brand's growing reputation, on July 1, 1972, Austin Nichols bought the Ripy Brothers Distillery. From then onwards, all Wild Turkey was made at this distillery.

Back at the entrance to the visitor's center, the stark modernity of this barn is immediately offset by the individual waiting for us. He appears — by his walking cane, his posture, and his age — to be from another time. Jimmy Russell is both the oldest and longest-serving master distiller in the US.

Perched on a bar stool with bourbon in hand, Jimmy recounts to me his long relationship with the Wild Turkey brand. "I started here in 1954," he says. I'm trying my best to digest the numbers, but it just doesn't seem to make sense coming out of a living human being's mouth.

So that's 64 years in the same job at the time of writing. Think about that for a minute. During Jimmy's tenure, billions of people have been born, gone to school, trained in their profession, worked a long career, and retired. Even now, Jimmy still turns up to work every day. Still tastes whiskey every day. I ask him when he feels he might retire, to which he responds, "The first day it feels like work."

At the age of 84 Jimmy does need a bit of help completing all of the tasks that a master distiller is required to do. So he shares the role with another Russell: Eddie, his son. Eddie has been making whiskey at Wild Turkey for a paltry 37 years and is today the driving force behind consistency and innovation at the distillery.

Although the current distillery building was built in 2010, much of what defines the unique production facets of Wild Turkey can be traced back to the 1950s which, coincidentally (or not), was when Jimmy Russell first appeared on the scene.

The non-GMO corn that Wild Turkey uses has been sourced from the same farm for generations. Rye is a significant part of the mash bill here too, not least of all in Wild Turkey Rye, and Wild Turkey sources a baker's grade rye from Germany for this (it comes at a premium price but the belief is that it contributes a richer spice and avoids the mustiness that lower-quality rye can manifest).

The yeast the Russells use is proprietary and was first developed in the 1950s. It's stored in multiple locations to insure against disaster. I joke that staff have to take it in turns to look after the yeast at the weekend and it's met with serious sideways glances.

Wild Turkey is primarily a bourbon distillery but with an increasing focus on rye. Rye mashes are run twice a year, once in the spring and once in the fall. Ten years ago that meant rye was made for a single day in the spring and a single day in the fall. In 2018 they mashed rye for a full week in spring and another week in the fall. So we can reasonably assume that of the 180,000 barrels that get filled here every year, about 7,000 of them contain rye whiskey.

Fermentation is conducted across 23 open-top fermenters for a target time of 72 hours, and the spirit comes off the doubler at 130 proof. It's cut to 115 proof before entering the cask.

Wild Turkey uses casks that are toasted to their own specification, then charred to a number 4 char. All Wild Turkey whiskeys are aged for a minimum of five years, but beyond that self-imposed rule, casks are bottled based entirely on taste. Russell's Reserve is a super-premium bourbon that is aged for a minimum of 10 years and blended from selected casks from specific warehouse locations that produce a richer, more concentrated style of whiskey.

Next to their oldest Warehouse, "Warehouse A," which was built in 1894, is the old Southern Rail track that passes through the property then bridges across the Kentucky River gorge, parallel to the Tyrone

ABOVE Jimmy Russell has probably influenced the contents of more bottles of whiskey than any other living person.

road bridge. The last passenger train crossed it on December 27, 1937. It remained in use for freight traffic, which had dwindled by the late 1970s, and the last train to cross the bridge was in November 1985. Prior to its retirement, the railroad delivered grain, transported bottled product, and even supplied coal, which was used to power the steam furnace. These days the bridge is a popular spot for bungee jumpers. Looking at the warehouse itself, it's difficult to find the beauty in the massive, boxy structure. But the blenders here take the view that each warehouse is like paint on an artist's palette. Each of the 20 buildings (there are a further six in other locations and Wild Turkey have a track record of building about one warehouse a year) possesses its own unique flavor-making properties, so the liquid from each warehouse needs to be carefully blended with other warehouses to create a balanced composition—to create art.

Like many other distilleries in Kentucky, Wild Turkey has seen a fire or two. The most recent was in

OVERLEAF The old rail crossing of the Kentucky River gorge was once a major artery for the Wild Turkey distillery.

2002. Jimmy recalls that it was a bright, sunny day when a fire broke out in one of the warehouses. He tells me that "17,192 barrels went up."

Wild Turkey Honey Liqueur was launched in 1976 and was followed up by a maple-flavored bourbon called Signature. Both products were "ahead of their time," which is a nice way of saying they flopped.

Austin Nichols was acquired by French spirits giant Pernod Ricard in 1980 for $100 million, and it was during their tenure, in 1991, that they released Rare Breed, a barrel-proof-mingling of 8, 10, and 12-year-old bourbons. In 2001, the distillery released Russell's Reserve, which was originally a 10-year-old bottling but has since grown into a small range of limited release and single-barrel bourbon and rye bottlings. In 2009 Pernod Ricard sold Wild Turkey to Gruppo Campari, the current owners, for $575 million.

101 STRAIGHT BOURBON (50.5% ABV)

The extra heat here gives the aroma a pronounced rye note, with cracked black pepper and a green nuttiness that's a bit like pumpernickel. That soon dissipates however, making way for toffee apple and barrel char. The taste is nutty, grippy, and sweet, with a green cardamom or eucalyptus note bringing up the rear.

STRAIGHT RYE (40.5% ABV)

This whiskey is fresh and clean-smelling, like mint toothpaste on a hot deck. The taste continues this theme with green jalapeño and fennel along with darker, toasty notes. Soft and quite accessible, this is a great entry-level rye.

RARE BREED (56.4% ABV)

Extra maturation begins to play its part here, with dried fruits (golden raisin and regular raisin) emerging, alongside the greener notes of the distillery's character. Next follows toasted nuts and a darker, bread-y aroma that builds on the idea of Christmas pudding. The taste is concentrated and bold, with the alcohol combating the residual sweetness from the barrel.

KENTUCKY SPIRIT (50.5% ABV)

Strong cornmeal and sweet sponge pudding aromas, with a liberal helping of vanilla custard. It's super-sweet on the palate with notes of barrel char balancing it out. This is a deliciously indulgent bourbon: perfect for after dinner.

ROAD TRIP PLAYLIST

"Old Man" – Neil Young

"Drunk" – Jimmy Liggins

"End of The Line" – The Traveling Wilburys

ABOVE One of Wild Turkey's rick houses. Beauty is only skin deep—it's what's on the inside that counts!

ABOVE See: much better! As with most of Kentucky's distilleries, the barrels are rolled into position on each floor.

VIEUX CARRÉ

35 ml/1¼ oz Wild Turkey Straight Rye
15 ml/½ oz VSOP Cognac
25 ml/generous ¾ oz Cinzano Rosso
5 ml/1 teaspoon Benedictine
1 dash Peychaud's Bitters
1 dash Angostura Bitters

Add the ingredients to a mixing beaker and stir over cubed ice for a minute. Strain into a rocks glass filled with ice. Garnish with a twist of lemon peel. (The original recipe, which the Carousel Bar honors, suggests optionally garnishing with a slice of pineapple and a cherry… I'm not a fan.)

Contrary to the name, the oldest buildings in New Orleans' "French Quarter" were in fact built during the Spanish occupation (1762–1802). But fires between 1788 and 1794 destroyed the "first generation" French Creole properties, so the majority of the buildings we see today were raised during the early part of the 19th century after the US had taken possession. At that time, Mississippi steamboats facilitated excellent trade routes with more northerly states and the Gulf of Mexico offered a gateway to transatlantic trading, making New Orleans the largest port in the south. The city grew at a staggering rate through the 19th century, with the population skyrocketing from 17,000 to 170,000 in the space of 50 years. With it came extraordinary wealth, which created a need for fancy hotels and decadent bars.

One such hotel was The Commercial, which was founded by Antonio Monteleone on the corner of Royal and Chartres, in 1886. This French Quarter hotel has remained in the Monteleone family ever since, having been expanded numerous times, before being mostly demolished and rebuilt into its current state in 1954.

Perhaps the most notable feature of the hotel is the Carousel Bar, which was originally built in 1949. The bar is a circular "island" style, seats 25 guests, and rotates at a rate of one revolution every 15 minutes— slow enough so you don't get dizzy but fast enough to disorientate (especially after a few cocktails).

Speaking of cocktails, it was an earlier, non-rotating, iteration of the Carousel Bar where the Vieux Carré was first mixed. Walter Bergeron was the head bartender there during the 1930s, and following the drink's creation, the cocktail featured in the 1937 publication *Famous New Orleans Drinks and how to mix 'em*.

In structure, the drink sits somewhere between a Manhattan and a Sazerac. There are some provocative pairings of ingredients here though: rye does battle with cognac and two varieties of bitters have a face-off. In many ways it is both a Manhattan and a Sazerac in the same glass, where the absinthe has been replaced with Benedictine. That last part is a critical element to the success of the drink, however, as it brings sweetness and harmonizes the floral, fruity cognac with the spice of the rye.

WILLETT

WE ARE FAMILY

"… the tall honey locusts, the stately old houses, some in disrepair, some with tourist's signs on their lawns, but gracious, still with dignity the could not be destroyed by years or weather; It's a fairly lively town… We have as much activity per capita here as Lo'ville or Cincinnati. You won't get bored."

ON BARDSTOWN, FROM THE NOVEL *WE'LL SING ONE SONG* BY OLIVE CARRUTHERS

The next stop on our tour is the town of Bardstown, which is less than an hour's drive heading south west. Bardstown is to bourbon what Nashville is to country music. Very close by are the towns Clermont, Boston (home to two Jim Beam distilleries), and Loretto, home to Maker's Mark, and combined with Bardstown, this area accounts for around two-thirds of all the bourbon in America. In Bardstown itself, home to 13,000 folks, we'll find the Willett distillery (where we're heading right now), Barton 1792 distillery (our next stop), and much of Heaven Hill's warehousing along with their distillery-turned-visitor's center.

There are also two very new additions to the Bardstown distilling scene.

The first is the hyper-modern Bardstown Bourbon Company, which began making whiskey in 2016. At the time of our visit they had already bottled some older whiskey, sourced from Tennessee, but were yet to bottle any of their own. As we go to print, they have released a blended Straight bourbon, which is made up of 60% of their own spirit blended with older whiskey from another Kentucky distiller.

Then there's Lux Row Distillery, which began distilling in April 2018. This facility is owned by a spirits bottler called LuxCo, based out of Missouri.

The company already owns something like 100,000 barrels of bourbon, but high demand and insufficient product has prompted them to build a $70 million distillery in Bardstown. The company also owns the Limestone Branch distillery in Lebanon, Kentucky, which opened in 2012 and produces the historic Yellowstone Bourbon brand.

Although Bardstown has been home to whiskey distillers for over 150 years, it was after Prohibition ended that things really took off and Bardstown became a bit of a party town. Distilleries were kicking back in to action and the easiest place to get your hands on whiskey was to head to Bardstown. People came from Lexington and Louisville and sometimes as far away as Cincinnati to witness "The Partiest Town in America."

According to bourbon historian Dixie Hibbs, there were 27 distilleries in the Bardstown area in 1896 but only a dozen by the time Prohibition came along in 1920. Amazingly, eight of those 12 reopened after Prohibition was repealed in 1933 and were joined by three new ones. There are currently five operational distilleries in the area.

North Third street was known as "Distiller's Row" because of all the distillers based there. Among others, the Beam and Noe families lived there, two doors

down from the Samuels family (founders of Maker's Mark—see page 180).

Bardstown is where the Kentucky Bourbon Trail begins and it's the location of the annual Kentucky Bourbon Festival, which is draws in around 50,000 people to the town in September each year, quadrupling the population for a week.

William Willett, Sr. was the first of the Willett family to get into the distilling business, after he married his wife, Mary, in 1738 in Maryland. The Willetts lived in Prince George's County, not far from where Washington, DC, would eventually spring up from. Some accounts suggest that William owned a tavern there and that he made Maryland Rye. When William Willett Sr. died, he left his distilling business to his son William Willett Jr., who moved to Kentucky in 1792, the same year in which the state was founded.

John David Willett (born in 1841) became the next member of the family connected to the whiskey industry. He established the Willet & Frenke Company, which traded whiskey out of Louisville and owned a distillery in Morton's Spring, just south of Bardstown, in Nelson County.

In 1874 he employed a man called Thomas Selvin Moore, whose sister had married into the Willett family. Moore was a Nelson County native, who would go on to be one of the key figures in establishing Bardstown as a whiskey Mecca. In 1876, due to "Failing health and eyesight," John David Willett transferred all his interest in the Willett & Frenke and distillery to his daughters. Enter: Benjamin F. Mattingly, husband of Catherine Willett, and son of John Graves Mattingly, the builder of distilleries that we touched upon in the last chapter.

The Willet & Frenke operation was now run by Tom Moore and Ben Mattingly, and the distillery become known as the Mattingly & Moore Distillery. The pair made a bourbon of that name (which is today made by Heaven Hill Distillers), along with "Belle of Nelson" named for a racehorse owned by John Willett, and "Morton's Spring Rye," named for the limestone spring that serviced the property. We'll discuss what happened to this distillery in the next chapter.

Having secured their place as "bourbon royalty," the Willett empire continued to spread and grow. Aloysius Lambert Willett, who went by "Lambert" (who can blame him), was the next-generation patriarch, having been born in Bardstown in 1883 and started work at the Mattingly & Moore Distillery at the age of 15. He also spent time in the Willett & Frenke offices in Louisville as well and worked at the Bernheim distillery. His son, Aloysius Lambert Thompson Willet, who went by "Thompson" (who can blame him either), co-founded the Willett Distillery in Bardstown in 1937. The chosen location had previously been the Willett family hog farm. Along with his brother Johnny "Drum" Willett, Lambert created the Old Bardstown bourbon and Johnny Drum brands.

During the 1970s energy crisis, when America faced gas shortages (and bourbon whiskey was losing market share to vodka), the distillery switched to making industrial ethanol. This turned out to be a poor strategy when fuel prices settled towards the end of the decade. The distillery ceased operation altogether in 1981. Thompson went bankrupt.

Enter, Even G. Kulsveen, a decanter maker from Norway, who was married to Martha Willett, and therefore the son-in-law to Thompson Willett. Kulsveen purchased Willett Distilling Company on July 1, 1984, and formed Kentucky Bourbon Distillers, Ltd.

For a time, the company operated solely as a bottling plant, earning it the moniker "the big daddy of bourbon and rye bottling." Despite not being a true producer of whiskey (a Non Distillery Producer or NDP if you will), they still managed to garner quite a cult following for their own products. These labels included the 1994 releases of their "Small Batch Boutique Bourbon Collection" featuring Rowan's Creek, Noah's Mill (we'll come back to that one shortly), Kentucky Vintage, and Pure Kentucky.

Of course it wasn't just a case of taking someone else's product and popping it in a bottle. Selecting barrels, managing their continued maturation, and blending to a specific flavor profile requires skill. A good distillery would be lost without a good warehouse manager and blender, which proves the point that there's craft in the final stages of whiskey making. Not only that, but Willett was buying older stocks up and letting them mature for even longer, so for a while some of the oldest bourbon expressions around were coming out of their warehouses.

If American whiskey hadn't seen such unprecedented growth over the past decade, perhaps the Willett Distillery would never have found a need to start distilling again. But with mature stocks (mostly from Four Roses and Jim Beam) becoming increasingly difficult and expensive to source, it became an essential step for survival. After a significant refurbishment, in 2012 the distillery kicked back into action. As of 2019, it is producing around 20 brands, labels, and variations of bourbon and whiskeys, some of which are still maturing.

Perhaps you haven't seen many bottles with Willett or even Kentucky Bourbon Distillers on the bottle? Well, that's for good reason. That's partly down to the sourced nature of the liquid, the labels of which do not identify KBD as the producing company. Instead the company does business under various superficial company names. These other business names often correspond to the bottling brand names (such as the Old Bardstown Distilling Company for the Old Bardstown bourbon brand and the Noah's Mill Distilling Company for the Noah's Mill bourbon brand). I can certainly appreciate why some people might find this kind of thing misleading, as if the distillery is deliberately trying to create confusion to hide the true source of the whiskey. But in some ways, I like the mystery of the liquid and the pseudo-heritage around each individual product.

Even Kulsveen and Martha Kulsveen (née Willett) continue to operate the facility to this day, and the next generation of the family, including their son Drew Kulsveen and his wife Janelle, their daughter Britt Chavanne, and her husband Hunter Chavanne, are also highly active participants. Britt Chavanne is now president of the distillery, Drew Kulsveen is the current master distiller and manages production, while Janelle Kulsveen runs the gift shop and hospitality side of things, and Hunter Chavanne

covers sales and marketing. Willett is among Kentucky's last significant family-owned distilleries and in spite of the scale (which is modest among the Kentucky set but big compared to most) this really is still a family business.

The distillery building is a beauty, featuring a timber-clad roof supported by beautiful limestone columns. Being relatively small, everything is within touching distance too.

There are two mash cookers, a 6,000-gallon one and a 3,000-gallon one. A total of six mash recipes are made here: two bourbon, two rye, and two wheat. However, these are sometimes blended after distillation and after maturation, so you're not necessarily getting one single mash in the bottle. One of the bourbon mash bills is a historical recipe, based on 72% corn, 13% rye, and 15% malted barley. The other is a newer, wheated recipe comprising 65% corn, 20% wheat, and 15% malted barley.

Two small mashes or one big mash fill a single fermenter, of which there are seven. Each fermentation lasts around three days. I started to do the maths in my head, and couldn't fathom why the distillery needed two mash cookers, since the big one alone could easily fill two fermenters a day. I wish I hadn't asked as it turns out it's all to do with the capability of ancillary equipment like steam boilers and how that balances with shift patterns. Sometimes it's nice to remind yourself that a distillery is a working alcohol factory, and that decisions are not always taken towards some subtle pursuit of flavor.

The column still here is at least 100 years old and was originally used to make the Waterfill and Frazier brand of bourbon. Column stills rarely garner the fetishism that traditional pot- stills do, but this particular column has an interesting story to tell. During Prohibition, the owner of Waterfill and Frazier, Mary Dowling, instructed Joseph L. Beam (cousin of Jim Beam) to dismantle the still and move it down to Mexico. Beam reinstated the still at the Tequila distillery he was working at but it seems that

167

WILLETT: WE ARE FAMILY

Beam was also making whiskey, since Mary Dowling continued to import contraband "bourbon" whiskey into the states. Whether Beam was complicit in this, I'm not sure, but the actions of Dowling are one of the reasons that it became necessary to codify bourbon as an American product.

When Prohibition ended, Joseph L. Beam returned to Kentucky and became an investor in the Heaven Hill distillery. His son, Harry Beam, was the distillery's first master distiller.

The column still found its way back too.

Spirit comes off the column at around 120 proof then up to 135 proof after pot distillation.

"Our copper pot-still is more in the shape you would expect to see in Scotland," says master distiller Drew Kulsveen. "We get more fruit and a lighter bodied whiskey coming off it."

This pot, which is manufactured by Vendome, is peculiarly-shaped for a bourbon still. It has a large, bulbous bottom, then a very tall, slender neck. It is indeed more reminiscent of a Scotch whisky still, although I've not seen one like this there either. It also has some weird gadgets on it, including a series of plates in the head that help to direct heavier compounds back to the bottom of the still. Willett are pretty proud of this still, so much so that one of their bottle designs is modeled on it.

A typical day's production bears fruit to the tune of 1,000 gallons of un-aged whiskey, or enough to fill about 20 barrels.

"We're actually on the highest altitude point in Nelson County," says Britt, "and all through the summer we open up the warehouses to allow as much airflow as possible. That breathing of the barrels is one of the things that makes our whiskey unique."

The distillery is in a beautiful setting. Half a dozen-or-so warehouses (it's actually eight) line the drive that leads down to the still house. They're smaller than what is typical in the area, holding around 5,000–6,000 barrels a piece.

Back in the dark years of the early 1980s, the distillery was still home to a substantial number of cows and pigs. So all the warehouses are equipped with livestock gates on the doors, to prevent an inquisitive cow from wandering in while the warehouse men were moving barrels around. Some members of the extended Willett family were put to good use though. As we walk in to one warehouse, Britt points out a winch system that was used to raise barrels up through the floors. It worked by clamping the barrel then running a rope through a pulley, the other end of which was tied to a mule (or other working beast). The mule would walk forward and the barrel would rise up. One slap on the back told the mule to walk only so far as for the barrel to reach the first floor. Two slaps was second floor. And so on.

Unsurprisingly, given the company history, a lot of what goes in to the bottle is the product of good blending. Brands like Old Bardstown (named after a racehorse, not Bardstown) and Johnny Drum are distinguished based on how the rye in the mash presents itself after maturation.

For the real whiskey geeks, the most recent significant releases came in 2008, when Drew Kulsveen introduced Willett Family Estate Bottled Bourbon and Willett Family Estate Bottled Rye. These products went on to become regular releases of single-barrel whiskeys, garnering a cult following and often exceeding 20 years maturation. In early 2009 the family released Willett Pot Still Reserve. This was another popular release, since the whiskey came in a bottle shaped like a pot still, copied from original still blueprints of the plant back in 1936. Remember though, that these releases all took place before the Willett distillery was back in operation—so at the time of its release the Pot Still Reserve was in fact the only pot still this whiskey had ever seen.

The first release celebrating the newly renovated distillery came in 2015, with a two-year-old edition of Willett Family Estate-bottled Rye that was entirely the product of the Willett pot still. Bourbon followed,

TOP LEFT Inside and out, the still house at the Willett distillery is one of the most beautiful in Kentucky.
FAR LEFT With it's bulging base and slender neck, the Willett pot still is entirely unique.
LEFT The warehouses feature some exceptional casks, many of which can be tasted in the Family Estate range.

LEFT The barrel bung is always located on the top of the barrel, so the blender will sometimes drill a hole in the side to obtain samples.

in 2016, and we expect to see more ongoing releases of whiskeys born and bred at the KBD facility.

Before we leave, we walk towards the old Noah's Mill gristmill, next to Rowan's Creek. Both lend their name to whiskeys made here. The mill is being refurbished back into a functional gristmill. Sadly, it'll only produce a tiny amount of grist, to make grits for guests staying in the B&B on the property. This distillery has come a long way in the past 20 years.

The conversation descends into discussion around the subject of grits. Britt leaves us with the parting advice: "Order shrimp and grits wherever you go. It's always going to be different." Then she pauses for a second, considers something, and finishes with, "Don't order the hot brown."

NOAH'S MILL (57.15% ABV)

Caramel and chocolate ice cream on the nose. Sweet and spicy on the palate, well structured but reasonably light. A touch of bitterness through the finish.

JOHNNY DRUM (43% ABV)

Big and meaty aroma, with notes of beef stock and bone marrow. Things sweeten on the palate, where cherry and maple syrup come into play, which altogether gives the impression of wood-smoked meats. The finish is candy cane and subtle spice.

ROWAN'S CREEK (50.05% ABV)

Bright orange soda and soft leather on the nose. There are notes of ginger beer and root beer on the palate, feeling herbal, bright, and fragrant. Overall, it's really delicious and super-accessible.

WILLETT RYE (53.7% ABV)

Quite repressed and nutty, with a touch of marmalade on the nose. Dry and spicy on the palate. Feels quite concentrated with bread crust, baking spice, and hot leather coming through.

WILLETT FAMILY ESTATE–BOTTLED 6 YEAR OLD BOURBON (59.9% ABV)

Waxy leather, orange blossom, ground ginger, coriander seed, and just a touch of praline on the nose. Peppered and lively, delivering black pepper and pimento, which softens quickly with a licorice finish.

ROAD TRIP PLAYLIST

"She Bangs the Drums"– The Stone Roses

"Having a Party" – Sam Cooke

"Boulevard of Broken Dreams" – Green Day

BOULEVARDIER

40 ml/1⅓ oz Rowan's Creek
20 ml/⅔ oz Campari
20 ml/⅔ oz Martini Rosso

Add all of the ingredients to a mixing beaker and stir over cubed ice for at least 90 seconds. Strain into a chilled coupe glass and garnish with a small twist of orange. You may like to add a splash of water to the mixing beaker too, to help cut through the syrupy Campari and lighten the drink a little.

This drink, like many others, was created by Harry MacElhone of Harry's New York Bar in Paris. It is mentioned only briefly in his book *Barflies and Cocktails* (1927), not among the cocktail recipes, but in the epilogue that follows the recounts the antics of his regular patrons:

"Now is the time for all good barflies to come to the aid of the party, since Erskine Gwynne crashed in with his Boulevardier Cocktail: 1/3 Campari, 1/3 Italian vermouth, 1/3 bourbon whisky."

Erskine Gwynne was a wealthy young journalist who came to Paris from New York, and in 1927 launched a literary magazine for posh men about town called—you guessed it—*The Boulevardier*. A famous cocktail bartender with his own written account of the drink's creation and a catchy name attributed to a known journalist. On appearances this seems like a straightforward origin story. But there is just one outstanding matter: how did Harry MacElhone come to have bourbon in his bar in 1927? There was no prohibition in France at that time of course (besides absinthe) but the production of spirits in the US. had been on hold for nearly a decade, and the only whiskey produced there was for medical purposes. MacElhone must have gathered quite a stock of the stuff prior to the 1920s and would likely have charged a high premium for drinks that contained it.

The Boulevardier bears more than passing similarity to a Negroni, but unlike a Negroni the bourbon in a Boulevardier is less inclined to be swamped by the other ingredients than gin is. The use of bourbon shifts the drink further in the direction of a Manhattan. Indeed, if you were to draw a Venn diagram with circles that represented a Negroni and a Manhattan, the Boulevardier would sit in the intersection.

BARTON 1792

THE BOURBON CAPITAL OF THE WORLD

"Bourbon!"

THE LAST WORD OF TALLULAH BANKHEAD (1902–68), ACTRESS

Back when we visited Heaven Hill, we covered some of the legend around the earliest Kentucky distillers. At Jim Beam and Woodford Reserve, we learned about some of the first families of whiskey in the region and the practices that they adopted. Now it's time to focus specifically on bourbon whiskey. We'll explore the origins of the category and how its growing popularity made it the de facto brown spirit of America, and how its dominance in the 20th century threatened to consume the wider categorization of whiskey.

It's accepted by most Kentucky whiskey producers that bourbon got its name from Bourbon County, Kentucky. The story goes that barrels of whiskey, arriving by riverboat in New Orleans, were invoiced to traders as "Limestone [the name of the port], Bourbon County, Kentucky". The long trip downriver (which took many months) gave the whiskey time to mature in the cask, mellowing the flavor and improving the quality. These barrels became highly prized, and "Bourbon county" became synonymous with the style of whiskey and was used to distinguish it from other styles, like Monongahela rye. The "Limestone" barrels would have originated from the junction of the Ohio River with Limestone Creek, where the Bourbon County settlement of Limestone Landing was formed. So, this story all seems to add up: a whiskey made in, or near, Limestone, with a direct route along the Ohio to New Orleans.

The problem is that Limestone was only a part of Bourbon County between 1786 and 1789, after which it switched to Mason County. But what's even more problematic is that both Bourbon County and Mason County were still part of Virginia in 1789. It was only in 1792 that Kentucky became a state, which coincided with Limestone being renamed Maysville. So, "Limestone, Bourbon County, Kentucky" has never actually existed as an address.

A far more reliable reference to bourbon comes from the Bourbon County newspaper, in 1821. It featured an advert for "Bourbon whiskey by the barrel or keg" offered by the Maysville-based firm of Stout and Adams. The term didn't seem to catch on, however, which is evidenced by the scant references to bourbon through to the middle of the century.

Sometimes a lack of reference can be just as telling as a direct mention, however. Although a fictional account of a man hunting a whale can hardly be classed as solid citation, the fact that Herman Melville lists three types of whiskey, "old Orleans... old Ohio... old Monongahela," in *Moby Dick* might indicate that bourbon whiskey still wasn't very well established by the time the novel was published 1851.

With that in mind, it is possible that the Stout and Adams reference to bourbon is just a random coincidence and that bourbon whiskey was named much later, via a different etymological pathway.

What we know for sure is that New Orleans merchants and traders had adopted the terms "old

Bourbon" or "old Bourbon County whiskey" by the 1860s. Two men from New Orleans that are sometimes credited with the early marketing of bourbon in this way are the Tarascon brothers, who arrived in Louisville from south of Cognac, France, and began shipping local whiskey down the Ohio River to Louisiana's bustling port city in the 1820s.

New Orleans was the third largest city in the US by 1840, and around half of the white population were French speakers. The word "bourbon", being of French origin, played to the French connection, and the spirit itself, being aged in barrels, appealed to the French taste for Cognac, which was at the time quite expensive to import. The Tarascon brothers knew all of this. In addition to this, one of New Orleans busiest thoroughfares was Bourbon Street, which was named independently of the Kentucky county and could suggest another etymological origin for bourbon whiskey. Could bourbon have gotten its name from the whiskey traders of Bourbon Street?

Speaking of the French, when Prince Napoléon (1822–1891), a member of the dynasty whose namesake had supplanted the royal French House of Bourbon, visited Staten Island in 1861, he drank whiskey from a flask offered by one of the soldiers there. "What is it?" he asked. "Old Bourbon, sir," came the response. "Old Bourbon indeed," was the prince's reply. "I did not think I would like anything with that name so well."

You might recall that one of the distilleries owned by Paul Jones Jr. (of Four Roses fame; see page 141) was J. G. Mattingly & Sons in Louisville, built in 1845. Well, John Graves Mattingly also built another distillery, The Marion County Distillery, in 1866.

John's son Ben Mattingly sold his share of the Mattingly Moore distillery, which he had acquired in 1876 with partner Tom Selvin Moore, to a group of Louisville investors in 1881. Tom Moore continued to work at the distillery for another 18 years, and finally left in 1899. It was at that point that Tom Moore built his own distillery on a 118-acre plot adjacent to the Mattingly Moore operation. The distillery was constructed mostly from wood but –for reasons that will become clear very shortly—the only

thing left of that distillery is some white limestone block work and gold brickwork which was added in the early 1900s. Tom Moore made a few whiskey labels here, including Tom Moore, Dan'l Boone, and Eleven Jones Whiskey. By 1905, Moore was mashing 8 tons of cereal a day and the warehouses held 20,000 barrels. Tom Moore Whiskey became nationally celebrated, with aged expressions in particular helping to establish the brand.

Meanwhile, the Mattingly Moore distillery was struggling, and finally fell into bankruptcy in 1916. Tom Moore was able to buy the distillery, merging it with his own, to create a super-distillery that sat on 196 acres of land. This is the site upon which the Barton 1792 distillery sits today. The distillery ceased production during Prohibition and was handed to Tom's son, Con Moore, in 1934. Tom Moore died in 1937 in Bardstown at the age of 84.

The most popular brands made there in the 1930s was Tom Moore and Kentucky Gentleman (which was a allegedly a nickname that Tom Moore had attracted from the Bardstown locals). Like many distilleries of the time, Tom Moore Distillery was repurposed for making munitions fuel (or "torpedo juice" as Josh puts it—which would be a fantastic name for a whiskey) during World War II. In 1944, Con sold the distillery to a group led by the Chicago whiskey trader named Oscar Getz.

Getz had been a customer of the Tom Moore Distillery, blending together a bourbon that he called "Barton." Once he had acquired the operation, he changed the name to match the brand. As for the origins of Barton, Getz freely admitted that it was completely made up.

Shortly after the Getz deal was done, the entire operation burned to the ground. There's a bit of controversy around the fire, which turned out to be quite beneficial for Getz, since the government issued war bonds that allowed him to rebuild Barton to three times its previous capacity.

Barton Brands changed owners in the latter part of the 20th century, being bought up by the Canandaigua Wine Company, which eventually became Constellation Brands. In the late 2000s,

ABOVE Looking almost divine in the evening twilight, Barton is devoutly committed to making great Kentucky bourbon.

Constellation Brands began focusing more on their wine business and so sold off a lot of their distilled spirits portfolio. That's when the Sazerac Company, the present owner, came along in 2009 and snatched up Barton.

Sazerac were more interested in the brands than the property. As Josh puts it, "the Sazerac MO is to take value brands and make them big." The deal doubled the size of their company though, and landed them with a historical distillery in the heart of the "Bourbon Capital of the World." The Barton distillery was closed down but Sazerac started shifting barrels over from the highly productive Buffalo Trace distillery.

The purchase also included the Glenmore distillery in Owensboro, Kentucky. Glenmore was founded by James Thompson, a Northern Irish immigrant who came to America in 1871, aged 16. Like many of the big names in Kentucky whiskey, he made his money as a whiskey wholesaler, at one time working alongside his cousin, George Garvin Brown (see page 191). In 1901, Thompson paid $30,000 for the failing Monarch Distillery on Owensboro's Ohio River banks. The distillery had already been known as

Glenmore prior to Thompson's purchase, but historians would later attribute the name change to Thompson on account of his Northern Irish heritage. As for the real reason why Glenmore was chosen… well, probably because it sounded Scottish and because Scotch whiskey was enjoying a boom time in the 1890s. James' sons, Frank and James P. Thompson took over the running of the distillery during World War I and through Prohibition.

⁕⁕⁕

It's evening by the time we arrive at Barton. Not that it makes much difference, because like most distilleries around here, it's operating 24 hours a day. The private road that cuts a line through the center of the distillery buildings used to be the main Bardstown thoroughfare, called the Bardstown Green River Parkway. The massive distillery buildings are intimidating in the evening light. They're so dark and so large that they could almost be the night sky, but with just enough contour visible for your mind to recognize the abnormality.

Josh Hollifield is the man who greets us. His official job title is "Distillery Visitor Manager" but we soon come to realize that he's an expert in many areas, including the whiskey-making process at Barton, but also as a chronicler of Bardstown.

Barton is one of the few distilleries that still runs on coal. Well, not exclusively coal, but one of the three boilers that power everything here is fuelled by coal, the other two by natural gas. The coal boiler was installed in the 1960s and munches through 50 tons a day.

"If it ever breaks down," says Josh "the EPA (Environmental Protection Agency) probably won't let us replace it."

The distillery runs a total of six mash bills: straight corn, straight rye, wheated bourbon, and three variations of bourbon with rye as the flavor grain. Corn is sourced almost exclusively from Kentucky and

there are trucks arriving every few hours. Josh contextualizes it in acres: "thirty acres a day."

The trucks are weighed when they arrive and when they leave to calculate the weight of cereals that has been deposited. This is a system that's consistent with all large distilleries. Most distilleries will test a sample of the cereal too, to check its water content. Anything above 14% water content is bad, because the grain is more likely to spoil through mold or bacterial infection, but also because water itself has no value. The difference between 45 tons of 12% water corn and 14% water corn is nearly a ton of water, but its water sold at corn prices.

After milling, the grains are sent to one of two 13,000-gallon mash cookers. In most bourbon distilleries, the non-malt cereals (corn, rye, wheat)

TOP LEFT The water tower at Barton, which sits just above their doubler, which is located outside.
ABOVE The doubler isn't the only thing outside. Two-thirds of each fermenter is situated outside the distillery building.

TOP RIGHT Deer roam the grounds, especially in the quiet area around the warehouses.
ABOVE The Barton operation is a mash-up of mid-century and modern technology working in parallel.

are cooked first to gelatinize the starch and make it more soluble in water. This speeds up the enzymatic digestion of the starch once the malt is added. Each cereal type tends to prefer a certain temperature of cook to achieve this. Corn likes to boiled, which causes the starch to swell irreversibly, breaking hydrogen bonds, and causing no end of disruption to the starch matrix. Some distilleries, like Four Roses, do this in a massive pressure-cooker, which can heat the mash up to over 130°C/266°F, dramatically speeding up the process. Rye tends to be added next, at around 78°C/172.4°F. Adding rye at higher temperatures can make the mash turn gluey. Malted barley and wheat are added around 65°C/149°F— any hotter and the enzymes in the barley become denatured. The whole thing is a bit like making a casserole, where all the different ingredients must be cooked to different temperatures and times for the best results.

Unlike most bourbon distilleries, Barton cook their corn and rye together at the beginning of the mash. Barton's logic behind adding rye in at high temperature is purely one of flavor: "We're trying to extract as much flavor from the rye grain as possible," says Josh.

Mashing takes around three hours: 90 minutes to heat it up and 90 minutes to cool it back down again. A lot of the equipment here has some age on it, which is contrasted by computer screens here and there. Barton underwent a significant upgrade back in 2015, which included installation of various autonomous gadgets. Now the entire operation besides mashing can be run by a single person in front of a computer screen.

The distillery has accumulated a total of 17 fermenters over the years, each of them 50,000 gallons. Fermentation takes around 4 days and results in a beer of between nine and 12% alcohol. Interestingly, Barton has three fermenters located outside of the main building. They will undoubtedly produce a unique style of ferment that will change through the seasons.

The still house is home to four enormous columns, but three of them are legacy items from a time when the distillery produced neutral grain spirits in the 1980s. The still that is operational is a monster though—six feet in diameter and five stories high.

"Our still is bigger than Buffalo Trace," says Josh, "but it runs slower. At Buffalo the column is just stripping the beer and the rectification is done in the doubler. Here, we have a copper top to the still, which cleans the spirit of impurities before it reaches the doubler."

It's for that reason that the Barton still needs to be run slower than the likes of Buffalo Trace, so that the copper can do its job. After the column, the spirit goes into a stainless steel doubler, which, unusually, is located on the roof of the building, like a water tower. After passing through the doubler, the spirit increases its strength by about 10% and flows off there at 70% ABV. The spirit is cut down to the maximum-permitted filling strength of 62.5% before entering the barrel. This distillery fills between 700 and 900 barrels a day.

We hop in the car and drive over to tour one of the warehouses. It's proper nighttime by this point as we wind along the service roads. The domineering silhouettes of warehouses pass us by, marked by a lone spotlight lighting their doorway and number. As we pass a knoll we're stopped in our tracks. Three wild deer are stood on top of it, so still that they appear not to be real.

Josh takes us in to what he describes as "one of the largest whiskey aging buildings in the world." It used to be the packaging and distribution center, but now it holds 80,000 barrels of whiskey. Here, the whiskey is palletized, so the casks are stood upright on pallets and can therefore be carted around the place by fork-lift. Lights switch on automatically as we venture in to the cavernous space, illuminating row upon row of barrels (and perhaps the Ark of the Covenant?!). Being a bourbon maker, the barrels are mostly of the American oak variety, but I spot casks from other industries too: port, sherry, pinot noir, rum, and Madeira, for example.

By this point it's become clear to me that Barton is a special place, and yet it doesn't garner the romantic fixation that distilleries like Buffalo Trace and

ABOVE Palletized warehousing is a more modern method of whiskey storage, which allows for the speedier movement of barrels around the place.

Woodford Reserve do. It's one of the best-kept secrets in Kentucky (and I hope it stays that way!).

Whether it's the coal-powered boiler, unique mashing process, a doubler that sits on the roof, or an aircraft hangar full of whiskey, Barton is doing things a little differently. But there's one more surprise this place has in store: the dryer house.

Distilleries produce enormous amounts of waste that can't simply be loaded into the sewage system. Most distilleries have to pay farmers to come and take it away. A dryer house flips this on its head though, allowing distillers to charge a premium for their waste. The Barton dryer house was installed in the 1940s, shortly after the fire, and it's still functional to this day. The process involves separating the spent grains from the liquid then running them through a centrifuge to dry out. The liquid meanwhile is evaporated to reduce it down to a syrup. Then the dried grains and syrup are mixed back together to form little balls of nutritious animal feed. Apparently there's so much protein in these tasty nuggets that farmers have to cut it back with other feed to stop the cows from bulking up too much.

The original dryer house was becoming a huge maintenance burden so was decommissioned in 2018 and a new one fitted. The plan is to convert the old one into a new visitor's experience, but first someone needs to go around and map the hundreds of pipes that run between the steam boilers and dryers to work out what's needed and what can be torn down.

VERY OLD BARTON (40% ABV)

Red apple, nutmeg, and slightly spirit-y on the nose. Vanilla and apple turnover on the palate followed by nutmeg, mace, and more apple sauce.

1792 SWEET WHEAT (45.6% ABV)

Apple oatmeal, green grape, and ginger on the nose. It's light and slightly hot but quite pleasant on the palate. A touch of piquancy and slightly hollow feeling to finish.

HIGH-RYE BOURBON (47.15% ABV)

There's a slight engine oil aroma, with hard-working grease, pecan, and flaxseed. Dried mango follows. It hums on the palate: spicy and tight. Tasty.

FULL PROOF (62.5% ABV)

The aroma is wine-y elegance, intense, fresh paint, and leather armchair. The taste is concentrated, with a prickly heat. A long finish follows.

ROAD TRIP PLAYLIST

"Jack & Diane" – John Mellencamp

"Moon Over Bourbon Street" – Sting

TURBO WHISKEY SOUR

50 ml/1⅔ oz Very Old Barton Bourbon
20 ml/⅔ oz lemon juice
10 ml/2 teaspoons Barrel Syrup (see below)
½ an egg white

Shake the ingredients with plenty of cubed ice then strain into a chilled rocks glass (no ice).
Garnish with a strip of orange zest.

BARREL SYRUP

100 g/3½ oz dried banana chips
100 g/3½ oz desiccated/shredded coconut
500 g/17 oz water
20 g/⅔ oz roasted carob powder
200 g/7 oz caster/granulated sugar
20 g/⅔ oz maple syrup
5 g/1 teaspoon vanilla extract
50 ml/1⅔ oz Very Old Barton Bourbon

Blend the banana chips and coconut, then add to a saucepan with the water and carob powder. Heat to a boil then remove from the heat and strain through a paper coffee filter. Add the sugar, maple syrup, and vanilla extract, along with the bourbon, which will help to extend the life of your syrup. Store in the fridge.
The recipe makes approximately 500 ml/17 oz.

For a subtle twist on a sour, I like to modify the sugar syrup component, introducing flavors that pair with the bourbon and highlight certain subtleties that might normally be suppressed by the lemon juice. It's easy to make most flavored syrups by brewing ingredients in boiling water like you're making a pot of tea, then straining and sweetening at a ratio of two parts sugar to one part infused water (it's easiest to use kitchen scales for this).

This recipe uses a handful of ingredients that feature in my tasting notes for bourbons and are therefore designed to complement its flavor.

MAKER'S MARK

MEETING THE MAKERS

*"Hugo, I don't much care for your law, but, by golly,
this bourbon is good."*

HARRY S. TRUMAN (1884–1972), 33RD PRESIDENT OF THE UNITED STATES

Tailor William (T.W.) Samuels inherited the distilling bug from his father when he established the family's first commercial distillery in 1844. He was actually a third-generation distiller, being the grandson of Robert Samuels Jr., a Revolutionary War veteran who ran a domestic distillery and served as a captain in the Cumberland County militia (a combination of professions that led to George Washington commissioning him to make whiskey for the army). Robert had three children: James, William, and Robert, Jr., and it was William that sired T.W.

Like his father, T.W. was the Nelson County Sheriff, and like his grandfather, he was a bit of a war hero. On July 26, 1865, Quantrill's Raiders, a group of pro-Confederate rogue guerrillas, took refuge in the house of T.W. Samuels in their namesake hamlet of Samuels Depot (not far from the present-day Jim Beam Distillery). Among their gang members was Frank James, elder brother of Jesse James, who was also a member of the group. In fact, the reason the group were in Samuels Depot in the first place was because Frank James's mother had married Dr. Reuben Samuel, a cousin of T.W. Samuels. After a late-night chat in the kitchen, the Quantrill's Raiders surrendered the porch of the family's general store. This story is corroborated by

PREVIOUS PAGES We're in the heart of Kentucky's beautiful Bluegrass region. Nothing to see here, people.

Frank James's .36-caliber revolver, which was handed over to T.W.'s wife Ora, and can be seen on display at Maker's Mark Distillery.

The Raiders received pardons and went down in history as the last Confederate soldiers to surrender in the American Civil War. A year after the war ended, Frank and Jesse James stole $17,000 from a bank in Russellville, Kentucky – their first bank robbery and not their last.

Meanwhile, T.W. Samuels got busy making whiskey. They relocated the distillery when the business was almost 50 years old, and by then, the Samuels family had amassed a cache of 8,000 barrels. William Isaac Samuels (T.W.'s son) had also joined the business and bought himself a house next-door to the Beams in Bardstown. Their most popular brands were the top-selling Old Deatsville and T. W. Samuels bottles, which carried the memorable slogan "There's a barrel of satisfaction in every bottle."

Tragically, in 1898, both T.W. and William Samuels passed away within months of each other. The distillery passed on to William's son, Lesley Samuels, who was at one time the mayor of Bardstown and the first State highway minister. Unfortunately, the distillery burned down in 1909 (you may have noticed this used to happen quite a lot), levelling all six warehouses and burning $100,000 worth of booze. Following that little incident, Lesley sold the distillery and its brand interest to the Star Distillery

Co. of Cincinnati, who had been a wholesale customer for some years. Prohibition shut down the operation, but when it was repealed in 1933, Leslie Samuels was already ahead of the game and had begun building a new distillery in Deatsville, about a mile up the road from the old family farm. This new distillery could process 40 tons of corn a day and had warehouses capable of storing 19,000 barrels of whiskey. It was around this time that Lesley's son, T.W. "Bill" Samuels, came on board as the master distiller. Bill petitioned his father to let him make a more modern, smoother-tasting bourbon, to which conservative Lesley said "no."s

Following Lesley's death in 1936, Bill ran the distillery for a further seven years, until pressures (including the government, who fancied the T.W. Samuels Distillery for making torpedo propellant) forced him to sell the distillery to a New York-based company. The quality of whiskey made there quickly deteriorated and the distillery closed in the early 1950s. These days, the warehouses at the Deatsville site, which are architecturally quite unusual, are used to house Heaven Hill whiskeys.

After six generations, the line of Samuels distillers seemed to have come to an end. Bill went off and served in the US Navy for three years. Then he returned home. And then he became restless. Which made his wife, Margie, very restless too. We'll get to what happened next very shortly. First, let me tell you another story:

Back around the time that Bill Samuels's great-great-grandfather was learning how to make whiskey on his dad's 60-gallon still, around ten miles away, in the area known as Hardin's Creek, Charles Burks built a gristmill and distillery. The year was 1805. Although Burks died in 1831, his family kept the 200-acre operation going. In 1878, George Burks joined the company and began to rebuild the facility, adding a bottling house and a manager's residence. Prohibition forced their descendants to shut down and leave. But the compound of 10 buildings that they put up in the 1880s was left intact.

In 1953 Bill Samuels bought the Burks Spring Distillery near Hardin's Creek for $35,000 and the

following year he distilled whiskey there. The motivation was allegedly born out of Margie's need to get Bill out of the house. "She said 'I don't care what you do,'" Maker's Mark's Education Manager Alex Bowie recounts, "'I just need you out of the house in the daytime.'"

One of the first things Bill did, in a truly theatrical display, was to burn all of the old whiskey recipes that had been handed down through the family. This ceremony was conducted in front of the Samuels family as Bill declared, "We will start from scratch!" The dramatic effect was lessened slightly when the drapes caught on fire.

Bill developed a new mash bill for his whiskey in a rather unconventional but fiendishly clever way. He made bread. Experimenting with every type of corn, rye, wheat, and barley combination, the mash bill he eventually settled on was the one that made the tastiest bread. Comparing whiskey to bread makes more sense than you might think. If you can imagine the difference between a light wheat bread and a dark rye bread, then you're some way towards understanding how these cereals impact liquor, too.

Bill renamed the distillery Star Hill Farm and employed Elmo Beam, the eldest son of Joe Beam, as the first master distiller. The Samuels knew him from the days of the old T. W. Samuels Distillery and he came out of retirement to make what they were at the time calling "Old Samuels". Elmo Beam died on April 5, 1955.

The idea of calling the whiskey Old Samuels died pretty soon after. The Samuels name had been sold with the distilleries, so Bill needed to think of a new name for his new whiskey.

He had time to think though.

Like many of today's new distilleries, Samuels sourced whiskey to bring in some cash and to start building relationships with distributors and retailers. Some of it came from what is now Beam's Booker Noe Distillery, then owned by Barton.

The name Maker's Mark came from Margie Samuels, who, to be frank, probably contributed more to the brand than even Bill Sr. did. Besides coming up with the name, which derived from her love of English pewter (which is stamped with the mark of the maker), Margie also designed the typography on the label, selected the paper, chose the square-shaped bottle, and came up with the idea of dipping it in red wax—something she borrowed from the Cognac industry. This started in the home kitchen, where Margie hand-dipped the first bottles using a home fryer to melt the wax. Margie's fried chicken was never quite the same, and neither was the whiskey business.

Those distinctive long ribbons of wax that run down the neck of the bottle are now protected by U.S. trademark 73526578. Registered in 1985, the trademark description reads, "The mark consists of a wax-like coating covering the cap of the bottle and tickling down the neck of the bottle in a freeform irregular pattern."

The literal maker's mark for Maker's Mark Whiskey is a star, to represent Star Hill Farm, an "S" for the family name, and a "IV" to signify the fourth generation since T.W. Samuels. I'll confess that I hadn't noticed the mark formed into the front of the bottle and on every label of Maker's Mark until someone pointed it out to me. Now it's the first thing I look at.

In 1975, Bill Samuels Jr. and Margie Samuels took over the running of the company. The only words of advice from Bill Sr. were: "Don't screw up the whisky." In time, Bill Jr's own son, Rob Samuels, joined the team too. Rob has the privilege of being able to refer to himself as an eight-generation distiller, and in his official capacity as Chief Distillery Officer, he is unofficially tasked with not "screwing up the whisky".

It's this sense of preservation that seems to permeate the entire Maker's Mark operation. "We are control freaks," says Alex. "We're trying to manage every stage of production to keep things exactly the same. If Bill Samuels Sr. did it in 1953, there's a good chance we're doing it the same way today."

New employees at Maker's Mark receive two things on their first day on the job. The first is a bottle of Maker's Mark. The second is an instruction: "Don't f**k this up!"

ABOVE The tranquil setting of Star Hill Farm belies the huge volumes of whiskey that Maker's Mark turn out annually.

As we walk down the pathway into the distillery grounds, we pass a small hut on the left. Alex waves a hand toward it without breaking stride, "that is the oldest licensed package liquor store in the country." It turns out there used to be a road running through the distillery, so it may be the oldest drive-thru in the country too.

The water used by master distiller Denny Potter comes from a 52-million-gallon spring-fed lake, perched up on the hills adjacent to the distillery. A reliable water source is of course essential, but it brings with it some issues. For instance, the distillery has to stock the lake with algae-eating fish to help prevent the growth of the chemical compound geosmin, which is a non-toxic but organic compound with a musty taste and odor.

"We don't change the mineral content or filter," says Alex, "we bring [the lake water] straight into a tank, preheat it with steam and then it goes on to the cooker."

If you want complete control of a lake though, you need to manage the entire ecosystem around it. That's why Maker's bought up all the land surrounding the lake too, guaranteeing the watershed contains no fertilizers, pesticides, or cow poo. Maker's Mark even employ someone to manage this area, with the job title "Environmental Champion."

Interestingly, that same lake used to generate power for the distillery. Prior to 1943 there was no electricity there, and a small steam engine powered everything. In 1943, the lake was constructed above the distillery and the line from it to the distillery delivered enough static pressure to operate the cooling coils.

The mash bill of Maker's Mark is made of 70% corn, 16% soft winter wheat, and 14% malted barley. That was all they made here until a few years ago, when a separate bourbon mash bill was introduced containing rye. That product was launched in Spring 2019.

The use of wheat was of course a Bill Samuels Jr. innovation and has been something that's gone on to define the product. The distillery uses a roller mill that crushes the grain between two big rolling cylinders. The roller mill has the advantage over the typical hammer mill that you find in most bourbon distilleries, in that it can be set to a very precise width and therefore defines the coarseness of the grist exactly.

There are eight original cypress-wood fermenters at Maker's Mark, which is more in the style of a traditional Scotch malt whisky distillery. They date

TOP LEFT Sample vials of whiskey, which are not for drinking but for analysis in the lab using gas chromatography.
ABOVE LEFT Oak treatments that Maker's Mark use for Maker's 46 and Private Select programs.
LEFT A Maker's Mark bottle without its trademark (literally) wax-dipped cap looks strangely naked.
ABOVE Maker's Mark may be big, but with these hand-printed labels, it's difficult to argue it isn't "craft".

back to the late 19th century, but have since been joined by a further 56 steel fermenters, which are the same shape and size as the original wood ones. Fermentation takes about three days. The "Samuels" yeast strain is the same yeast that Bill Samuels introduced in 1953.

The stills at Maker's are 100% copper and slightly shorter than normal. They contain 16 plates and, at the top, something called a "disc and donut." This device replaces the bubble plates that sit at the top of most beer-stripping columns. It's basically a 17th plate, comprising a small central hole with a large disc suspended above it. Its purpose is to stop spirit vapor from shooting up to the top of the still. The absence of plates with "bubble caps" is simply down to the all-copper design, which strips out heavier compounds at every stage. The result is a medium-to-light spirit with good structure on the palate. The spirit comes off the stripping column at 120 proof.

That's quite a low-strength spirit, and so too is the barrel entry proof: 110 proof. This means less water is needed before distillation and after maturation, preserving the character of the ferment. There are four old warehouses up on the hill next to the lake, but those hills make further construction of warehousing quite tricky. So the vast majority of Maker's Mark is matured in 20 huge warehouses on the other side of the nearby town of Loretto.

It took until 2009 for Maker's Mark for launch their second expression: Maker's 46. The idea behind Maker's 46 was "Maker's on steroids" and this was achieved by double-maturing Maker's Mark in re-fill bourbon barrels with 10 toasted French oak staves suspended inside them. The distillery even has a coopering area that was purpose-built for it. Production of 46 then inspired their single barrel program, called Private Select.

This program was developed by Alex's wife, Jane Bowie, who is the current master blender at Maker's Mark. "We take a fully mature Maker's Mark then put it in a new barrel," says Jane, "then we insert ten staves in the barrel, from a selection of five types or treatments of wood. This gives us 1,001 different stave combinations."

These staves are sourced from both France and America then toasted to varying degrees using infra-red or convective heat. Each type of stave imparts unique flavors into the spirit based on its toast level and origin. The staves are all assigned a delicious sounding esoteric name like "Seared French Cuvée" and "Roasted French Mocha". The staves for Maker's 46 and Private Select are thinner than regular barrel staves, and some of them have ridges cut into them too, to increase surface area and speed up the infusion process.

For Private Select, the finishing process takes just nine weeks, but the results can be clearly tasted. Customers are invited to come and taste from a library of hundreds of samples of pre-finished whiskeys, then based on their preferences, they get their own cask loaded with the appropriate combination of staves. A few months later the process is complete and you're the proud owner of 240 bottles of Maker's Mark.

"We've never entered our spirits into spirits competitions," says Alex, "but some of our single barrel customers have won awards with the whiskey they made here."

I think this is one of the shrewdest single-barrel programs around (Maker's Mark are not alone in offering services like this): essentially charging customers upfront to run experiments on their behalf. It's customer funded R&D, which is still very much necessary when it comes to mystical art of maturation. "As an industry, we're only just scratching the surface on wood," says Alex. "We're learning more about it all the time. Things we thought we knew a year ago, we're now finding out are simply not true."

Perhaps the most recognized element of the Maker's brand is that trademark splurge of red wax on the neck of every bottle. This is applied by a team of four who, with the dexterity of ninjas, lift, dip, and roll the bottles on a relentless conveyor belt. A few years ago, a machine was installed to complete this task, but the bottles lost the "handmade" look. The machine was promptly uninstalled.

Walking around the village that is the Maker's Mark distillery, it occurs to me that it is the epitome of what every craft distillery wants to be — big, but retaining authenticity. So many of the working practices here would, under normal circumstances, have been phased out by the accountants for their high cost or inefficiency. But Maker's are either careless of profit margins or deeply respectful that attention to detail comes at a cost, and that it's a cost that's worth putting up with if quality is to be preserved. In the 1970s, Maker's ran the advertising tagline, "It tastes expensive ... and is."

Take the labels, for example. Any normal distillery would simply order up a batch of labels from the printer and store them ready for use. Not at Maker's Mark. Here they have a small outbuilding with a single operator who prints every single label using a vintage mechanical printing press. Why do this? It would certainly be cheaper and easier to outsource label printing, not to mention easier to create new designs and change old ones. But cheaper and easier don't seem to be factors that are considered here. And when you strip away cheaper and easier you can begin to make decisions that improve the product rather than limiting it.

Although the captions of "hand crafted" and "family run" are entirely deserved, Maker's hasn't been in family ownership for nearly 40 years. Canadian company Hiram Walker bought the distillery and brand in 1981, and through a series of mergers and acquisitions, the company ended up in the hands of Illinois-based Fortune Brands in 2011. The spirits division of that company was then snapped up by Beam Inc., later becoming Beam Suntory. So as it stands, Maker's Mark and Jim Beam are siblings.

MAKER'S WHITE (45% ABV)

A warm hay and stale, cut-grass aroma greets you. Sweet and cereal on the palate. Touch of orange cream soda appearing on the nose. Granddad's old wardrobe.

MAKER'S MARK (45% ABV)

Typical bourbon characteristics of butterscotch, vanilla, and coconut, are joined by baking spices and candied citrus zests. The taste is indeed smooth, thanks to the wheat, which gives a clean style that's easily affected by the oak and soft spice flavors of the barrel. Finish is relatively quick but pleasant.

MAKER'S 46 (47% ABV)

Big top notes of glue and gasoline quickly give way to cherry and almond cake. The taste is far softer than the nose suggests: clean and fruity with gentle wood spice complementing soft mint and herbal notes. The finish is clean, like fresh laundry dumped in a barrel.

ROAD TRIP PLAYLIST

"Everyday is a Winding Road" – Sheryl Crow

"Life's Been Good" – Joe Walsh

"The Weight" – The Band

LEFT The bottle archive from Maker's Mark Private Select program. Every bottle represents a unique barrel, and therefore every bottle is different.

WHISKEY SMASH

10 mint leaves
60 ml/2 oz Maker's Mark
20 ml/⅔ oz lemon juice
10 ml/2 teaspoons gomme

Drop the mint into the base of a cocktail shaker and give it a gentle brushing with a muddler or rolling pin. This helps to liberate some of the oils. Be sure not to crush the mint, as it can release bitter, chlorophyll notes.

Add the rest of the ingredients, followed by some cubed ice. Shake well, then strain into a rocks glass filled with ice. Garnish with a slice of lemon and a mint sprig.

This drink sits somewhere between a Whiskey Sour and a Julep, combining mint, citrus, and a little sugar into the same glass. Oh, and bourbon. Always bourbon.

It was created by one of the living legends of the bartending world, Dale DeGroff, the man who also had a hand in creating the Cosmopolitan. This drink featured on the end of New York's Rainbow Room back in 1998, while Dale was working there.

The recipe is simple and delicious, so like most drinks that earn that description, it's much open to customization: top up with soda and you basically have a bourbon mojito. Switch the sugar for maple syrup, honey, or brown sugar syrup and you get something a little more indulgent. Trade the mint for another herb (thyme and basil both work well) and you have yourself yet another variation.

BROWN–FORMAN

DOCTOR'S ORDERS

"Whiskey is by far the most popular of all remedies that won't cure a cold."

JERRY VALE (1930–2014), ACTOR AND SINGER

The period between the Civil War and the turn of the 20th century was a time of huge industrial transition and economic growth for the United States. Steam and electricity replaced human muscle, iron replaced wood, and steel replaced iron. Products that were previously moved by boat or cart were now loaded on to trains, and by 1900 there were 193,000 miles or railroad traversing the nation.

Prior to the Civil War, it took about 60 hours of labor to produce an acre of cereal. By 1900, it took under four. Steam, created from burning coal, drove the next generation of mechanized farm machinery. But these advances in efficiency and the advent of the railroad demanded investment on behalf of the farmer, which most of the time wasn't possible. Many borrowed money from either the bank, hoping for good harvests to pay back the bank loan, the railroad (which was owned by the bank), or the broker who was handling their whiskey and cereals. The prices of both the commodity and the overheads were set by the monopolist railroad and banker/broker however, so they could set whatever prices they liked. Most farmers were unable to pay their debts, so sold up and either became tenants on their own property or gave up altogether and emigrated to the city. This contraction in the market made big distilleries even bigger and led to big companies buying big distilleries.

No place in Kentucky embodied the new industrial era of distilling like the Louisville suburb of Shively

(Shy-vlee). And what Shively lacked (and lacks) in beauty, it makes up for in distilling history. Following the end of Prohibition in 1933, eight distilleries opened in the area, which was known at the time as St. Helens. Given the volume of whiskey it produced, the city of Louisville ended up annexing the lucrative St. Helens area, so that it could tax the businesses there. Rather than let that happen, the residents incorporated the area, including all of the distilleries, and became part of an extended Shively. Some of the biggest names and most important individuals in bourbon history came out of this area. Some built state-of-the-art distilleries or made innovations in their liquid products, while others became the original whiskey marketeers. It's worth taking a quick tour around Shively to explore their stories...

Just up the road towards Louisville proper is the enormous Bernheim distillery, which was the first Kentucky distillery we visited on our journey. Prior to Prohibition, this place was run by Isaac Wolfe Bernheim, a German-Jewish immigrant who, so the story goes, arrived in the US in 1867 with only $4 in his pocket.

Bernheim was later joined by his brother, Bernard, and the pair launched the I.W. Harper brand of bourbon whiskey. Issac took the brand's initials from his own name, and the Harper came from... well, actually nobody is sure about that one. The pair invested in a distillery called Pleasure Ridge Park in

1890, located a few miles out of Louisville. When that one burned down six years later, they built a brand-new distillery in Shively. The brothers divested from the business over the years that followed, correctly anticipating Prohibition. The Canadian company Schenley Co. acquired the business after Prohibition. Various mergers and acquisitions took place after that, until Heaven Hill finally acquired it in 1999.

One Shively distillery that ceased operations in 1983 but at the time of its opening was claimed to be "the largest in the world" is the old Seagrams (or Kessler) Distillery. It was built between 1933 and 1936 for the production of neutral spirits, but also made bourbon whiskey. The build was undertaken by Distillers Corporation Limited, who acquired Joseph E. Seagram & Sons (later renamed The Seagram Company Ltd.) in 1928. The Art Deco brick warehouses here included a system of underground tunnels, so that barrels could be moved around the complex without being seen by the public.

The Frankfort Distillery, although named after the town of Frankfort, was actually built in Shively following the repeal of Prohibition. The original Frankfort Distillery was based in Frankfort itself and was bought by Paul Jones & Co. (of Four Roses fame) to make medicinal whiskey, but the distillery had closed by the end of Prohibition. The architect of the new Shively distillery, Carl J. Epping, described it as, "the last word in modern distillery construction." This was another distillery that Seagram's later acquired.

Confused yet? You will be...

After their Frankfort operation closed, the Frankfort Distilling Company bought medicinal whiskey from another distillery on Main Street in Louisville, called A. Ph. Stitzel. This distillery was originally founded by the Stitzel Brothers, Arthur and Frederick. Although it was Arthur's name on the sign above the door, it was arguably Frederick who contributed the most to the whiskey industry. He was the man who developed and patented the barrel "ricking" system that's still used to store and organize barrels today.

Prior to Prohibition, the Stitzels sold a lot of whiskey to a wholesaler called W.L. Weller and Sons. William Larue Weller established his Louisville business shortly after he returned from the Mexican-American War, in 1849. He is often credited as the inventor of "wheated" whiskey: a bourbon-style mash bill with wheat instead of rye. Perhaps his greatest move, however, was to employ a 19-year-old salesman by the name of Julian Procter Van Winkle. Van Winkle would go on to run the Weller company, eventually partnering with Arthur Stitzel to form a new company called Stitzel-Weller. The combined might of a sales legend and whiskey-making genius allowed the new company to market numerous brands, including Old Fitzgerald, Old W.L. Weller, and Old Rip Van Winkle. Stitzel-Weller marketed whiskeys as being "made the old fashioned way," which meant pot stills and low barrel entry proof. They also made exclusively wheated bourbons—true to the Weller way.

When Prohibition came along, Van Winkle—who was now 45 and beginning to be known as "Pappy"—was able to piggyback on A. Ph. Stitzel's medicinal license, allowing Stitzel-Weller to continue to bottle spirits for the many sick people across the nation. Following repeal, the company opened a new distillery in Shively, which is historically known as the Stitzel-Weller distillery but was known popularly as the Old Fitzgerald Distillery.

Stitzel-Weller ceased operations in 1972, but re-opened—sort of—as the Bulleit Bourbon Frontier Whiskey Experience in 2014. Bulleit, a brand launched by Seagram's in 1997 but driven largely by Diageo since 2000, has been contract-distilled at the Four Roses distillery for most of its existence. The brand was in need of a visitor's center however, and the old Stitzel-Weller distillery was the perfect place (or would have been if the whiskey was actually made there). As of 2017, Bulleit Bourbon is being distilled at a new distillery in Shelbyville, which is 30 minutes east of Louisville.

Over 100 million whiskey prescriptions were issued during Prohibition, always in standardized one-pint bottles, which were usually packaged in cardboard

ABOVE Looking south across the Ohio, to downtown Louisville and, in the distance, Shively.

and occasionally in tin boxes. It seems bizarre to think that it would be necessary for a government to regulate production of liquor for medical reasons, but whiskey has a far longer history as a medicinal curative than it does a social one. To frontiersmen, for example, whiskey was more than a drink: it was an anesthetic, disinfectant, and either a stimulant or a tranquillizer, depending on the situation and the individual. President Andrew Jackson even advised his old friend John Coffee, who was suffering from arthritis, to bathe himself in whiskey.

Only ten medicinal licenses were authorized by the government during Prohibition, but only six companies applied and obtained one. They were Glenmore, Frankfort Distilling Company, Schenley, A. Ph. Stitzel, American Medicinal Spirits (a government-approved company formed after Prohibition, which had scooped up whiskey from various warehouses), and Brown-Forman.

Let's talk about Brown-Forman.

George Garvin Brown, one the most influential figures in bourbon's history, was born in Munfordville, Kentucky, in 1846. He moved to Louisville to attend high school, where his older half-brother, John Thompson Street Brown, had already established himself as a successful whiskey trader on "Whiskey Row" in downtown Louisville. The block-long stretch from 101–133 W. Main Street in

downtown Louisville was once packed with whiskey traders who would blend and bottle products from nearby distilleries.

George worked for a drug company for a few years, until the Brown brothers joined forces in 1870, forming J.T.S. Brown & Brother Co. They sold Sidroc Bourbon, among various other brands. A couple of years later, George Forman (no, not that one) joined the Brown business, first as a salesman but later working as an accountant.

The following year, Henry Chambers joined the firm. He previously worked in the pharmaceuticals industry and was the man who gave George Brown his first job. Chambers became a major stakeholder in the company, and pretty soon afterwards, John Brown left.

It was around this time that Old Forrester bourbon (one 'r' was later dropped) was introduced. This product was allegedly named for the local celebrity physician William Forrester (although the official line is that it was named for Civil War hero General Nathan Bedford Forrest). As far as historians can tell, Old Forester was the first to trade exclusively in glass bottles, that is, you couldn't buy it any other way. The modern-day Brown-Forman will tell you this was a move that guaranteed product quality, and while that may be partly true, it's likely the real reason for the move was to grow sales in the lucrative "prescription whiskey" market. Most whiskey at the time was sold only in large containers, and by offering their product in small glass bottles it became much easier for physicians to prescribe the whiskey to patients (for all manner of ailments) and to have some assurance of its quality. This marked the beginning of a new era of brand marketing for bourbon producers and brand following for consumers, along with counterfeiting activity by those looking to make a few bucks off the back of a successful bourbon brand.

In 1876, George Brown's cousin, James Thompson joined the firm, which was now called Brown, Chambers & Co. Then a bit more reorganization ensued, wherein Chambers retired and Thompson ran off to open the Glenmore distillery (which we touched upon two chapters ago) leaving Brown and Forman, who formed Brown, Forman & Co. with 90% and 10% of the company respectively. The year was 1890.

Forman died in 1901, and in 1902, the company acquired another distillery owned by Ben Mattingly (of Barton notoriety), called—appropriately—Ben Mattingly Distillery. This distillery became known as the Brown-Forman Distillery Co. and was located in the small village of St Mary's in Marion County, until it burned down in 1919.

George Garvin Brown, who died a couple of years before the fire, is remembered as one of whiskey's greatest advocates. Back in 1894, Brown was elected both the first President of the National Liquor Dealers Association and President of the Wine & Spirits Association, the latter being an organization founded to fight the rising tide of Prohibitionist activity. In 1910, Brown even published a book entitled The Holy Bible Repudiates Prohibition, which basically listed hundreds of bible references that mentioned liquor, "proving that scriptures commend and command the temperate use of alcoholic beverages."

Following George Brown's death, the entire business (including the doomed distillery) was handed to his son, Owsley Brown. Despite the minor setback of not having a distillery, Owsley was able to secure one of the medicinal licenses, and kept the

company afloat during Prohibition by buying up the entire stock of Early Times whiskey. He also moved the company back to Louisville into a government-designated warehouse.

There's a lot of history between Brown-Forman and the city of Louisville. In 1937, intense rainfall caused the Ohio River to flood its banks, so an 1,800-foot floating pontoon bridge was constructed from empty Brown-Forman casks to move people from Jefferson Street to Baxter Avenue and dryer areas in Crescent Hill and the Highlands. Over 75,000 people crossed the makeshift bridge in four days.

Following Prohibition, Brown-Forman bought the old Labrot & Graham distillery (see page 135) and their current distillery in Shively, as well as opening the nearby Bluegrass Cooperage. This business was originally a rifle stock manufacturing company but

today makes 45% of the world's supply of new whiskey barrels. The Bluegrass Cooperage raise around 2,500 casks a day and approximately 90% of them are filled with Jack Daniel's. The rest are used for Early Times, Old Forester, and Woodford Reserve. These barrels once used then go on to other whiskey distilleries around the world, or to tequila and rum makers.

Brown-Forman passed down to the next generation in the 1940s, who made the well-informed decision to purchase the Jack Daniel's Distillery in Lynchburg, Tennessee. From then onwards, sensible further acquisitions turned this family run business into one of the largest American-owned companies in the spirits and wine business, turning over $3 billion in sales.

The Brown-Forman distillery in Shively makes Old Forester Bourbon and Early Times Whiskey. The distillery today is not open to visitors, and has an unashamedly "let's get down to business" feel. It's clean, efficient, functional, and not at all pretty. Old Forester uses a higher rye content mash bill than Early Times, and is aged entirely in new charred oak as opposed to Early Times, which uses some re-fill casks—hence the non-bourbon denomination.

One major point of interest in the distillery is the use a "thumper" instead of a "doubler" (see page 124) for distilling, wherein the alcohol vapors from the beer still are pumped through a small pot-still containing water.

The warehouses on site hold a whopping 320,000 casks, and are split between Early Times, Old Forester, and Woodford Reserve stock. Heat is cycled here using steam, going from 15°C/59°F up to 26°C/78.8°F and back again over the course of eight weeks. The benefit of this is that it improves consistency and avoids stocks at the top getting hotter than those at the bottom. This also means that evaporative losses are more consistent throughout the warehouse and the alcohol content from cask to cask

is consistent too. Secondly, it speeds up certain elements of the maturation process by emulating seasonal effects. It doesn't quite make sense from my end, but Brown-Forman believe the effect can be compared to two complete seasonal rotations in the space of time that it takes to do one (for those struggling to maintain attention, that's a year).

In 2018, Brown-Forman finished construction of a new 70,000-square foot Old Forester distillery in the heart of downtown Louisville, which took three years and the princely sum of $45 million. Located on the site of Brown-Forman's original headquarters (which it vacated in 1922), this distillery has a production capacity of 100,000-proof gallons a year, as well as an on-site cooperage and warehouse space. But like Woodford Reserve (which is also owned by Brown-Forman), this operational distillery functions as a shop window for the brand more than it does a whiskey factory.

EARLY TIMES (40% ABV)

Coconut, cotton candy, and bullets of popcorn appear on the nose. On the palate there's more dark candy in the taste, but it's layered over a backdrop of pipe weed and musty warehouse notes. The finish is sweet and surprisingly long.

OLD FORESTER (43% ABV)

Green apple (which was an aroma that powerfully emanated from the fermenters when I visited previously) is polished with toffee and allspice. There's crème anglaise and vanilla popcorn too, with some more bubblegum rye surfacing after a few sniffs. The taste is spiced and woody, leaving a slick caramel finish. It's the less-refined twin of Woodford Reserve.

ROAD TRIP PLAYLIST

"Down The Road" – The Forester Sisters

"I Wanna Be Sedated" – The Ramones

"Whiskey Is a Medicine" – Tyler Lyle

OPPOSITE ABOVE Old Forester has returned to Louisville's Whiskey Row—the site of the distillery's founding in 1870.
OPPOSITE BELOW The warehouses at Brown-Forman are carefully climate-controlled through pipes in the floor.

GRANDPA'S OLD COUGH MEDICINE

700 ml/24 oz Old Forester
150 g/5¼ oz maple syrup
1 cinnamon stick
5 whole cloves
3 bay leaves

Add all of the ingredients to a sterilized glass bottle and leave to infuse. The flavors will extract slowly over time, and I suggest waiting at least six weeks. You can speed up this process by leaving the bottle in a warm place, or running it through a dishwasher a few times.

One of my favorite pre-Prohibition whiskey adverts came from Walter B. Duffy's Rochester Distillery. He claimed his malt whiskey could cure malaria, "sluggish blood," and "weak women."

Now, I'm unable to promote the medicinal benefits of whiskey without receiving nasty letters, so I won't be doing that. I would, however, still like to proffer a recipe for a medicinal whiskey infusion, purely to satisfy historical intrigue and certainly not to be used as guidance for those wishing to manufacture a curative that might be administered to oneself during periods of sickness.

Whether or not you agree that whiskey can help to cure the common cold or not, few of you will argue that certain choice herbs and spices can alleviate the symptoms. Indeed, liqueurs (which are basically sweetened spirits infused with herbs, fruits, or spices) have their origins tied up in medicine, and it's essentially a liqueur recipe that I offer below.

As for what you choose to infuse, well that's up to you, but certainly warming winter spices are a good place to start. So too are citrus peels, warming herbs (like rosemary and thyme) as well as bitter roots, such as gentian.

Also you may want to consider infusing wood chips into the bottle (maybe taking a lead from Copper Fox owner Rick Wasmund and using toasted fruit woods—see page 19).

MICHTER'S

MAKING THE DREAM A REALITY

"If when you say whiskey you mean the devil's brew, the poison scourge, the bloody monster, that defiles innocence, dethrones reason, destroys the home, creates misery and poverty, yea, literally takes the bread from the mouths of little children; if you mean the evil drink that topples the Christian man and woman from the pinnacle of righteous, gracious living into the bottomless pit of degradation, and despair, and shame and helplessness, and hopelessness, then certainly I am against it.

But; if when you say whiskey you mean the oil of conversation, the philosophic wine, the ale that is consumed when good fellows get together, that puts a song in their hearts and laughter on their lips, and the warm glow of contentment in their eyes; if you mean Christmas cheer; if you mean the stimulating drink that puts the spring in the old gentleman's step on a frosty, crispy morning; if you mean the drink which enables a man to magnify his joy, and his happiness, and to forget, if only for a little while, life's great tragedies, and heartaches, and sorrows; if you mean that drink, the sale of which pours into our treasuries untold millions of dollars, which are used to provide tender care for our little crippled children, our blind, our deaf, our dumb, our pitiful aged and infirm; to build highways and hospitals and schools, then certainly I am for it."

NOAH "SOGGY" SWEAT (1922–96), STATE REPRESENTATIVE FOR MISSISSIPPI

By the late 19th century, Kentucky had become so synonymous with bourbon that traders with questionable ethics would move to Kentucky to sell rectified, un-aged spirits, just so that they could call it Kentucky bourbon. This blatant abuse of the term "bourbon" became the basis of the "What is Whiskey?" debate of 1906. The debate was spurred by the US Congress passing the Pure Food and Drug Act of 1906, which set out to define American whiskey. While the Act was good news for Kentucky distillers, it was bad news for anyone making imitation products (and for imported whiskey). So upset were the producers of these counterfeit whiskeys that they forced the matter into the courts for three years, during which time no solution could be settled upon.

Newly elected President William Howard Taft (in office 1909–13) stepped in at this point and spent six

months reviewing arguments from both sides. From the Kentucky corner he received statements from prominent figures like E. H. Taylor, Jr., Isaac Wolfe Bernheim, and George Garvin Brown. Then, on December 27, 1909, the "Taft Decision" was issued, ruling in favor of the Kentucky distillers, laying out the definitions of what could be defined as "Straight," "Blended," and "Imitation" whisky (all of the records from this time omit the 'e' from whiskey). Taft also defined bourbon as being "made from mash that consists of at least 51% corn (maize)." This makes Taft—in some people's eyes—the father of modern bourbon. And it's for that reason that he was inducted into the Kentucky Bourbon Hall of Fame, just 10 days before the 100-year anniversary of the Taft Decision.

Today, there are 68 distilleries in the state of Kentucky, which represents a 250% increase in the

last decade. These operations are spread across 32 counties, compared to only eight counties in 2009. More than a third of all distilling jobs in the US are in Kentucky, boasting an average salary of $95,000—up 23% since 2009. Between them, they filled a whopping 1.7 million barrels of whiskey last year—more or less one for every Kentucky household—the highest since 1972.

There have only been two amendments to the rules set out in the Taft Decision in the past 110 years, but they're two quite important ones! On July 1, 1938, the Alcohol and Tobacco Tax and Trade Bureau ruled that bourbon whiskey must be aged in "charred new oak cooperage." This piece of legislation occurred at the tail end of the Great Depression, when unemployment was at 25%.

The timber industry was among the hardest hit of the affected industries, but they were highly effective lobbyists. It's thought by many that the decision to force bourbon producers to use new oak barrels was influenced by woodcutters looking to increase jobs and revenue. Since the use of charred new oak casks is arguably the most significant contributor of flavor to the bourbon style, this is a fascinating example of politics and economics steering the course of history in a way that most of us would never imagine.

The second amendment to the rules of bourbon came about in 1964, when Congress declared bourbon "a distinctive product of the United States." The passing of such a bill was certainly driven by a sense of pride and patriotism in America's native spirit, but there was a commercial impetus too. Lewis Rosenstiel, the head of Schenley Distillers at the time, had more barrels of old whiskey then the rest of the entire industry combined. In fact, he had way too much. Supply far outstripped demand and it looked as though Schenley would be forced to sell whiskey at a loss if something didn't change quickly. So Rosenstiel poured $35 million into a global advertising campaign and sent promotional cases of bourbon to US embassies around the world. His competitors followed suit, stirring up bourbon hysteria in all the right places. A few years later Rosenstiel retired as one of the richest men in America.

Our next stop is Michter's Shively distillery, which is only a short drive from Early Times: "Back on to the Dixie Highway, head north a few blocks, then hang a right," were the directions we received. This is a new distillery, nestled into the railway tracks (another reason why Shively became an industrial hub) on the other side of which is the old Seagram's Distillery.

A new distillery it may be, but the brand goes back a bit further (and the story of its founding even further still). The Michter's brand was originally created by Lou Forman in the 1950s. He was an advertising executive, who had a share in an old distillery in Schaefferstown, Pennsylvania. The name Michter's came as a result of a portmanteau of the names of his two sons: Michael and Peter.

Now when I say "old distillery," I really do mean old distillery. Schaefferstown was, like much of Pennsylvania, settled by German immigrants in the early 18th century. One group of Germans who were particularly partial to settling these parts were the Mennonite Christians, who were escaping sectarian prejudice in Europe. John Shenk and his brother Michael settled on Snitzel Creek near present day Schaefferstown and he built a distillery in 1753. Handed down within the Shenk family for more than a century, it was sold to Abraham Bomberger in 1860. He was a Shenk-descendant through his mother, Elizabeth Shenk Bomberger. Bomberger transformed the distillery from a shed on a farm into a full-scale commercial operation. The distillery enjoyed some success (at one time marketing something called "Pure Rye Rum") but like most of its contemporaries, it discontinued production during Prohibition.

The distillery changed hands a few times following Repeal, but managed to teeter precariously on the edge of financial ruin through each of its tenancies. Then Lou Forman came along and launched Michter's, which became the name the distillery adopted in 1975.

This was at the beginning of a downturn in bourbon sales, and by the 1980s, production had shrunk to just a single barrel a day. Michter's hobbled along until 1989, when the government threatened to take action for missed mortgage payments and around $180,000 in unpaid taxes. The company filed for bankruptcy and abandoned the distillery in 1990, leaving stills, equipment, documents, personal belongings, and about 40,000 barrels of whiskey. Lebanon County officials seized the property but struggled to keep looters at bay. Much of the whiskey ended up being re-distilled into industrial ethanol!

Flash forward a few years and Joe Magliocco, a former Michter's sales rep in the 1980s, is now the president of Chatham Imports, a New York-based supplier of wines and spirits. He teamed up with his mentor Dick Newman, former President of Austin Nichols (the originators of Wild Turkey) and acquired the abandoned Michter's trademark. Intent on reinstating the brand, Joe sourced whiskeys from various Kentucky distilleries, on the hunt for the style of whiskey that he wanted Michter's to be. Working backwards, he could then formulate a recipe (since he had only acquired the trademark for the brand, not the business assets, so he had no recipe to work from).

By this point, he seemed to be on a roll, and the dream was becoming a reality. Now all he had to do was raise enough money to build a full-scale distillery. Seeing as distilleries aren't cheap to build, Joe hedged his bets, and in 2003, he began buying contract-distilled spirits from an undisclosed Kentucky producer. Michter's are keen to emphasize that their involvement with the contract distiller went beyond the normal "send me some six year old bourbon" sort of relationship.

"We were the chef in someone else's kitchen," says Michter's John Shutt. "We knew how to cook, we just didn't have a kitchen yet." This arrangement meant commissioning mash bills and managing whiskey stocks, then identifying good casks and monitoring their progress.

And for ten years it all worked out rather well for the brand, allowing them to develop cult status among bartenders and whiskey aficionados, and to sell rather a lot of whiskey. The Michter's packaging has aided this: with its gothic typography and casual torn paper styling, it has the sense of a brand that's been around since the Middle Ages. The heritage element is helped along by the "Est 1753" statement on the label, which does feel like a little bit of a stretch given the number of times it has changed hands. However, despite the brand's growth, it feels to its fans like it's small enough to seem exclusive, but big enough to be available in good bars and spirits shops all over the world.

Selling all that whiskey is what helped to fund the building of the Michter's distillery in Shively. The building is a former GM auto-parts shop, which took two years, between 2013 and 2015, to be converted into a working distillery. Now that they're making their own liquor they can begin to bottle from this distillery, but it takes time to mature whiskey, and it's unlikely that customers will be tasting whiskey from the Shively distillery until 2020.

"The transition will be determined by one thing only," says Andrea Wilson, Michter's master of maturation. "The quality of the liquid."

As we embark upon a tour, Andrea talks more about their production processes and I begin to see some of this quality commitment in action. Michter's are ruthlessly dedicated to controlling and protecting their process. There is no public access to the Shively distillery, no mash recipes are divulged, and no age statements appear on most of their bottles. So let's dig around and see what we can learn:

Michter's use only non-GMO corn, rye, and malted barley. These are milled on one of two "cage mills," which are rarely encountered in distilleries. They're more expensive than your average mill, and Andrea describes their operation like two hamster wheels, one inside the other, spinning in opposing directions. Micro adjustments can be made to these "wheels" to calibrate a specific grind size.

There's one mash cooker sized at 10,000 gallons and the fermenters here are 18,200 gallons, so two cooks are needed to fill one fermenter. Although only one Michter's bottling is called "Sour Mash" (based on a historical bottling from the old distillery), all of their products are in fact made using the sour mash process.

Michter's are tight-lipped about how many mash recipes they run and what the contents of those recipes are. If I had to guess, I would say that they are only running two mashes: one bourbon (with a low rye content of around 12%) and one rye (probably at around 60% rye). Andrea does admit that they use

TOP LEFT The railroad is just one of the reasons why Shively became a distilling powerhouse.

ABOVE Bottles of aged spirit in one year iterations, with the youngest on the left. As you can see, a great deal of color comes from those first twelve months.

TOP RIGHT The Michter's Vendome doubler is, like everything else in this distillery, beautifully clean and perfectly efficient.

multiple yeast varieties to make their whiskeys though, and fermentation takes three to five days.

Distillation is done on a shiny new 46-ft copper column manufactured from 11,000 lbs of copper by Vendome. We've encountered stills made by this Louisville firm all over Kentucky, and it's fair to say that their significance to the bourbon industry is on a par with that of the farming or coopering. The exact origin of Vendome is a bit murky, but the company's founder, Elmore Sherman, was supplying stills by 1910 and probably for a few years before.

The spirit comes off the stripping column at 129 proof, then increases to 138 proof once it passes through the doubler. The doubler at Michter's is actually capable of functioning as a thumper too, giving the distillery team a little more control over the character of the distillate. All that copper is going to have a powerful purifying effect on the spirit, which Andrea confirms. "Our objective is to create a really high-quality, clean distillate."

Next, we move on to barrel filling, which is one particular area where Michter's really set themselves apart. "Of any distiller of scale we are the lowest entry proof," says Andrea. "It's one of the main signatures of our brand."

Fill strength is a phenomenon that most brands are still exploring. When a higher percentage of the whiskey you are aging is water, the result is a higher percentage of water soluble compounds extracted from the oak. These have different flavors than the ethanol-soluble compounds. Lower-strength liquids tend to extract more tannin and sugar from the wood, leading to a darker color and sweeter, fuller mouthfeel. Higher-strength spirits tend to extract more lactones (think coconut, varnish, and butter) and, since they extract less tannin, less color too. Paradoxically, higher-strength spirits also make more sugars available by breaking down hemicellulose and lignin more rapidly. On average, a new oak cask will dump 3–5 lbs of sugar into a spirit over a five-year period. Barrels filled at lower strength will tend to be towards the higher end of the scale.

There's also an argument that when you buy whiskey aged at lower strength, you're getting more of the barrel in the bottle, since less dilution is required to reach bottling strength. The downside of filling at low strength is that you need to buy more barrels and you need more space to store them. A distiller needs five barrels to hold 260 gallons of 125 proof spirit, but they would need six barrels to hold that same spirit once it's been cut with water down to 105 proof. Increase the scale by a few orders of magnitude and you're talking about millions of dollars worth of wood and 20% more warehouse space, just because you like the way whiskey tastes when it's aged with more water.

Barrels at Michter's are both toasted and charred. They have a capacity of around 14,000 barrels in their warehouses which are all heat-cycled. This means Andrea can artificially replicate conditions of day and night by warming and cooling the buildings. This is only done in the winter, when maturation typically slows to a crawl.

"We slowly increase the temperature of the warehouse in increments," says Andrea "then slowly reduce it back down again. There are probes in barrels all over the warehouses, ensuring we're hitting the right temperature gradients."

She won't tell me what temperature they heat the warehouse to, or how frequently these cycles occur. But however you choose to look at it, heat cycling is a way of speeding up maturation, avoiding the slump that the winter brings. However, due to Michter's bottling policy, it's important for consistency too.

"We do so much single barrel and small batch that we need to guarantee uniformity between barrels wherever they are in the warehouse," says John.

We've already talked about "small batch" and its lack of definition, but at Michter's, "small" does mean small—never more than 20 barrels and generally between five and seven years old.

The whiskeys here are chill-filtered prior to bottling, but it's not a one-size-fits-all approach. In fact, the chemistry of every expression is analyzed and then an appropriate filtering method applied. "It's a skillful, thoughtful approach to filtration," says Andrea. "We're not doing it just for aesthetics; it's managing the filtration media, micron size, and temperature to make the absolute best version of the whiskey."

Among the core range of bottlings are the Bourbon and Rye expressions, plus Sour Mash and American Whiskey. It's stated on Michter's website that Sour Mash, "with it's unique grain selection, cannot be categorized as a rye or a bourbon." This suggests to me a roughly equal billing of rye and corn, with malted barley taking up the reminder of the bill. "Sour Mash is our homage to the style of American whiskey that they were making in the Pennsylvania distillery," says John. In reality this is probably achieved by blending together barrels of rye whiskey and bourbon whiskey. Michter's American Whiskey is more than likely made from a bourbon mash bill, but matured in a combination of new and re-fill casks to achieve a different flavor profile (and disqualify it from bourbon classification).

More recently, Michter's have opened an all-new downtown Louisville visitor's center and distillery. Amazingly, they have been able to retrieve some of the stills and cypress-wood fermenters from the original Pennsylvania distillery. While I'm not sold on the 1753 claim, I am definitely excited about the prospect of whiskey fans getting to see these relics from America's oldest distillery.

ABOVE This device is used to both stir and cool the hot mash before it is sent to begin fermentation.

SOUR MASH (43% ABV)

The aroma is like melted ice cream spiked with black pepper. On the palate it's both peppery and sweet, beginning with wood spice then transitioning to malt loaf, sour plum, and finally toasted grain.

STRAIGHT BOURBON (45.5% ABV)

The aroma is soft, sweet vanilla milkshake. On the palate, it's dry wood, white chocolate crunch with rice crispy cake. Leather conditioner follows and the finish is reminiscent of Krispy Kreme donut.

STRAIGHT RYE (42.4% ABV)

Rye is present but not overwhelming on the nose. Spiced plum pie, black olive, licorice emerge on the palate. The taste is peppery, joined by refreshing, lighter notes of orange and a mid-palate of

butterscotch. Great for cocktails where you can't decide whether to use rye or bourbon.

BOURBON TOASTED (45.7% ABV)

The aroma is all the toasted things: coconut sugar, roasted pecan, hazelnut, and coffee. The taste is nutty and dry, with toasted marshmallow and créme brûlée. The finish dries right out, leaving banana pancake.

ROAD TRIP PLAYLIST

"The Times They Are A Changin'" — Bob Dylan

"A little Less Conversation" — Elvis Presley

KENTUCKY BUCK

50 ml/1⅔ oz Michter's Sour Mash Whiskey
20 ml/⅔ oz Homemade Spiced Ginger Syrup
20 ml/⅔ oz lime juice
soda water

Add the first three ingredients to a chilled highball glass filled with ice and stir. Top up with soda and stir, adding more ice if necessary. Garnish with a fresh strawberry.

SPICED GINGER SYRUP
(MAKES 1 LITER/QUART)

500 g/20 oz water
150 g/5¼ oz coarsely grated ginger
5 g/1 teaspoon ground coriander
12 black peppercorns
500 g/17½ oz sugar

Add all the ingredients except the sugar to a pan and simmer with the lid on for an hour. Strain the infused water through a cheesecloth, then add the sugar while it's still hot.

This drink is traditionally a combination of bourbon with ginger ale and a squeeze of citrus, so not dissimilar to a mule (for which I have provided a recipe on page 347). Most bartenders agree that ginger ale doesn't give the necessary "kick" that the name of the drink suggests, though. So if you have the time, it's far better to make your own ginger syrup.

Make the syrup in advance and store in the fridge for up to a month. I've provided a guideline recipe for the syrup, but feel free to spice it any way you see fit.

PRICHARD'S

MELLOW COUNTRY

"Alcohol may be man's worst enemy, but the Bible says love your enemy."

FRANK SINATRA (1915–98), SINGER AND ACTOR

Leaving Louisville, we join I-65 and make ourselves comfortable for the next few hours of driving. This interstate drops south in an almost perfect vertical line, taking us over the Kentucky border into Tennessee and then further south still, coming close to the Alabama state line.

About 90 minutes in, we pass through Nashville, the home of country music, which, of any genre of music, probably has the greatest connection with whiskey. Indeed, the songs on local radio in these parts seem to mention whiskey, bourbon, beer, and "sweet wine" with uncanny regularity, usually in the context of cheating, fighting, or repairing a broken heart. Despite some resistance, over time we get drawn into the stories that these songs tell, such as Kris Kristofferson's "Whiskey, Whiskey," in which he sings, "Whiskey, whiskey, my old friend, I've come to talk with you again. Milk of mercy, please be kind and drive this feeling from my mind." And then there's Chris Stapleton's smash hit "Tennessee Whiskey," which gets played, on average, every fifth song.

In the mid-1980s, country music legend Merle Haggard inked an endorsement deal with George Dickel. The distillery sponsored Haggard's "Ain't Nothin' Better" Tour and plastered his face on advertisements that announced, "Water's for teardrops. Dickel's for drinking."

Given how often whiskey is employed as a narrative tool in country music (and vice versa), it's not surprising that Nashville has become one of the nation's premier locations for drinking and making whiskey. There were no distilleries making whiskey here ten years ago; now there are at least 10. One of county's biggest stars, Dierks Bentley, has a bar on Lower Broadway called Whiskey Row. Bob Dylan is currently in the process of building a distillery inside a 160-year-old church in downtown Nashville where he'll produce his "Heaven's Door" brand amongst an arts center and concert venue.

Besides celebrity operations, others include Corsair (who have two distilleries in Nashville) and have made a good name for themselves bottling many experimental mash bills and weird cereal varieties.

There's also Nelson's Green Brier distillery, which is a modern revival of one of the biggest Tennessee brands of the 19th century. Charles Nelson was a German immigrant who came to Nashville from Cincinnati before the Civil War. He opened a grocery store in Nashville and began buying whiskey from the Robertson County Distillery in Greenbrier. Back then, Nashville was to Tennessee whiskey what Louisville was to Kentucky Bourbon, and Charles Nelson established a successful whiskey wholesale and blending business there. Besides selling whiskey, Nelson was a coffee trader and supplied it to the Maxwell House hotel in Nashville, which later gave its name to the coffee brand. After selling off his grocery interests, Nelson purchased the distillery in

Greenbrier and expanded production. By 1885, the Green Brier Distillery was employing 25 people and manufacturing 8,000 barrels of whiskey a year. The brand went on to be widely distributed and exported internationally, putting Tennessee whiskey on the map before the likes of Jack Daniel's and George Dickel became household names. The operation ceased production when statewide Prohibition took effect in 1909. Almost exactly 100 years later, Nelson's great-great-great grand-children, Charlie and Andy Nelson opened Nelson's Green Brier Distillery in Nashville, resurrecting one of Tennessee's first great whiskey brands.

With Nashville behind us, we penetrate even further south, approaching Alabama at pace. There's not a lot to see in this part of south central Tennessee besides highways and the occasional church sign displaying messages designed to strike the fear of god into passing motorists. Southern Tennessee is smack-bang in the middle of the Bible Belt, and the state has the highest percentage of Evangelical Protestants of any state, at over 50% of the population. The first European settlers here were a similar breed to that of Kentucky, bringing with them the word of the Presbyterian, Baptist, and Anglican Churches.

They also brought a taste for alcohol.

To begin with, this meant rye whiskey, since that was the dominant grain in pre-Revolutionary America and seeing as many Tennessee immigrants came from big rye states like Maryland and Pennsylvania. Take Colonel Evan Shelby for example. He became the father of Kentucky's first governor and moved his family from Maryland to the Holston River area in the 1770s. Shelby owned and operated Shelby's East Tennessee distillery, possibly the first in the state (though this was before the state of Tennessee actually existed) located at Sapling Grove near Shelby's Station on the Holston. Many similar operations popped up in the years that followed, and some that were dissimilar, like John "King" Boyd's Red Heifer distillery and bar in Nashville.

Both East and Middle Tennessee were well suited for the production of whiskey, having good soil for growing corn, an abundance of firewood, white oak for the manufacture of barrels, and a good network of rivers to ship the whiskey to marketing centers like Knoxville, Chattanooga, Nashville, and Memphis.

Nowhere fit this description better than the counties of Robertson and Davidson, between Nashville and the Kentucky border. The earliest state records show that by 1799, Davidson County was home to 61 stills that were servicing fewer than 4,000 people. In 1820, the Fourth Census showed that New York, Pennsylvania, Ohio, and Tennessee had more capital invested and employed more men in the production of spirits than any other state in the Union. The industry continued to grow right up until the Civil War.

During the Civil War, occupying Union forces banned the distillation of whiskey because corn and other grains were needed to feed both humans and livestock. In Robertson County, distilling was one of the first businesses to start up after federal troops pulled out in April 1865. The timing couldn't have been better for distilling. Limestone water, corn, and firewood were readily available in spring, and a still could be set up easily and cheaply. Nearly everyone in the county started making whiskey for the simple reason that it was the fastest way to make money and required virtually no capital. A major advantage was the fine reputation that Robertson County distillers such as Wiley Woodard already enjoyed. The 249 gallons of whiskey Woodard shipped to Lyon & Company in Nashville on September 21, 1865, went for $3.75 a gallon, compared to 40 cents a gallon before the war.

In 1886, the Nashville Union newspaper reported that the distilling industry was the largest manufacturing industry in the state of Tennessee, annually consuming 750,000 bushels of corn. By the late 1880s, however, the industry had begun to decline. Smaller and less successful distillers had gone into other businesses, faced with intense competition from the larger distillers on the one hand, and mounting pressure from church and temperance groups on the other. Tennessee's first Women's Christian Temperance Union chapter had formed in 1874 and would be joined by the Anti-Saloon League in 1899.

One early Davidson County distiller was Benjamin Prichard, who in 1822 passed his "still, tubs, and utensils thereto" to his son, Enoch. What happened next is anyone's guess, but this story became the inspiration for Enoch's great-great-grandson, Phil Prichard, who, in 1997, set about opening the first new Tennessee whiskey distillery in living memory.

Now, in my mind, anyone opening a small independent distillery prior to 2000 can claim to have their origin story rooted in the ancient history section of modern distilling. Prichard's is a trailblazer for the "craft" distillery movement, being one of the first five of its kind in the US and the first the state of Tennessee had seen for decades. Phil Prichard, the founder, gave up a life of farming and technical dentistry, moving back to his home state of Tennessee with the dream of making American rum.

This started with a homemade still, pieced together from copper pipes and a large turkey baster, but he eventually took the plunge and snapped up two old pot-stills from a seller in Vermont. Then all he needed was a license and a location.

"My brother-in-law, who was the former governor of Tennessee," says Phil, "told me, 'if you put it in one of the more depressed counties in the state, the governor might look favorably on it.'"

Phil Prichard chose the small settlement of Kelso as the home for his distillery, and an old grade school as the premises. It started in just the back room to begin with but, as the company has grown, the 30-strong team have begun to occupy the entire building and branched out to open a second site in Nashville.

Over 20 years later, and at the ripe age of 77, Phil remains the dominant force at the distillery and can still be found giving tours and tastings in his white suit and Panama hat, like some eccentric principal.

The exterior of the school in Kelso would have you believe that some unsavory types were squatting inside. The building looks like, well, an abandoned school. There are a bunch of shipping containers dumped in the playground, which we later discover are used for maturation. There's also a large, steel barn that's used for distribution and storage. Inside though, there's a hive of activity going on. The still

house is the old cafeteria, the offices and bottling line are the old classrooms, and the gymnasium has been converted into a stock holding area. Phil Prichard's office is the old staff room.

"This is one of the funniest things I ever got involved with," says Phil with a chuckle as he leads us from classroom to corridor, past the school sports trophy cabinet, which has been re-tasked as the Prichard's awards cabinet.

The focus at Prichard's is split between rum and whiskey, but it's the whiskey that pays the bills here. Prichard's single malt is made from 100% malted barley and aged in new 15-gallon oak casks. There's a rye whiskey too, as well as a Tennessee whiskey (more on that shortly), and bourbon. Double Barrel Bourbon is sourced from Heaven Hill and made from a mash bill of white corn, rye, and wheat. It's is aged for nine years by Heaven Hill, cut from 120 proof to 95 proof, and then re-barreled in new charred oak barrels.

The term "Tennessee whiskey" doesn't actually have a legal definition in the US Federal regulations. Instead, it's defined by the North American Free Trade Agreement (NAFTA), which defines Tennessee whiskey as "a straight Bourbon Whiskey authorized to be produced only in the State of Tennessee". On May 13, 2013, Bill Haslam, governor of Tennessee, signed House Bill 1084, requiring products produced in the state labeling themselves as "Tennessee whiskey" to be "filtered through maple charcoal prior to aging." That means if you're making something called Tennessee whiskey in Tennessee and not filtering it through maple charcoal, you're in danger of getting your license revoked.

The purpose of the charcoal mellowing, which is popularly known as the Lincoln County process (which is where it's thought to have originated), is to remove impurities present in the distillate, leaving a cleaner canvas for the barrel flavors to decorate. It was probably first developed as a response to poor-quality distilling practices and a clear need to correct it. Distillers of yesteryear would have filtered the spirit in whiskey barrels that were perforated at the bottom. A flannel would be laid over the base of the cask and a layer of charcoal added. Then the white whiskey would be poured into the cask and the resulting drips of "clean" whiskey collected from underneath. When technology improved, sugar maple trees were used to make the charcoal because it's an abundant but not terribly useful wood, and it doesn't impart much flavor.

Interestingly, the charcoal filtration does affect the pH of the whiskey, raising it by a point or two and likely contributing to the "mellowing" effect that Jack Daniel's likes to talk about. Jack Daniel's long-time master distiller, Jeff Arnett, describes the effect of the process as "removing the bitterness associated with the grain bill." The point is, it really does make a difference to the final flavor of the product and is therefore an important production stage in defining the taste of Tennessee whiskey.

Now that we're all familiar with the rules, it's time to drop a bombshell: Prichard's do not filter their Tennessee Whiskey through charcoal prior to aging and they aren't legally required to either.

You see, Prichard's had already been producing their own un-mellowed Tennessee whiskey for a few years when the new bill was passed in 2013. So Phil Prichard sought an exemption from the bill under a "grandfather clause" and was successful. The revised bill now states that for any distillery granted a license between January 1, 2000 and January 1, 2001, charcoal filtering is optional. Prichard's is the only Tennessee distillery that meet this requirement and unless the law is changed further down the line, no other Tennessee whiskey will ever be able to claim the same status. Ironically, Prichard's are one of only two Tennessee distilleries located in Lincoln County.

Having said that, House Bill 1084 deliberately omits details around the mellowing process, like how much charcoal? For how long? Does the wood need to be from Tennessee? It's possible that millions of liters of spirit could pass through a handful of charcoal and it would be sufficient to keep the feds happy.

Prichard's Tennessee Whiskey is made from a mash of 70% corn, 15% rye, and 15% malted barley. The mash undergoes a six-day ferment before being doubled-distilled in the 700-gallon and 500-gallon Vendome copper-pot stills. The spirit comes off the still at a modest 125 proof and is proofed down to 110 for maturation. Barrels here are a mixture of 15 gallons all the way up to standard 53-gallon casks.

In 2014, Prichard's opened a second distillery in Nashville. It's on the grounds of the Fontanel Mansion, which is a 186-acre property that was previously owned by country music singer Barbara Mandrell. Since 2010, it has been a tourist attraction, including a winery, public walking trails, an amphitheater with live concerts, and the mansion itself, which is one of the largest log-built homes in the world. The distillery is small, but very much notable on account of the still. Prichard's commissioned Vendome to make a 400-gallon Alembic copper still in the style of a French cognac still. They're going to use it to make Tennessee brandy.

PRICHARD'S TENNESSEE WHISKEY (40% ABV)

There's a healthy hint of rye here that the other Tennesseeans don't have, along with banana bread, golden raisins, and dried apricots. The taste also announces rye pepperiness and good action on the mid-palate. The dry grippy-ness continues, even exhibiting some tannin that both adds structure and flattens any subtlety that might have been there.

PRICHARD'S SINGLE MALT WHISKEY (40% ABV)

Aromas of green malt, golden syrup, chestnut and damp meadowsweet reach the nose. It's viscous, nutty, and sweet on the palate. I find it highly approachable, clean and delicate, but it's lacking some balls. It's more like an Irish Pot Still whiskey than a Scotch Malt.

PRICHARD'S DOUBLE BARREL BOURBON (45% ABV)

Hard-ball caramel, sticky toffee pudding, and the overwhelming sensation of being locked in a oak coffin. On the palate, it's like you're lickin' your way out! Massive resinous oak notes crush the fragile world around you. There's a long, dry finish with spikes of oak lactones that hiccup through you.

PRICHARD'S RYE WHISKEY (43% ABV)

The initial hit of diesel fumes is followed by brilliant sour plum, nutmeg, cocoa, and cherryade. The taste is pleasant, but lacking the exuberance that the nose alerted us to. There's nuttiness, spice, and some vanilla, but distinction is sadly lacking.

ROAD TRIP PLAYLIST

"Tennessee Whiskey" – Chris Stapleton

"Good Times" – Sam Cooke

"Coal War" – Joshua James

FRUITY LUCY

500 ml/17 oz Prichard's Tennessee Whiskey
100 g/3½ oz dried peach
100 g/3½ oz dried apricot
50 g/1¾ oz dried plums
50 g/1¾ oz dried mango

Add all of the ingredients to a sealable glass jar. Store in a warm, dark cupboard and allow to macerate for at least six weeks. Stir occasionally (and have a taste to check the progress). When you think it's ready, and the fruit has leached most of its color, strain the liquid and bottle.

Wait! Don't throw away the fruit. It's infused with delicious whiskey and can serve as a boozy garnish for other cocktails, or baked into a cake. Alternatively, you can dry the pieces out in the oven and eat them as a high-fiber, low-sugar snack.

Prichard's bestselling product is not technically a whiskey but a whiskey liqueur. It's called Sweet Lucy and is based on the Tennessee tradition of packing a flask of fruity whiskey liqueur when exploring the great outdoors and killing ducks with shotguns.

Tradition requires one to make their own infusion of whiskey, fruit (peaches, oranges, and apricots are common) with lots of sugar and whiskey. Great pride would often be displayed by its maker as the bottle made its rounds for a sip among friends.

My version is unsweetened and made only from whiskey and dried fruit, which front up all the sugar. The result is a certain natural harmony between the oak barrel and the fruit that added-sugar liqueurs tend to miss. If you like your liqueurs really sweet, though, you may opt to add a little sugar in there.

JACK DANIEL'S

JACK AND HIS STILL WENT DOWN THE HOLLOW

"Jack Daniel's, if you please
Knock me to my knees,
You're the only friend
There has ever been
That didn't do me wrong."

FROM THE SONG "JACK DANIEL'S IF YOU PLEASE" BY DAVID ALLAN COE

Lynchburg is a mere 20 minutes from Kelso. The drive takes us through rural southern Tennessee, where the Lynchburg Highway undulates through trees and past fields. Progress is slow because we're stuck behind a grain truck, which is probably heading to the same place we are. Five minutes later, another truck appears in the rear view mirror. This is the reality of this road—a conveyor belt that feeds the biggest whiskey distillery in America.

Jack Daniel's is the largest-selling single distillery whiskey in the world. Its iconic square bottle, with its black and white label, is a brand icon that, in many ways, transcends the American whiskey category as a whole. Indeed, a recent brand awareness survey conducted in the US saw Jack Daniel's hit an unprecedented 99% among people of legal drinking age. In 2017, 135 shots of Jack Daniel's were poured every second. Every day, 750 tons of corn arrive at the distillery—enough to fill over 15,000 barrels with white whiskey every week. Brown-Forman currently commands 89 warehouses to hold all this stock, and have experimented with gigantic 54,000-barrel warehouses that were so big they buckled under their own weight and are now held together by huge steel cables.

It's strange then that the product originates from the town of Lynchburg in Moore County with a population of less than 6,000 people. It's even stranger, though, that Moore County is classified as a "dry county." It's this kind of head-scratching logic that embodies the confusing relationship that Americans, and in particular Tennesseans, have had with alcohol for over 200 years.

By the looks of things, Lynchburg has done well off the back of Jack. The buildings and shops in the central square are immaculately presented, and the streets are clean. In fact, it's a little bit too clean. We walk around for 20 minutes and begin to get that feeling of being in a theme park, where on the surface everything is normal but you're only really seeing a façade.

Mr. Jack, as he is affectionately referred to, was the youngest of ten children, born around 1846 to a farming family based in Southern Tennessee. Jack was—not to put too fine a point on it—the runt of the litter; measuring only 5'2" as a grown man, he was up against it from an early age. Jack's mother died giving birth to him and his step-mother showed little love. Some legends suggest that Jack ran away from home at the age of six, but it actually wasn't until his father died in the Civil War that orphaned Jack moved in with his neighbor, in 1864. Two years later, under the watchful eye of his adopted father, Dan Call, and former slave Nathan "Nearest" Green, Jack was tutored in the art of distillation, learning about the value of corn and the importance of good water. How long Jack, known as the "boy distiller", had been distilling before that is anyone's guess. On November 27, 1875, after almost a decade of distilling whiskey and moonshine, Jack registered his own company, Daniel & Call, and began distilling on Call's farm.

In 1884, the operation moved to its current resting place in what is now known as "The Hollow." The Hollow caught Jack's attention due to its cave spring, the water of which is still used to make Jack Daniel's today. Such was Jack's relationship with Nearest that he employed two of his sons, George and Eli Green. Then, at least four of Nearest's grandchildren joined the Jack Daniel's team: Ott, Charlie, Otis, and Jesse Green. In total, seven generations of Nearest Green's descendants have worked for the distillery, with three direct descendants still working there today including his great-granddaughter.

A story like Nearest Green's doesn't come along every day: former African-American slave improbably becomes master distiller and mentor to the biggest name whiskey has ever known. So it's surprising that it took until 2017 for anyone to capitalize on it. But in July of 2017, Uncle Nearest, Inc. debuted its Uncle Nearest 1856 Premium Whiskey, and they have since added an 11-year-old expression to the line up. The originator of this brand is Fawn Weaver, an African-American writer and whiskey historian who took a keen interest in the story of "America's first African-American Master Distiller." With no distillery to speak of, Uncle Nearest is currently sourced from a couple of Tennessee distilleries (not Jack Daniel's). As of April 2019, it is sold in 47 states and eight countries, which explains why the brand was able to buy up Dan Call's old 330-acre farm along with another 270-acre plot near Nashville, where plans are afoot to build a distillery, museum, and "history walk." I'd like to say that this is a brand that's worth keeping any eye on, but the chances are it'll be hard to avoid over the coming years.

Back to Jack Daniel's distillery, we discover that it was originally called "Old Time," and at some point around the turn of the century, they began making a whiskey with the Jack Daniel's name on it. Despite appearing for some time before, the "Old No. 7" brand wasn't registered until 1908 and is the subject of many a tall tale and a good helping of intrigue. Tour guides at the distillery today prefer to play dumb and perpetuate mythical stories of Old No. 7's origins: "Seven was the number of times Jack was engaged," says our guide. What follows is the likely truth behind the whole thing:

Every distillery in Tennessee was registered in a tax district and within that district, given a unique number. Originally, Daniel & Call was registered in the 4th district, which was later merged with the 5th district. During the merger, Daniel was given a new unique number, "16." Their old number, with which they were recognized by wholesalers and customers alike, was lost. So they made the decision to put it on their bottle: "Old No. 7."

Despite reportedly being engaged seven times in his life, Jack neither married nor had any children. In 1887, Jack's nephew, Lemuel Motlow, came to work for him, having been a part-time errand boy since 1880. Jack saw the opportunity, and began grooming "Lem" as his successor. And a fine choice it was, for Lem drove the Jack Daniel's brand into the 20th century and established the brand for what it is today.

As for Mr. Daniel himself, sadly, his money got the better of him, but in a more literal sense than you might imagine. At the age of 55, Jack looked like a man who enjoyed rich foods and whiskey. One day in 1904, he arrived at his Lynchburg office and after struggling with the combination lock on his safe, he kicked it in a fit of rage. His foot was badly bruised, and perhaps broken, but it went untreated and over time eventually became gangrenous. Successive amputations over the coming years left him with no leg at all, and Jack eventually died from an infection on October 9, 1911. The guilty-looking safe can still be seen at the distillery in Lynchburg today.

When Prohibition in Tennessee took effect in 1909, Lem Motlow moved the entire operation to St. Louis

in Missouri. A fire in 1913 ravaged the distillery however, and Lem barely had it back in working order before nationwide Prohibition took effect in 1920. Production stopped altogether during this period and even when the Volstead Act was repealed in 1933, much of the state of Tennessee, including Moore County, remained dry (and still does today). It wasn't until November 11, 1938, after a great deal of petitioning from Lem Motlow, that the law was relaxed to allow production in Lynchburg and the first new barrel of Jack Daniel's was rolled into warehouse after 30 years of inactivity.

By the time World War II had begun, the brand had barely had time to surface for air. Even in the years following the war, production slowed and even stopped due to unavailability of the correct grade of corn—a stubborn move on Lem Motlow's part that later granted Jack Daniel's a reputation for superior quality. Even as late as 1951, a reporter for *Fortune* magazine wrote an article with the opener, "If you've never heard of Jack Daniel's whiskey, so much the better. Its relative obscurity is part of its charm."

After Motlow's death in 1947, the company was run by his four hands-on sons, who grew the business successfully until selling it to Brown-Forman (the current owners) in 1956. It was the clever "backwoods" advertising campaign that propelled the product to stardom, by playing off the small-town, slow-paced, lifestyle that the square black-and-white bottle stood for—similar ad campaigns can still be

seen today. Not before too long, the well-kept secret that was Jack Daniel's Tennessee Whiskey had become not well-kept at all.

Among the famous historical imbibers were President Harry S. Truman, who sent a bottle to Winston Churchill (Truman allegedly drank bourbon for breakfast), and J. Edgar Hoover, founder of the FBI, who would relax with a glass of Jack. Then came the Hollywood set, influenced by the legendary Rat Pack, who took a bottle of Jack Daniel's on stage during the Las Vegas shows. On stage in the 1950s, Sinatra famously proclaimed Jack Daniel's the "nectar of the gods." Sales doubled following Sinatra's endorsement and the brand was sold purely on allocation for the following 20 years, during a time when American whiskey as a whole was really struggling. The working class embraced the product too, as it became synonymous with motorcycle clubs and particularly the Harley Davidson brand.

There are about 400 folks working at the distillery in Lynchburg. Only one mash bill is used, comprising 80% corn, 8% rye, and 12% malted barley. The cereals are cooked with water from the Cave Spring Hollow, which runs at a constant temperature of 13°C/55.4°F all year round. Jack is the brand that made "sour mash" famous, and in their case, around one-third of the mash water comes from sour stillage.

Fermentation takes place across 56 steel vats, each of them holding 40,000 liters. The distillery uses a proprietary yeast strain, which dates back to the repeal of Prohibition. They actually employ a full-time microbiologist (who literally wrote the book on yeast) who is in charge of managing the yeast culture. The yeast is held in a cryogenically controlled vessel at a constant temperature of -80°C. Once a week a new culture is bred to avoid the possibility of mutation.

"We're constantly monitoring for shifts in character," says Jeff, "and through our lab we can crosscheck distillate character with the mother culture to check things are working okay."

The fermentation is actually quite drawn out, and takes around six days, resulting in a beer with a strength of 11–12 percent.

There's a total of six column stills at Jack Daniel's distillery, capable of outputting a combined 25,000 proof gallons of whiskey a day, which is enough to fill about 50 hot tubs. The four larger stills are 6¼ ft wide and 45-ft tall. The "smaller" ones are a mere 4.5-ft wide. Each still works independently, and there are no attached doublers or thumpers. The resulting distillate is 140 proof.

Next, the spirit is filtered through charcoal in accordance with Tennessee State law. The distillery actually manufactures their own sugar maple charcoal, and has a yard space that the distillery tour passes through where visitors can see huge ricks of wood stacked in flaming towers like a game of giant Jenga that got totally out of hand. When it's time to make the charcoal, someone from the distillery team douses the rick in 140 proof Jack Daniel's spirit, then sets light to it.

"Once the flames have gone out and the embers are glowing, we put the fire out and compact the charcoal together" says Jeff.

These pellets of charcoal are then sent to the mellowing room, where there are 72 vats, each of them 14-ft deep, containing 10 ft of charcoal. This room is right next to the still house, so the newly made spirit can be pumped straight over there. "Mellowing" hardly feels like the right term though, since spirit is flowing at a rate of 60 gallons a minute. Because of the sheer volume of liquid, the charcoal has a 12-month lifespan before it needs to be replenished. The charcoal at the top of the vat

becomes saturated with whiskey first, which renders it redundant after a week or two, handing over the filtering work to the charcoal further down. This continues, as the line of active charcoal slowly drops towards the bottom of the vat, until all 10 ft of charcoal is saturated like a wet sponge and the whole vat needs topping up. It's for this reason that the filtered spirit can taste quite different depending the age of the charcoal, so everything gets blended together prior to maturation.

"Most of our barrel entry is 120 proof," says Jeff, "but we have filled at 110 at times."

This is all going into brand new 53-gallon American oak barrels, of which the Jack Daniel's distillery is the most greedy consumer in the world. Old No.7 is typically matured for three to four years, giving it enough time to develop the distinct aroma of a maturation warehouse. The warehousing for Jack Daniel's covers a total of 2,000 acres around the town of Lynchburg. There are around a dozen warehouses on the distillery grounds, but the balance are located a mile or so south of Lynchburg. In total, the entire inventory sits at around 2.5 million barrels.

For some time now there's been debate around whether Jack Daniel's is a bourbon. I really don't think it matters whether it is or isn't, but for the curious folk among you, the simple answer is "yes". But it's also a Tennessee Whiskey. Just like all straight bourbons meet the minimum federal requirements to be classed as "whiskey," Tennessee whiskey meets all the requirements of straight bourbon whiskey.

Although No. 7 accounts for 99% of the whiskey made here, Brown-Forman have released an impressive number of bottles over the years.

The distillery's second release came about in the 1980s as a response to the rising tide of vodka brands. Gentleman Jack is made from the same base as Old No. 7, and right up to maturation follows the same production process. However, once fully matured, it undergoes a second charcoal-filtering process, further mellowing the flavor.

Then came Single Barrel in 1997, which is whiskey sourced only from the casks stored on the higher floors of the warehouses. Around 5,000 of these barrels are selected every year, each yielding around 230 bottles. At the time of its launch it cost $45 a bottle, which was an almost unheard-of price for a bottle of whiskey back then.

Since then, the distillery has released something like 60 expressions, most of them commemorative bottles and limited edition releases. In 2016, they launched Jack Daniel's Single Barrel Rye, which of course uses a rye mash bill, but every other bottle is made from the same mash, same fermentation, same charcoal-filtering, and same distillation.

JACK DANIEL'S OLD NO. 7 (40% ABV)

The aroma is unquestionably banoffee pie and BBQ. There's glazed pecans too, a hint of butter and pancake batter. On the tongue it is sweet and slick, like banana custard, with plenty of vanillin, a little hint of tobacco ash, and a kind of vacant finish.

GENTLEMAN JACK (40% ABV)

Crisper, cleaner, and generally more gentlemanly. The aroma is softer and less smoky, allowing the vanilla and banana to take a stronger grip. Softer and supple in taste, the finish has a lick of soft fruit and drifts off quite quickly.

JACK DANIEL'S SINGLE BARREL (45% ABV)

Maple wood floor, banana, peanut butter milkshake, and superglue hit the nose. This leads on to more wood aromas, with treacle tart, anise, and plenty of vanilla. On the palate there's darker suggestions of some wood spice and a hint of pepper… and a neutral heat that's quickly covered up with honeycomb and clotted cream.

ROAD TRIP PLAYLIST

"Holiday Road" – Lindsey Buckingham

"Hit The Road Jack" – Ray Charles

"That's Life" – Frank Sinatra

JACK & COKE

40 ml/1 ⅓ oz Jack Daniel's Old No. 7
125 ml/4¼ oz Coca-Cola

Add the ingredients to a highball glass filled with ice and stir for a minute. Garnish with a slice of lemon.

A Jack & Coke might not seem like a particularly fancy drink. It's certainly easy to construct and ubiquitous enough to feel a bit mundane. But that shouldn't detract from the simple genius of it. The mix of cinnamon and nutmeg spice with orange and lime that coke brings has a strong affinity with the flavors extracted from a barrel. The whiskey, with its flavors of vanilla and banana bread, complements coke, creating a new, unique flavor that is enjoyed by many. And for good reason!

GEORGE DICKEL

CASCADING CHEMICALS

"My own experience has been that the tools I need for my trade are paper, tobacco, food, and a little whisky."

WILLIAM FAULKNER (1897–1962), AUTHOR

Leaving Lynchburg to the north, we head towards the city of Tullahoma. This sprawling place is everything Lynchburg isn't: modern and a little rough around the edges. Tullahoma was once an important railroad town in the late 1800s, which explains why John F. Brown and F. E. Cunningham were compelled to establish the Cascade Hollow Distillery there in 1877. The other good reason to put a distillery there was that it was near to Cascade Springs, which provided all the water required for the operation.

Over the ten years that followed its opening, the distillery changed hands a few times until the Geo A. Dickel company bought it in 1888. George Dickel himself was a German immigrant, born in 1811, who practiced as a cobbler until he opened a liquor wholesale store in Nashville in the 1860s. His brother-in-law, Victor Schwab, joined the firm some time later and the company became well known for blending and rectifying (flavoring) whiskey, including that sold by the Cascade Distillery. Their Cascade Whiskey was marketed as being "As mellow as moonlight". George Augustus Dickel died in 1894 and left the majority of his shareholding to his wife Augusta.

Schwab kept things running well up until 1903, when a new bout of prohibition fever took hold. Schwab fought tooth and nail against the Temperance

PREVIOUS PAGES The Great Smoky Mountains on the Tennessee/North Carolina border live up to their name!

movement and those demanding Prohibition, spending thousands of dollars trying to convince Tennessee politicians to vote against any legislation aimed at limiting the sale of alcohol. But in 1910 the distillery closed, and Cascade Whiskey sought asylum in Kentucky where, for a time, it was made in limited quantities at the A. Ph. Stitzel distillery—that is, until Prohibition was enacted there too. There's some evidence to suggest that the Cascade brand was made and sold as medicinal whiskey during this period, which makes sense because the Stitzel distillery did have a medicinal license. In 1937, after Prohibition had ended, the Schenley group purchased Geo. A. Dickel & Co. and shoe-horned production into the George T. Stagg distillery (now Buffalo Trace).

As the 1950s saw the Jack Daniel's empire begin to swell, Schenley put in an offer for the brand, but when Brown-Forman bought it instead, Schenley made the decision re-build the Cascade Hollow Distillery.

In 1958, while their stocks matured, Schenley began bottling a very young corn whiskey, which they called "Pride of Tennessee." Early aged Tennessee whiskeys were still bottled under the Cascade brand, but since it conflicted with Cascade Bourbon, also owned by Schenley, in 1964, it went on sale as George Dickel's Tennessee Whisky (they spelled it without the "e"). By this time the recipe had almost certainly changed compared to the pre-Prohibition Cascade, but Schenley did go to great

efforts to flavor-match the old bottles that they had acquired.

Following various mergers and buyouts, the distillery ended up in the hands of Diageo in the 1990s, and promptly fell victim to over-production, which forced its closure. Diageo then reopened the distillery in 2003, frantically pumping out whiskey in an effort to meet growing demand for "alternative" Tennessee Whiskey.

Cascade Hollow Road runs north out of Tullahoma amongst densely packed trees that conceal the adjacent Cascade Spring and Cascade Falls. After a mile or so, the trees form a clearing and you're driving right through the center of the George Dickel Distillery. To the west, the spring widens next to the gift shop and tasting room. On the other side of the road is the distillery itself.

Master distiller Allisa Henley is here to greet us. She's a 12-year veteran at Dickel, having started here when she was 28. In an industry that's dominated by men, it's extremely refreshing to see a young woman running a distillery of this scale. (Since the time of our visit, Allisa has left the distillery and now works for Popcorn Sutton distillery in Nashville. She's the second Dickel master distiller to make that move.)

The standard Dickel mash bill is 84% corn, 8% rye, and 8% malted barley. These ingredients are weighed on an antique scale and recorded with a pen and paper. There are two mash cookers, each with a 9,600-gallon capacity, and after a four-hour cook, the cereal soup is pumped in to one of nine 20,000-gallon fermenters, so two mashes per fermenter. Dickel uses a proprietary yeast strain, and fermentation takes around four days, producing a beer of 8% ABV. Distillation is done in two stages, first the copper beer-stripping column (45 inches in diameter and three stories tall) which increases strength to 115 proof, then on to the doubler, which fortifies the spirit up to 125–130 proof. This is a relatively low strength, which means the spirit preserves a little more of the cereal's character.

As is required by the state of Tennessee, George Dickel charcoal-mellows their whiskeys. Dickel approaches the process slightly differently to Jack Daniel's however, by steeping the spirit in the charcoal pellets for seven to ten days, as opposed to dripping it through continuously. This gives a much longer contact time between the charcoal and spirit and I liken it to steeping coffee in hot water (as in a French press) as opposed to percolating water through coffee.

"George Dickel noticed that the mellow spirit tasted better in the winter time than the summer," says Allisa, "so we chill the spirit to 40°F all year round now."

This chilling will make a different range of compounds available to the filtration medium, but will also assist with the clarity of the final product and the removal of fatty acids in the same manner to chill-filtering.

The effect of this proprietary filtration technique is distinguishable when comparing the potent aroma of Dickel straight off the still, and the soft, buttery nuances of George Dickel No. 1, which undergoes mellowing, but no maturation in oak. (Given that the mash bill is over 80% corn, Dickel No. 1 is classifiable as a corn whiskey and therefore doesn't need maturing to be called whiskey.)

Next, we tour the warehouses, which are a sheet metal construction. These buildings are nowhere near the height of the warehouses we've seen in Kentucky, or even at Jack Daniel's. Each one is only a single story, stacked just six barrels high, which means there's far less temperature variation from top to bottom and therefore more consistency between casks.

There is one particularly unique practice that stands out: as is the norm, the racked warehouses are loaded one barrel at a time by rolling each cask down the shelf. Besides the weight of the cask, one of the biggest problems with rolling casks along their rack is ensuring that the bung resides on the top of the barrel when it stops in its final resting place, so as to minimize the risk of leaks. If the barrel is rolled into position with the bung on the bottom this presents a problem, since all 770 lbs must then be turned in the highly restricted space at the end of the rack. Well, the burly barrel-men at George Dickel have devised an ingenious method to stop this happening, by marking each rack with a series of numbers that represent the hands on a clock face. Before being rolled into position, the bung is rotated to a "minute" that corresponds to its position in the rack. For example, position three in the rack requires the barrel to be loaded at "25P"—positioning the bung at 25 minutes past the hour. With this key piece of information, every cask can be loaded onto the lift in the correct position, then rolled into its final resting place safe in the knowledge that the bung will finish on the top. Genius.

While we ponder the intricate nature of warehouse management and walk among the wooden library of maturing whiskey at Dickel, it's as good a time as any to revisit the process of aging spirits and discuss the science of what takes place in the cask.

Much of what goes on in the perpetual twilight of a warehouse is unpredictable without analyzing every stave of wood that makes up every cask and every drop of liquid that goes in to it. The impracticality of this is obvious, which is why the cellar manager or blender must take regular samples to evaluate progress and gauge the optimum time that a whiskey should spend in a given barrel. Besides systematic testing and tasting, the aging process is most often a simple guarding of treasure that is yet to accomplish its full worth. Having said that, the changes that take effect in the murky realms of the vessel are, even today, being scrutinized and tested to better understand the effects of the barrel and the optimum maturation conditions for the whiskey.

Oak itself contains over 100 volatile compounds capable of contributing aroma, flavor, and mouthfeel in a whiskey. If an oak barrel is analogous to a tea bag, we can view these compounds as flavors that will infuse in a non-linear fashion into the whiskey, with an increasing presence as time goes on. The additive effects of the wood come from four potential sources that make up much of the composition of oak: lignin, hemicellulose, extractives, and oak tannins.

Lignin makes up around 25% of the oak and it's the breaking down of lignin that produces much of the aromatic qualities of wood smoke, as well as some very important acids, phenols, and aldehydes that influence whiskey. One example of a compound, derived from the heating of lignin during toasting or charring, is guaiacol, an aromatic oil that contributes roasted qualities reminiscent of coffee or toast to the liquid. Guaiacol is also a precursor to other flavorful compounds, like vanillin, which gives us vanilla, white chocolate and toffee aromas, and eugenol, which encompasses a whole family of dry spicy flavors like nutmeg and cinnamon.

Hemicellulose is the breeze block of oak's secondary cell walls, and is thought to react with complex acids in the spirit, causing simple wood sugars (around 200 different types) to be extracted, which provide body and "smoothness" to the liquid. The treatment of the wood during coopering causes some of these sugars to undergo caramelization too. The sugars provide little in the way of actual sweetness, but they are thought to knock back some undesirable bitter or sour notes, and the caramelized sugars can give plenty of associated aromatic sweetness. This includes compounds like furfural (an aldehyde formed from the sugar xylose), which has a nutty aroma, and cyclotene, which is all about maple syrup and licorice notes.

Extractives are basically free-running compounds that are "washed" out of the wood. Also attending this party are oak lactones that offer glossy, coconut, and honey aromas. Then there's a whole range of other mostly unpronounceable compounds that give us subtle grassy, baked, wood-sap, peachy, and even greasy aromas.

Wood tannin gives the familiar drying sensation on the palate (like sucking on a tea bag), and when managed correctly, it supplies balance and grip to an otherwise flabby spirit. Tannins also help to combat sulphur (egg) aromas in young whiskeys, and act as a crude marker of overall wood influence by stabilizing color. Tannins, although odorless, are also catalysts for oxidative reactions and can indirectly affect whiskey aroma.

Other compounds are formed during maturation through the oxidation of wood extracts and volatile components that are already present in the distillate spirit. These are brought about through chemical

ABOVE Before being filled, the spirit undergoes charcoal-mellowing, in one of several tanks, which takes 7–10 days.

ABOVE Each rack is marked with numbers, symbolizing the hands on a clock, to ensure the bung is in the right place.

processes between alcohol and oxygen, ultimately producing esters—the building blocks of fruity and floral aromas. Besides ethanol, there are numerous other trace alcohols present in the spirit. Each alcohol has its own style and is subject to the effects of oxidation, resulting in the formation of an aldehydes and acids. For example, the oxidation of the ethanol (alcohol) in the cask forms acetaldehyde and acetic acid. Aldehydes play an important role in whiskey aroma, like benzaldehyde (oxidation of benzyl alcohol), which smells like almond. Acetic acid, along with other oxoacids, are crucial for the formation of esters. Esters provide all of the fruity and floral top notes—everything from geranium, or jasmine, right through to apple, sage, pineapple, and many more. Because these reactions occur in the spirit itself, they require only the presence of oxygen and lots of time.

There are also certain subtractive effects caused by the char of a barrel, which serves as a small filtration layer in a similar way to charcoal mellowing. It does this by leaching onto undesirable compounds that may be present in the whiskey, like dimethyl sulphide (DMS), which asserts a vegetal cabbage-like aroma on new whiskey.

Finally there is color. I am of the opinion that too much emphasis is placed on whiskey color. Although color plays an important part in flavor perception, bending our better judgment towards grass, fresh fruit, and heather when a whiskey has a green tinge, and plums, florals, and jam when the whiskey is red—it is in truth little more than an indicator of cask type and condition. I have tasted 40-year old malt whiskeys with only a soft straw colour and 3-year old bourbons the color of Fanta. Perhaps some approximate forecasting can be made of a whiskey's flavor profile based on the assessment of color alone (dark hues are sometimes an indication of tannin), but how much of this is our mind's curious ability to make red things taste "red," I don't know.

Extraction of color is for the most part a linear process: the longer the time in cask, the darker the color gets. The exception to this is the first 6–12 months of aging, especially in new oak casks, and therefore particularly applicable to the bourbon industry. During the early stages of maturation, the spirit will take on an increased initial splash of gold, as free extractives invade the liquor. Once these "easy-pickings" compounds are exhausted it's back to the usual breakdown of lignin and other color contributing wood components over time.

Dickel No. 8 is aged for five-to-seven years in charred oak barrels. Dickel No. 12 is seven-to-nine years old, aged in the same oak barrels as No. 8. Then there's Dickel Barrel Select, bottled at a minimum of 10 years old. This is a small batch whiskey, comprising a vatting of 10–15 barrels in total.

In 2013, George Dickel launched a rye whiskey made from a mash comprising 95% rye and 5% malted barley. This spirit is actually distilled and matured by MGP (see page 300) in Indiana and would be difficult to differentiate from the many other rye whiskeys made there were it not for the fact that George Dickel put it through their charcoal mellowing process prior to bottling.

"The mellowing softens the initial hit of spice and brings up some of the fruitiness in the spirit," says Allisa.

GEORGE DICKEL NO. 8 (40% ABV)

A big punch of vanilla, with apricot and tangerine in the background. This is followed up by some solid oak lactones and a generous helping of maple syrup. The plate is heavily vanilla'd, with clear and present early maturation characteristics—glossy candy and more maple syrup. Finish is soft and subtle, with just a touch of rye spice or smoke carrying the flavor through.

GEORGE DICKEL NO. 12 (45%)

The wood aromas here are more butch and burly. Hardwood resin, sticky vanilla toffee and a welcome, spiced dark fruit compote—a result of the wood getting in its stride and working in cahoots with the rye. More voluptuous on the palate than No. 8, this is a golden-corn oil slick of a whiskey, flexing its muscles and showing off deep black pepper spices and a refreshingly dry finish.

GEORGE DICKEL BARREL SELECT (43% ABV)

Soft stone fruits shine through, like canned peaches and ripe plums. The backdrop is undoubtedly wood though, but it certainly does not overwhelm. Vanilla sugar, coconut surfboard wax, and chamois leather all paint a vivid oak picture. On the palate it is perhaps flatter than I would like, but when the prickly finish subsides, you come to realize that it wasn't the finish at all.

GEORGE DICKEL RYE (45% ABV)

Absurdly sweet aromatics bounce off this glass, like a bag of banana, strawberry, and especially chocolate orange-flavored candy. The palate offers little in the way of argument either as the candy shop continues … but this candy is evil. The sting in the tail is hardy rye spices, which wage bloody warfare with the sugar-coated candy.

ROAD TRIP PLAYLIST

"Graceland" – Paul Simon

"One Bourbon, One Scotch, One Beer" – George Thorogood

POPPED OLD FASHIONED

50 ml/1⅔ oz George Dickel No. 1
15 ml/½ oz Popcorn Syrup (see below)

Stir the ingredients with ice and strain into a rocks glass filled with ice.

POPCORN SYRUP

200 g/7 oz water
100 g/3½ oz plain un-salted popcorn
100 g/3½ oz sugar
5 g/1 teaspoon salt

Heat the water in a pan until nearly boiling, then mix with the popcorn and allow to cool for ten minutes. Transfer to a blender and blend until fully mixed. While the popcorn/water mush is still warm, pour through a mesh sieve. Return the filtered liquid to the pan and add the sugar and salt. Heat gently until the sugar is dissolved. Transfer to a bottle and keep refrigerated.

Perhaps it's the effects of the Lincoln County Process, but for me, Tennessee-style whiskey tends to amplify flavors of corn in the mash bill more than bourbon does. In fact, it's probably the barrel I'm tasting, not the corn (since, if anything, charcoal-filtering the distillate is likely to soften the flavor of the base material), but my mind is incapable of not connecting corn with those sweet, oily caramel flavors that the barrel contributes.

So I've designed this drink to accentuate some of those flavors, in a boozy concoction that joins together two American institutes: the distillery and the movie theater.

You can, of course, buy off-the-shelf popcorn syrups that will do the job just fine, but I personally prefer to make my own because you can achieve a much more natural flavor and it's easier to control the sweetness.

ROCK TOWN

STILL HOUSE ROCK

"What can an ex-president of the United States do except get drunk?"

FRANKLIN PIERCE (1804–69), 14TH PRESIDENT OF THE UNITED STATES

As we bid Cascade Hollow farewell and embark upon the next leg of our journey, we are at the same time bidding farewell to big whiskey (for now) and are destined for smaller, newer operations. We'll be in the car for the rest of the day now, heading west to Memphis, then across the Mississippi River and into the state of Arkansas.

Of course, Memphis has a history with whiskey, both as a trading and blending center, and with some distilleries of its own. Memphis' Old Dominick Distillery is one example of a new whiskey business that's aiming to revive some of that old whiskey history. Chris and Alex Canale are the great-great-grandsons of Domenico Canale, an Italian immigrant who established a grocery and whiskey blending business in Memphis in the 1840s. The Old Dominick Distillery opened in 2016 and released its first batches of two-year-old bourbon and Tennessee whiskeys in late 2018. With a production capability of 500,000 bottles a year, this is another one to watch.

Thomas Jefferson acquired about half of the land west of the Mississippi River in the Louisiana Purchase of 1803. Thought to be one of the biggest land purchases ever made, this little deal secured Jefferson 828,000 square miles of the North American continent (approximately a quarter of the US) and included the present-day states of Louisiana, Missouri, Arkansas, Iowa, North Dakota, South Dakota, Nebraska, and Oklahoma, along with most of Kansas, Colorado, Wyoming, Montana, and Minnesota. Factoring in interest due to English and Dutch banks, Jefferson paid $27 million for the lot.

The first US exploration of this vast swath of land was undertaken by Capt. Meriwether Lewis and Lieut. William Clark, who, over a two-year period, mapped rivers and mountains all the way from St. Louis, Missouri to the Pacific Northwest. The Lewis and Clark Expedition contributed significant geographic and scientific knowledge of the West, aided the expansion of the fur trade, and fostered good relationships with some Native American tribes while simultaneously strengthening US claims to the Pacific.

There was very little in the way of whiskey-making going on in this region before the mid-19th century, and it's fair to say that the next eight distilleries are all located in non-traditional places to make spirits. That's not to say whiskey has never been made in these parts, only that no reputation for aged spirits has survived.

This presents some exciting opportunities for a new distillery. When there's no operational manual to work from you, get to enjoy the freedom of writing your own rules. Obviously, any whiskey made in the US will still need to conform to federal regulations, but the sense I get is that consumers and whiskey-makers alike want to see original products with their own sense of place.

PREVIOUS PAGES We travel through the beautiful Ouachita National Forest on our way towards northern Texas.

But how do you go about defining whiskey with place where no whiskey has been made in that place for over 100 years, or ever at all? Does a distiller need to take conscious action to instill a sense of place in their products, or does it occur more organically, through geography, climate, the abundance of local cereals, or consumer tastes? These are the questions I'm asking myself as we leave Memphis on I-40, crossing the Mississippi into Arkansas.

Per square mile, Arkansas has one of the lowest concentrations of distilleries of any state. There are a couple of moonshine distilleries in the north of the state, but Rock Town distillery in Little Rock has basically enjoyed free rein since their opening (as the first distillery in the state since Prohibition) in 2010.

The distillery is right on a highway intersection, which is a clue to its former use as a Cadillac dealership. Now re-purposed, it houses the entire distilling operation as well as a popular bar and tasting room, which is the #2 rated Trip Advisor destination in Little Rock.

Phil Brandon is the proprietor and master distiller of Rock Town.

"I got laid off from my job in telecommunications and thought to myself, 'screw you corporate America—I'm going to make whiskey!'"

Phil has built himself a little bit of an empire in Little Rock. The distillery employs 16 people in total, and the bar and shop are full of locals watching sports and sipping whiskey. The walls are decorated with press cuttings from various local and industry publications, documenting Phil Brandon's rise to whiskey celebrity.

"We're primarily a bourbon maker, but we also make rye, single malt, and other bourbon variants," says Phil. He's actually underselling it. Rock Town run around ten different whiskey mash bills, which is a lot for a distillery of this size. "We do what I call our 'flavor grain series' where we switch the middle grain in bourbon for other cereals," he tells me. This program has seen Phil experiment with chocolate malt, golden promise malt, and un-malted barley.

Even amongst the malt whiskey, Phil tells me he's trialing Irish malt, caramel malt, and other roasted malts. At this point he starts listing even more cereals and mash recipes, and I seriously begin to doubt his claim of "ten mash bills." Rock Town is a lot like one of those craft breweries that seems to continually turn out new product after new product, always trying new things. Everything is an experiment and every experiment is for sale.

The problem I've found with these kinds of operations before is that so much of the stuff they make tastes weird at best and bad at worst. Initially, Phil's laidback manner and "It's all good!" responses crystallize this thought in my mind—nice guy makes nice whiskey for a captive audience. Well if that's what he is, he's been blessed with an extensive range of accidentally delicious products, because this is the where the disarming nature of Rock Town comes into play. Pretty much everything Phil touches tastes delicious. In fact, I'd say he's one of the most understated distillers in the country, with a good eye for detail and a real knack for formulating the right recipe.

Now, given the range of recipes here, it's comforting to learn that the rest of the production is relatively consistent. Fermentation is a three-day process. Mashing is always done on a Thursday, fermented over the weekend and distilled on Monday. Another mash is done on Sunday and Monday to be distilled on Thursday and Friday. Wednesday is when the first distillations are mixed and re-distilled to create the finished spirit. The open-top fermenter is currently filled with a rice-based whiskey mash. Arkansas happens to be the largest rice producer in the nation, and by request of the Arkansas Rice Federation, Phil is now making rice bourbon (one of the first of its kind), made entirely from Arkansas corn and rice.

"The rice gives the mash a brighter, whiter color," he says. "We dip a finger into the ferment, which is pale, sour, and boozy."

All of the products here are double-distilled on a highly versatile 250-gallon still that has been with the business since the start. The same still is also used to make vodka and gin.

Most of the whiskeys made at Rock Town are aged between 18 and 24 months, but some are matured for much longer. Barrels are all 15 and 30 gallons in size and evaporative losses can be as high as 15%.

The main three products here are bourbon, rye, and hickory-smoked whiskey, all three of which come in standard and single-barrel versions.

"Then there's a three year old bourbon variant," says Phil, "a four-grain sour mash, peated bourbon, barley bourbon, barley whiskey, four-grain sour mash anniversary edition, sherry cask bourbon, rye…" I'm about to remark on the breadth of the range at this point but he continues, "…chocolate bourbon, single malt, golden promise single malt, rice bourbon."

Needless to say, it's a busy roster of products here and an impractical range of products to market if this were a larger operation. But since nearly all of Rock Town's sales take place in the state of Arkansas, Phil can afford to try new things, knowing that his followers will be scrabbling to get their hands on whatever his next experimental bottle is. Brown spirits drinkers are perhaps even more receptive to unusual products, too, as an established level of discernment encourages further exploration.

One product of particular note is the hickory-smoked whiskey, which is made using smoked wheat that Phil smokes in 400-lb batches on a smoker he built himself. This smoker was made from a converted filing cabinet, where the drawers hold the cereals and the smoke is generated from a small fire at the bottom. "Screw you corporate America," indeed!

We're heading for northern Texas next. It's a six-hour drive, which will take us through the beautiful Ouachita National Forest. Unfortunately, most of the beauty is lost to us, as the sun has already set by the time we get there. Ouachita is an extremely sparsely populated area of the south, and we drive over an hour without seeing another car or even any buildings. The headlights occasionally reflect a pair of eyes however: deer, mongoose, and even a family of black bears crossing the road.

Time becomes arbitrary in the blackness of the night but at some point we cross the imaginary line that marks the border between Arkansas and Oklahoma. There are only two whiskey distilleries in this state, Oklahoma Distillers, in Tulsa, and

Scissortail, just south of Oklahoma City. The combat veterans who run the Scissortail distillery make a rye and a bourbon under the Scissortail brand and an additional range of whiskeys under the Leadslingers brand: a bourbon, which features an emblem of an eagle carrying an assault rifle on the label; a single malt called "Minuteman," named after the militia from the Revolutionary war; and a rye called "Fighting Spirit." They also make a cinnamon whiskey called "Napalm," for which they ran a special "Make America Great Again" bottling for Donald Trump's election. We keep on driving.

Finally, we arrive in the city of Duncan, which is just 30 miles north of the Texas border. We rest there for what's left of the night.

ARKANSAS BOURBON (46% ABV)

The aroma is initially of Honey Smacks, slick caramel, a little engine oil and cream soda. The taste is dryer than expected, with a kind of blackened banana note, and waxed orange flavor. Dryness continues into the finish, which makes it quite a quaffable whiskey.

FOUR GRAIN SOUR MASH (46% ABV)

More herbal and spiced, with notes of fennel seed, spice drawer, baked apple, and vanilla fudge. Canned sweetcorn juice comes through with time. It's gentle on the palate, well-rounded, and buttery.

HICKORY SMOKED WHEAT (45% ABV)

The smoke is reminiscent of gasoline-style fumes with a touch of canned peach. It's dry on the palate, with a continuing gentle smoke.

ROAD TRIP PLAYLIST

"I Drove All Night" – Cindi Lauper

"Alabama Song" – The Doors

"Arkansas Traveller" – George Pegram

WHISKEY & TONIC

50 ml/1⅔ oz Rock Town Hickory Smoked Wheat Whiskey
120 ml/4 oz Fever-Tree tonic water

Add the ingredients to an ice filled highball and stir gently. Garnish with a strip of lemon zest.

Tonic water is more traditionally served with gin, but tonic water can work equally well (if not better) with other types of spirits, whiskey included. I can hear the cries of "blasphemy!" already, but bear with me here for a second.

Tonic water contains sugar and quinine, which is what gives it that mouth-puckering bittersweet flavor. All of the world's quinine comes from the cinchona tree, which is native to South America. Whiskey gets much of its flavor from trees too so, in principle at least, there is a synergy that can be established here. The quinine will serve to highlight some of the tannic notes in the whiskey and the sugar will bring out some of the caramel flavors —effectively amplifying these sections of the wood flavor spectrum.

I have experimented quite a bit with pairing different types of whiskey with tonic water to see where the best results can be found. It turns out that it's the whiskeys that you wouldn't normally pair with soda water that work best with tonic. I'm talking about smoky whiskeys and whiskeys matured in wine casks.

Rock Town's excellent Hickory Smoked Wheat Whiskey is the absolute ideal candidate for this treatment, where both the lighter, fruitier notes of the spirit and the rich smoky flavors interplay perfectly with the tonic. As you might imagine, this is a great drink to enjoy on a warm evening, but thanks to the smoke, it also feels just as at home in the cooler winter months.

OPPOSITE TOP Every single barrel of Rock Town whiskey is held within this one room, to the north of the main distillery building.
OPPOSITE FAR LEFT Here we see Rock Town's multi-purpose copper pot-still and, in front of it, a fermenting batch of rice whiskey!

OPPOSITE LEFT While the range of mash bills at Rock Town is extensive, the barrels—thankfully—are consistently new American oak cooperage.
FOLLOWING PAGES Just before the border with Oklahoma, we pass by this mercantile store in Caddo Gap, right in the heart of Ouachita National Forest.

AP MERCANTILE Co. IM

DRINK
Coca-Cola
IN BOTTLES

SOUVENIRS
TOYS ·· GIFTS

JAMS ◆ JELLIES
RKANSAS MADE!

ANTIQUES
AND COLLECTIBLE

BALCONES

TECTONIC RUMBLINGS IN TEXAS

*"Sleep late, have fun, get wild, drink whiskey, and drive fast on empty streets
with nothing in mind but falling in love and not getting arrested."*

HUNTER S. THOMPSON (1937–2005), AUTHOR AND JOURNALIST

Dawn breaks as we head south from Duncan, crossing the border into Texas and turning southeast on Route 81, towards Dallas. This road traces the line of the old Chisholm Trail, which was used during the post-Civil War period to drive cattle from the ranches in southern Texas, through the Great Plains, all the way up to the railheads in Kansas, where they were sent to market. I don't think it's too much of a stretch to assume that bottles of whiskey were carried along the route by cowboy drovers looking for some respite during the long and arduous beef drive.

Past Dallas, we join I-35 heading south. This road traces the Balcones fault line, which probably formed when the land east of here crashed in to the rest of North America 300 million years ago. The fault has remained inactive for the past 15 million years (thankfully) and it's likely that I would never have even heard of it were it not for a certain distillery in Waco, Texas.

Our first stop in Texas is at what is arguably Texas' best-known distillery. Founded in 2008 and distributing to Europe by 2010, Balcones was the distillery that introduced me to the potential of Texas as a whiskey-producing region. From the perspective of someone who lives and works in the UK (mostly), Balcones felt like a maverick departure from most of the other American whiskey brands. Not only were Balcones' spirits not produced in Kentucky, they

weren't even bourbon! Or whiskey! (They omit the 'e' at Balcones.) Put all that together and what they're basically saying is, "we're not interested in what you're making and where you're making it. We're making our own thing, and we're making it here."

The early roster of products was made up of a rye, a malt, and two corn-based spirits, plus a smoked whisky, most of which display "TEXAS" front and center on the label, with the lone star emblem rockin' the bottom label.

My first taste of the Balcones stable of products was in 2011, at The Whisky Show in London. The team from Balcones was hard to miss. Amongst the sweaty clusters of tweed-jacketed whiskey geeks, they stood out like a 10-gallon hat in an elevator, and nobody more so than Balcones' founder, Chip Tate.

However, on September 14, 2014, Balcones' board of directors suspended Tate from his position as President and a few months later, Tate agreed to be bought out of his shares and signed a non-compete agreement that prevented him from making whiskey until March 2016. He was a whiskey celebrity by this point—the embodiment of the American craft whiskey movement—and the whiskey world watched with keen interest as all this played out. Tate has since gone on to set up Tate & Co., his second Waco whiskey venture.

Meanwhile, Balcones got big. In 2016, the distillery relocated to a 65,000-sq ft former self-storage

building that dates back to the 1920s. This distillery is 25 times bigger than the previous location and it's a far cry from the original welding shop operation located six blocks away, where space was so tight that the copper still had the dual-purpose function of both distilling and mashing.

What's most interesting about this transition from micro distillery to… midi distillery (we're not yet at the size of the Kentucky juggernauts) is the consideration of the product itself. How do you go about upscaling all of your equipment by at least an order of magnitude while maintaining the same flavor profile? Well, we were about to find out.

Co-founder and head distiller Jared Himstedt and distillery manager Thomas Mote take us on a tour of the operation. Jared is the embodiment of the hipster vagabond look, with dusty baseball cap, scraggly beard, and all-black attire. Thomas looks more normal. These guys are the rock stars of the industry though, key characters in the story of modern American whiskey and—jumping ahead a little—producers of some really delicious booze.

The cereals at Balcones are milled in one of two ways depending on their type. Malt gets the roller mill treatment, while corn and rye go through the hammer mill. The mills are unusual, as is their "chain and disk" grain transportation system, because both are sourced from a brewery equipment supplier. Thomas admits, "a lot of our team—myself included—have come from the brewing industry, so you'll notice that in the terms we use which are sort of a mish-mash of American brewing, American distilling, and Scottish distilling."

The distillery runs ten different mash bills, comprising various corn mashes, various malted barley mashes (including peated and Texas-grown malt) as well as bourbon (high-rye and wheated) and rye (Elbon Rye from Northwest Texas accompanied by crystal, chocolate, and roasted rye).

The two mash cookers and seven fermenters are all 25,000-liters capacity. The fermenters are outside of the main building but are connected to a temperature sensor that pumps coolant when necessary (pretty much all the time). Fermentation takes seven days, of a mish-mash of American brewing, American distilling, and Scottish distilling."

The distillery runs ten different mash bills, comprising various corn mashes, various malted barley mashes (including peated and Texas-grown malt) as well as bourbon (high-rye and wheated) and rye (Elbon Rye from Northwest Texas accompanied by crystal, chocolate, and roasted rye).

The two mash cookers and seven fermenters are all 25,000-liters capacity. The fermenters are outside of the main building but are connected to a temperature sensor that pumps coolant when necessary (pretty much all the time). Fermentation takes seven days, though Thomas reckons most of the alcohol has been made by the end of Day 3. This extended ferment has the effect of lowering the pH of the beer, creating new aldehydes and esters that will provide character in the whiskeys.

"We don't do sour mashing," says Thomas, "but because of our long fermentation we reach a pH in the low threes region."

"We do it backwards." Jared chips in, continuing: "The backset on American sour mashing brings a lot of acetic acid, which translates to acetone (solvent) aromas in the product. Our long fermentation generates more lactic acid, which we think has a less aggressive, softer note to it."

Distillation is done in copper pot stills made by Forsyths in Scotland.

Now, before we go any further, I have to tell you that these stills are like nothing I've ever seen before. The still is the beating heart of any distillery, and the most important part too since it's what facilitates spirits production. But after over 350 distillery visits, I thought I had seen them all. I hadn't.

First, a little background: back in the old distillery, where space was tight, the 250-gallon still was backed into a corner, and with no room for the condenser, the lyne arm of the still had to run through a wall and into another section of the building. This long, upward-slanting lyne arm was a trait of the still, removing sulphurous compounds in the spirit through extended copper contact and creating prejudice against heavier volatile aromatics.

So when it came to upscaling the distillery, it was essential that the new spirits stills had a lyne arm that was much longer and wider than the original, so that it remained in proportion with the bigger still base. When Forsyths did the calculations, they quickly realized that the lyne arms on these stills would need to be at least 165 ft long and the condensers would need to be located in the next block. This was considered a little impractical, so Forsyths came up with the idea of coiling the lyne arm on top of the still, which gave the arm the length they were after.

"It takes so much power to get the necessary vapor pressure to push spirit through," says Jared. "So any corrections, we do."

The condensers cool over two stages, first changing the state of matter of the spirit from gas to liquid, then reducing temperature from 110°F to 60°F: the temperature that the hydrometers are calibrated to.

Balcones Single Malt is produced as true to the Scottish style as is possible in Texas. The malt is sourced from Simpsons in Berwick-upon-Tweed, a 70-year-old lauter mash tun (a vessel that separates the wort from the solids) is used (sourced from the Speyburn distillery), and of course the stills were made in Scotland too. Most of the barrels used to make it are new American oak casks, but some re-fill casks are used too.

Balcones are currently making 250,000-proof gallons a year. This is achieved in one shift a day, five days a week. Jared and Thomas reckon the distillery, in its current form, could triple production if it became a 24-hour operation. In spite of their enormous facility, most of Balcones maturation takes place in another location on the outskirts of Waco, though. The distillery loses around 15% a year to the angels' share (the romantic term for volume lost due to evaporation), meaning that by the time they come to bottle some of their older, 4+ year expressions, the barrel is only half full.

"We haven't filled small barrels in two years," Jared tells me.

Everything here is in 53-gallon casks made from American, Hungarian, or French oak, using custom toast and char levels. That presents quite a few or finishing to get there, then so be it."

Balcones is an example of what happens when a small distillery gets really successful. A decision has to be made. Do you remain the same, knowing that you can't produce any more spirit and that the only way to make more money is to charge more? Or do you expand your operation? Visit any farmers' market and you'll encounter dozens of cottage industry types that, I imagine, are quite happy making what they can and selling what they make. Building a brand doesn't have to be an exercise in building revenue, and achievement is measurable in more ways than just a bank balance. A lot of the time it's the producers that don't seem to be valuing growth above all else that get me enthusiastic. Because that means they're focusing on something else, which more often than not is their liquid. It takes a certain kind of obsession to disregard the commercial aspect of your business in favor of some creative goal. Sure, the two are not mutually exclusive, you can have an eye on the accounts while allowing yourself room to enjoy mastering your product.

TEXAS SINGLE MALT (53% ABV)

On the nose, we find coconut oil, dusty flaked almonds, and a light spreading of Nutella. Sweet orange oil and treacle is awarded to those who are persistent. Hot tree bark, burnt cedar, and a whole ton of residual sugar emerge in the taste. The sweetness carries through a long toasted finish of grape skin, luscious caramel, and maple syrup.

TRUE BLUE (50% ABV)

The initial hit of booze-soaked crispy corn fritters slowly dissipates, revealing beautiful barrel aromatics, including toffee apple, smoked caramel… and do I detect some sherry? Over time, this whiskey begins to smell suspiciously like a malt. It's gooey on the palate, with soft tortilla, toasted wood, and sweet almond. Stunning.

BABY BLUE (46% ABV)

Steamed asparagus, hemp oil, and green banana skins are the first to show in the smell. Sweet cut grass and baked sponge cake come next, with thyme, cornbread, and vanilla. There's a texture of coagulation on the palate, like it's self-aware and unwilling to be swallowed. The finish is breezy, sweet, and really rather more-ish.

ROAD TRIP PLAYLIST

"Ride Like The Wind" – Christopher Cross

"Have a Drink on Me" – AC/DC

"Paranoid" – Black Sabbath

BARBECUE SAUCE

50 ml/1⅔ oz Balcones Baby Blue
20 ml/⅔ oz carrot juice
10 ml/2 teaspoons lemon juice
10 ml/2 teaspoons sherry vinegar
10 ml/2 teaspoons Demerara (brown) sugar syrup
fresh thyme
soda water, to top up

Add the first five ingredients to a highball glass filled with ice and give a stir. Next add two or three sprigs of fresh thyme, followed by more ice and the soda. Give another brief stir and serve with a slice of lemon on top.

Okay, this isn't actually a recipe for barbecue sauce, but rather a cocktail that's perfect for drinking alongside food at a barbecue, and that plays on the slang term for alcohol: "sauce."

Barbecue and bourbon are quite possibly the only two major food and drink traditions that can truly be considered American in their origin. Both of them have their roots in the colonial era (George Washington once attended a "barbicue" in Virginia) and both have strong ties to Southern culture too. Within the broader categorization of barbecue, the state of Texas is representative of one of four regional styles (Memphis, Carolina, and Kansas barbecue are the other three) and it's epitomized by a liberal use of beef over pork.

For me, a barbecue presents one of the best opportunities for food and drink pairings in the culinary world. The food tends to be salty, smoky, and fatty, with perhaps a little sweetness and spice. To cut through all that richness and balance the meal you need a nice clean acidity, such as barbecue sauce or vinegar slaw. Unfortunately, those condiments don't have any alcohol in them (typically) and are therefore irrefutably a lot less fun than a cocktail.

My Barbecue Sauce cocktail combines Texas whiskey with ingredients that can already be seen on many a good pit master's chopping board. This is a long, tangy drink that, despite its delicate appearance, is easily up to the challenge of a hunk of smoked short rib.

FOLLOWING PAGES The "sparging" of malted barley in the mash cooker at Balcones, which involves spraying hot water through the mash to collect the sugar. This process is rarely seen in American distilleries and is more common in brewing and in the production of Scotch whisky.

GARRISON BROTHERS

MANAGING THE ANGELS' SHARE

"Whisky is liquid sunshine."

GEORGE BERNARD SHAW (1856–1950), IRISH PLAYWRIGHT

When Mexico gained independence from Spain in 1821, it was a seriously big nation that encompassed the present-day US states of Texas, New Mexico, Arizona, California, Utah, and even parts of Colorado. No sooner had Spain been removed from the picture that unrest among Tejanos (Texas Mexicans) began, provoking insurrection and inspiring yet another revolutionary uprising. In late 1835, Mexico deployed an army to take care of the unruly Texans, resulting in a number of conflicts, including The Battle of the Alamo, a 13-day siege at a mission in San Antonio that ended in the defeat of the rebels. Meanwhile, while the siege was ongoing, the Republic of Texas was declared on March 2, 1836.

Mexico refused to recognize an independent Texas, however, and various conflicts occurred in the decade that followed. In 1845, the US Congress passed a bill that authorized the United States to annex the Republic of Texas, which was popularly approved by Texan voters who were mostly American anyway. Texas was admitted to the Union and became the 28th state on December 29, 1845.

A casual drive along the Texas/Mexico border, from Brownsville to El Paso, takes around 14 hours by car. It's for this reason—the sheer size of Texas—that it's difficult to summarize the culture of the state. Sure, there's Southern culture here, but Southern accents and Southern food are less apparent as you head further south. Most of the churches here are Roman Catholic and the food is quite far removed from

barbecue and gumbo. When I asked Robert Likarish from Ironroot distillery what the difference was between Mexican food and Tex-Mex, he told me simply: "Tex-Mex has more cheese."

On the road out of Austin towards Garrison Brothers, we drive past the Deep Eddy Vodka distillery in Dripping Springs. Thanks, in part, to the success of Tito's "Handmade Vodka" (the brand currently sells over 60 million bottles a year), Texan vodka seems to be experiencing a its golden age. Dripping Springs is also home to San Luis Spirits, who have been making vodka and gin since 2005, as well as Treaty Oak Distilling, who make whiskey.

The area in and around Austin is packed with whiskey distilleries, too. There's Still Austin Whiskey Co., which opened in September 2017, making it the first distillery in the Austin metropolitan area since Prohibition. It's a substantial operation, so it seems likely we'll be seeing their products everywhere in the coming years.

One thing that all of these distilleries have in common is the heat. There's no escaping it here, and in the height of the summer, 97°F is a fairly typical midday high. Of course, on particularly hot days it can easily creep up beyond 110°F, from "dang hot" to "oh sh*t!"

From a whiskey-making perspective, this presents a new set of challenges, particularly with respect to maturation, where some of the interactive processes between spirit and wood are wildly accelerated by the temperature. I don't expect George Bernard Shaw intended us to take him literally when he said that "whisky is liquid sunshine," but in southern Texas, the blazing ball of gas in the sky has as big an impact on the whiskey as anything else.

In 2008, Dan Garrison became the first whiskey maker to produce a legally defined bourbon in Texas since Prohibition. But despite being a native Texan, he wasn't quite prepared for the heat. "It nuked the barrels," he tells me. "They leaked. Cracked. Broke altogether. Hundreds of gallons were lost."

It turns out you can't just apply Kentucky methodology to south Texas whiskey-making and expect end up with a similar product. A fresh approach is needed.

Fortunately for us, it's the need for "fresh approaches" that has shaped the world of spirits that we enjoy today. It's when innovation becomes essential, not optional, that spirits of place and of people begin to manifest. The requirement to adapt is an attribute that spirit lovers should seek out, as it quite often results in an interesting product.

The Garrison Brothers distillery is located in Texas Hill Country, near the Pedernales River. If you own property around here, the chances are you own a few thousand acres of it. Ranches easily exceed 4,000 acres in this part of the world and it can take a few minutes to get down the driveway.

This distillery sits on a modest 70 acres—a mere patch of lawn relative to its neighbors. When Dan bought the place, there was nothing save for a wooden cabin, which has since become the shop and hospitality area, and is the first stop for visitors as they arrive. And what a welcome they get! There are pitchers of iced tea, dozens of chunky wooden rocking chairs, and a hardworking beer fridge leaning against the cabin wall dispensing ice-cold cans of local lager (take note, other distilleries).

Dan Garrison makes his appearance and immediately ticks all the boxes you would hope a Texan ranch owner/whiskey maker would tick: Stetson hat, silver hair, button-down shirt, beaming grin.

Looks can be deceiving though. Dan previously worked a long and mostly successful career in advertising and marketing, working for Saatchi in New York and a Texan software company called Extraprise during the dot-com bubble. When Extraprise collapsed during the economic downturn of the early 2000s, Dan's substantial shareholding was vaporized. Having just filed a tax return, the IRS still insisted on taxing the full $125,000 based on his holdings in the now-dead company. Without a job or the means to pay it, Dan scraped together everything he could, around $65,000, and headed over to his tax office to plead with the IRS to accept the payment.

"I told them 'I don't want to declare personal bankruptcy,'" he says, "'but I will if you don't accept this check. But the first thing I'll do is go to the nearest bar and spend all of the $65,000 on bourbon.'"

Fortunately, the IRS accepted his plea bargain and absolved his debt.

The idea of bourbon must have lodged itself somewhere in his head though. Feeling the need to clear his head, the very next day Dan hopped on a plane to Kentucky and toured the Kentucky bourbon trail. It was his first trip to the home of bourbon.

"I walked in to the Maker's Mark distillery in Loretto," he recalls, "and I looked up at that big still and said to myself, 'that's what I'm going to do for the rest of my life.'"

We hop into an open top 4x4 (or perhaps "dune buggy" would be more appropriate) and Dan drives up the track towards the distillery buildings. It's late afternoon and the sky has taken on gentle pink opacity. The vehicle wiggles its way up a loose track, kicking plumes of dust into the afternoon air. Dan yells something at me, but it's lost under the roar of the engine and the only word I can make out is "snakes." It brings to mind those wise words spoken by comedian W.C. Fields: "Always carry a flagon of whiskey in case of snakebite, and furthermore always carry a small snake."

The various small buildings on the ranch really give you the sense that this distillery has been built from the ground up. But slowly, over time. And they've not stopped yet—a big ranch expansion is underway. A new still arrived 24 hours before we did. Garrison

ABOVE One of Garrison Brothers' drive-thru whiskey aging warehouses.

Brothers is not a big operation, but they make whiskey 24 hours a day, 365 days a year. With distribution currently spanning 26 states and half a dozen countries, you can appreciate Dan's eagerness to ramp up production and lay down fresh stocks.

The fact that there is a lot of land to build on will set this distillery in good stead for further expansion, but its remoteness also causes operational headaches, too. The first of which is water. In the arid Texan climate, rivers and lakes are scarce, so most ranches source their water from aquifers and wells beneath the surface. Distilleries are thirsty operations, though, and groundwater depletion is no joke. A distillery that drinks all the well water faster than it can be replenished won't last long, and plundering aquifers can cause deteriorating water quality and even land subsidence. Perhaps Dan asked God for a solution, because the heavens answered: rain. This

distillery has over 10,000 sq ft of roof space capturing rainwater and channeling it into above-ground and below-ground storage tanks. Annual rainfall in Hill Country is in the region of 36 inches, so that's 30,000 cubic feet of rain a year, or 190,000 gallons of water—good for about 60 mashes, or 20 days' worth of production.

Drainage is similarly challenging, "We're out on the middle of nowhere, with no sewage system. If we screw up, we're in big trouble."

We start the tour out the back of the main distillery building, where three grain silos store all the cereals. There's one 60,000-lb corn silo and two 40,000-lb silos for wheat and barley. At odds with the rustic feel of the place, the milling system here (which uses a hammer mill) is state-of-the-art and can hydraulically shift cereals around the place for milling and mashing with complete automation.

ABOVE This copper pot still was joined by an identical sibling just hours before our arrival at the distillery.

ABOVE Dan Garrison: marketing expert, distiller, and devout Texas Longhorns fan.

Only one mash bill is in use here, with corn making up 74%, wheat 15%, and malted barley 11%. The corn and wheat are both products of Texas, but the barley (which is all but impossible to grow in Texas, apart from areas of the Panhandle) comes from Montana. They cook together 325 gallons of water and 1200 lbs of cereal, resulting in a very sweet 20–25 brix mash. The beer here ferments in one of 16 open-top fermenters for four or five days, and runs off at a whopping 17% ABV—one of the highest-strength ferments I've seen.

Any given quantity of cereal can only produce a certain given quantity of alcohol; the strength is governed by how much water is used in the cook. Garrison Brothers eye-watering beer is an example of what happens when water is rationed and you brew a super-concentrated mash (high ratio of cereal to water). Of course, you need special yeasts that can tolerate very high alcohol concentrations and continue to work, and the team here are tight-lipped about the specific strain they use. As we have already learned, different yeasts produce a different array of flavors from the substrate, so this is yet another example of the environment forcing the hand of the distiller and shaping the finished product.

Dan bought his first still from the long-time master distiller at Buffalo Trace Distillery, Elmer T. Lee (more on him on page 151).

All of the barrels at Garrison Brothers are of the "midi" 30-gallon persuasion, and are sourced from a few different cooperages. This is intentional, because it guarantees the oak is sourced from different forests and therefore produces a different-tasting product that's ideal for blending. The casks undergo a slow toasting for 20 minutes and brief 53 second char.

We've already learned a lot about wood and barrels: how casks are made, what flavors they contribute, and how they are stored. But we haven't yet addressed exactly what happens to a spirit as it rests inside a cask. And is "rest" even the correct word?

Garrison Brothers is as good a place as any to discuss the physics of maturation, since most changes that occur during aging occur here at a far greater pace thanks to the absurdly high temperature of southern Texas.

When it comes to the barrel, we know two things for sure: the temperature outside the barrel is constantly shifting (daily and seasonally), and the spirit is constantly evaporating. We can plug these variables into a formula called the Ideal Gas Law, which can tell us some interesting things about oak penetration. Bear with me here…

Pressure, volume, temperature, and the amount of gas are all variables that are relative to one another. When temperature increases, more spirit changes from liquid to gas, so the pressure or volume must increase to maintain a balanced ratio. In practice, both of them increase, forcing the liquid into the grain of the wood. However, when night falls, or the seasons turn colder, the amount of gas decreases, which means that pressure and volume must also decrease, sucking the liquid back out of the wood.

This is also relevant to evaporative losses. While the volume of liquid in a cask remains relatively constant in most distilleries, at Garrison Brothers it can drop by over 10% every year. When spirit vapor evaporates, the liquid in the cask replenishes the (increasing) space with more vapor. This is why filling barrels close to the top will achieve greater penetration of the oak, because a smaller volume of air will achieve a higher pressure when it gets hot.

Distillers should take care not to fill too close to the top though, especially when it's cool outside. Liquid expands when it gets warm too, and in the right circumstances the pressure inside a cask and pop the bung off and caused precious whiskey to spill out.

All Garrison Brothers whiskeys are aged for a minimum of four years, which in this climate and in those casks, is a long time. The Small Batch bourbon is an annually released blend of 498 casks, all of them a shade over four years old.

"We've changed processes along the way," says Dan, "and that's evident in the differences each year. We're not changing anything anymore though. The 2018 bourbon is the best we've ever made."

They also bottle a 375ml "boot flask" version of Small Batch, which, as Dan says, "you can take to the game on Friday, the dance on the Saturday, or the church on Sunday, and nobody's going to know!"

Any barrels that taste a little unusual, perhaps exhibiting notes of fig or dried fruit, after four years, are set to one side and closely monitored. These casks are earmarked for their Single Barrel releases, or sold direct to customers.

The epitome of the single barrel bottlings is "Cowboy Bourbon" a single-barrel, barrel-proof expression that isn't even filtered, usually resulting in splinters of wood and chunks of carbon sitting at the bottom of the bottle. This is the only time I've heard a distiller recommend decanting a whiskey (to avoid getting splinters in your throat!).

Lastly, there are a couple of special releases: Balmorhea (named after a local spring) which is a double-matured, first for four years in new American oak, then for an additional year in another new American oak cask; and Estacado, which is aged three years in a new American white oak barrel and finished for six months in Llano Estacado Winery Port wine casks.

"It should be like a warm blanket of caramel, butterscotch, and chocolate," he says, grinning. "That's good bourbon."

TEXAS STRAIGHT 2016 (47% ABV)

Chamois leather, corn bread, corn on the cob. Light, soft, and creamy on the palate. Delicate and sweet.

TEXAS STRAIGHT 2018 (47% ABV)

Drier and more buttery on the palate, still with some sweetness there, but with more grip and a longer finish than the 2016.

ESTACADO (53.5% ABV)

A bourbon layered with red jammy fruits, like strawberry and blackberry. Strawberry ice cream and a little bit of black pepper on the palate.

ROAD TRIP PLAYLIST

"Paradise By The Dashboard Light" – Meat Loaf

"Have You Ever Seen The Rain" – Creedence Clearwater Revival

"Oh My Sweet Carolina" – Ryan Adams

ABOVE Dan Garrison committed to buying this enormous longhorn bull sculpture now on display at the distillery after a night of bourbon drinking. He broke the news to his wife the day it arrived.

FOLLOWING PAGES In the words of Dan (stood out of shot): "Well now you've seen a genuine Texas sunset, gentlemen."

BLINKER

60 ml/2 oz Garrison Brothers Texas Straight Bourbon
30 ml/1 oz ruby red grapefruit juice
7.5 ml/1½ teaspoons grenadine

Shake all the ingredients with ice and fine-strain into a chilled cocktail glass. Garnish with a twist of lemon.

Here's a massively underrated whiskey cocktail that contains ruby red grapefruit juice—a fruit that is a most appropriate ingredient in Texas.

The US is the world's largest producer of grapefruits, producing over 1.5 million tons of grapefruit each year, which is more than one-third of the world supply. That's rather impressive considering only three American states grow commercial citrus fruit: California, Florida, and Texas.

And had the grapefruit not ended up in Texas, it is highly unlikely that America would have much of a grapefruit industry today. Grapefruits were unpopular in Texas for many years, but fruit farmers continued to persevere with it. Their hard work eventually paid off when they discovered that the grapefruit was prone to mutation. In 1929, a Texan orchard owner discovered a red grapefruit growing on a pink grapefruit tree. With its striking red flesh and sweet taste, the fruit was an instant hit. The effect was to transform Texas into a grapefruit growing superpower and to change the face of the nation's breakfast table forever.

Back in 1934, lawyer and cocktail author David A. Embury wrote of the Blinker, "One of the few cocktails containing grapefruit juice. Not particularly good but not particularly bad."

Well, perhaps tastes have changed, because I think this is a cracking drink and pretty much everyone I've ever handed one to feels the same way.

IRONROOT REPUBLIC

THE FRENCH CONNECTION

"Always carry a flagon of whiskey in case of snakebite.
Furthermore, always carry a snake."

W. C. FIELDS (1880–1946), COMEDIAN

We have one more distillery to visit in Texas, before we head north, towards Colorado. Seventy-five miles north of Dallas is Denison, the birthplace of Dwight D. Eisenhower (1890–1969). Like many towns across this nation, its exploits are few and far between and they could have ended with the 34th President, but for anyone with a passing interest in alcoholic beverages, there's another reason to make a stop.

It surprised me to learn that Texas is home to over 4,000 acres of vineyards and that wine making here is a multi-billion dollar industry. Spanish missionaries established the first vineyards in Texas—the first vineyard in North America, actually—back in 1662, and there are dozens of native grape varieties floating about. Many of these varieties were categorized in the late-19th century by the Denison horticulturalist, T.V. Munson, who, as well as writing things down, was a dab hand at creating weird hybrid vines that produced grapes the size of plums (everything is bigger in Texas).

Munson gained notoriety during the *phylloxera* epidemic of the late-19th century, which decimated most of the vineyards in Europe. He pioneered methods in creating phylloxera-resistant vines using the Texas native variety *Vitis berlandieri*, which enjoyed similar limestone-rich soil types to that of France. Of course, the French wanted to grow Sauvignon Blanc and Chardonnay, so Munson grafted

European vines onto the Texan rootstock and enabled hundreds of vineyards to begin producing wine again. As a thank you, Munson earned an induction into the French Legion of Honor (only six Americans have achieved this, one of which, coincidentally, is Dwight D. Eisenhower) and sister-city status for Denison, which is twinned with Cognac, France.

This leads us effortlessly on to our reason for visiting Denison: Ironroot Republic Distillery. Now, with all this chat about grapes, you might imagine that Ironroot is a brandy-focused distillery. And you would be wrong (although they do make a little). Ironroot is a modern-day mash-up of French and Texan spirits production, borrowing techniques and processes from both sides of the Atlantic to create a unique product.

The exterior façade of Ironroot is sufficiently "non-distillery" looking to make us wonder whether we're in the right place. It's a big, beige box that has the look of a boat showroom about it… because that's exactly what it used to be (Denison is right next to Lake Texoma, one of the largest reservoirs in the US). The 30-ft sign on the wall, "Ironroot Republic Distillery," gives the game away, though.

We're met by Robert and Jonathan Likarish, who represent two-thirds of this family-run operation. They both epitomize that relaxed Texan style, but this is no hobbyist operation. Jonathan has enough degrees to furnish an entire family, with a BSc in industrial engineering, and MSCs in both biomedical

engineering and mechanical engineering. Robert is no slouch either, with degrees in both economics and law. Now that I think about it, as collecting degrees goes, that's a solid range for starting a distillery. That was what Robert thought at least, and after years of joking about it, he convinced Jonathan to make the leap. The brothers began interning in 2010, on a mission to work out what kind of distillery they wanted to make.

To sum it up in one word, it would have to be "corn."

Now, I grant you that corn is not the most romantic of the whiskey-making cereals. It doesn't tend to have the honeyed fruitiness of malted barley or the gritty spice of rye. But I suspect that it was exactly corn's uncharismatic reputation that piqued the curiosity of the Likarish brothers, who describe it as "the red-headed step-child of the whiskey family."

But corn is also every bit a Texan crop. Being indigenous to Mexico, and given that Texas was once part of Mexico (and accounts for around two-thirds of the US/Mexico border today), it's likely that the first North American corn was grown in the state of Texas. Indeed, corn in Texas pre-dates the Spanish conquest, and Texans were major transmitters of prehistoric corn culture from Mexico into the lands that make up the eastern half of the US. Corn was an economic necessity to Texans; it was an integral part of their way of life. Indigenous cultures used cobs for jug and bottle stoppers, smoking pipes, tool handles, back scratchers, torches, fishing floats, and firewood.

When most of us picture a cob of corn, it's a huge yellow truncheon of a thing that we think of. But back in the 19th century, corn of all colors was grown, from blue to red to black and purple. Many of these native varieties were introduced to settlers in the 1840s, by Texan natives. By 1859, Texas was growing 15-million bushels of corn a year. Over time, commercial pressures forced low yielding heirloom varieties out, and the high yielding, sweet "yellow dent" corn that we're all familiar with became the variety from which virtually all other cultivars have spawned.

The Likarish brothers use yellow dent too, grown about 15 miles from the distillery. It makes up to 95% of the four mash bills they produce, but they also use about a dozen other heirloom varieties, or "flavoring grains," each contributing a unique aroma and taste to their whiskey. By blending these varieties into a mash, Ironroot can create a balanced product, with spice, fruit, sweetness and fragrance, by using only one cereal type: corn. In fact, for most of their whiskeys they don't use any cereals besides corn: their corn whiskeys are 100% corn and one of their bourbon whiskeys is 100% corn, too!

"A lot of people don't believe that 5% of a different corn can affect a whiskey, but it can," says Robert.

"Bloody butcher" is one of their favorites of the weird corns. It's red, of course, with black speckles and very large kernels. Robert tells us it was one of the first hybrid corns developed by a collaboration between the Native Americans and the settlers. Another popular variety is "Floriani," which was exported to Italy some time ago to make polenta, then discovered growing on a single random farm in Texas.

"It's a flint corn. When it comes off the still it's very spicy, almost like a cayenne pepper," explains Robert. "There's a slight umami note on it too," chips in Jonathan. And I agree. It does have a savory, spiced tomato note to it. It's really eye-opening to experience the differences that a 5% change in the mash bill can make, especially given it's still corn, nothing else.

Thanks to Munson and those that followed him, corn has been blessed with great varietal names. Besides those mentioned already, Ironroot use Black Aztec, Green Oaxacan, Magic Manor, Amanda Palmer... "One day I'm going to grow up and name corn varietals," says Jonathan.

The total cereal count here is about 15, with a few types of wheat featuring here and there (including a malted wheat), three barleys, and a couple of different ryes. 95% of all the cereals used at Ironroot are sourced from within 60 miles of the distillery. This is set to drop slightly as the brothers start making more single malt, as most of the barley in Texas is grown in the cooler Panhandle region to the west of here. There's a contingency for that, however. New strains of barley are being developed all the time, and Robert believes more heat-resistant varieties should be available locally in the coming years.

The stills are custom-made, but designed in the most face-palmingly simple manner: buy a bunch of whiskeys, decide which ones you like best, then take a look at the stills they use and copy them. It's refreshing to see such an honest approach to an aspect of distillery engineering that is usually beset with smoke and mirrors, especially given Jonathan's engineering background. The result of this qualitative assessment is a 1,000-liter still that is around 20-ft high, with a steep, downward-facing lyne arm. This setup produces a heavy distillery character, which is necessary to retain all the nuances from the cereals.

When making single malt whiskey, the mashing is outsourced to a local brewery. The aim is to produce a Scottish-style malt, which requires the mash to be filtered through a lauter screen prior to fermentation.

Over in the warehouse, the French connection really starts to factor in. There are American White Oak bourbon barrels, but nearly half of all the casks in the warehouse are European oak—even the bourbons are matured in them.

The casks are treated like they are in France too. The brothers follow the cognac practice of elevage ("marriage") in their warehouse, which sees partially matured spirits moved around and combined together, like slow-motion teenage speed-dating. They also practice an ongoing regime of "proofing down" barrels as they mature. In the Ironroot warehouse, more water is lost to evaporation than alcohol. This means that the proof of the spirit is constantly rising, which has an effect on the range of compounds extracted from the wood. The Likarishs are after vanillin more than they are the wood spices that get extracted at very high proofs, and adding a liter of water to the cask on schedule keeps the proof in check.

Most of the casks are the standard 53-gallon "bourbon cask" size that we saw in Kentucky and Tennessee. Unlike 99% of new American distilleries, Ironroot has never released a product aged in anything smaller. But just like the rest of the craft-distilling industry, Ironroot are looking to size up.

"We're starting to fill a bunch of 60s," Robert tells me. "Honestly, I think this is the direction we're going… probably even larger actually, maybe 70-gallon barrels. We're just trying to see what is the best size barrel for Texas. It's been ten years and nobody has spent much time trying to figure it out."

As of early 2019, the oldest whiskeys in the Ironroot warehouse are just over four-and-a-half years old, and they're currently filling 20 barrels a week. Each cask contains one of the four main mash bills and once it's aged between two and three years they will be blended in to one of the expressions or, in some instances, released as a "single barrel" bottling.

Now, if three years doesn't sound like long, it's worth remembering that many of the mechanisms in maturation occur much quicker in hot climates. And this is Texas. That said, Ironroot have a fairly well-insulated warehouse, losing only around 8% a year in evaporation. That means these are relatively youthful spirits that are still representative of their base material. After all, wouldn't it be counterproductive to put all that effort into sourcing unusual, low yield, big flavor corn varieties, only to smother them with cask character and homogenize flavor?

Jonathan and Robert duck, climb and dive their way around the warehouse, pulling cask samples for us to try. I've rarely seen producers with such an intimate knowledge of their casks.

"Do you wanna do #195 or #199?" asks Robert.

"I was going to get #148 first," replies Jonathan.

"Okay, let's do that, then I'm voting #195."

"They're like your children," I comment.

"That's really the fun bit about elevage. You're tasting everything every four to six months, so you really get to learn the personalities of each individual cask, their special quirks," says Robert.

About 80% of the current production goes in to char #1 bourbon casks with a heavy toast. Robert

ABOVE Stills, fermenters, and mash cookers at Ironroot Republic —an entire distillery in a single photograph.
LEFT Another example of Vendome's handiwork. The green patina is caused by water and copper reacting with air.

notes that the heavier chars were too extractive in the Texan heat, and had a tendency to filter flavor from the spirit. The two core bourbon expressions are Promethean and Harbinger. They also produce corn whiskey, single malt whiskey (due for release in 2020), and various experiments.

"We're really fallen in love with these casks," explains Robert, "especially with the purple corn mash bill. You get an almost molasses type character, a little cinnamon. They're really great casks."

"Promethean" is the more entry-level of the bourbons, though it's still bottled at a mighty 51.5% ABV. The mash bill is made up of 80% Yellow Corn, 5% Purple Corn, 5% Bloody Butcher Corn, 5% Flint Corn, and 5% Rye. "Harbinger" (of intoxication perhaps?) is bottled at 57.5% ABV, with a mash of 90% Yellow Corn, 5% Purple Corn, and 5% Bloody Butcher Corn.

Finally there's "Hubris," a corn whiskey, which became the least aptly named of the three after winning World's Best Corn [Whiskey] at the World Whiskies Awards in 2017. It's made from a mash of 95% Yellow Corn and 5% Purple Corn. Take away some of that new-oak flavor and we start to discover the true nature of the corn(s).

While bourbon must be made from a mash bill containing a minimum of 51% corn, corn whiskey must be made from a minimum of 80% corn. In order to distinguish high-corn mash bill bourbons from corn whiskeys, the maturation of corn whiskey is different to that of bourbon: straight corn whiskey must be aged in either used or new un-charred containers for a minimum of two years. Corn whiskey without the "straight" designation is not required to be aged (but if it is, it must be in used or new, un-charred containers) and can be colored and/or flavored.

On reflection, perhaps Ironroot isn't a mashup of French and Texan spirits after all. When you dig deeper, you discover that there's not really much that's Texan about the operation. They mature spirits the same way as cognac, they use the same wood as cognac, and they distill in much the same way as cognac. The only difference is the raw material, but even then, the careful consideration in blending corn

varieties for flavor is conducted in an altogether French manner. Corn is treated with the same respect that a winemaker might treat a grape, which is why I say they're not making whiskey here really, they're making corn brandy——or perhaps corngac?

PROMETHEAN (51.5% ABV)

First impression is hot butter and marmalade on brown toast, then broken timber, a touch of sloe, and nutmeg, giving it a slightly festive edge. There's a little rose on the taste plus plenty of heat, which is delivered like hot fat rather than peppery spice. The finish is fairly short, with cracked toffee and cream.

HUBRIS (58.9% ABV)

Banana custard, butterscotch, and basically any yellow thing you can think of. There's a dairy-like quality that meshes with vanillin from the cask in the most delightful way. The nose holds back on the incredible texture and taste of this spirit, though. It's oily and thick, with creamy corn fritters, jalapeño, and lots of baking spice. Wood provides a solid, nutty backdrop for these flavors to play on. A masterpiece!

HARBINGER (57.5% ABV)

The aroma is more suppressed than Promethean, which is to be expected at this strength. Chewy caramel/fudge, a touch of ground coffee, and a slight suggestion of corn tortilla. Substantial depth and great tactile balance on the palate. Anise, licorice, some dried fruits shine through——many of the things I would associate with cognac… only hotter.

ROAD TRIP PLAYLIST

"Road Trippin'" – Red Hot Chili Peppers

"Helplessly Hoping" – Crosby, Stills, and Nash

"I Heard it Through the Grapevine" – Creedence Clearwater Revival

SOUR GRAPES

60 ml/2 oz Ironroot Hubris
20 ml/⅔ oz verjus
20 ml/⅔ oz red grape juice concentrate

Shake all of the ingredients with cubed ice and strain into a rocks glass. Garnish with grapes.

Given the Likarish brothers' fascination with all things French, it would be negligent of me not to attempt to incorporate one of Ironroot's delicious, corn-based whiskeys into some kind of grape/corn mongrel drink.

I've chosen concentrated red grape syrup for sweetness (available from most home-brew stores) and verjus (a very acidic juice made by pressing unripe grapes) for sourness. Verjus has a similar acidic quality to white wine, but without the booze. It was actually a common staple in medieval kitchens before the tropical invasion of lemons and limes.

Use the recipe below as a starting point for this cocktail but be prepared to adjust it based on the sweetness and acidity of the grape concentrate you use. Ultimately, the drink should have the same sweet and sour balance as a classic whiskey sour, only with a lengthier acidic bite and more fruity aromas.

DISTILLERY 291

STILL IN THE DARK ROOM

"I'm here to kick ass and drink whiskey.
And pilgrim, I'm all out of whiskey."

JOHN WAYNE (1907–79), ACTOR

We head northwest from Denison, following the contour of the Oklahoma State line as we pass through Wichita Falls, on our way to Amarillo. Texas's most northern reach, which forms part of the cooler "Panhandle" region, is another place where the state's whiskey movement is changing agricultural communities. This area of Texas is mostly flat and mostly empty, save for the occasional tornado, but they're starting to grow barley here for making whiskey. Mustering up all of the intrepidity we can, we head to the Whiskey River music bar and spend the remainder of the night drinking bad cocktails while watching farmers dance to classic rock covers.

Bad bars aside, Amarillo serves as the perfect stopover on the route to our destination: Colorado. Shortly after leaving Amarillo, we touch the northern tip of New Mexico before joining I-25, heading north. It's at this point that we first set eyes on the Rocky Mountains, which take up almost half of Colorado's landmass. In fact, the state of Colorado contains 75% of all the land in the US with an elevation higher than 10,000ft. We don't know it yet, but the Rockies are set to be a constant presence for the next week or so of driving and drinking (not at the same time).

The Centennial State (Colorado became a state on the 100-year anniversary of American Independence) is actually the fourth-biggest barley-growing state, although it lags some way behind Montana, Idaho, and Washington State. Over a third of all Colorado

barley is snapped up by one company: MillerCoors, the US business unit of Molson Coors. In total, they buy barley from 180 different farmers across 47,000 acres of Colorado farmland. In fact, many of the farmers in the state are basically part of the Coors family, having been tied to the brewery since the 1870s. The biggest barley growing area is in the San Luis Valley, in the south of the state, at the headwaters of the Rio Grande. In the 1940s, this area was earmarked as a test site for "Trinity," the codename for the first nuclear weapon test. Had Colorado been selected (New Mexico was chosen in the end), a decent chunk of barley-growing land would still be radioactive. Instead, it's home to 80% of Colorado's barley.

Approaching Colorado Springs from the south, we spot Pike's Peak to our east, the highest of the summits that make up the Front Range of the Rockies. The slogan of "Pike's Peak or Bust!" was painted across many of the covered wagons when the whole area was consumed by the Gold Rush of the 1860s. Only a handful of those who flocked to the region ever found gold, though. One of the big names of that era was Spencer Penrose, a mining entrepreneur and spirits bootlegger who used his wealth to open the Broadmoor Hotel in Colorado Springs. One of his old safes was busted open a few years ago, and dozens of bottles of pre-Prohibition spirits were found inside.

Today, we are we seeing a new kind of gold rush as distillers frantically establish "whiskey mines" in tactical locations across the nation. The number of craft distilleries in Colorado grew by 25% between 2017 and 2018, from 80 to 99, which puts it at the top of the list alongside Texas, Tennessee, and Pennsylvania, who have all seen similarly explosive growth. But where have all these whiskey makers come from?

I'm generalizing slightly, but from what I have seen, there are three different routes to becoming a distiller: the first is to go and work in a distillery, learn the ropes and gradually ascend to the top while you "learn on the job." This is the route that most of the "master distillers" at the big Kentucky operations have taken. Another option is to go to college and study. A relevant qualification might allow you to move straight into a production role and avoid the more menial jobs like hosing down floors. The final option is that you read a bunch of books, trawl Internet forums, visit other distilleries, ask lots of questions and then open a distillery.

The final option really wasn't really an option at all until a few years ago. But the likes of Rick Wasmund (Copper Fox distillery owner/operator; see page 19) have not only demonstrated to wannabe distillers that they can start their own distillery—they've also helped inspire people who never dreamed of making whiskey to turn their hand to distilling. There are something like 18,000 people directly employed in distilling jobs across the nation now, but from what I've seen, most of them don't hold an appropriate qualification. Distilling has become democratized, and we're in a new era of the common man, where anyone can become a distiller and see the their dreams realized so long as they have the time and tenacity to assign to the task.

Perhaps there's no better example of such a person as Michael Myers, founder and master distiller of Distillery 291 in Colorado Springs.

Now, imagine you drew a Venn diagram with three circles labeled "rock star," "distiller," and "fashion photographer." At the point of their intersection, it would say "Michael Myers." He greets us at the

entrance, tall, dressed in black, with his long, silver hair tied back in a knot.

We start the tour the right way, which means two or three glasses of Colorado whiskey to get the conversation flowing. Whoever it was that came up with the idea of doing tastings at the end of a tour was entirely misinformed.

Michael had already enjoyed a long career as fashion photographer in New York when 9/11 happened. But the events that took place on that day changed everything for him. He couldn't get back into his apartment after the towers fell, so did the obvious thing and... moved to Colorado Springs. From his new base there, he commuted to New York for a few years, then eventually moved back to New York. But the whole thing wasn't working.

Then, in August 2010, he read an article about Hendrick's Gin and Sailor Jerry Rum in a magazine, and like most people who read articles about liquor, immediately decided he could make a whiskey brand. Michael was no stranger to whiskey, though. He grew up in Georgia and his family owned a Tennessee farm, along a road we drove a few days ago, right between Jack Daniel's and George Dickel. Accustomed to drinking whiskey as he was, he didn't really have the first clue how to make it. So he called in help from his friend, Mike Bristol, who owned a local brewery called Bristol Brewery.

"I wanted to create a rye whiskey that reflects Colorado—rough and tumble but beautiful at heart," Michael tells us. "And it had to look like the kind of whiskey you see in a western movie. The bottle gets slammed on the bar along with a glass, and it stays there until you're done."

When most people start a distillery, one of the first things they do is speak to a still manufacturer, like Vendome in Louisville, Forsyths in Scotland or Christian Carl in Germany. Not Michael Myers. He built his still from scratch, soliciting the help of a local welder to hammer and weld it from copper plates. The plates themselves were not an off-the-shelf variety either...

It turns out that copper plates are also used in the photography world, where they are chemically etched

ABOVE Colorado Springs is tucked into the eastern edge of the Southern Rocky Mountains, and it makes for quite a sight.

with an image to create a printmaking plate known as photogravure. The technique dates back to mid-19th century, and at the time of its invention it produced the highest standard of photographic reproduction available. Michael arranged for seven photographs from his portfolio to be etched on to copper. He then printed and framed the images, before rolling the copper into still-shaped pieces and welding them together into a still.

"Distillation reminds me a bit of the dark room," he says. "You have complete control over what comes out, and you have to be sensitive to each variable."

Now he has the only still in the world that doubles up as a printer.

It's perhaps little wonder then that the name of Distillery 291 came from the internationally renowned gallery "291," which was located at 291 Fifth Avenue, New York City, from 1905–17.

"291 was the first ever photo gallery in the world," says Michael. He tells us that the gallery was originally known as the "Little Galleries of the Photo-Secession," and opened and managed by photographer Alfred Stieglitz. This place was responsible for the first US exhibition of autochrome (color) photography, and featured works by Cézanne, Picasso, and Matisse.

"My dorm room number when I was doing my photography major was also 291," he says. "So I was like 'cool, obviously I'm meant to be a photographer!'" It turns out he was meant to be a distiller, but there was still some way to go before he could call himself one.

The business started in a basement space a few doors away from the current distillery, which was at the time occupied by the Bristol Brewery. The early setup was very modest indeed, comprising 55-gallon plastic fermentation barrels, a 55-gallon mash cooker (which doubled up as a beer stripping still) and Michael's chemically engraved spirits still. Everything ran on a domestic water heater, which unfortunately had an automatic shutoff that kicked in every 45 minutes. Rather than tamper with the

ABOVE Some rare experimental bottles at 291 that I'll unfortunately never get the chance to taste again!

ABOVE RIGHT Look closely and you'll see the etching of one of the Tetons on the side of the still.

electrics ("because I wanted to use it for my home shower at some point"), Michael reset the button manually every 45 minutes.

"I'd go cook dinner, then pop back and reset the button," he says. "I'd go sell whiskey and have to rush back to reset the button."

At that time Michael was making just over a barrel of whiskey a month. Demand easily outstripped what he was making, and it became clear that he needed to upscale the operation.

As of 2013, the distillery has inhabited the 7,500-sq ft space formerly occupied by the Bristol Brewery. It's a lot bigger than Michael's basement space, though you certainly wouldn't call it large. Bits of legacy equipment are still hanging around from the original operation, such as the 55-gallon mash cooker, which is now used as a reservoir for bottling. Also hanging around is a stainless steel tank that looks like a submarine, which used to double up as both mash cooker and stripping still.

Michael shows us the 1,500-gallon corn cooker and two Louisiana cypress fermentation vats. Distillery 291 have a very strange mashing protocol, which is basically a sour mash, except Michael buys IPA from Bristol Brewery, which he strips the alcohol out of and uses the left over stillage to flavor his mash. He believes that the stillage, with its slight hoppy aromatics, makes for a really tasty ferment.

The flagship rye whiskey at 291 is made from 61% malted rye and 39% corn. Their Colorado bourbon is produced from 80% corn, 19% malted rye, and 1% malted barley. Each mash is available in two expressions: "barrel proof" and "single barrel." "Single barrel" is bottled at 50.8% ABV and "barrel proof" at around 64%. I don't pay too much attention to awards, because pretty much every distillery seems to have won a few, but 291's Barrel Proof Rye has seen a considerable haul of awards, including the coveted "World's Best Rye" at the World Whiskies Awards in 2018.

The beer for these mashes is fermented to around 10% ABV, then goes through three stages of distillation. The first is the stripping stage, which takes place in a stainless steel still and turns 1,000 gallons of beer into 270 gallons of low wine at 35% ABV. Then it's on to Michael's 300-gallon copper pot still (a scaled-up replica of Michael's original 45-gallon copper pot-still).

"I had some local guys from the Department of Defense come over," says Michael. "They really liked whiskey and helped me build this still out of sheet copper. It's total overkill, but they were used to fabricating parts for military use, so I just let them get on with it."

The third distillation takes place in Michael's original 45-gallon copper pot still. The whole process produces 100 gallons of spirit at 150 proof—double his monthly output of a few years ago. Michael invites us to take a better look at the little still, and upon closer inspection, we can trace the fine lines of the Grand Teton peak delicately engraved into the side.

The spirit is then proofed down to 125 gallons before filling into barrels. All of the barrels here are of 10–30 gallons in size. Small casks never fail to generate a shudder from me, and I begin to imagine a massively over-oaked spirit that has none of the oxidative nuance and esters that only long maturation affords. Having tasted Michael's whiskey already though, I know that this simply isn't the case here. They're great.

"I got lucky," says Michael. "Something I'm doing is right." So how is he doing it?

Well, there might be a bit of luck involved, but there are some clever ideas too. Small pieces of aspen wood, sourced from Monarch up in the Rockies, are toasted and popped into the cask for two to three weeks. "It shifts the caramel notes in to more of a maple characteristic and adds a little smoke and spice," Michael says.

Besides the core range, 291 produce a high-rye bourbon called "HR," a wheated four-grain bourbon called "Bad Guy," and an experimental range called "E." The E range is released once a year in extremely limited quantities and has featured malted barley and malted rye mashes. Michael digs around his spirits cabinet and finds a half bottle of release#3, which he reckons is one of the best whiskeys he's ever made. It's made from 100% malted rye—check out my tasting notes to find out what I thought of it.

AMERICAN WHISKEY (45% ABV)

Aromatically, this whiskey seems young—more of an adolescent than a child. There's plenty of pear and orchard fruit on the nose, paired with violet and eucalyptus. There's little sign of the barrel, though. It's creamy and long on the palate; the distillery character is certainly preserved as waves of dry stone fruit crash around your mouth with a suggestion of marker pen. Ironically, this is a great whiskey for Scotch lovers.

COLORADO BOURBON (50% ABV)

Sweetly aromatic on the nose with notes of toffee and pecan. A darkness underpins it though, with licorice and date coming through. The finish is dry and tannic, which makes it exceptionally more-ish.

COLORADO RYE (50.8% ABV)

Maple bacon, incense, and a touch of tobacco comes in initially, then it gives way to confectionery notes, especially cherry. Taste is dark and concentrated, like a thick porter that's been spiked with gasoline. The finish is subtly smoky and prickly with heat.

EXPERIMENTAL RELEASE #3

Where to begin? "Candy store" is probably the best way to summarize, but this whiskey smells so good it would be shameful not to elaborate: cola candy with bright orange citrus balanced by cinnamon and orange blossom, then vanilla bon bon with toffee and powdered sugar. It's super-concentrated on the palate, with chewy toffee, baking spice, tobacco, and a Jägermeister finish. This is one of the best whiskeys to have ever come out of a 30-gallon cask.

ROAD TRIP PLAYLIST

"Rocky Mountain High" – John Denver

"Come Join The Murder" – The White Buffalo

"Colorado" – Stephen Stills

MANHATTAN

60 ml/2 oz 291 Colorado Rye
30 ml/1 oz Italian sweet vermouth
2 dashes of Abbott's Bitters (or bitters of your choosing)

Add all of the ingredients to a mixing glass and stir over cubed ice for a minute or two (take your time, dilution is important here). Strain into a chilled cocktail glass and garnish with a booze-soaked maraschino cherry.

Given the strong connection that Distillery 291 has to Manhattan, and the fact that we won't actually visit any distilleries on the island of Manhattan, this seemed like the best time to feature one of the best loved and most enduring whiskey cocktails of all.

There is a popular story associated with the creation of the Manhattan that is so perfectly apt that it could only be a complete fabrication.

The story goes that one Dr. Ian Marshall invented the drink in 1874. Apparently he was attending a banquet hosted by Jennie Jerome (aka Lady Randolph Churchill, Winston Churchill's mother) at the Manhattan Club in NYC. The banquet was being held to honor presidential candidate (and governor of New York) Samuel J. Tilden. Allegedly, the drink was a great success and, as word spread, guests in other bars began ordering the cocktail made famous at the Manhattan Club.

Sadly, there is a big problem with that story. On the date of the supposed banquet, Lady Randolph Churchill was actually in Blenheim, England, christening her newborn son, Winston. This is something of an inconvenience since it would be fitting that a legendary drinker, such as Winston Churchill, was present (even if unborn at the time) at the creation of one of the grand masters of the cocktail world.

It is a strange thing that you can take virtually any spirit, mix two parts of it with one part sweet vermouth, add a dash of bitters, and be confident in the knowledge that it'll probably taste pretty damn good. Perhaps no iteration works so well as the Manhattan, though. The boisterous, working-class bourbon or rye is tamed by the perfumed aromatics of the vermouth, and the relationship held together by just a touch of bitterness. God bless America.

LEOPOLD BROS.

THE WHISKEY KINGS

"I struggled into a trench coat and made a dash for the nearest drugstore and bought myself a pint of whiskey. Back in the car I used enough of it to keep warm and interested."

FROM *THE BIG SLEEP* BY RAYMOND CHANDLER

From Colorado Springs, we drive north for an hour until we reach Denver.

It was back in the mid 1990s when Denver natives Scott and Todd Leopold decided they wanted to open a sustainable brewery. German-style lagers were their passion, although it had gone much further for Todd Leopold, a graduate of the malting and brewing course at the historic Siebel Institute of Technology in Chicago and a former apprentice at the Doemens Academy in Munich, Germany.

At the time, in 1999, there were around 12 microbreweries in Colorado, and the brothers quickly (and incorrectly) concluded that the market was already oversaturated (there are more than 140 breweries in Colorado as of 2019). So they decided to base themselves in a place where the craft-brewing scene was still nascent and ended up relocating to Ann Arbor, Michigan, in the Great Lakes region.

Eight years later, with the brewery business going okay and some distilled spirits being added to the product range, the landlord did what landlords do and raised the rent. The business became untenable, so the brothers relocated Leopold Bros. to their home state of Colorado. The move presented them with an important decision. You see, you can't sell beer and spirits under the same license in Colorado. It's one or the other. They chose distilling (and we should all be grateful they did).

With Todd handling the technical aspects of brewing and distilling, Scott's expertise filled in the gaps in the business. He has a B.A. in Economics and a B.S. in Industrial Engineering from Northwestern, and an M.S. in Environmental Engineering from Stanford, which explains why their Denver distillery is one of the most sustainable distillery operations in the country. All the water here is filtered and recycled, and the stillage is collected by farmers. The general code at Leopold Bros. is that if it isn't sold to customers or farmers, it's composted or recycled. In fact, the distillery fills just one large trash bin a week with non-recyclable waste. That's it.

The distillery actually meets all of the requirements for LEED (Leadership in Energy and Environmental Design) Certification, which is almost unheard of in this industry. The standard requires low to zero waste, use of renewable energy, resource-efficient buildings and as little as possible stress on the environment in all areas of the operation. Todd and Scott are related to Aldo Leopold (1887–1948), considered the father of wildlife ecology in the US and the author of "The Land Ethic," which called for an ethical, caring relationship between people and nature. So maybe the sustainable approach runs through their veins.

We arrive at the distillery tasting room late in the morning. The distillery is clean and modern; it's only

a single story high (save for a turret that contains the top of their column still) but commands a broad footprint. It's a typical Colorado morning: blue sky but freezing cold. Scott Leopold isn't around today unfortunately, but when the bearded Todd Leopold—clad in his trademark brown dungarees—strides into the room and shakes my hand, I'm immediately very grateful there's only one of them. Todd is a big guy and I have no reason to doubt that his brother is too. Both of them at the same time might be a little intimidating. However, I quickly come to realize that it's not Todd's size that strikes a feeling of awe, it's his knowledge. I don't think any American distiller would disagree that Todd is one of the most important distillers in the country. The extent of his research and refinement of the whiskey-making process has made him a hero of the craft spirits movement, and his spirits are quite frankly some of the best around.

So a visit to Leopold Bros. is a little like a masterclass in how to make spirits. You could drill Todd on virtually any aspect of spirits production and he'd be capable of taking the conversation to a level that nobody in the room—and perhaps in the world—would be able to keep up with. As we are about to see, nothing is left to chance here and everything is scrutinized.

We begin the tour.

Leopold Bros. is one of the rare distilleries that has its own malting floor. Prior to building the floor, Todd had trained on the malting floor at the legendary Springbank distillery in Scotland. The floor at Leopold's is a little smaller than Springbank, and can take up to 20,000 lbs of barley at a time. That said, when they first built the malting floor in 2014, it was the largest of any US distillery. It's not anymore, but that's set to change. As we go to print, Leopold Bros. is completing a new 24,000-sq ft "Malt House," which will be about ten times the size of the existing floor and one of the largest floor maltings in the world.

As we've already learned, malting is a laborious process and a terrible idea from an economic standpoint. But for the Leopolds, malting was a chance to take control at the beginning of the spirits-making process, including the variety of barley they use and the types of sugars produced during the malting process (which we'll talk about more shortly).

"When we first started this, we couldn't get farmers to return our phone calls. Most of them had been growing whatever Coors told them to for so long that they had forgotten flavorful varieties existed."

Now, the tide has turned, and new relationships have developed mutual benefits for distiller and farmer, as Todd gets the cereals he wants and the farmer gets a better price.

Once the barley (the "two-row" variety) has steeped in the tanks for a couple of days, up to a moisture content of 50%, the "Colorado CrossFit" begins as it's spread on the floor using wheelbarrows and rubber boots. Germination takes seven-to-nine days, where the barley is regularly turned to ensure even temperature distribution and prevent the growth of mold.

"Colorado is too dry for malting barley," says Todd "so we have an energy-efficient humidifier and temperature controller, which recreates the conditions you might find in Scotland." In between batches, the entire area is scrubbed down and sanitized using the leftover "heads" from distillation.

Next, it's on to the kiln, which is heated by an electric fan. No smoke is used, which is particularly important here because there's a malted barley component to 22 out of the 24 products that Leopold Bros. currently bottles.

On the mash bill side of things, Leopold Bros. currently runs three mash bills: Maryland Rye (65% rye, 20% malted barley, 15% corn); straight bourbon (64% corn, 17% malted barley, 15% rye), plus some brewers' malts including Chocolate Rye.

The distillery has 16 x 200-gallon open-top wooden fermenters made by an old company called Hall-Woodford based out of Philadelphia. Wood was

ABOVE LEFT A pagoda roof indicates the presence of a malting kiln, an unusual feature of a US distillery.
ABOVE RIGHT Todd Leopold explains the workings of the three-chamber still to me. I'm mildly befuddled.
BOTTOM A warehouse that is both light and airy, which is something of a rarity in the whiskey world!

chosen for its ability to coax in certain natural bacteria that would create interesting secondary fermentations. The oldest three are made from cypress wood, the others from Douglas fir. The shift in timber type was not a flavor consideration but rather one of cost and sustainability of the timber. "They're located right next to the window," says Todd "because we do some spontaneous ferments which rely on airborne yeast to get things going. We plant lilacs and lavender out there and the blossoms are a good source of yeast."

Leopold Bros. uses a standard distillers' yeast, as well as its own proprietary strain, and whatever is floating around in the air. It shouldn't be too surprising that Todd Leopold places so much emphasis on fermentation, given the company's background as a brewery. "It is, without question, the most important thing we do," he says.

Fermentation produces many other things besides ethanol, including various other alcohols, aldehydes, acids, and ketones. These are the building blocks of the final liquid's flavor profile. Fermentation is where all of the flavor in an un-aged spirit is made—the distillation is merely a selector of flavor.

Once the yeast and mash come into contact, there's a period called the lag, which can last between three and six hours. Here, the yeast is acclimatizing itself to its new surroundings and preparing for the challenges ahead. The next stage is the log, where the yeast kicks into action. Deprived of the oxygen it needs to sustain itself, it begins to ferment the sugars, producing ethanol, CO_2 and heat, all at a serious pace, as well as multiplying rapidly. The output of CO_2 in particular causes the mixture to eddy and foam. In fact, foam can sometimes become a bit of a problem during fermentation, leading some distillers to use anti-foaming agents.

The time it takes for fermentation to complete (i.e. convert all of the available sugar into alcohol) is typically around 36–48 hours. But the exact time will depend on the virility of the yeast strain that's used and the temperature of the fermentation. Most yeast strains require a minimum temperature of 68°F to be effective but will become stressed and eventually die at temperatures above 95°F. Creating a warm environment for the yeast to work in isn't normally a problem, since the fermenter is filled directly from the hot mash cooker and most often needs chilling before yeast can be pitched. But keeping that temperature stable can be an issue, particularly in hotter climates.

Fermentation is exothermic (i.e. the reaction releases heat), and when you have thousands of gallons of fermenting beer in an insulated container, it can easily get hot enough to kill the yeast. Some distilleries combat this by installing a metal coil around the circumference of the fermenter, which can circulate cool water when required.

Temperature is more than just physical factor that needs to be kept within a specific margin, however. A quick, warm fermentation using the same yeast and mash will produce a different set of compounds compared to a slow, cool fermentation. Todd tells us that cooler ferments—typical of the German lager-style—also limit the production of higher alcohols and ethyl acetate that might give rise to solvent aromas or a "burn" on the palate.

Fermenting slower and longer can help initiate secondary ferments caused by wild yeast or bacteria, which aid in the development of wild, fruity, and floral flavors that will carry through to the distillation stages. The downside of dragging it out for too long is that some of the shiny new alcohol that has been created in the wash can be expended in the production of aldehydes through the alcohol's oxidization—in other words, long fermentations make interesting flavor, but they take up space and eat into your profits a little. Leopold Bros. actually encourages the growth of the bacteria *Lactobacillus* in their ferments, because of the flavor that it generates and imparts.

Todd tells me that "There are basically two types of bacterial fermentation, homofermentative and heterofermentative. The first just makes lactic acid, but the second makes lactic and acetic acid."

The acetic acid is where you get flavors like raspberry, but when it reacts with certain alcohols produced during the ferment (namely 1-Octanol), it

produces the octyl acetate ester, which is commonly used in fragrance manufacture and smells of citrus. "Orange marmalade is becoming our house aroma note thanks to that lactobacterial fermentation," Todd tells me.

The materials that go in there impact this hugely too. Their malt makes less dextrin available to the yeast, which stabilizes the ferment and slows it down. This is why they value their floor malting at Leopold Bros. so much. It's really an extension of their obsession with fermentation.

Leopold Bros. has a total of eight stills, ranging from columns used to make neutral spirits, through to Christian Carl pot stills, Vendome pots, and a one-of-a-kind "Three Chamber" still.

Todd proceeds to give me a detailed description of how the still works. The best way I can describe it is as a primitive form of a column still mixed with a solera aging system.

The still comprises three chambers stacked on top of each other that each work like a pot still. The beer is loaded into the system in batches via a heating chamber that's on top of the third section. It's basically a fourth chamber, but think of it like a warming bucket. The bottom kettle is heated via steam injection and valves on the outside allow Todd to fill each of the three chambers with hot beer. Each chamber then begins distilling the beer, which occurs more rapidly at the bottom, nearer to the heat source. In each chamber, the distillate then rises up through and inverted 'J' pipe into the chamber above. At the top, the third chamber outputs to a thumper, which sends the spirit on to the condenser to be collected.

When the liquid in the bottom pot is spent of alcohol, the stillage is drained, making room for the next batch. A valve is opened to allow wash from the next kettle up to pour into the pot below. Each kettle is successively gravity-fed into the next distillation chamber down, and then filled from the one above, until the cycle is complete and the top chamber is charged with fresh wash. Thus, the still receives wash in batches and produces spirit continuously.

The process is far slower than that of a column still, and as such, produces a far richer, oilier distillate. But Todd also says it can be used in such a way to remove many of the spicy characteristics we normally associate with rye, giving over floral notes instead. As far as anyone knows, Todd's chamber still is one of only two in the world that are currently operational. His was custom-made by Vendome, based on 19th century schematics. "It's the only one in the world for that very reason. It gives whiskey a rounder, more flavorful character."

On to maturation: the barrels here are all 53 gallons in size and always have been. They're sourced from Independent Stave in Missouri, but the wood itself is grown in the Ozark region, or in some cases sourced from France. Nearly everything goes into new oak, but there are a handful of sherry casks hanging around. Todd tells us he's a big fan of low-barrel-entry proof, arguing that higher fill-strength is purely a cost-saving exercise and—if it wasn't already apparent—that's not something that motivates Leopold Bros.

All of the whiskeys that Leopold Bros. currently bottle are single-barrel expressions, with the barrel number written on the bottle. Due to the seasonal temperature variation (and the effect this has on fermentation and maturation), as well as the unpredictability of the barrel itself, it's likely that their American Small Batch and Straight Bourbon whiskeys will differ from bottle to bottle. Their

Maryland Rye will be a little more consistent, since it's spontaneously fermented only in the summer months, and bottled and made available to purchase two and half years later, in the winter.

It's frightening to think that we're only really scratching the surface with what Leopold Bros. is doing with whiskey…

STRAIGHT BOURBON (45% ABV)

Charred corn on the cob, toasted coconut, and carob. The taste is clean and quite dry. In fact it's very dry, with a caramelized bitter note and just the right amount of heat for an apricot jam finish.

TENNESSEE STYLE (45% ABV)

Although there's no escaping the buttery corn in the aroma, it's accompanied by a touch of orange jelly and syrupy sponge pudding. There's a lovely polished note to this whiskey. Chocolate and a vague nuttiness follow; the finish is a massive hit of sweet cherry.

MARYLAND STYLE RYE, BARREL #146 (43% ABV)

An initial aroma of nori seaweed is displaced by dark brown bread, hazelnut and raw lavender honey there too, which all together conjure up the image of a

breakfast table in Germany. A little fruit, perhaps damson or dark cherry reveals itself on the palate. Utterly delicious.

AMERICAN SMALL BATCH, BARREL #1162 (43% ABV)

Toffee sauce and coffee cake lead the way with this spirit, which immediately speaks to after dinner sipping. Sweet and spiced in the taste, once the heat from the rye dissipates you're left with boozy poached pear and apricot tart.

❧

ROAD TRIP PLAYLIST

"Two of Us" – The Beatles

"Go Your Own Way" – Fleetwood Mac

"He Ain't Heavy, He's My Brother" – The Hollies

RIGHT Leopold Bros. has a large tasting room and distillery shop where you can sample products or arrange a tour.

REMEMBER THE MAINE

50 ml/1⅔ oz Leopold Bros. Maryland-style Rye
20 ml⅔ oz Italian vermouth
10 ml/2 teaspoons Leopold Bros. Michigan Tart Cherry Liqueur
5 ml/1 teaspoon Leopold Bros. Absinthe Verte

Add the ingredients to a mixing beaker filled with cubed ice. Stir for at least 90 seconds,
then strain into a chilled cocktail glass. Garnish with a strip of lemon.

A rather clunky name it may be, but don't let that put you off. Remember the Maine is one of the best cocktails to come out of the mid-20th century.

A good cocktail should be at least as good as the sum of its parts. And no one part should dominate any other part. Crunch those two rules together and what you get is a drink that is balanced both aromatically and from a taste perspective. The two modifying liqueurs in Remember the Maine perfectly pair with rye whiskey, amplifying the fruit, nut, and herbal components of the spirit.

The vermouth—which pairs well with brown spirits on most occasions—adds subtle spice and more warming herbal notes. No single ingredient stands above another. It is as if the rye was simply made that way—and made delicious in the bargain.

This cocktail was penned by Charles H. Baker, one of the most distinguished drinks writers of all time. He was the author of *The Gentleman's Companion: Being an Exotic Drinking Book Or, Around the World with Jigger, Beaker and Flask*, a book documenting his booze-fueled escapades around the globe, which included recipes (not all of them great).

The *Maine* we're being urged to remember is the United States Navy ship that sank in Havana Harbor in 1898, contributing to the outbreak of the Spanish–American War. The phrase "Remember the *Maine*! To hell with Spain!" became a rallying cry for action.

WYOMING WHISKEY

BIG PLANS IN THE GREAT PLAINS

"Whiskey has killed more men than bullets. But most men would rather be full of whiskey than bullets."

WINSTON CHURCHILL (1874–1965), FORMER PRIME MINISTER OF THE UK

We set off from Saratoga Springs, near the Colorado border, and head north into the heart of Wyoming. You can drive a long way in this state without seeing much. Wyoming is the 10th largest state in terms of landmass, but the smallest by population. In fact, only Alaska has a lower population density than Wyoming.

Fresh snowfall disguises the few landmarks that Wyoming can muster, presenting us with a lunar-like feeling of remoteness. An hour of driving goes by and we fail to encounter another vehicle on the road, save for the most important kind of vehicle in a Wyoming winter—the snow plow.

We drive through Carbon County, past Atlantic City, South Pass City, and Miner's Delight, all places with a single commonality—nobody lives there. These ghost towns are all relics of Wyoming's Gold Rush era.

Atlantic City sits on the edge of the South Pass shelf, which, as of 1812, became the preferred route through the Rockies and into the Pacific West. When the California Gold Rush kicked off in 1848, bringing 300,000 people to the state, most traveled with haste through the South Pass, which is ironic since gold was discovered there 15 years later.

One newspaper of the time reported "slathers of it," and mines with colorful names like Young American, the King Solomon, and the Mary Ellen popped up in quick succession. By 1880, nearly all

of them had closed and their respective towns were all deserted.

Some geologists believe there's still plenty of gold to be had in Wyoming, just not enough people to find it! Besides cattle ranching and tourism, the economy is still supported by mining activity, though nowadays it's coal and gas rather than precious metals.

There's still a precious kind of liquid gold to be found in these parts however, and we are just the kind of prospectors to mine it!

The Wyoming Whiskey distillery is in Kirby, a town in Hot Springs County, in the northern part of the state. The population of Kirby is 92. It's close to the Bighorn River, which cuts a vertical line through the Great Plains, with Bighorn National Park to the East and the world's first national park, Yellowstone, to the West. A little further north from the distillery, on the Montana border, is where, in 1876, the Battle of the Little Bighorn took place between federal troops commanded by Lieut. Col. George Armstrong Custer and Lakota and Northern Cheyenne Indians led by Sitting Bull. Even though the battle was a decisive victory for the Northern Plains people (who vastly outnumbered Custer's army), it marked the beginning of the end of Native American sovereignty in the West.

The Battle of the Little Bighorn was just one of many conflicts that came about following President Ulysses S. Grant's "Peace Policy" that relocated various tribes from their ancestral homes to parcels of lands established specifically for their inhabitation. Wyoming's Wind River Reservation is a 2.2-million acre square of land that was formed during that time for the Shoshone tribe. We drive through the heart of it, and past the town of Shoshoni. As we do, our gaze turns to the west. Somewhere, about 30 miles away, in the belly of the mountains, there's an 11,000-ft peak that's home to the largest concentration of bighorn sheep in the Rockies. Of greater interest to us, is the allure of its name: Whiskey Mountain.

It's early afternoon when we arrive in Kirby. The roads here are made of gravel, and the buildings are few. There's not a lot going on in Kirby, besides a railroad crossing and the Mead family's 1,200-acre ranch. It's one of two ranches that the family own, the other being in Spring Gulch, near Jackson Hole, in the heart of the Teton mountain range that forms part of the Rockies. The Kirby farm was purchased as a new place to pasture cattle after bison and wolves were reintroduced in Grand Teton National Park as part of the conservation effort. The Meads literally traverse the state like this, seasonally driving cattle on horseback from the Tetons to warmer pastures, then back again when the plains get hot. The Mead name is known across Wyoming since the time of the gold rush. Now, it's quickly becoming known across the nation, because they're the founders of the Wyoming Whiskey distillery.

Brad and Kate Mead started the distillery with their attorney friend and Kentuckian David DeFazio in 2009. At the point of its conception, Wyoming Whiskey became Wyoming's first commercial whiskey distillery. Brad and Kate now oversee the operations of both ranches while Brad also acts as CEO of the whiskey distillery. As the Wyoming Whiskey website rightly states: "They are pretty much like other business executives, but they do most of it on horseback and with a much better office view."

The distillery's general manager, Blair Woodall, greets us in the distillery parking lot. She recently moved up to Wyoming from Colorado, having previously worked at the Stranahan's distillery there. It's the weekend, and both the town and distillery appear completely deserted. Either everyone's at nearby Thermopolis (the largest town in the area, though that's not saying much) or they're really good at hiding. It's cold outside, which might go some way towards explaining the absence of life, though. There's black ice on the ground, and the whiskey barrels lined up near the door have formed discs of ice from the pools of water collected on top.

We enter the distillery through the front door, and find ourselves in a large room with a 38-ft column still rising up through the center.

"Kate Mead was standing in here one day," says Blair, "and said to her husband, 'you know what, we should do a winery.'"

At that time, what is now the still house was a large roping arena, used for, well, slinging ropes around horses. Brad reminded Kate that they knew nothing about growing grapes, but they did know what good bourbon tastes like. So Brad attended the Kentucky bourbon festival for research purposes, and called up Kate a few days later to tell her he was bringing a still back with him. "Will it fit in the garage?" was Kate's response. "No," was the reply. In fact, the still was so tall, the only way to fit it in to anything was to pour the concrete onto the ground, put the still in position, then erect the building around it. This work began in 2008 and was completed the following year.

In a similar vein to stories we've already covered, this whiskey-making project began as a diversification program but quickly developed into a passion. And with that growing passion, their ambition grew too. The mantra now is as simple as they come: "We will be the bourbon of the American West."

So how do you go about making whiskey in Wyoming? Well, you make bourbon and you make it more or less the same way as they do in Kentucky. While some young distilleries are content with establishing new categories of whiskey that are specific to their state or region, Wyoming Whiskey seems to have its sights set on beating Kentucky bourbon at their own game.

An important part of the beating-Kentucky-at-their-own-game-strategy involved getting the right distiller on board. Steve Nally was the man they

LEFT There is basically only one reason to find yourself in Kirby, WY, but it's a very good reason…

BELOW LEFT The paintwork of the distillery seems to complement the only other visible color in this town: green.

BELOW If it wasn't for the distillery, visitors to Kirby in the winter would have cause to assume it's another ghost town.

ABOVE There's still plenty of arable land available to grow corn on, should Wyoming Whiskey need it.

picked. Not only had he worked at Maker's Mark for 33 years, he was also born in Loretto right next to the Maker's Mark distillery. You couldn't have hoped for a more traditionalist Kentucky distiller.

His experience is what has helped to shape the whiskeys made here, and it also explains the wheated mash bill, which is a trademark of Maker's Mark. Steve got the distilling side of things off the ground when he joined the team in 2008 and continued to run the operation until he left the company in 2015, moving back to Kentucky to run the Bardstown Bourbon Distillery.

Day-to-day whiskey-making is now taken care of by Kate and Brad's son, Sam Mead. Besides being a fifth-generation rancher and now first-generation head distiller, Sam Mead's resumé includes winning the USASA Halfpipe and Slopestyle Nationals competition. Oh, and he's also the mayor of Kirby. Perhaps it's because there are so few people in Wyoming, or maybe the Mead family are just a really gifted bunch, but we soon learn that everyone does a little bit of everything around here. While maintaining and growing their ranch operations over

the past 100 years, the Mead family has had their share of US Senators, lawyers, extreme skiers, and two Wyoming Governors.

The water used here comes from a mile-deep limestone aquifer located 42 miles north of the distillery. For the first three and a half years, the 12,000 gallons of water required for production was trucked to the distillery. Now the water is piped in from the source.

The distillery makes two whiskey recipes: a wheated bourbon, with a mash bill of 68% corn, 20% wheat, and 12% malted barley; and a high-rye American whiskey comprising 48% rye, 40% corn, and 12% malted barley.

Cereals are sourced from one farmer whose land stretches no further than 100 miles away. In the context of Wyoming's remoteness, that might as well be next-door. Brent Rageth has supplied Wyoming Whiskey with cereals from the start, helping to select strains of non-GMO corn, wheat, barley, and winter rye for specific starch and sugar. Blair tells me that the corn strain that Wyoming Whiskey use matures in just 92 days.

The mash cooker holds 2,500 gallons and supplies seven 2,500-gallon open-top steel fermenters. The distillery uses two types of yeast in concert with one another: a wine yeast and a beer yeast. The beer yeast is designed to produce the maximum yield of alcohol, while the wine yeast is called in to target specific alcohols and esters.

Spirit is distilled up to 130 proof and enters the barrel at 114 proof. The overall goal here is softness and fruit flavors.

Although Sam Mead has taken over the reins from one of the Kentucky greats, he hasn't let that stand in the way of advancing the product. The Meads were unhappy with a sour apple note that their young whiskey displayed, so Sam brought in the help of a chemist. They found that due to their fermentation parameters, the yeast was becoming stressed and kicking out a lot of acetaldehyde. Sam was able to adjust the fermentation to limit the production of the sour apple compound and refine the spirit that came off the still.

The only problem then was that the Meads were sitting on thousands of barrels of stock that had high concentrations of acetaldehyde. The solution they found was to bottle during the summer months, when the acetaldehyde (which has a boiling point of 62°F) would flash off the spirit and never enter the bottle. The Bighorn Basin experiences massive temperature fluctuation from summer to winter, which is good for getting rid of undesirable compounds and useful for speeding up certain parts of maturation chemistry.

"Sometimes it can be 130°F in our warehouse. Right now it's about 12°F," says Blair.

With around 10,000 53-gallon barrels of whiskey currently maturing across six warehouses, there's enough whiskey at Wyoming Whiskey to furnish every resident of Kirby with over a hundred barrels each. Although the distillery released some early expressions that were a shade over three years old, now all the whiskeys here are matured for a minimum of five years.

In spite of its youthfulness, the first 3,000 cases that were released in 2012 sold out to alcohol retailers in less than four minutes. The appetite for Wyoming

Whiskey hasn't settled down much since then. So it was that in early 2018, the Meads announced a strategic partnership with Edrington, owner of The Macallan Distillery in Scotland, among other operations. Now Edrington own a minority stake in the business and will be handling sales and distribution of Wyoming Whiskey across its substantial global network. With a force like Edrington behind the brand, Wyoming Whiskey stands a good chance of putting Wyoming on the global whiskey map.

SMALL BATCH BOURBON (44% ABV)

There's sugared pecan and banoffee pie on the nose, with a touch of sweetcorn soup. There's a nice balance of sweetness and dryness on the palate, beginning with foam banana candy and ending on white pepper and sticky wood resin.

DOUBLE CASK BOURBON (50% ABV)

Initially raw-feeling and spiced, like barbecued meat, before quickly dissolving into sweeter vanilla, coffee, and coconut barrel aromas. It's concentrated and hot on the palate, but not overwhelmed by wood character. There's plenty of sweetness, however, which draws the finish out over a long period.

SMALL BATCH AMERICAN (50% ABV)

The aroma here is more savory than the two bourbons, beginning with pistachio and ginger, then becoming herbal with notes of mint tea. The taste is beautifully balanced, with sweeter barrel flavors and a suggestion of cedar wood, balancing out those lighter, spicy, herbal elements.

ROAD TRIP PLAYLIST

"Take the Money and Run" – Steve Miller Band

"Jackson" – Johnny Cash and June Carter

"Heart of Gold" – Neil Young

BLOODY COWBOY

40 ml/1⅓ oz Wyoming Whiskey Small Batch Bourbon
120 ml/4 oz tomato juice
20 ml/⅔ oz brown sugar syrup
10 ml/2 teaspoons soy sauce
10 ml/2 teaspoons cider vinegar
3 ml/½ teaspoon liquid smoke
2 g/½ teaspoon sweet paprika
hot sauce, as needed

To make the drink, add ice cubes (I've used ceramic baking beans, which I froze) to a battered old (but clean!) bean can followed by the rest of the ingredients. Pop a spoon in there and give it a good stir. Garnish with some fried strips of bacon and serve with a straw.

Back in 2015, a bright spark decided it would be useful to compile all the Google searches of cocktail recipes on a state-by-state basis. Using data spanning a decade, they were able to map the most popular drink searches in each state. In Wyoming, the Bloody Mary was searched for more than any other mixed drink. What does this tell us about Wyoming? Not a lot, other than that the people who live there suffer from hangovers more than most (it would be interesting to see what time of day these internet searches were conducted).

Of course, you can make a Bloody Mary with bourbon whiskey and it's an okay drink. But with a few tweaks of the classic recipe, it can be very delicious thing. I've chosen to serve it in a bean can, but you can use a regular glass.

FOLLOWING PAGES The Rockies truly are a natural wonder, but it's surprising how easily one becomes accustomed to their constant presence.

HIGH WEST

APRÈS–SKI

"I'm still waiting for the whiskey to whisk me away.
I'm still waiting for the ashtray to lead me astray.
From the northwest passage,
To the great divide.
Everybody's looking
For the other side."

FROM THE SONG "OTHER SIDE" BY JOSH RITTER

Like bank robbers on the run, the Rockies have served as a colossal roadblock hampering our escape west, which we've spent about a week trying to navigate around. But now, finally we've found a way through (if only for a moment). From Kirby, Wyoming, we're heading to Utah.

We could drive south for six hours, back through the Wind River Reservation, then cut through the Rockies via Evanston on I-80. But Wyoming's great and wild expanse is a slow form of intoxication that threatens to become paralyzing in its lack of variety if things don't change. The mountains have beckoned us for days now, and it's futile to resist any longer.

So instead of driving south we drive west out of Kirby into Yellowstone National Park. The gain in elevation is almost imperceptible as the peaks around us match our climb. Skirting around Yellowstone Lake we then head south, into Grand Teton National Park, and down to Jackson Hole ski resort. We had been wondering where all of the people in Wyoming were, and it turns out they're all here, skiing and drinking. We spend the night drinking boilermakers in the legendary Million Dollar Cowboy Bar, which has been intoxicating cowboys since 1937.

We leave Jackson the following morning, which is when it dawns on us that we'll be spending the next night in a ski resort too.

High West distillery is located in Park City, Utah, around 30 minutes east of Salt Lake City. High West is the world's first and only "ski-in, ski-out" whiskey distillery and was the first distillery to open in Utah since 1870. You'd have to say that at 7,000 ft above sea level, it is undeniably both "high" and "West." And if there's anything that we can learn from the French, it's that skiing and alcohol go hand in hand.

Whiskey in Utah goes back well before the founding of the state in 1896. From 1825–40, the "Rocky Mountain Rendezvous" was an annual summer gathering of mountain men to exchange pelts for supplies. Alcohol was not one of the "supplies" at the first rendezvous in Wyoming, which lasted a day. This oversight was corrected with a generous supply of whiskey at the second annual rendezvous in Utah's Cache Valley, creating a month long celebration of mountain culture that was so popular the mountain men repeated it as an annual event. In time, the large fur companies established teamster-driven mule caravans, which packed in whiskey and

LEFT Utah is one of the most geographically diverse states, featuring arid deserts, rock formations, and thriving pine forests in mountain valleys.
ABOVE During the ski season, High West probably has the busiest bar and restaurant of any distillery in the United States.
OPPOSITE Sun, snow, and a saloon—what more do you want? Well, a whiskey distillery please.

supplies to a pre-announced location each spring/summer. The annual rendezvous was known to be a lively, fun place, where anyone was permitted to attend, even tourists who would venture from as far as Europe to observe the festivities. Explorer James Beckwourth (c.1800–67) described the event as: "Mirth, songs, dancing, shouting, trading, running, jumping, singing, racing, target-shooting, yarns, frolic, with all sorts of extravagances that white men or Indians could invent."

Given that roughly 62% of Utahans are Mormon (and that figure is rising) and that Mormons are forbidden to drink alcohol, modern-day Utah doesn't seem like an obvious place to open a whiskey distillery. But the number of Mormons in Salt Lake City is actually in decline. In any case, historically, the Mormon Church didn't seem to have too much of an issue with making whiskey in the state.

Probably the biggest name in Utah's whiskey history was Brigham Young, a key figure in the history of the Mormon Church. Also known as the "American Moses," Young organized the migration of about 16,000 Mormons from Illinois to Utah. He founded Salt Lake City and became the first governor of the Utah Territory and would in time impart significant influence on the religious and political landscape of the American West.

It is said that Brother Brigham hated whiskey, once proclaiming that, "If I had the power, I would blow out the brains of every thief in the territory, and I despise the whiskey maker more than I do the thieves." In spite of his adamant distaste for it, Young was also known to go to great lengths to get it for medicinal purposes—a fact confirmed in the following line from his "Journal of Discourses" (1862): "When there was no whisky to be had here, and we needed it for rational purposes, I built a house to make it in."

At the height of his power, Young controlled much of the goings-on in Utah. That meant distilleries and numerous taverns too. In Salt Lake City, Main Street, south of 2nd Avenue, was familiarly known as Whiskey Street on account of the many taverns located there. The revenue collector's record shows, that between 1862, when the internal revenue system went into effect, and December 1869, the advent of the railroad, 37 distilleries were founded, all of which were owned by Mormons, with Brigham Young

TOP LEFT This copper pot still makes only a fraction of the spirit that ends up in High West bottles.
ABOVE RIGHT These columns are actually only used for producing High West's "7000" brand of vodka.

LEFT Underground, in the mashing and fermenting room, which looks a bit like a chemistry classroom, we discover some of the experimental recipes that High West is developing.

among them. So what were they making in Utah? Well, Sir Richard Burton, one of the greatest explorers of the 19th century clears it up for us: "The whisky of Utah Territory, unlike the Monongahela or rye of Pennsylvania and the Bourbon…of Kentucky, is distilled from wheat…"

In 1868, Young founded the ZCMI (Zion's Cooperative Mercantile Institution), which was dubbed "America's first department store" and stocked a range of whiskies. It was there that the pharmacist, C.E. Johnson, began selling his own

brand of "Valley Tan Mormon Whiskey." "Valley Tan" was a Mormon term, traditionally referring to leather-making, but it eventually applied to any product that was made locally. According to Mark Twain's *Roughing It* (1871) though, Valley Tan is a "kind of whisky, or first cousin to it; is of Mormon invention and manufactured only in Utah. Tradition says it is made of [imported] fire and brimstone," whatever that means.

We're visiting Park City in the middle of the ski season, which means the distillery is overrun with customers. In fact, I'm not sure I've ever seen so many people drinking and eating at a distillery. The guy running security on the door refuses us entry with a level of autonomy that can only be achieved through millions of repetitions.

Fortunately Steve Walton, lead bartender at High West, comes to our rescue.

"I came over here to be a ski-bum for one winter," he says, "now I've been with High West for eight years and have a house and wife and two kids."

Lead bartender is probably a bit of an undersell with Steve. He's seen the brand grow by an order of magnitude during his time there, and is a font of knowledge for all things relating to the brand and to Park City (and snowboarding).

Steve explains to us that half of the distillery building (which is actually two buildings joined together) used to be horse livery, servicing the animals that transported all the mining equipment up in to the mountains. Long before the first après ski was consumed in Park City, it was a mining town. The completion of the first Transcontinental Railroad in 1869 was a game changer for Utah. Built by three private companies, the six-year construction period sought to connect existing rail lines in San Francisco to those in Omaha, Nebraska. Two thousand miles of railroad later, the two sides finally converged on Promontory Summit, Utah, on May 10, 1869. The railroad brought hopeful miners by the droves to Utah with their eyes set on becoming rich overnight. Modern conveniences like electricity and running water, plus the promise of silver and copper in the hills, made Park City one of the most sought-after mining towns in the West.

The livery building is actually one of the oldest buildings in the city, and when the mining industry collapsed in the 1950s, the structure became the first gas station in Park City, dubbed "National Garage." Park City is no stranger to a few flames; one fire, in 1898, destroyed three-quarters of the town. Another, across the road from the National Garage, where the Caledonian Hotel is now located, burnt so furiously that it caused the paint the on the facade of the National Garage to bubble and crack (a little like when a barrel is charred), revealing a hidden sign underneath. The building has since been added to the National Register. The adjacent building, which is connected by a glass-fronted corridor that houses the stills, is the historic Ellsworth J. Beggs house, a two-story box house that was built in 1907. It too is on the National Register and now serves as a bar and tasting room.

Next to and behind the distillery are what look like stunted electricity pylons, but are in fact the old iron head-frames that were used to winch copper from the mountains down into the city.

Steve tells us that this old gas station now serves up to 1400 people a day between 11am and 11pm. "We don't do reservations," he says, "because as soon as someone leaves, someone else is ready to take their place."

The National Garage had been empty for years when Dave Perkins viewed it as a potential site for his distillery. Dave was a biochemist, which is what attracted him to distilling.

Taking occupation of the buildings wasn't exactly straightforward either. Both the house and garage were in poor states of repair and more space was needed to create the distillery, bar, and restaurant operations. So, over the course of two years, both buildings were carefully deconstructed so that new foundations and basements could be built, then pieced back together in more or less their original locations. An extra, smaller building was constructed between them, and it's this bit where the distillery lives.

In spite of the scale of such a build job, High West was a brand that, from the start, had bigger aspirations than it was able to keep up with. The Saloon distillery in Park City is more saloon than it is distillery, and the still itself is a mere 250 gallons. That's big enough for a mom and pop-sized operation, but far too small for a brand looking to compete in international markets. To make up the deficit, High West did the same thing as WhistlePig (see page 81), sourcing whiskey from other producers and blending it with their own.

One of the great advantages of buying sourced whiskey is that you can divert the capital you'd otherwise be using for raising a distillery, or building up aged stocks of whiskey, into sales instead. And if the brand is strong (which it should be, given all the money you've saved) it can quickly turn into a lucrative business with minimal cash tied up in assets. In the case of High West, they did a fantastic job of brand building in their early years, both through their sales team and international distribution network, but also in the visitor experience in Park City.

In fact, High West experienced double-digit year-over-year volume growth between 2013 and 2016, topping out at around 150,000 cases of whiskey in 2018. "It's been unbelievable," says Steve. "We're now in all 50 states and have growing international distribution." All that revenue is what has enabled High West to build another distillery in Wanship, a few miles north of Park City. The same year that distillery came on-line, Dave Perkins sold the High West brand and both distilleries to Constellation Brands in a deal worth roughly $160 million.

The Wanship distillery, which is less food-focused, fits more of the classic mold of a distillery and tasting room. It's equipped with a new 1600-gallon Forsyths copper pot still with a column attached to it. That distillery is now running 24 hours a day, and has already been upgraded once.

But even with both distilleries pumping out spirit, around 80% of the whiskey in High West bottles will still be sourced from other producers. And this is unlikely to change.

High West eats through very large volumes of seven to ten-year-old whiskey in their blends. If they wanted to start making all of that whiskey themselves, they would need to build a distillery big enough to handle not just the current volume of spirit that the brand sells, but the projected volume in five or ten years time. And they would need to keep as much of that spirit in barrel as possible for the next decade. That would require both enormous upfront capital investment and negative cashflow while the product matures for eight to ten years.

Not only that, but any new distillery would inevitably produce a different tasting product to the spirit being sourced from Indiana and Kentucky.

If the whiskey High West are making themselves constitutes only 20% of a bottle, any taste changes can be mitigated at the time of blending. You can't blend in such a way to create a different style of whiskey to the one your distillery is making!

The whiskeys that High West makes are distinctive in their blending of young and old spirit. Born out of a necessity to incorporate their own young whiskey in to a tasty mixture with sourced older stocks, these liquids make formidable blends and have in some ways established this style of whiskey making.

American Prairie is a blend of three straight bourbon whiskeys, all of them sourced, and aged from two to 13 years. Double Rye is a blend of two rye whiskeys: High West's own 80% rye mash bill and a 95% rye whiskey sourced from MGP (the next distillery on our hit list), aged for three to seven years. Rendezvous Rye is a blend of the same whiskeys as Double Rye, in different proportions, aged between four and seven years. Campfire is a blend of sourced bourbon, High West-distilled rye, and peated Scotch whisky sourced from Scotland, ranging in age from four to eight years old.

It's worth noting that all of the formulas for these whiskeys are subject to change and, indeed, have changed over the years. Whether it's a shift in the mash bill, the age statements, or the specific blend of whiskeys that goes into the bottle, High West will from time to time subtly alter numbers and statements on their labels to keep things up to date. The important distinction here though is that while they may not divulge the specifics of the liquid in the bottle, they are not ashamed to admit that they use a great deal of sourced whiskey in their blends.

"What we're doing with whiskey is really around the sensory," says Steve "We blend according to flavor, so that sometimes means more of this or that, and sometimes means the age of the whiskey differs."

Besides the core four bottlings mentioned above, High West is mashing various other recipes that are occasionally released in limited supply. One that I am particularly fond of is a young wheat whiskey called Valley Tan, which features the image of Porter Rockwell on the label. Rockwell was one of the

ABOVE Never drink and ride (this applies both for horses and snowboards.)

Mormon "Destroying Angels" (that is to say, hitmen) who was known to drink his valley tan with no water before "disappearing" unruly citizens.

RENDEZVOUS RYE (46% ABV)

Guns & Roses. Gun oil, leather, and hot plastic, swimming in a vat of rose-water. There's soft tropical fruits too, including lychee and melon. On the palate, the whiskey is sweet and juicy, erring on the fruit side of things and drilling home some good spice to boot. There's a long finish of oak lollipop.

CAMPFIRE (46% ABV)

The name says it all. The nose is white chocolate, hot honey, and banana, along with melted plastic and a subtle whisper of smoke in the finish. Concentrated spice hits you up front in the mouth, leading into sweet and juicy cantaloupe and then trails of smoke. It's like someone struck a match on your tongue (in a good way).

VALLEY TAN (43.5% ABV)

Green and creamy. On the nose, the aroma is pistachio oatmeal, with some soft vanilla leading into spearmint and soft greasiness. There's a luscious texture on the palate, like buttery mashed potato, with a good amount of heat to remind you it's there.

ROAD TRIP PLAYLIST

"Leave the Bourbon on the Shelf" – The Killers

"Sweet Child O' Mine" – Guns N' Roses

CAMPFIRE COCKTAIL

60 ml/2 oz High West Campfire
10 ml/2 teaspoons Marshmallow Syrup
(see below)

Stir over cubed ice for a minute then strain into a chilled rocks glass. Garnish with a toasted marshmallow.

I was really smitten with High West's Campfire expression when it was released. I loved the idea of blending whiskey to meet a certain, specific flavor and disregarding the notion that whiskeys from different producing countries shouldn't be mixed. I believe that food and drink that bring about a feeling of nostalgia or transportation are among the most powerful sensory forces we can experience.

So, I copied the idea and created a cocktail called Campfire that featured on the inaugural menu at my whiskey bar, Black Rock, in London, UK, back in 2016. At Black Rock, we also mixed bourbon with peated single malt, but since the drink was going to be based on an Old Fashioned cocktail, we sweetened it with marshmallow syrup. The marshmallow flavor contributes a giddy, indulgent quality that pairs beautifully with the peat smoke. I source a concentrated marshmallow extract that can be diluted into regular sugar syrup at a ratio of 20:1.

In this recipe, I'm using Campfire as the base spirit and simply mixing it with marshmallow syrup. If you're struggling to get a hold of Campfire (as I was in 2016), try mixing three parts bourbon with one part peated malt and using that as your base.

CATCHERS OF THE RYE

*"Too much of anything is bad, but too much whiskey
is barely enough."*

MARK TWAIN (1835–1910), AUTHOR

Although it makes little sense from a logistical perspective, our trajectory must point east once again for the sake of broadening our historical journey. This 2,000-mile drive will take us from the Rockies to the Ohio border, passing through six states and three time zones—all for the love of whiskey.

We leave Park City and, through mostly deserted roads, skirt along the lower quadrant of Wyoming, through the state capital, Cheyenne, and across the border into Nebraska. Known as the "Great American Desert," I've also heard people describe this state as "unbearably flat"—and they really weren't joking. For six straight hours we existed only in an animated version of Springsteen's Nebraska album cover.

The "Cornhusker state" is well-suited to making whiskey, with its hot summers, cold winters, more miles of river and underground water than any other state, an economy that relies heavily on corn and wheat, and the patience exhibited by its residents. Seemingly few Nebraskans got the memo though— there are only a dozen or so distilleries here and only a couple of them make whiskey.

Iowa is yet another central state that's primed for whiskey making. It's right in the heart of the corn belt, the huge smear of land that passes through Illinois, Iowa, Minnesota, and into the Dakotas, and has dominated corn production in the US since the mid-19th century. In 1956, former Vice President Henry A. Wallace declared that the Corn Belt was the "most productive agricultural civilization the world has ever seen." By the year 2000, the corn belt was growing around a quarter of all the world's corn.

If the corn belt is indeed a belt, Iowa would be the buckle. The state grows and harvests almost 3 million bushels a year, around 20% of the nation's supply. Only a fraction of US corn gets made into whiskey, though; most of it is used to make animal feed, although around a third of it is distilled into industrial ethanol. Combine corn farming and industrial ethanol production and you have a decent chunk of the Iowan economy right there.

For us, I-80 is like a 300-mile drive-thru of this corn belt buckle, touring the best distilleries that Iowa has to offer in the process. There aren't many here, but there's still some good stuff going on. Lonely Oak is a farm distillery based just outside of Earling. Dave Pickerell consulted on this operation in its early years, which now bottles a two-year-old bourbon made from estate-grown corn.

Then there's Cedar Ridge, situated just north of Iowa City, which was the first distiller in the state to appear since Prohibition when it opened in 2005. Owner, Jeff Quint launched Iowa's first bourbon from here in 2010, which came about after voicing frustration that Iowa was growing so much corn but making no whiskey. The corn is sourced from the family's own farm and distilled on a Christian Carl

pot still. Cedar Ridge also make malt, malted rye, and wheat whiskeys.

The "Quad-Cities" of Bettendorf, Davenport, Rock Island, and Moline span the Mississippi River and the state line between Iowa and Illinois. A few miles to the north, in Le Claire, is the Mississippi River Distilling Company, which makes Cody Road whiskeys, named after William "Buffalo Bill" Cody (1846–1917), who was born in Le Claire.

From the Quad Cities, it's a quick blast through Illinois along I-74 until we reach Indiana. We pass by Peoria, Illinois, on the way, once considered the "whiskey capital of the world." A total of 73 distilleries operated in the greater Peoria area between 1843 and 1919, at one time making Illinois the biggest producer of whiskey in the US. Indeed, if some historical accounts are to be believed, when the distilleries were operating at peak production, the state contributed nearly half of the federal government's entire tax revenue!

Next, we find ourselves in Indiana. The state motto here is "Crossroads of America," which is fitting because Indiana has more miles of Interstate Highway per square mile than any other state, and more major highways than any other state. It's also apt because, like any crossroads, Indiana is the kind of place where people quietly pass, focused on the somewhere else they're headed. For us though, this is an important stop. If you have even a passing interest in exploring new whiskey brands, there's an extremely strong chance that you've tasted whiskey from a single distillery in Lawrenceburg, and it's quite possible that you had no idea that it was made there.

The town of Lawrenceburg sits on the northern banks of the Ohio River in Indiana, on the tri-point with Kentucky and Ohio. Lawrenceburg is practically surrounded by traditional whiskey-making territories, with Ohio and Pennsylvania to the East, Kentucky and Tennessee to the south, and Illinois to the West. So why have we never heard of Indiana whiskey?

Well, there are two good answers to that question. The first is quite simply that we have forgotten about Indiana's distilling history.

ABOVE The control room does feel a little bit like an air traffic control center at an airport.

The second is that Indiana's biggest distillery would prefer to keep itself under the radar. You see, Lawrenceburg is home to the Midwestern Grain Products distillery (MGP), which is not only the biggest distiller in Indiana, but one of the largest in the entire nation. They produce around 10% of all American whiskey here, but only bottle a few brands that are not particularly well known. The rest of the spirit made here is contract-distilled for other customers who wish to market a whiskey brand but perhaps don't have the cash or desire to open a distillery of their own.

But before we get into that, let's explore the first answer: commercial distilling in Lawrenceburg goes back at least as far as 1847 and to the founding of the Rossville distillery, which evolved into the present-day MGP operation. The immediate proximity of the Ohio River made Lawrenceburg a good spot for making whiskey but the greater benefit came in the period from 1850–60 when the railway came to the city. This innovation enabled distilleries like Rossville to source their cereals from further away, like Indiana's fertile central plains.

Some years later, Schenley (see page 218) built a distillery very close to the Rossville operation. The reason? Water. An underground aquifer provides an almost limitless supply of water, which is essential if you're planning on making loads of booze. Seagram's bought up the site in 1933, at which point they were the largest spirit maker in the world, owning multiple Kentucky distilleries, one in Maryland, and one in Canada.

In 2001, following a calamitous foray into the music and entertainment business, Seagram's assets were liquidated and the distillery was acquired by the French drinks giant Pernod Ricard. This was an important transitional period for the Lawrenceburg distillery, as the shift in focus moved away from own-brand products to contract-distilling for other brands. CL Financial (owner of the House of Angostura in Trinidad) came in and bought the distillery in 2007, then sold it to the current owner, MGP, in 2011.

The site is essentially a 30-acre fortress, with the distillery in the center protected by half a dozen warehouses on the perimeter.

Mike Templin, the plant manager, leads us on a walk around the facility, first towards the tower-block control room before a long walk through the vast central courtyard of the distillery. Like an abandoned metropolis, the gigantic brick buildings loom all around us, their long windows and scale giving them a vaguely Kremlin-esque vibe with a dash of Brick Expressionism on account of the white bricks spelling out "SEAGRAMS SINCE 1857". The typography communicates a sense of endurance, like these building were built to last. And last they have, even if Seagram's itself is no longer an entity.

Midwestern Grain Products as a company dates back to 1941, when they were founded to make high-strength alcohol for torpedo fuel during World War II. They only make drinkable alcohol now.

When MGP bought the distillery, another company, Proximo, bought the bottling hall, which is located on the other side of the US-50 highway. Proximo still bottles some of the products that MGP produce, and there's a 500-m long trench that connects the two operations together.

This distillery makes neutral spirits and gin, as well as a range of aged products from various mash recipes. MGP publishes 12 different mash recipes on their website, including a high-rye rye (95% rye, 5% malted barley), a low-rye rye (51% rye, 45% corn, 4% malted barley), high-rye bourbon (60% corn, 36% rye, 4% malted barley), and bourbon (75% corn, 21% rye, 4% malted barley). Various wheat and corn whiskeys are also on the roster, as well as unpublished recipes that are customer-specific.

"Internally, we designate recipe by letters of the alphabet," says Mike. "And now we're running out of letters." It's extremely likely that no other distillery in the world is making as many whiskey recipes as MGP in Indiana. Only MGP know the true extent of their customer database, but I wouldn't be surprised if the number of products containing MGP juice in the marketplace exceeds 250. Oh and speaking of the number 250, that's MGP's minimum order quantity in barrels for a bespoke recipe.

The product range doesn't end at spirits either. As the name suggests, Midwestern Grain Products make loads of types of flours, proteins, and starches that end up in basically any type of processed food you can think of with a cereal component.

"Demand for our whiskey has shot up in the last couple of years." says Mike "People are calling up and saying 'I have an idea for a brand and a distillery, can you sell me something to get things started?'"

Of course, MGP are only too happy to oblige. However, what often happens next is that the customer's sales volume exceeds the planned distillery and warehouse size. So they can't build the small distillery they wanted to since it would be unable to keep up. The obvious thing then would be to build a bigger distillery, but that requires a lot of capital investment. So what do they do next? "Our hope is that they keep on buying from us," says Mike. "It's worked out okay so far—we've got a lot of entrepreneurs up and running."

We walk past the corn silo, which is a couple of hundred yards away from where the mashing and fermenting takes place. The silo holds up to 2,000 tons and automatically sends parcels of corn to a smaller silo near the mill whenever the level in that silo drops. All of the cereals here are delivered by truck, except for the malted barley, which—perhaps because it's the most noble of the cereal varieties—arrives the old fashioned way, via rail.

"It's a smaller component of the mash bill so easier to manage inventory," says Mike. "We couldn't rely on corn to be delivered like this because rail isn't reliable enough and it could shut the plant down if we don't get it on time."

MGP also uses the rail line to transport out leftover processed stillage to be sent to farms to use as animal feed. The water, which comes from the same aquifer, emerges at a constant 58°F all year round.

Riding the elevator up to the control room, Mike explains that the grain containers are located at the top of the tower block and that the processes are then dictated by gravity. The control room has all the look, feel, and altitude of air traffic control at a busy airport. Here, the processes are managed by computer, which dictates which grain containers dump cereals into the mill and at what time. The grain is ground on a hammer mill, then sent to a pre-cooker where it forms a hot slurry with water and backset. This is sent to the mash cooker where steam heats the whole mixture up to the necessary temperatures depending on what recipe they are making.

There are two fermenting rooms, one on each side of the street. The one we visit has 14 27,000-gallon open top fermenters. We're told that there are 21 fermenters in the other room and that they're "about twice the size." The larger fermenters are also of a closed-top design, and the CO_2 that they produce is actually collected and compressed by a third party, allowing it to be sold on to medical and soft drinks industries. This kind of technology can be seen in many distilleries around the world, but it's surprisingly rare to find in an American distillery.

MGP uses its own proprietary yeast strain that was developed during the Seagram's era. However, some customers ask that MGP uses a yeast that they have selected themselves, which is a clever way of defining a specific style of spirit and may improve your chances of potentially transitioning the style of whiskey when production moves to your own distillery.

Fermentation takes around three days, and then the product is sent over to the beer still. I ask Mike if there's only one beer still to which he responds, "We have several." An exact number wasn't forthcoming! Mike does tell me that the stills are run slightly differently based on the mash bill, though. The spirit passes through a doubler and comes off the still at around 130 proof.

The majority of the product made here goes into barrels and is matured on site. Some whiskey is matured in other locations, and some un-aged whiskey is sent directly to customers so that they can mature the whiskey in the barrels and location of their choosing. Standard barrel entry proof is at 120, though some customers are managing that side of things themselves, so it's prone to vary.

"Despite our size, there hasn't been a whole lot of technical innovation here," says Mike "The warehousing team, which is around six or seven people, house the barrels up on to the racks and roll the barrels in by hand."

He's right with respect to that part of the process, although other parts are a little more autonomous. Barrels are filled on conveyor belts, where gas station-style nozzles rapidly dispense liquid into batches of eight barrels, which are promptly whisked away to make space for another batch of barrels. The warehouse we're shown around is racked in the traditional way, but there are palletized warehouses on site too.

MGP does bottle a range of own-brand whiskeys, which I had assumed were simply re-labellings of whiskeys that are also sold to contract customers. It turns out, however, that for their own-brand bottlings, MGP actually blends together whiskeys made from different mash recipes to create original, proprietary formulas.

Total production here is at around 24 million bottles of whiskey a year, or somewhere in the region of 10% of the entire American whiskey market. Rye whiskey is what the distillery has become really famous for, and MGP probably makes as much rye whiskey as every other American producer put together. "We're big," says Mike, "And it's misleading how quiet it is around here, but that's how it's supposed to be when things are running well."

TOP LEFT A delivery of rye arrives at the distillery. And when a delivery comes in, you need a guy with a hardhat and a clipboard.

MIDDLE LEFT One of two huge fermentation rooms at MGP, where hundreds of variants of whiskey begin their lives.

TOP RIGHT As you can probably tell, MGP is not the kind of place where you turn up for a distillery tour unannounced.

RIGHT This area is used for filling and dumping whiskey in preparation for bottling. It's strangely reminiscent of a milking parlor.

Leaving MGP we drive northwest, towards Indianapolis. The many highways here are organized in a grid system, which means you can travel over 50 miles without needing to use the steering wheel. The novelty of driving with no hands wears off after five minutes, then boredom sets in, and boredom is always followed by tiredness.

We skirt past Indianapolis and head north, to Kokomo. Our accommodation for the night is on an alpaca farm. Indiana must be a confusing place for an alpaca, an animal that has evolved to live at 5,000-m altitude in the sparsely oxygenated air of the Chilean Andes—not the pancake landscape of the Midwest. It's dark when we arrive and we fail to spot a single alpaca. Perhaps they died of oxygen poisoning.

Tonight we're staying in a log cabin on the edge of the farm. The rain is falling in sheets, and as we step inside the sound of it shifts dramatically, like Gatling gun shells hitting the roof. The Gatling gun was invented in Indiana by Richard Gatling, in 1861, the same year the Civil War started. It's also about the same time as our cabin was built, and goes some way to explaining why it's decked out like what I imagine one of Abraham Lincoln's Civil War command posts

looked like: flags draped over the walls, wood-burning stove, gas lanterns, and chunky oak furniture.

Lincoln grew up on a farm in Indiana but moved to Illinois in his twenties, where he lived for most of his adult life as a lawyer before running for office. And Illinois just so happens to be where we're heading next. But first—sleep.

GEORGE REMUS BOURBON (47% ABV)

Plenty of barrel aroma on the nose: caramel and vanilla notes, plus some winter spices such as cinnamon, allspice, and nutmeg. This follows through to the taste, where sweet caramel and vanilla ice cream are coupled with spice-drawer dryness and toasted oak. Lightly textured and quick to finish.

ROSSVILLE UNION MASTER CRAFTED STRAIGHT RYE (47% ABV)

A nice balance of fruit (cherry and damson) and nut (brazil and hazelnut) on the nose, which melds together nicely with some barrel influence. On the palate, there's vanilla, charred oak, and white pepper. The finish has a little more of that fruitiness found on the nose, and dry japaleño spice brings up the rear.

TANNER'S CREEK BLENDED BOURBON, (42.5% ABV)

Fruit comes through nicely on this whiskey, with cherry juice and lavender honey taking center-stage. There's a touch of golden raisin in there too, giving a kind of Danish-pastry aroma. The taste is dry and crisp, with a hint of orange zest to accompany more traditional vanilla and butterscotch from the barrel.

ROAD TRIP PLAYLIST

"Shelter from the Storm" — Bob Dylan

"The Passenger" — Iggy Pop

"Riders on the Storm" — The Doors

WALDORF

50 ml/1⅔ oz Rossville Union Rye
20 ml/⅔ oz Sweet Vermouth
5 ml/1 teaspoon Absinthe
2 dashes Angostura Bitters

Stir in a mixing beaker then strain into a chilled coupe glass. No garnish required.

The Waldorf Astoria Hotel in New York sits among the list of the most legendary drink spots in the world. It was built in 1931, which was only a couple of years before Seagram's got to work on the distillery now known as MGP.

One of the signature cocktails of the hotel's bar was the Waldorf, which is basically a Manhattan with a measure of absinthe. Depending on who you listen to, the absinthe either moves the drink in the direction of the Sazerac or turns it into an outright absinthe-fest. In *The Old Waldorf-Astoria Bar Book*, A. S. Crockett calls for equal parts of whiskey, vermouth, and absinthe, which results on a drink that tastes of little but anise. I suggest using around 5 ml of absinthe—enough for it to be noticed but not so much that it becomes a nuisance.

KOVAL

THE BLACK SHEEP

"Ashes to ashes, dust to dust, if the women don't get you then the whiskey must."

CARL SANDBURG (1878–1967), AUTHOR

It was in the 1840s that Chicago emerged as a major transportation hub thanks, in part, to the opening of the Illinois and Michigan Canal, which allowed shipping from the Great Lakes, through Chicago, down to the same Mississippi River that was shipping bourbon to New Orleans. As Carl Sandburg's 1916 poem put it, Chicago was the "Hog Butcher, Tool Maker, Stacker of Wheat, Player with Railroads, and Freight Handler to the Nation."

In 1840, Chicago ranked as the 92nd most populated city in the US. By 1890, over one million people called Chicago home, making it second only to New York. And while New York perhaps has the most famous skyline in the world, it was Chicago that had the first skyscraper—the ten-story Home Insurance Building, which opened in 1885.

When you combine the industrial capability of the city with the nearby availability of grain in the Midwest, Chicago also proved a logical place to make beer and whiskey. There were eight distilleries here in 1860, which doesn't sound like a lot until you consider their scale. The Shufeldt Distillery, established in Cook County in 1849, produced 8 million gallons of whiskey a year at the height of its powers.

However, there was another city in Illinois that was producing even more than Chicago: Peoria, which was once considered "the whiskey capital of the world."

Most of Peoria's successes in the whiskey industry came as a result of the infamous Whiskey Trust. In 1882, John D. Rockefeller created the Standard Oil Trust. It was designed to allow Rockefeller and other Standard Oil stockholders to get around state laws prohibiting one company from owning stock in another company.

Five years later in Peoria, Joseph Greenhut (owner of the Great Western Distillery), and other distillery owners used the Standard Oil Trust as a model and created the Distillers & Cattle Feeders Trust (known as the Whiskey Trust). A total of 65 distilleries joined the trust at the time of its creation, 24 of them in Illinois, and 12 of them in Peoria. Additionally, three of the nine founding members of the Trust were from Peoria, including the president, Joseph Greenhut. The Whiskey Trust would go on to become one of America's most notorious organizations, operating a whiskey monopoly with a reputation for ruthlessly shutting down distilleries throughout the Midwest.

Distillers that joined the Trust had to incorporate their distilleries, sell shares, and effectively hand over control of production and pricing to the Trust. This allowed the Trust to control supply and demand in the region and therefore control competition and pricing. Distillers were often given managerial jobs in their former sites once they had joined the Trust. Such was the success of the Trust that some of its operations became incredibly large producers of spirits. Some reporters called it "the octopus." One of the early members of the Trust were the Clarke Bros, who built a distillery in Peoria in the 1860s. They produced "Clarke's Pure Rye" there from 1888 onwards, advertising themselves as "The Largest Whiskey Distillers in the World" on branded playing cards.

If you owned a distillery and didn't want to join the Trust, you might find that the Trust would move into your community and undercut your prices. If that didn't work, you might receive threatening letters, or an evening visit from some nasty men. Remember the Shufeldt Distillery in Chicago? They were bullied by the Whiskey Trust and in 1888 discovered a Trust spy working on their payroll who reportedly gave a full confession. The distillery's owner, Thomas Lynch, told reporters, "The Trust might easily put up the price of spirits but it cannot do so as long as Shufeldt holds out, and it would be a mighty good thing for the Trust if Shufeldt is out of the way."

The same year as the spy was rooted out, it was discovered that a valve on a vat of high-strength spirits had been tampered with to make it an explosive risk. Shortly after its discovery, two packs of dynamite containing seven sticks each were thrown on to the roof of the distillery. One of them cut a big hole in the roof and the other failed to detonate. The Trust was accused of sponsoring the crime and the Trust secretary, George J. Gibson, was arrested for attempting to sabotage the plant. However, in spite of significant evidence, including a statement from an excise officer who told police that he had been offered $25,000 to plant a bomb under a vat of alcohol, all charges against Gibson were mysteriously quashed by a judge in Chicago.

The explosion may not have destroyed the Shufeldt distillery but it was enough to rattle the nerves of Thomas Lynch. He sold the distillery to the Whiskey Trust in 1891 for a reported $1.75 million (equivalent to $50 million in 2019). The distillery was closed and relocated to Pekin, Illinois.

By 1890, the federal government and several states became concerned with the monopolistic tactics of the Trust. So, to avoid trouble, they incorporated under Illinois law, becoming the Distilling and Cattle Feeding Company. The trustees became the company's directors. Everyone still called it the Whiskey Trust.

One of the weirder chapters in the history of the Whiskey Trust occurred in 1891, when the Trust solicited the help of the Japanese scientist Takamine Jokichi. Jokichi came from a family of sake brewers in Honshu, Japan. He would go on to be the first person to isolate adrenaline, but prior to that, he founded a company that studied the enzymes found in koji (a rice mold used in sake brewing) that break down starch during mashing. Jokichi resided in Peoria for four years, assisting in the development of a faster, more efficient fermentation of whiskey mash. His laboratory, under heavy security, was located in the malt house of the Woolner Grove distillery. A few years into his tenure, in 1894, the Manhattan distillery in Peoria adapted its fermentation process according to his findings.

Production among the Whiskey Trust's growing catalogue of producers continued to increase in the 1890s, reaching its zenith in 1894, when the Whiskey Trust accounted for more than 80% of the nation's total production of alcohol spirits and around 70% of all whiskey. Peoria remained its headquarters, with six distilleries in Peoria accounting for 50 percent of the trust's production. Do the math and you'll come to conclusion that six distilleries in the city of Peoria were making over a third of the nation's whiskey.

As you might imagine, the Whiskey Trust was viewed by many with abhorrence, but with strong-arm tactics and powerful links to government officials, there was little that could be done to loosen their grip on the market. That didn't stop Max Reefer, a whiskey blender based in Kansas City, Missouri (where local newspapers described him as "irrepressible" and "indispensable") from bottling his "Green Mountain Distillery Anti-Trust Whiskey." The label on the bottle read:

"The whiskey we send is distilled from the purest grain (no seconds), is matured and ripened in wood and will cost you but a few cents over $2.00 per gallon. We guarantee that no Trust house ever sold the same quality goods for less than $3.00 to $4.00."

As phenomenally successful as the Whiskey Trust was, its reign was short. Such was the aggression of the growth strategy that, in 1893, they began to

lower dividends to shareholders in order to purchase even more distilleries. This was not a popular move for many shareholders, which meant the Whiskey Trust was becoming unpopular to pretty much everyone. This included the government, who had by this point got their act together and begun to recognize the Whiskey Trust for what it was: a cartel. What ensued was a series of court decisions starting in 1893 and ending 1895, that found the Distilling and Cattle Feeding Company "exceeded powers granted by its charter, destroyed competition, and was repugnant to public policy... and therefore was illegal."

One 2002 study on the Whiskey Trust, published by the University of Pittsburgh, concluded that, "the primary cause of the demise of the Whiskey Trust was market entry. According to industry observers, as the trust gained market share it also tried to raise prices. This attracted new firms to the market, who in turn, undercut the trust."

Greenhut came out of the whole arrangement okay, though. Long before most of the Kentucky Whiskey barons had made their first million, Greenhut was lounging in his 35-room mansion in Peoria, complete with its glass conservatory and turrets. In 1899, he even entertained President William McKinley (in office from 1897 until his assassination in 1901).

As Prohibition crept over the land—by 1913, nine states were completely dry and another 31 were dry by local option—things began to get grim for the alcohol industry, and for distillers in particular, with brewers and winemakers trying to throw them under the bus in an effort to keep beer and wine legal.

In 2008, Sonat and Robert Birnecker founded Koval, the first new (legal!) distillery to open in Chicago since the 19th century.

Before then, Sonat and Robert were based in Washington, DC, with Sonat working as a German professor and Robert employed at the Austrian Consulate. Instead of spending the $30,000 they had saved on an apartment in DC (which would possibly be more like a closet), they moved to Chicago, where Sonat's family came from. Then, instead of spending their savings on an apartment there, they naturally decided to buy a 300-liter pot-still. Robert was an Austrian native who grew up around distilling and winemaking at his parent's winery, so this kind of thing was already in his blood.

At that point, in 2008, there were still Prohibition-era laws in affect in Chicago. So Sonat headed down to Springfield and set about attempting to repeal the laws. The endeavor was a success, allowing not only for the Birneckers to start a distillery but also for them to contribute to the laws that governed what made a craft distillery "craft", which at the time meant producing no more than 75,000 gallons of spirit year. (These regulations have since been updated and now constitute two separate classes of licenses, the more flexible of the two allowing up to 100,000 gallons of spirit produced a year).

Whiskey was being produced right from the start. They started with rye, oat, wheat, spelt, and millet whiskeys, exploring the individual grains and seeing what they tasted like on their own. "We had this sort of academic approach of looking at it in many

different ways," says Sonat. They then tried maturing each of these cereals individually in toasted barrels and charred barrels. This approach, while no doubt interesting, doubled the number of whiskeys they were making, forcing them to cut down to the core expressions they bottle today.

The name they chose for the brand was Koval, which means "blacksmith" in several Eastern European languages. However, in Yiddish it also refers to a "black sheep" or someone who forges ahead or does something new or out of the ordinary. This was the moniker that Sonat's grandfather was labeled with when he moved to Chicago in the early 1900s.

In 2017, they expanded considerably, and now have a 46,000 sq ft area to produce, bottle, and distribute whiskey from. That meant a new roof, new skylights, a tasting room, whiskey museum, and additional distillation equipment. There's a reason for all this expansion. This distillery makes six core expressions of whiskey and at least the same again in special releases and one-off editions. Plus, as of 2018, Koval is distributed in all 50 states and a total of 55 export markets. Of the new set of American distilleries, I don't know of a brand with better distribution. Indeed, Koval's distribution rivals even that of the older Kentucky distilleries!

Water comes in from Lake Michigan and is charcoal-filtered before being used by the distillery. Koval sources all their cereals from within a 150-mile radius. Their bourbon is made from a mash of 51% corn and 49% millet; their rye whiskey is 100% rye, and millet whiskey is 100% millet. Then there's the Four Grain whiskey, which is made from 37.5% malted barley, 37.5% oats, 12.5% wheat, and 12.5% rye. Enzymes are used for conversion in all of these mash bills, and they all utilize the same type of yeast.

"When the distillery first started they trialled a bunch of different yeasts, says Mitch Conti, Koval's

TOP A big sack of Illinois corn at the Koval distillery, preparing itself to be turned into bourbon.
MIDDLE One of the main emphases that Koval places on production is in its distillation cuts.
BOTTOM A row of barrels in a rick house can be beautiful, and so too can a bunch of barrels placed here and there.

marketing manager, "but really didn't notice the difference after the spirit had been distilled. We're looking to get the best possible alcohol yield on these mashes, then to make a clean, flavorful spirit."

The mash cooker holds 5,000 liters, which feeds four fermenters, each of them a little over 5,000 liters, which ties in nicely with Koval's enormous 5,000-liter German still. If only all distilleries were this simple! The still, by the way, is the biggest still of its kind that I've seen. Koval have a second one on order.

The still has a couple of attached columns, which allows Koval to make their own neutral spirits for vodka production. When making whiskey, they can distill in a single run by closing five of the 16 plates on the column. Bourbon comes off at the maximum permitted strength of 80%. The other whiskeys come off the still even higher, at a whopping 86%. This means a single 5,000-liter run will produce about 460 liters of spirit for Koval bourbon, or enough to fill three of their 30-gallon barrels.

Spoiler alert there. Yes, Koval have up until recently used exclusively 30-gallon barrels coopered by The Barrel Mill in Minnesota. More recently they have bought larger, 53-gallon barrels from a cooperage in Tennessee. The policy here is to use them only once. All of the whiskeys Koval makes are proofed down to 113 and are generally aged between three and five years. Perhaps most interesting of all is that every bottle is unblended and from a single barrel. Crunch all of this distillery data together and what do you get? Well, there's a lot of focus at the start of the process, with interesting mash bills that utilize unusual grains. Then comes mashing and fermentation, which are, by their own admission, designed to make alcohol. Distillation is clearly an area of expertise for the distillery, with particular focus on the hearts cut. But when a spirit comes off a still at such a high strength, it's inevitable that some of the flavor will have been stripped out in the pursuit of purity. Also, filling at such a strength will require some Koval's spirits to be diluted with 50% of water before they enter the barrel.

Finally, the casks, which being that little bit smaller and exclusively virgin oak, will be extremely active,

especially on a spirit with a relatively light character. So the ultimate conclusion is a whiskey with quite a lot of barrel character, even in low-age expressions.

BOURBON (47% ABV)

Subtle at first on the nose, but what shines through most is the sense of new oak, with butterscotch, maple, and coconut being the dominant forces. On the palate, it has a good body and seems to balance alcohol and sweetness well. Pleasant cereal notes and a French-toast flavor come through in the finish.

OAT (40% ABV)

The aroma immediately suggests the unconventional cereal. There's a strange emulsion paint smell that disputes after a while, revealing a preferable smells of honey and porridge. The taste is a lot dryer than expected, where cask character dominates. The spirit is also quite light bodied with just a suggestion of citrus coming through in the finish.

RYE (40% ABV)

Notes of bread crust and bagel lead the way with this rye, which certainly seems to err on the side of bread-y rather than nutty or spicy. The taste continues this theme, with a delicious bran flavor that at times feels almost agricultural, like hay and cut grass. The finish softens out slowly, showing that this is a super accessible rye for the masses.

FOUR GRAIN (47% ABV)

The aroma is like an oat cake that's been slathered in hot butter. There's a really great harmony between cereal notes and maturation character. The taste is salted oatmeal with a touch of maple syrup.

ROAD TRIP PLAYLIST

"Chicago" – Sufjan Stevens

"Long Train Runnin'" – Doobie Brothers

"Eyes to the Wind" – The War on Drugs

WHISKEY HIGHBALL

40 ml/1⅓ oz Koval Four Grain
120 ml/4 oz ice-cold soda water

Add the whiskey to a chilled highball glass filled with ice and stir briefly. Then top up with soda and give another brief, gentle stir. Garnish with a slice of lemon.

I'm a big believer in highball drinks and consider them one of the best entry routes into whiskey appreciation. There aren't many things I like more than sipping on a nice rye or single malt and appreciating the distinctions of its crafting, but one of the things I do like just as much is enjoying an ice-cold, effervescent highball on a warm afternoon.

The origins of the drink are actually English. The original highballs were brandy-based drinks that became popular in Europe in the mid-19th century. Then, when Scotch whisky came into vogue, it supplanted brandy as the base spirit. New York barman Patrick Duffy claimed the highball was brought to the US in 1894 from England by actor E. J. Ratcliffe (1863–1948). Duffy wrote, in his 1934

The Official Mixer's Manual, that, "it is one of my fondest hopes that the highball will again take its place as the leading American Drink."

The drink achieved peak popularity in the mid-20th century, when it appeared regularly on British television and was consumed by everyone from Winston Churchill to James Bond (who in the Fleming novels drank more highballs than he did martinis). It didn't ever regain the popularity in the US that Duffy hoped for, and until quite recently has fallen out of fashion in the UK, too.

That is set to change though. I believe that highballs are the next big thing in mixed drinks. Don't believe me? Well how about you make one and tell me how good you think it is…

FEW

FOREVER WET

*"Prohibition makes you want to cry into your beer
and denies you the beer to cry into."*

DON MARQUIS (1878–1937), JOURNALIST AND AUTHOR

Leaving Koval, we head a few miles north to the Chicago suburb of Evanston, where our next distillery stop is located. We almost immediately pass the Rosehill Cemetery, where many notable Chicagoans are buried, including one Frances Elizabeth Willard.

Willard became president of the United States Woman's Christian Temperance Movement (WCTU) in 1879, a position she held until her death in 1898. The WCTU was originally organized in December 1873, for the purpose of creating a "sober and pure world" through abstinence. In the same year, more than 200,000 retailers sold liquor in the US, a whopping 120,000 more than just 10 years before. So the cause for concern was understandable.

The WCTU based themselves out of the then-distinct city of Evanston, a few miles north of Chicago (though today very much part of the urban sprawl). The reason they chose Evanston was because it was already dry. Amendments to Northwestern University's charter, granted by the State of Illinois General Assembly in 1855, established that the City of Evanston was to be devoid of alcohol. The trustees of the city later adopted an ordinance prohibiting spirits, which is what drew Willard and her family to move here. In time, Evanston became recognized as the birthplace of the entire prohibition movement.

While most of you reading this book are unlikely to sympathize with Frances Willard's cause, it's difficult not to marvel at her commitment. Willard's seemingly boundless energy took her on a 50-day speaking tour in 1874, and an average of 400 lectures a year for a 10-year period, during which time she covered an average of 30,000 miles of travel a year.

She really didn't like whiskey.

Another prominent figure from the WCTU was Carrie Nation. Standing six feet tall and weighing 175 lbs, this colorful Kentuckian believed that Jesus was talking directly to her and that his commands included the complete destruction of all saloons. She took the edict literally, and personally smashed apart a saloon in Kiowa, Oklahoma. She was famous for wielding a hatchet, which became her go-to method for tearing apart bar tops and breaking down saloon doors. She went on to publish a newsletter called *Hatchet* and another known as *Smasher's Mail*.

Others took a slightly more passive approach to causing saloons problems. WCTU members would often join together outside saloons to pray and harass the customers, to attempt to drive the establishments out of business. On most occasions, these acts were not well received by saloon keepers or patrons. Sometimes beer was thrown on the sidewalk so that the women wouldn't kneel down for prayer. Other times the beer was simply thrown on the women.

The WCTU also inspired the formation of other anti-alcohol conventions, such as the Anti-Saloon League of America, in 1893. This organization

lobbied for state laws that would ban the sale of alcohol and they also endorsed political candidates that would help further their cause. By 1900, many of the smaller temperance societies had either given their support to or had become part of the Anti-Saloon League.

Most saloons at that time were extremely unruly places that served liquor, wine, and beer to almost anyone—young or old, sober or drunk, morning, noon, or night. George Ade, author of *The Old Time Saloon* (1931), noted that, in Chicago, once a saloon keeper got his license, he would throw the key to his bar into Lake Michigan so that his doors could never again be locked.

The temperance movement got its way, however, and Prohibition began on January 17, 1920, when the Volstead Act went into effect. A total of 1,520 Federal Prohibition agents were tasked with enforcement. However, the 1920s turned out to be some of the "wettest" days in American history. Booze was smuggled in from Canada, the Bahamas, and Mexico, or it was manufactured in barns and backwoods by one of the thousands of moonshiner operations that sprouted up to meet demand. While quality surely suffered, the Prohibition era did a good job of shifting American tastes away from beer and towards hard liquor.

In just the first six months of 1920 alone, the federal government opened 7,291 cases for Volstead Act violations, and criminal empires began to blossom. At one end of the operation was the illegal stills, and at the other end was the speakeasy. Agents from the Bureau of Prohibition pursued them both vigorously. This era gave rise to legendary gangster syndicates like the Chicago Outfit. Led by Johnny Torrio and Al Capone, the Outfit became the most powerful crime organization in the Midwest. Rarely out of the headlines, Capone's empire made millions and waged a bloody war on the streets of Chicago until his conviction in 1931 for tax evasion.

Another prominent Midwest bootlegger from the Prohibition era was George Remus. By 1920, Remus was one of the best criminal attorneys in the Midwest. In the 1920s, his acute knowledge of the

Volstead Act allowed him to buy up distilleries and create his own drug company, and it's thanks to this that Remus became an enormously successful bootlegger, serving as both buyer and seller, and then cooking the books to "lose" shipments in-between. He called his system "The Circle" and referred to himself in the third person. At the height of his powers, Remus had 3,000 employees working three shifts a day and was doing millions of dollars worth of business a year.

In 1925, Remus was indicted for violating the Volstead Act 3,000 times. It took the jury less than two hours to find Remus guilty and he was sentenced to two years in federal prison. When he got out, he shot his wife for betraying him, was tried in court, and was found not guilty on the sole ground of insanity. It's said that F. Scott Fitzgerald's Jay Gatsby was based in part on George Remus.

One interesting side effect of Prohibition came about when bootleggers began modifying their cars and trucks to make them faster and handle better, so as to improve their chances of outrunning and escaping agents. Robert Glenn "Junior" Johnson (1931–), was one such moonshine driver, who became particularly adept at outrunning the authorities in North Carolina in the 1950s. He went on to become one of NASCAR's greatest ever drivers, dubbed "The Last American Hero," and was eventually pardoned by Ronald Reagan 1986 for a moonshine conviction in 1956. During an interview with the BBC, he once said, "If it hadn't been for whiskey, NASCAR wouldn't have been formed. That's a fact."

When Prohibition finally ended in 1934, Chicago began to return to normality. But when the city of Evanston was given the option to be "wet" or "dry" under an amendment to the Illinois Liquor Control Act, the citizens took the dry option. The ban on alcohol was more symbolic than anything, since Chicago and the nearby suburb of Skokie were both "wet" and only a short drive away. Perhaps that's why the ban remained in effect for so long.

It wasn't until 1972 that the City Council voted to allow restaurants and hotels to sell liquor on their premises. The Council later approved the sale of alcohol at retail liquor outlets in 1984.

But you still couldn't make spirits in Evanston. Then Paul Hletko came along.

Undoing 160 years of Prohibition history was no easy task. Paul made many trips to Evanston City Hall, dealing not so much with resistance to his wants but more just the inertia it takes to affect any kind of change in local government.

So Evanston is the spiritual home of temperance in the US. But it's also the spiritual home of FEW Spirits, which is located only a half-dozen blocks away from Frances Willard's former home, on 1730 Chicago Avenue. There's a plaque outside the property that commemorates her time there. Now, in case you haven't noticed, "FEW" happen to be Frances Elizabeth Willard's initials, although Paul Hletko insists this was purely a coincidence.

FEW Spirits doesn't have a plaque and is actually not all that easy to find—even when you know the address. There's that same sense of adventure and discovery that you might experience when trying to track down a speakeasy bar. We wander around for a few minutes until we find the distillery tucked down an alleyway between a thrift store and the American Toby Jug Museum (who knew?). Only painted bricks with the faded "FEW" logo signify that you're in the right place.

Inside we're greeted by Paul, FEW founder and master distiller. He is a patent lawyer-turned-distiller, whose family has a background in making booze. His grandfather ran a renowned Czech brewery many years ago (by Paul's own request it shall remain nameless). Establishing FEW spirits in 2011 was in part a continuation of the family legacy.

The distillery is small—surprisingly small for a brand that has managed to gain some good international traction with their product. Plans are afoot to expand, but for now Paul takes us on a tour of the place that FEW has called home for the past eight years (which really only requires standing in the middle of the distillery and spinning around).

Given that we're in Illinois, it's not that surprising to learn that cereals can be sourced quite locally, mostly from farming co-operatives. FEW doesn't currently have milling capability, however, so the corn, rye, and malted barley arrive pre-ground in 50-lb sacks. Paul tells us they go through 4,000 lbs of grain a day at FEW, which means 200 bags of grain must be dumped (by hand) in the mash cooker each day—now that's what you call handmade!

Fermentation is temperature-controlled and they use a different yeast for each product. Paul reckons that the yeast plays at least as big a role in the flavor of each expression as the mash recipe does. The fermenters are also agitated, to ensure even distribution of heat. Fermentation takes three days.

Distillation is done in a Vendome steel beer-stripping column, which is linked to a copper doubler. It's more common to see distilleries of this size using pots instead of columns, which is why the column at FEW is one of the smallest column stills that Vendome have ever made. "I don't think there's an advantage or disadvantage to using columns over pots from a flavor point of view," says Paul, "but what I will say is that when it comes to efficiency the column takes the place of eight pot stills." The spirit comes off the doubler at 67% ABV.

The spirit is then cut with water to 59%, ready for filling into barrels. Virtually everything at FEW starts its maturation in new American Oak casks, with the exception of some single malt spirit that goes into its own used bourbon barrels. Paul also has a range of wine barrels, coffee barrels, and even a 100-year-old Irish whiskey barrel reserved for special projects and perhaps for some future experimental releases.

The distillery is currently filling around eight barrels a day, which then get sent to one of two (soon to be three) warehouses a mile or two away from the modest distillery building.

I'm interested in the expansion plans and relocation, and quiz Paul on the challenges of chasing all of his equipment while producing the same quality of whiskey.

"We want to make whiskey taste the way we want it to taste," says Paul. "As long as we can accomplish all those goals, everything else is just a tool." Paul reiterates many times that the policy here at FEW is to "chase the liquid not the technique." This means that nothing is done here unless it needs to be done and anything that is done a certain way is done for a certain reason. And that reason is always the taste of the spirit.

The FEW bottles are some of the prettiest in the industry, each one labeled with an illustration inspired by the 1893 Columbian Exposition (a.k.a. the Chicago World's Fair). World's fairs showcased the latest in technology, the arts, and products and were known to attract tens of millions of visitors.

"That fair was a turning point for Chicago and the rest of the world," says Paul. "There was all sorts of cool stuff there that nobody had seen before."

He's not wrong. At the time, it was seen as impressive that Chicago was even able to host the fair in the first place, beating out the likes of New York and Washington, D.C. for hosting rights. Prior to the fair, Chicago had a reputation as a dangerous, dirty city in the industrial Midwest. The Columbian Exposition changed all of that.

This was the first World's Fair to be electrically lit, having followed the recent face-off between rival inventors George Westinghouse and Thomas Edison in the so-called War of the Currents. Westinghouse won the contract to power the Fair with his AC electricity, installing over 120,000 incandescent lamps. Electricity allowed for other innovations to be present, such as the first "moving sidewalk," the first movie theater, the first automatic dishwasher, the first vacuum cleaner, and the first neon and phosphorescent lamps.

The world's first Ferris wheel was in operation there too, built by George Washington Gale Ferris Jr. (1859–1896). You'd think they might have tested the idea with something smaller, but this wheel was a massive 80 meters high and had 36 cars, each of which could accommodate 40 people. George C. Tilyou (1862–1914), later credited all the fun of the fair for inspiring him to create America's first major amusement park, Steeplechase Park in Coney Island, New York, in 1897. Besides boosting the image of Chicago, the fair left a legacy of American industrial optimism that continues today and set the stage for the most popular of all the world's fairs: Disneyland and Disney World.

FEW's Bourbon bottle shows an illustration of the Statue of the Republic, a 65-foot statue that dominated the fair's skyline. The original was destroyed, but a 24-foot bronze replica exists in Jackson Park that was created for the 25th anniversary of the fair in 1918. The bourbon is a mix of 70% corn, 20% rye, and 10% malted barley.

The rye shows an image of the world's first electrically powered fountain, which was also on show at the Fair. This whiskey is a mix of 70% rye, 20% corn, and 10% malted barley.

The single malt features an illustration of the South Side Rapid Transit Railroad, which connected the downtown area with the Fair and other parts of the South Side.

Paul tells me their newly released American Whiskey is "about half rye whiskey, half bourbon whiskey, then about 5% of this weird single malt we did, that I wouldn't even really call a single malt." Incidentally, the category of "American whiskey" is one of the loosest out there, and it even permits the blending of un-aged high-strength spirit into aged whiskey. It's also one of FEW's best products to date.

BOURBON (46.5% ABV)
Cherry juice and peach lemonade on the nose, which is joined by vanilla custard spiked with mace on repeat smells. It's dry and nutty on the palate, with

TOP LEFT I wasn't lying—I told you it was difficult to spot the FEW sign!

ABOVE Sacks of pre-ground cereals stacked up, ready for mashing. The expansion plan will do away with these bags and introduce grain silos and mills.

TOP RIGHT The stainless steel beer-stripping column still at FEW—an unusual feature for a small distillery

RIGHT The pot still here is used as both a doubler for whiskey making, and as a gin still for, well, gin making.

ABOVE The Statue of the Republic watches over the Grand Basin at the 1893 World's Fair in Chicago.
RIGHT FEW's bottles and labels are among the prettiest around. The bourbon features the statue shown above.

pecan and Brazil nut lingering until spice trickles in. The finish has just a touch of tannin, delivered in such a way that you really want another sip.

RYE (46.5% ABV)

A slight touch of caraway seed brings about a menthol note, and that's supported by a hint of bay leaf. There's a warming cinnamon note here too, plus notes of bittersweet chocolate and coffee liqueur. The aromatics continue on to the palate, bolstered by sweetness and spice that together make for a chewy mouthfeel. The linger is long and satisfying. A cracking rye!

SINGLE MALT (46.5% ABV)

The aroma reminds me of a genever with its nutty, malty smell supported by herbal freshness. More of that herbaceousness presents itself on the palate, with a green tea-like umami kind of flavor, which speaks of Japanese teppanyaki more than it does Chicago pizza! The finish has a soft lick of smoked almonds. This is an unusual malt—but I love it.

AMERICAN WHISKEY (46.5% ABV)

This whiskey is wonderfully finessed on the nose: there's loads of fruit, like apricot and fig jam and possibly a touch of raspberry. A little Scotch character comes through in the taste (more so than the malt!), and it's not especially "American" tasting, really. What it is, however, is rich, sweet and slightly spicy. Oh, and delicious.

ROAD TRIP PLAYLIST

"Roll On" – Josh Ritter

"Here I Go Again" – Whitesnake

"Bootleg" – Creedence Clearwater Revival

SCOFFLAW COCKTAIL

50 ml/1⅔ oz FEW American Whiskey
25 ml/generous ¾ oz dry vermouth
15 ml/½ oz lemon juice
10 ml/2 teaspoons grenadine
½ an egg white

Add all of the ingredients to a cocktail shaker and shake with cubed ice. Double-strain into a chilled coupe glass. Garnish with a strip of lemon.

A 2019 Nielsen study showed that the most popular cocktail in every major US city has one thing common in that they begin with the letter "M": Margarita, Mojito, or Martini. Chicago seems to be the only exception to this rule and it's the Old Fashioned that tops the list here. That's a pretty cool accolade, which arguably makes the Windy City one of the best places to drink whiskey.

But we already enjoyed an Old Fashioned back when we visited Dad's Hat in Philadelphia. In Chicago it feels more appropriate to enjoy a Prohibition-era drink and there are few better than the Scofflaw Cocktail.

This drink, like most of the cocktails invented during the 1920s, was actually conceived in Europe, at Harry's Bar in Paris. The word "scofflaw", however, is American in its origin and was coined in 1924 when the *Boston Herald* ran a competition asking their readers to come up with a new term for describing "a lawless drinker or illegally made or illegally obtained liquor." "Scofflaw" was chosen as the winner from a pot of 25,000 entries.

The drink itself is a good one, and follows the basic formula of a popular gin drink called a Clover Club. Grenadine is used in place of sugar as a sweetener, and lemon and vermouth combine to give a strangely homogeneous, citric wine-y note. Most recipes call for a dash of orange bitters, but I think it's better without. Most recipes don't call for egg white, but I think it gives a much better texture to the cocktail.

DRY FLY

SPOKANE OF WHISKEY

*"When you work hard all day with your head and know you must
work again the next day what else can change your ideas and
make them run on a different plane like whisky?"*

ERNEST HEMINGWAY (1899–1961), AUTHOR AND JOURNALIST

As we leave Chicago, heading west, we embark upon the single biggest leg of our journey. Interstate 90 is a trans-continental road and the longest highway in the US, connecting Boston to Seattle. It will take us through Wisconsin, Minnesota, South Dakota, Wyoming, Montana, and Idaho, before we reach our destination: Spokane, WA. This section of driving cuts a line through the heart of the corn belt, but as we'll soon see, there's a distinct lack of whiskey distilleries in this part of the country.

We drive past the capital of Wisconsin, Madison, which is home to Yahara Bay Distillers. Founded in 2007, they produce Wisconsin's first aged whiskey since Prohibition (made from corn, barley, wheat, and rye). All spirits in Wisconsin have to pass through both a licensed wholesaler and a licensed retailer before reaching the consumer, which isn't particularly helpful for a young distillery. In 2009, the law changed and tasting rooms were permitted, which opened up new retail opportunities for distillers, and since then a growing number of new whiskey makers have appeared in the state.

To the northwest of Madison is the village of Prairie Du Sac, home of the Wollersheim Winery, with a history dating back 150 years. More recently, they became Wollersheim Winery & Distillery, making brandies alongside a Round Top Rye (65% rye mash bill, aged two years) and a "Curiosity Collection" of corn whiskeys, made from heirloom varieties and matured in white "port" casks.

We cross the Mississippi again, which this far north tracks the Minnesota/Wisconsin state border, and continue west, towards Rochester. Minnesota was more reluctant than most states to go dry during Prohibition, and thanks to its more remote northern regions near the border with Canada, it became a popular smuggling route. As such, the city of Minneapolis became a haven for gangsters such as John Dillinger (1903–34) and George "Baby Face" Nelson (1908–34). In certain rural areas, like Stearns County, about an hour northwest of Minneapolis, nearly every household was connected to the bootleg alcohol trade, many of them making whiskey as well as trading it. Minnesotan farmers adopted innovative strategies to speed up maturation of their spirits, experimenting with hanging barrels from trees over bonfires, or covering them with canvas and manure to create compost-style heat.

Just north of Stearns County, next to Lake Osakis, is the Panther Distillery. With warehousing and bottling spread around various towns in the area, Panther is one of the largest whiskey makers in the state despite being only eight years old. At Panther, they make bourbon whiskey in Vendome stills as well as a unique spirit called Minnesota 14, made from a corn variety with the same name. It was developed by the University of Minnesota in 1888 and was a popular bootlegger's choice during Prohibition. And it's this whiskey we're enjoying as we settle down for the night.

Leaving Rochester, we continue surging west, crossing state lines into South Dakota. West of the Missouri River, the landscape becomes more rugged, featuring rolling hills, plains, ravines, and steep flat-topped hills known as buttes. We enter the South Dakota Badlands, with their dramatic layered rock formations, steep canyons, and towering spires. A little further to the west of us, near Rapid City, is Mount Rushmore.

Neither of the Dakotas has much of a distilling industry, in spite of a very grain-heavy focus in the agricultural sector. One notable exception is Proof Artisan Distillers in Fargo, ND. They make "Crooked Furrow Bourbon" from local corn and malted barley, as well as "Glen Fargo" which, if you hadn't guessed, is a North Dakota take on Scotch single malt.

Dawn breaks on our third straight day of driving, as we cross the state line into Montana. The economy here is traditionally reliant on ranching and growing cereals, but the fastest growing sector in Montana is tourism. That, in my mind, makes Montana the perfect place to start a whiskey distillery.

Montana's first distillery in more than 100 years was Roughstock, which was one of the first small distilleries in the country when it was founded by Bryan Schultz way back in 2005. In 2017 it also became one of the first distilleries of the modern era to close, proving that there's no guarantee of success in whiskey even if you're one of the first to the table.

Glacier Distilling, in Glacier National Park, seem to have had greater success. As you might expect, they use glacier water in the production of their whiskeys. They make "North Fork" and "Bad Rock" rye here, as well as two malt whiskeys called "Wheat Fish" and "Two Med" with the beer sourced from the Great Northern Brewing Company. The packaging is some of the best I've seen in American whiskey, and the spirits are damn tasty too.

As we leave Montana, we cross the Idaho Panhandle before hitting the state of Washington.

Washington was one of those states that couldn't wait for Prohibition to be passed and, on New Year's Day 1915, a statewide ban on the manufacture and sale of alcoholic beverages came into effect, although alcohol could still be legally consumed in a limited fashion in private settings. Of course, that all changed with nationwide Prohibition on January 17, 1920.

When Prohibition ended in 1933, it once again became legal to purchase alcohol from stores, restaurants, and saloons, but new laws dictated that hard liquor could only be sold by state-run liquor stores and consumed in private. It was not until 1948 that Washington voters—partially thanks to an influx of war workers and returning veterans—approved the sale of spirits in restaurants and bars.

With one notable exception (which we will touch upon in due course), there were no distilleries in this state until Dry Fly came along in 2007.

Dry Fly is based in Spokane, near the Idaho border. Spokane grew at a furious rate in the late 19th century, becoming an important rail shipping and transport hub for mines and farms. After mining activity declined, the region began to rely more heavily on farming, particularly wheat. And with guidance from the Washington State Liquor Control Board, they began producing vodka and gin to be sold through state-run liquor stores.

Not long after the rebirth of distilling in Spokane, Dry Fly and other distilleries began lobbying for reform of the state's distilling licenses, which were, at that point, costly to acquire. Two Spokane-based legislators, Senator Chris Marr and Representative Alex Wood, helped introduce House Bill 2959 in 2016, which (when enacted) brought into effect a new license, built around agriculture and defining distilling as an "agricultural practice".

The new rules required that 51 percent of the raw materials come from within the state of Washington. The annual fee for a "craft" distillery license (the "craft" designation meaning that production is less than 20,000 gallons a year) was also reduced from $2,000 to $100. There were additional restrictions on how much the distillery could sell (no more than two liters of spirit per person per day) and how much they could sample (half-ounce samples only up to total of two ounces per person per day).

By January 2011, there were 32 licensed craft distilleries in Washington and 37 more in the application process. As of early 2019 there are around 120, probably half of them making whiskey in some shape or form.

"We were one of the first 20 small distilleries in the country," says Dry Fly founder Dom Poffenroth, "and we've always been very adamant about farm-to-bottle sourcing and knowing our agricultural side."

Establishing that link between the numerous farms that surround Spokane and the distilling industry did more than just fix a licensing issue; it's re-established the link between the two industries. Both industries succumbed to economic pressures over the past 50 years, which meant churning out products that can be sold globally. Now, products that these farms grow get to stay in the state, to be manufactured in to something that celebrates the uniqueness of the cereal or the land, which can then fly a flag for Washington state internationally.

"We only buy from a couple of farmers," says Dom, "but many more than that would tell you we buy from them. They take it as a source of pride."

Farming in Washington is of the "drylands" persuasion, meaning that the crops are non-irrigated and as such tend to be drought-resistant varieties. This also means that most crops are planted in the winter, to benefit from snow melt and spring showers. Spokane is on the northern tip of the Palouse Region (from the French word for "lawn"), which is characterized by gentle, undulating hills. The area was settled during the wheat-growing boom of the 1880s and wheat it is that remains the primary crop. The area is also known for barley and a kind of wheat/rye hybrid cereal called tricatale (more on that shortly).

"We wanted to make a rye whiskey," says Dom "but rye is considered a noxious weed in most counties of Washington, so we had to get a bit creative."

When wheat dominates the landscape, rye is seen as a pest. This is due to its tenacity of the plant, which drops seeds when it's harvested, that will overwinter quite happily, and then sprout up the following year.

This can go on for up to a decade after the rye was first sewn. Once you plant rye, it's very difficult to get rid of it entirely. This is why some farmers in Washington employ the help of young workers (including, many years ago, a young Dom Poffenroth) to weed out any random shoots of rye.

Dom wanted to create an image for his spirits that was representative of the Northwest. Trout fishing is an extremely popular activity in east Washington and, being a fly fisherman himself, it seemed like a good fit. I'm no expert on fishing, but I know it requires a fair bit of patience, which seems like a good opportunity to drink whiskey, right?

That said, I am always nervous about a whiskey brand that aligns itself too closely with politics, art, food, sport, modes of transport, or a historical person. In my opinion, a good brand should communicate what a product is and—at a stretch—how it might make you feel, not what it's trying to be or who it wants to appeal to.

So yes, I was a little nervous about Dry Fly Distilling, whose name, logo and website do more than hint at a connection with fishing.

I needn't have been.

"We're not edgy," says Dom, "we're trying to make kind, soft, gentle whiskeys."

The distillery runs eight different mash bills. The first whiskey they launched was (perhaps unsurprisingly, given the location) a wheat whiskey made from soft white winter wheat. The first whiskey they made, however, was a single malt. Dom was adamant from the start that this product needed to be at least eight years old, so the barrel was put to one side. However, it turned out that it needed even longer than eight years, and they finally got around to releasing it in February 2019. To my knowledge, this 10-year-old single malt is the oldest of its kind to be released by a small distiller this century. In fact, it's probably one of the oldest single malts ever to be released by an American distillery. Sadly, it was limited to just one barrel, constituting 160 bottles for $149.95 a piece.

"I wish I had a hundred barrels of that," Dom tells me. "If I did, I'd be fishing more!"

Back to the mash bills, and besides the wheat mash and two malt mashes, they also mash two bourbon recipes: 60% corn, 20% malted wheat, 20% malted barley; and 60% corn, 40% triticale.

Triticale is a hybrid of wheat (Triticum) and rye (Secale). Triticale has a strong presence in Washington, so using it is another way to reaffirm those values of people and place. This cereal has only become a commercially viable crop recently, but given that it features the yield potential of wheat and the disease-resistance and environmental tolerance of rye, it seems like a cereal with a future ahead of it. Dry Fly were the first distillery to ever use triticale for making whiskey, for which Dom is "very proud". There are a handful of distilleries around the country that have featured it since, but Dry Fly's 100% Triticale whiskey is by far the best known example.

Like many of the first new-wave distilleries, Don sought help from Michigan State University. That, in turn, connected him with Christian Carl still makers, who nursed him through the early years of production. Dom now has two stills from Carl, which are used in tandem to produce all of their whiskeys. That's set to change however, as Dry Fly will soon be moving to a new location and switching to a column/pot setup. This system will still work in two stages though, meaning that it will still be necessary to make spirits "cuts" from the second still.

"Single-step distillation is precarious," says Dom "because you have no ability to go in and make sensory evaluation. The cuts off the still are the defining factor. You can make a wider cut, but the product has to sit in a barrel for longer. Or you can narrow it down and then you're not asking the barrel to take care of defects."

All of the casks at Dry Fly are standard 53-gallon bourbon casks and this is the only size cask Dom has ever used for maturing new-make whiskey. At the beginning, this decision was more reflective of cost than anything else, balancing the time saved by maturing spirits in small casks with the additional up-front expense of tiny casks. Now that the distillery is 12-years-old and has an inventory of hundreds of barrels, Dom doesn't need to go through the painful

process of transitioning to bigger barrels and deal with the shift in spirit character that this process inevitably bring about. "As a category, I think small barrel whiskey ought to be its own thing," says Dom. "Whatever the type of whiskey, the spirit coming out of small barrels is so different from that which comes out of the 53s."

Every whiskey passes through one of these new, 53-gallon American oak casks, with the exception of the single malt, which is matured in the distillery's own ex-bourbon barrels.

"You've got a lot of guys aging single malt whiskey in new oak," says Dom "and that is a brutal approach to making that kind of whiskey."

Another exciting series of whiskeys they're working on, which Dom calls "circular projects," is a cask-exchange program. Dom loans his used barrels to local brewers, then when they're done they send them back again. He will then drop a mature whiskey back into the cask for it to be imbued with the flavor of whatever fermented product it previously held. He's definitely not afraid of an experiment...

STRAIGHT WHEAT (45% ABV)

The aroma here is lively and almost fizzy, with orange soda, cough candy, molasses, and licorice. I'd definitely place this whiskey in the "aromatic" camp of whiskeys. The taste is—as advertised—soft and gentle, but by no means bland. There's structure here and the finish is sweet and orange-filled.

BOURBON 101 (50.5% ABV)

The aroma has a slight medicinal, iodine note. This gives way to soft vanilla ice cream and corn aromas. The taste is a good balance between the lightness of the corn and the peppered, grippy effects of triticale. The finish is oily and bright, but without greasiness.

PORT-FINISH STRAIGHT WHEAT (45% ABV)

The aroma here has some floral notes of rose and strawberry, which are supported by softer, more citric smells and redcurrant. The taste is clean and quite dry, with an almost mineral quality that leads to just a touch of red grape juice in the finish.

ABOVE Visitors to Dry Fly's tasting room, making the most of their state-mandated 2-oz rations.

STRAIGHT TRITICALE (45% ABV)

The nose is green and fragrant with a touch of cracked hazelnut, tangerine, and ginger. The palate is a little prickly, but well integrated, with more of that tangerine note, along with vanilla and ginger beer. Candied citrus peels and black pepper take the finish.

SINGLE MALT 7 YEAR OLD

The aroma here is like a walk in the woods, with cedar and Douglas fir taking center stage. Next comes soft apricot jelly and orange marmalade, but in spite of the fruit there's an endearing savory quality to the smell. The taste is not overly complex but very satisfying. The finish is long and demands another sip.

SINGLE MALT 10 YEAR OLD

The nose on this malt is alive with huge orange esters, like a freshly opened can of Fanta. There are confected notes here too: gummy bears and orange sherbet. Fruit (mostly citric) continues on the palate, which is supported by cask character that brings about incense and baking spices.

ROAD TRIP PLAYLIST

"Little Red Corvette" – Prince

"Running on Empty" – Jackson Browne

"Walk on the Wild Side" – Lou Reed

DEATH BY WHISKEY IN THE AFTERNOON

20 ml/⅔ oz Dry Fly Straight Wheat Whiskey
5 ml/I teaspoon absinthe verte
5 ml/I teaspoon gomme
Champagne, to top up

Take a chilled Champagne flute and add the ingredients in the above order. Make sure the Champagne is extremely cold as the spirits probably won't be. No garnish needed, and if you're up to the challenge, Papa advised to "drink three to five of these slowly."

As someone who likes to read and drink (but not fish), the most famous fisherman I can think of is Ernest Hemingway. We needn't repeat the drinking escapades of this man, but suffice to say, he liked to drink and he liked to drink well.

Hemingway is credited for inventing a handful of drinks and popularizing many more. But one of the little-known Hemingway creations shares a title with one of his books: *Death in the Afternoon*, a book about the history of bullfighting.

The original printed recipe for a Death In the Afternoon comes from 1935, and it tells us that,

"this was arrived at by the author and three officers of H.M.S. Danae after having spent seven hours overboard trying to get Capt. Bra Saunders' fishing boat off a bank where she had gone with us in a N.W. gale."

The drink itself is a simple one: absinthe plus "iced" champagne. That's it. For modern palates it can prove a little challenging, and I've seen the drink get a better reception when another spirit is added into the mix and the absinthe dialed down. Cognac works well, but so too does wheat whiskey.

COPPERWORKS

PLAY IT BY BEER

"To alcohol! The cause of—and solution to—all of life's problems."

HOMER SIMPSON

We awake the next day in a new city. The memory of the previous evening drive from Spokane to Seattle is muted by the dimness of the night and the battle to remain conscious. Apparently we made it though.

In these closing stages of the tour, we're now afforded a couple of days of rest from driving as we explore what Seattle has to offer for the whiskey lover. Our base is near Discovery Park, on the shores of Puget Sound, which means we pass the Ballard Bridge on the way in to the city center.

Located underneath the Ballard Bridge is (as far as I knew at the time) Seattle's first distillery since Prohibition, Sound Spirits. They make gin and liqueurs, alongside a single malt whiskey called Madame Damnable, which is a fantastic name for a whiskey, not least of all because it's the nickname of the owner of Seattle's first brothel. Having married the captain of a whaling ship, it was said that Mary Ann Conklin could curse in six different languages (hence the "damnable" part). Madame Damnable is distilled twice in pot stills and aged in 30-gallon new oak barrels for around three years.

I found out later out that Sound Spirits wasn't actually the first distillery in Seattle since Prohibition. That accolade actually goes to Northwest Distilleries Inc. in Seattle, which was founded in January 1934 shortly after Prohibition ended. The fact that this distillery ever existed was not well known, since the Washington State Liquor Control Board (WSLCB)

either lost or destroyed many of its early records, which led many to assume the distilleries that arose in the 2000s were the first in 70 years.

Situated on 1733 Westlake Avenue, Northwest Distilleries had a rated capacity of 2,000 gallons of spirit a day—a substantial operation to misplace! The distillery was located in a three-story building that boasted $150,000 worth of equipment and employed up to 50 people. *The Seattle Times* claimed that the company's still was the "most modern apparatus obtainable."

The distillery made gin alongside "Mello Morn" Straight Bourbon, which was available for 65 cents a "fifth" (one fifth of a gallon). They later added Straight Blended Whiskey called "Briar Springs" to their roster. The company seems to have shut down by 1940, as no further records exist.

The distillery we're heading to was founded some 80 years after Northwest, in 2013. Copperworks is located in Downtown Seattle, only a few minutes walk from the world-famous Pike Place Market. The distillery is nestled under the Alaskan Way overpass, right by the piers of Seattle's waterfront area. Copperworks was founded by old pals Jason Parker and Micah Nutt, and it's Jason that greets us when we enter the tasting room, alongside Copperworks' Vice President, Jeff Kanof.

Jason has a long background in brewing. He was the first brewer at the Pike Brewing Company (then Pike Place Brewing) in Seattle when it opened in 1989.

Back then, there were only about 250 breweries in the US. There are now thought to be more than 7,000. During that time, he acquired qualifications in chemistry and microbiology and worked at various other breweries including Fish, Redhook, and Pyramid, the latter being the second biggest craft brewery in America at that time.

The craft-brewing scene has exploded in Washington in recent years. I say recent, but craft brewing is at least 35 years old in Washington, culminating in 400 small breweries in the state. Only California has it beat on numbers, but California also has five times the population of Washington.

"We came to Copperworks with a sensibility for making beer," says Jason. "And when we started practice distillation runs we used beer—real, drinkable beer."

With an address book full of brewers and the knowledge of what kind of beer he needed, it struck Jason that he didn't need to build grain stores and mash cookers at Copperworks distillery—he could just commission his brewer friends to make the beer he needed. It's important to recognize the distinction between brewing and fermenting here. By brewing, I mean mashing.

Copperworks brews beer at Pike Brewing, Elysian Brewing, and Freemont Brewing, then ferment it at their distillery in Downtown Seattle. This is made possible by the brewer-specific approach to beer making. That means the wort is boiled after brewing, which denatures the enzymes so that no more conversion takes place during fermentation. Jason tells me that this results in a loss of potential alcohol but a gain in mouthfeel. It also sanitizes the wort, killing the bacteria, meaning the wort is safe to transport and that natural fermentation will take place. Immediately after brewing, the sweet wort is loaded in to 550-gallon plastic "tote" containers and trucked to the Copperworks distillery for fermentation.

I ask Jason if all three breweries are cooking the same beer recipe. "Yes," he responds, "...and they're

making three different beers."

Beer one is a 100% pale malt, which comprises 50% Washington State malt and 50% malts sourced from various parts of the Northwest, which have been blended for consistency.

Beer two is a mix of 25% caramel/crystal malts and 75% pale malt. Jason describes this as "like a Scotch ale," remarking on the mouthfeel and body of the resulting ferment.

Beer three is the most exciting, but it can hardly be classed as a single beer since the parameters of the recipe are constantly moving. This is by design, as the concept is single-farm, single-variety, single-vintage barley. "Does terroir matter?" is the question Jason is asking, and it's a question that will be answered through an ongoing series of single malt releases that switch out variety, location, and vintage.

Over the past four years, Copperworks has been working with seven different Washington farms to produce five different malts for brewing. Jason tells me he wanted, "The same malt on two different farms, both dry and irrigated, coastal and inland. Or the same farm but two different varieties from the same year. Or the same farm and the same variety, but different years."

We've already learned that the flavor a cereal imparts on a spirit goes much deeper than merely the cereal type (corn, wheat, barley, and rye), and that the specific variety within that cereal can dramatically shift the character of a spirit. Jason says that the location of the farm and the year of the harvest also influence flavor in the spirit coming off the still. The final question is whether those nuances become muted by maturation or whether their presence in the spirit forces a different trajectory for the maturation profile that results in a distinctly different liquid.

"We may not get a fit on terroir on any of the malts growing in Washington State," says Jason. "There are over 10,000 different malts in the ground, but only 18 are in production quantities."

Copperworks is paying, on average, three times the price for these malts compared to what they would be if they weren't dictating the parameters. And they're

OPPOSITE Pike Place Market sees 200,000 visitors a week, so it's not a bad place to locate a distillery.

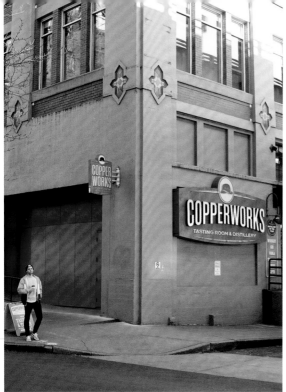

also taking a risk with the quality. Some of these cereals have never been grown on a commercial level and have certainly never been brewed before. And even at the brewing stage, the results have been mixed, with some malts producing low yields and others overachieving. On one occasion, an entire batch of barley had to be dumped when 22% of the grain died after harvesting. If you tried to malt a batch of cereal like this it wouldn't work because 20% would rot once it went into the steeping tanks.

Even once the sweet wort arrives at the distillery, Copperworks takes a brewer's approach to making beer by pitching (adding) a live brewer's yeast to start fermentation (the yeast gets transported from the brewery along with the wort). Jason says this puts less stress on the ferment, because the yeast is already virile, unlike dried yeast, which is pitched in a dormant state.

Fermentation of the beer is also undertaken at a lower temperature (70°F) than is typical for whiskey.

A lower temperature means a longer ferment of around seven days. They're then left with a beer of around 9% ABV, with fewer sulphites and a lower quantity of higher alcohols than a typical whiskey ferment (you may remember that Leopold Bros. take a similar approach to fermentation—see page 270). The beer is then left to condition for a couple of weeks, which allows the yeast to flocculate (form small clumps, which can be filtered out), leaving a bright, clear beer. This means less yeast is entering the stills, which limits the production of meaty flavors that are associated with yeast autolysis (the destruction of cells by their own enzymes) when yeast burns on the inside of the still.

By now we've been chatting for nearly 40 minutes, and it strikes me that we've barely touched on distillation, and yet we're in a distillery that—on the face of things—seems to covet that stage of production above all others. That's a false assumption though. This is a distillery founded on brewing sensibilities that happens to outsource the brewing stage of production to proper breweries. Jason tells me that these partnerships will remain in place as long as the breweries are happy to work with Copperworks and meet its required volumes.

"We hope to grow beyond their capacity one day," he says. "And we'd like to build a brewery. At that point we would own our own destiny, and we could make a beer—which would be fun."

One truckload of wort fills the 1,800-gallon fermenter. This arrives on a Thursday, which sets into motion a three-week cycle of fermentation, conditioning, and distillation.

The stills here are manufactured by Forsyths in Scotland, and modeled after the stills at the Aberlour Distillery in the Scottish Highlands. Distillation of the first wash (i.e. the product of fermentation) takes 950 gallons of beer at 9% ABV and turns it in to 350 gallons of low wines at 24% ABV. This is combined with the heads and tails from the previous spirits distillation, and loaded into the spirits still for a second distillation.

Around four liters of foreshots are collected and discarded before the heads begin to pass over. The heads cut is made when the spirit coming off the condenser drops to 73% ABV and the heart of the run is collected until the strength drops to 60% ABV. This makes for an average batch of around 100 gallons at 67.5% ABV, so enough to fill a couple of barrels a day.

Copperworks cuts their spirit to four different entry proofs for their whiskeys: 110 proof, 112 proof, 115 proof, and 120 proof, each intended to extract a different profile of flavors from the barrel.

Besides a handful of used bourbon barrels and some sherry casks, all of the barrels at Copperworks are either new oak or re-fill Copperworks barrels (i.e. ones that they have previously aged malt whiskey in). The oak is a minimum of 18 months air-dried, but Copperworks is transitioning towards 24 and 36 months as a minimum. These are sourced from three different cooperages: Kelvin, Independent Stave Company, and Canton. Jason is particularly fond of Canton, who have cooperages in Kentucky and Napa. "Those guys can trace back each barrel to the specific part of the forest that the tree came from," he says.

Copperworks ages their product indoors, in a controlled, warm environment.

"Every ten degrees you drop below room temperature, esterification drops in half," says Jason. "If whiskey is cold when it's maturing, it isn't maturing at all."

The warehouse temperature is set to 70°F and the humidity in Washington is around 60% in the summertime. When the warehouse gets heated in the winter however, the humidity drops to around 30%. As we stand in the warehouse space in March, it's reading 24%. That's very dry, which is why the evaporative losses here are made up more from water than alcohol. In other words, the alcoholic strength of the spirit goes up.

"It doesn't smell much like a warehouse in here,"

ABOVE LEFT Yours truly loitering around outside the Copperworks Distillery.
FAR LEFT They call it Copperworks for a reason! The stills here are beauties and appear to be polished daily.
BELOW RIGHT This is the kind of thing that makes me smile: tasting glasses and barrels.

says Jason. "And that's because we don't want loads of whiskey vapor in the air; we want air in the air because that's what will cause oxidation in the casks and help make the flavors we're after."

As we continue to discuss the various variables of maturation, we gradually slip into an extended tasting session with Jason and Jeff, as the two of them spend the next hour clambering around casks, dipping into barrels and sharing whiskeys with us that even they haven't yet had the occasion to try.

Copperworks releases their American Single Malt in numbered batches two or three times a year. The whiskey is aged for a minimum of three years and typically comprises a blend of four to nine barrels, which are selected because they evoke a particular style. That might be red or tropical fruits, or it may be a spice characteristic. It may be that a release contains one of the mash recipes or it may contain all three. It may have some sherry-cask influence in it, or it may not. The strength of each release is prone to wandering, too.

The current release at the time of writing is #21, which is the first to use all three malt recipes and a blend of nine different barrels: two barrels of Pale Malt, three barrels of the caramel and crystal malt blend, and four barrels of Alba Malt. A visit to Copperworks website awards the curious with extremely detailed production specifications, right down to the fermentation gravity and malt ratios down to the individual pound. I'm not sure there's another whiskey distillery on the planet that divulges so much information about their process.

While it's true that this distillery is outsourcing some sections of production, and that they're not committed to the farm-to-glass approach in quite the same way as somewhere like Hillrock (see page 77) where the cereals are grown and malted on-site, to say that they are in any way negligent of any stage of their process would be extremely misleading. No matter how insignificant the variable may appear, it's probably been thought about and tested and adjusted to meet reach a desirable outcome.

Jason Parker's whole approach is to scrutinize, then adapt—to take the things he knows work, and to

investigate the things he doesn't know. It's a "first principles" approach to whiskey making—acknowledging convention but then breaking the problem down into its most basic form. Then it becomes a case of picking the pathway that achieves the best results, but always with a focus on flavor rather than yield.

Perhaps Copperworks is not just aiming for great tasting malt whiskey, but the best tasting malt whiskey. Period.

COPPERWORKS AMERICAN SINGLE MALT RELEASE 20 (50% ABV)

Orchard fruits and autumnal spice lead the aroma on this one, with baked apple and cinnamon. A little cut wood aroma also creeps in, with coconut sugar and burned crème brûlée. The taste is dark and rich, with tobacco and ginger, followed by orange peel and butterscotch. The finish is dry, with a satisfying spice.

COPPERWORKS AMERICAN SINGLE MALT RELEASE 21 (50% ABV)

Perfumed and tropical on the nose, with banana and mango supported by jerk spices. The taste is spiced and dry, but also retains a Juicy-Fruit-quality presented with incredible clarity. The finish leaves a residue of nutty, malty flavors that eventually dry up into honey and nutmeg.

ROAD TRIP PLAYLIST

"Further On Up The Road" – Johnny Cash

"Rain King" – Counting Crows

"Copperhead Road" – Steve Earle

SEATTLE MULE

50 ml/1⅔ oz Copperworks American Single Malt
20 ml/⅔ oz lime juice
10 ml/2 teaspoons gomme
100 ml/3⅓ oz Rachel's Ginger Beer

Add the first three ingredients to a highball glass filled with ice and stir. Then top up with ginger beer and give another gentle stir to combine them. Garnish with a sprig of mint.

When vodka's main assault on bourbon began in the late 1940s, it was the Moscow Mule that lead the cavalry charge.

Early sales of Smirnoff vodka in the US weren't great. But in 1946, John Martin, of the Heublein Spirits Company, found himself in the Cock 'n Bull pub on Sunset Boulevard, chatting to proprietor Jack Morgan, who had made a similarly poor investment in ginger beer. John and Jack mixed the vodka with the ginger beer and capped it off with a squeeze of lime, then sourced copper mugs to serve it in (allegedly from another failed businessperson) and the Moscow Mule was born.

Shortly afterwards, the pair acquired one of the first ever Polaroid cameras and went from bar to bar photographing bartenders posing with bottles of Smirnoff vodka and copper mugs of Moscow Mule.

They would show Polaroid photographs to bar owners who didn't sell the product as a means of sealing the deal. Customers went nuts for the stuff and the vodka revolution began.

The thing is, as with most vodka cocktails, the Moscow Mule works just as well—if not better—when you switch out the vodka for a spirit with more flavor. Dropping whiskey into a mule brings about a depth of character that vodka can't compete with, layering sweet, caramel barrel characteristics with the spicy ginger notes. Once upon a time, ginger beer was made and stored in wooden barrels, and mixing whiskey into a mule goes some way towards replicating that flavor.

My recipe uses Rachel's Ginger Beer, a Seattle brand that I found in Pike Place Market. Obviously other brands will work too.

WESTLAND

PURSUING PACIFIC NORTHWEST PERFECTION

*"Never delay kissing a woman or
opening a bottle of whiskey."*

ERNEST HEMINGWAY (1899–1961), AUTHOR AND JOURNALIST

The distillery we're visiting today should prove to be a gem. Westland is one of the most respected distilleries in the country, famed for producing single malt whiskeys in the Scottish style but with a special emphasis on celebrating the Pacific Northwest. Their approach is reminiscent of a New World wine-maker making Old World-style wines. Westland's founders, Matt Hofmann and Emerson Lamb, saw Washington as one of the best places in the world to make single malt whiskey. The Skagit Valley (in the northwest of the state) and Palouse Region (in the southeast) offer some of the best cereal-growing condition in the world. Seattle's Cedar River Watershed, which is one of the last unfiltered water sources in a metropolitan area, provides a great water source for the distillery. Westland considers it a "national treasure." Then there's the climate, which is very mild and not at all different to that of the UK.

Like Copperworks (see page 341), Westland was also influenced by the craft beer movement in Washington, and recognized the natural evolution from brewing towards distilling. Lamb and Hofmann co-founded Westland in the South Park region of Seattle in 2011. They didn't stay there long, though, transferring to a refurbished space in the Industrial District a couple of years later.

Distillery visitors will no doubt be awestruck by the bright and airy timber-clad bar space and retail area, possibly forgetting that they're in a distillery at

all. For a company that started up only eight years ago, Westland certainly gives the impression that they're here to stay. Now, while the bar is a nice place to enjoy a dram, it conceals the real reason for our visit: the hard-working, well-regarded whiskey-making operation out back.

The first point of discussion on the tour is the raw materials used to make Westland's whiskeys. Although Westland makes only single malt whiskey, they use more than one type of malt. They call it a five-malt grain bill, which constitutes a blend of specialty malts: Washington Select Pale Malt, Munich Malt, Extra Special Malt, and Pale Chocolate Malt, as well as Brown Malt.

Specialty malts are malts that have undergone special heating processes in which the starches are converted to sugars by heat and moisture right inside the hull. As a result, these malts contain more complex sugars, some of which do not ferment, leaving a pleasant, caramel-like sweetness. They range from pale gold to dark or burnt browns.

We munch on each of the individual malt grains to identify their differences. Each one has a different flavor profile, ranging from nutty hay through to toasted bread, on to chocolate and coffee (the different malts also impart a range of colors too). An important consideration is that a darker, roasted malt, such as a chocolate malt, will yield up to 30% less alcohol compared to a standard pale malt.

It's worth mentioning at this point that, in addition to the treatment of the malt after germination, barley itself comes in two distinct formats: two-row and six-row. Scotch distillers prefer two-row because it's typically lower in protein and produces a higher yield of fermentable sugars. In the US, six-row barley is traditionally preferred, since the barley typically contains more enzymes, which is really needed for corn and rye mash bills. Of course, if you're making a single malt in the US, you're free to use either type. Westland use two-row.

Westland also uses peated malt for some of their expressions. Most of the peated malt they use is imported from Scotland. However that didn't sit well with Matt Hofmann, who, in his relentless pursuit of terroir began searching for privately owned peat bogs in the Pacific Northwest. Hofmann's search for peat brought him to Doug Wright, a retired sheriff's detective who operates a bog in Shelton, on the western point of Puget Sound. Wright mostly sells it to agencies for soaking up oil or chemical spills. The bog goes down 40 ft at least, and is home to thousand-year-old beaver dams and volcanic ash, presumably from the eruption of Mount Mazama in Oregon—now Crater Lake—more than 7,000 years ago.

Hofmann managed to convince Skagit Valley Malting to use dried pellets of peat to smoke a malt for him; that malted barley was duly mashed and distilled in 2017, and it is currently (patiently) sitting out its time in casks. The first batch consisted of 70 barrels.

Although location and climate can clearly impact fermentation, distillation, and maturation, they do not necessarily describe a place in the flavor they make. And while cereal varieties clearly have an impact on the flavor of a spirit, I'm not convinced that the location in which they're grown makes all that much difference. But peat is another thing entirely. Since it comprises all the local flora, compressed into flammable form, the constituent plant matter has a bearing on what kind of smoke gets produced. I've long maintained that one of the only truly reliable expressions of terroir in whiskey is peat, so these experiments that Westland is running are really exciting for the American single malt category.

The mash cooker here is 5,000 liters and runs two mashes a day. Mashing is done in the same way as Scottish malt whiskey, meaning the cereal is filtered out and only the hot sweet liquid (known as "wort") is collected. This is done using a lauter tun, which is basically a mash cooker with a slotted bottom to assist in the filtration process. The mash itself functions as the main component of the filter though, with the cereal husks working like a sand filter to capture mash debris and proteins. Westland will mash and filter three times, each time increasing the temperature of the water to extract the maximum amount of sugar from the grain. This repetition of filtering and watering is called "sparging." The third and final water is held back and used as the preliminary water for the next mash.

The five fermentation tanks here are 10,000 liters and made from stainless steel. Westland uses a Belgian Saison brewer's yeast, which has a ton of flavor but ferments slower and yields a little bit less. It's for that reason that fermentation times can go on for up to six days here. Unusually for a malt whiskey distillery, Westland also adds enzymes to their mashes.

"Enzymes are a concession we had to make when we chose to use the darker roasted malts," says Tyler Pederson, the production manager at Westland. "We could brew without them, but with them we know we're getting the maximum possible starch conversion," he tells me.

Their saison yeast is happiest when fermenting at low temperatures between 15–20°C (the Scottish influence at Westland extends even to a use metric volumes and temperature measured in Celsius). However, Westland ferments at around 26°C, which they believe helps to make a more ester-rich beer. The target here is bright fruity ester notes along with some phenolics. Tyler tells us that aromas of clove and banana come through in the third day of the fermentation. By the end of the fermentation, Westland has itself a beer of 8% ABV.

Westland products are distilled twice, true to the Scottish style. The stills are made by Vendome, with the wash still weighing in at 2,000 liters and the spirit still 1,500 liters.

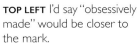

TOP LEFT I'd say "obsessively made" would be closer to the mark.

ABOVE It's nice to see a little Scottish terminology permeating distilleries thousands of miles away.

TOP RIGHT Another nod to Scotland—a "spirit safe" was historically used to prevent tax avoidance.

MIDDLE RIGHT The types and treatments of malted barley used at Westland.

RIGHT Distillery pets are really underrated. They help control pests and serve as a morale booster for the workers.

"Our process is very similar to how they operate in Scotland," says Tyler. "But we do have some things that are unique."

One of these unique things is that Westland make a cut in both their spirit distillation and their wash distillation. Tyler collects from the first distillation in two batches, switching when the low wines drop below 15% ABV. The first batch will be on average around 35% ABV. Tyler explains to me that if he dilutes this with water to below 27.5% ABV, a phase separation takes place and many of the fatty acids that were previously suspended in the solution float to the top of the vat. Tyler then draws off the liquid from the bottom of the tank, leaving the fatty acid oil slick behind. Now that this fraction of the low wine has been cleaned up, it's re-distilled as a spirits run. The purpose of forcing this phase separation is to remove some of the heavier, oily components from the spirit, which lighten the texture of the whiskey and helps promote clean, fruity aromas.

After removing the foreshots from the spirit run, Tyler begins collecting the hearts of his run at 75% ABV and stops collecting when the strength drops to 65% ABV. The heads and tails, along with the second cut from the wash distillation are then all mixed together and re-distilled in a feints run that takes place once a week.

On a typical day, Westland will collect around 900 liters of 70% ABV spirit. This is then diluted with water ready for filling into casks. Barrels are filled at 55% ABV if it's new American oak and 62.5% ABV for wine casks and other types of used barrels.

We touched on Washington's climate already, which is of course critical to how maturation plays out. Westland's warehousing is located on Washington's North Bay in a small town called Hoquiam. The 8,000-person town, which happens to be Westland founder Emerson Lamb's hometown, has a steady, predictable, and damp climate, similar to that of Scotland: an ideal environment for the maturation process. Westland has about one barrel there for every person living in the town.

There are three main bottlings coming out of Westland: American Oak, which is made from the five-grain mash bill and matured for a minimum of three years in a combination of new oak casks and refill bourbon casks; Sherry Oak, which is also made from the same mash bill but aged in a combination of new American oak and ex-Oloroso sherry and ex-Pedro Ximénez casks; and finally Peated, which is made from 100% peated malt, aged in new oak casks and refill bourbon casks, then blended after maturation with what is effectively the whiskey that goes into the American Oak bottling. Although Westland bottles don't mention how old the liquid inside is, all of their releases are aged for a minimum of three years.

In their pursuit of Pacific Northwest perfection, Westland are on a quest to use barrels coopered from indigenous oak. *Quercus Garryana*, more commonly known as the Oregon white oak or Oregon oak in the US and as the Garry oak in Canada, is native to the Pacific coast and can be found from southern California to southwestern British Columbia.

"It's more like a French oak barrel," says master blender, Shane Armstrong. "Low sweetness with a kind of blackberry note."

Westland bottles an annual Garryana release, which tends to contain around 20—40% Garryana-matured whiskey, blended with other whiskeys of Shane's choosing.

If you're worried about Westland chopping down loads of oak trees just so we can drink nice whiskey, fear not. All of the oak they're using is sourced from wind-fallen trees or trees that needed cutting down for safety or conservation reasons. And just to be sure they're doing their bit, they have partnered with a company that have planted more than 2,000 trees in the Tahoma region (the hope is that 10% of them grow to full maturity).

Westland is currently holding 173 Garryana casks, which are maturing a range of malt whiskeys including peated and unpeated mash recipes. Five of these casks are very special indeed because they are holding peated whiskey smoked with Skagit Valley peat—resulting in flavor derived entirely from Pacific Northwest ingredients. Very few whiskey distilleries in the world can claim such a feat.

The distillery holds an annual "Peat Week" festival (currently in its fifth year), which is inspired by the tradition of some Scottish distilleries of making peated malt whiskey for a single week (or sometimes two) of the year. They also release a special Peat Week bottling to commemorate the event.

Very recently, Westland has begun bottling an annual release called Reverie, which is basically their throw-the-rulebook-out experimental series. The 2018 release was a blend of peated and unpeated whiskeys, which have been through casks that formerly held Moscatel (a rich, sweet wine made from Muscat grapes).

Like Tuthilltown (see page 66) and High West (see page 288), Westland is another distillery startup that has captured the attention of a multinational. The French drinks giant Rémy Cointreau acquired the entire business in early 2017. However, the day-to-day running of the business remains in the hands of Matt Hofmann.

AMERICAN OAK SINGLE MALT (46% ABV)

The nose is lemon and orange custard, waffle ice-cream cone, crème brûlée, chocolate, and jasmine tea. It smells great. On the palate there's a rich fruit flavor, Rainier cherries, Swiss chocolate, almond, bananas, cream, and Turkish coffee.

SHERRY WOOD SINGLE MALT (45% ABV)

The aroma here is all yellow, with Mirabelle plum and peach, and soft golden raisins. This continues with yet another yellow thing: lemon peel. On the palate, it's soft and slightly sweet, with a little tannin on the finish. Delicate, fruity, and balanced.

SINGLE MALT PEATED (46% ABV)

Besides the more obvious smoked note of this whiskey, there's a general sense of toastiness too with a little iodine. The taste is really balanced, with a little spice, a touch of banana, and incense. Really tasty.

PEAT WEEK 2018 (50% ABV)

On the nose, the peat is more subtle, minerally, and fresh. There's big smoke and spice on the palate, with smoke building on the nose after the first sip. The finish is clean and elegant, with a subtle sweetness.

REVERIE (50% ABV)

It's quite light on the nose, but fragrant and juicy on the palate. Its subtlety makes it a very intriguing whiskey. Melon skin, grapefruit, and just a wisp of smoke in the mouth.

BLACK RAVEN (AGED IN COFFEE STOUT AND AMERICAN CHERRY SOUR BEER CASKS) (50% ABV)

Concentrated and full on the palate, with a touch of coffee and hot, red juice. Slightly spiced and a little hot with a long, coffee finish.

ROAD TRIP PLAYLIST

"Steady Rolling" – Martin Harley

"Wind of Change" – Scorpions

"Get It Right Next Time" – Gerry Rafferty

WEST COAST STIMULANT

50 ml/1⅔ oz Westland American Oak Single Malt
25 ml/5 teaspoons espresso coffee
10 ml/2 teaspoons sugar syrup

Shake all of the ingredients with cubed ice and strain into a rocks glass filled with ice.

Seattle's Pike Place Market was established in 1907, making it one of the oldest continually running markets in the US. The market is renowned for its fish (which are tossed like American footballs between the fishmongers who work there), but perhaps its biggest claim to fame is that it's the location for the first ever Starbucks Coffee Store, which opened in 1971. Like or loathe Starbucks, it has certainly played a role in the development of the West Coast coffee scene and helped to establish a level of espresso snobbery in the region before most states had graduated beyond the percolator.

Given the stimulating effects of caffeine and its potential to increase productivity, I don't think it's any coincidence that some of the most successful businesses of the last 40 years have emerged from the most caffeinated parts of the nation. Amazon and Microsoft are perhaps the best two examples. Both are headquartered in Seattle and their respective CEOs currently hold positions one and two on the global rich list.

Espresso coffee first found its way into a cocktail in the 1980s, when London's late great Dick Bradsell responded to a guest's request for a "drink that will pick me up, then f**k me up." The Pharmaceutical Stimulant was the result, which later became known as the Vodka Espresso, then the Espresso Martini.

The formula for these drinks is a simple one: booze, coffee, sugar. It's basically like making a coffee liqueur à la minute. And the great thing is you can interchange one spirit for another and mess about with the coffee itself to find the best affinity in the pairing. I've found that when using malt whiskey as the base, your best bet is to go with a light roasted, fruity coffee with notes of berries and chocolate (Central African coffees often fit this description). Certainly avoid anything roasted too dark, as this can give a kind of burnt wood effect to the resulting drink. Equally, it's best to avoid peated whiskeys in coffee cocktails, since smoke is considered an off note in coffee roasting.

HOTALING & CO.

OLD POTRERO, NEW PASTURES

"If, as they say, God spanked the town
For being over-frisky,
Why did He burn His churches down
And spare Hotaling's whiskey?"

CHARLES FIELD (1873–1948), JOURNALIST AND POET

On our way from Washington to California, we drive through Oregon, stopping for the night in Portland to drink whiskey and do all the things that hipsters do there, like go to farmers' markets and drink coffee. It turns out that hipsters also like to drink whiskey, so we're quick to book in a brief tour of the Westward distillery, which was formerly known as House Spirits. It's easy to get Westward confused with Westland, not only for their name and close proximity, but also because both focus on single malts made using brewer's yeast. Oregon has about a third fewer distilleries than Washington but nearly half the population, giving it the highest distillery-to-human ratio in the West.

The state with the most distilleries of all however, is California—with 156 according to the American Craft Spirits Association's 2018 report. So we're going to spend all of our remaining stops in the Golden State.

California was part of the Viceroyalty of New Spain from 1535 until 1821, when Mexico gained independence from Spain and took California with it. After the Mexican-American war ended in 1848, California became a State of the United States as a part of the Compromise of 1850 that divided territories acquired during the war. Distillation in California goes back well before it gained its statehood, but exactly how far is open to debate. What we do know is that there wasn't a lot of whiskey being made here.

Given the $35 billion value of the Californian wine industry today, it shouldn't come as too much of a surprise to learn that the history of distilling here is tied into wine. By 1823, there were 21 Franciscan missions in California. All of them had vineyards and all but four were successfully making wine and brandy. In the 1840s, tycoon Leland Stanford (1824–93) started to distill brandy in California. He quickly became one of the world's largest brandy producers and used the money he made to found a little-known university called Stanford.

In the latter part of the 19th century, the Californian brandy industry grew to a tremendous size. This was helped along in no short measure by the collapse of the French brandy industry in the 1870s, which encouraged eminent wine and Brandy producers to emigrate to California. Naturally, the industry in California fell apart when Prohibition came into effect. But unlike the whiskey industry in Kentucky, which had been afforded medicinal licenses, the Californian brandy industry struggled to regain traction after Prohibition was repealed.

The early 1980s brought about a shift in the tide of distilling, though, heralded by the arrival of two new brandy distilleries: St. George in Alameda and Alambic in Ukiah (around 50 miles north of San Francisco). Both of them were small, independent, and had interests that lay not only in running a commercially viable business, but also in re-establishing some of the spirit-making practices that had been lost to time.

We've traveled thousands of miles and passed through dozens of distilleries to get to where we are now, but finally, in Northern California, we find ourselves in the birthplace of the modern American craft spirits movement and nearing the original craft whiskey distillery.

We drive in to San Francisco on the 101, crossing the Golden Gate Bridge, passing through SoMa and on to Potrero Hill. The hill got its name back in the 1700s, when Spanish missionaries grazed cattle there. They called it Potrero Nuevo, or "New Pasture." The hill also lends its name to the whiskey made at the next distillery on our list: Old Potrero, which is produced by Hotaling & Co. (formerly Anchor Brewers & Distillers). For anyone interested in ranking brands by their age, Old Potrero is the oldest continually produced craft whiskey in the nation.

The distillery is housed within and kind of underneath the Anchor brewery. It's like a grotto, hidden along long series of corridors and down flights of steps. It's early evening when we arrive, so the brewery has been vacated, but the distillery has the feeling of somewhere that feels quiet most of the time. It's deserted, in fact. Save for one solitary figure: Bruce Joseph.

To talk about Bruce we must also talk about the history of the Anchor brewery, because he's been working there his entire adult life.

The history of brewing at Anchor goes back to 1896, when there was huge demand for booze from Californian Gold Rush prospectors. The brewery burned down and relocated a few times, but the modern chapter of its history really begins in 1965,

when Frederick "Fritz" Maytag III bought the dying operation, which reportedly had a bank balance of $128. The brewery then moved to its current location on 1705 Mariposa Street in 1979.

The craft brewing thing was just taking off back then. Anchor was making waves with their traditional "Steam" beer, which is a highly effervescent style of beer made by fermenting lager yeasts at warmer ale yeast fermentation temperatures.

Bruce joined the Anchor team in 1980. "I was fresh out of college," he says. "There were only thirteen employees back then. We were young and energetic—the distillery space you're standing in now was used as a basketball court."

Fritz Maytag will undoubtedly go down as one of the world's foremost alcohol innovators. He came from a very business-minded family that made rather a lot of money manufacturing washing machines in the 1930s. Fritz's acquisition of the Anchor brewery was met with disdain from the rest of his family, but he would go on to become one of the pioneers of the craft beer revolution, then cap it off with America's first craft whiskey and craft gin (Junípero).

Producing a rye whiskey in 1993 must have seemed like just about the craziest decision one could make. The category was on life support, all of the old distilleries had closed, and the only other American brands in production were Wild Turkey, Jim Beam, and Old Overholt. If you ordered a rye in a bar, you would likely be served a Crown Royal or Canadian Club. These spirits all had one thing in common—they were made on column stills.

Fritz, however, took the same approach to whiskey-making as they had to beer. That is to say, they made it flavorful.

"People didn't know that they wanted beer to taste of something," says Bruce. "Then Fritz came along and showed them that they did."

Bruce and Fritz worked together to make Anchor's first whiskey product: a pot-distilled whiskey made from 100% malted rye, named Old Potrero. In January of 1996, Anchor released a 13-month-old rye whiskey followed by a three-year-old straight rye a couple of years later. Then came Old Potrero 19th

Century Style Rye and 18th Century Style Rye (the latter is still around). In 2006, Anchor released Hotaling Rye, their first Bottled-in-Bond Expression (the first Bottled-in-Bond expression release from any small distillery). This was the first Bottled-in-Bond craft whiskey, a limited release that came out at various ages, including an 18 year old—one of the oldest whiskeys from a small independent distillery that has been released to date.

The name Hotaling was borrowed from the legendary San Francisco spirits merchant A. P. Hotaling. Hotaling came to California during the Gold Rush era and amassed a fortune selling whiskey to the growing population in the West. His name was immortalized during the devastating earthquake of 1906 and the fires that followed, which destroyed 28,000 buildings in the city, including most of the dive bars, dance halls, and brothels in San Francisco's former red-light district. A. P. Hotaling's whiskey warehouse on Jackson St was a rare survivor.

The story goes that when the army turned up on the second day of fires, they planned to dynamite the building as a firebreak to prevent the flames spreading into neighboring government buildings. However, when they found out that the Hotaling warehouse was full of whiskey, they pumped salt water from the bay and even sewer water in an effort to save it. Whether this was a result of a love of whiskey or a hesitancy to dynamite a building full of highly flammable materials, nobody is entirely sure. Somehow, they did save the Hotaling warehouse though, and it still stands today, although like much of the area it's now been converted into offices.

The fact that these whiskeys were associated with the growing Anchor brand was a major benefit, but what was even more beneficial to the distillery was that it didn't need to hit huge sales targets or production deadlines because the brewing side of things could easily support it.

"We were lucky enough to be around to watch Fritz," says Bruce. "He transformed the beer industry and then set his sights on spirits. He always put a lot of thought into what he wanted to do and then threw himself into it."

All the whiskeys that are currently being bottled are made from 100% malted rye, although Bruce is experimenting with malted barley too.

"All the malted rye we've used over the years has come from malt houses that supply breweries," says Bruce. "We've bought cereals from all of them over the years."

Mashing here is done without the need for enzymes. Because the mash is 100% malted rye it has all of the diastatic power (i.e. the power to convert starch to sugar) it needs in natural form. Bruce thinks enzymes are overused in the industry, and that many distilleries succumb to the sales pitch when they could function quite happily without.

"We ferment downstairs," says Bruce. I had already thought we were "downstairs" but it turns out there's another downstairs, which we follow Bruce to, like descending the levels of a submarine. This is a dark, moody, and industrial-feeling space, which is used to ferment the beer for the brewery as well as the distillery. We're well underground, so it's actually very cool too and apparently the temperature is reasonably consistent all year round.

As you might expect, the same yeast that's used to make Anchor beer is used to ferment the rye malt for whiskey. The good news there is that it makes a flavorful, fruity ferment. The downside of this is that some of the sugar in the mash isn't converted into alcohol, so it's less cost-effective.

As I already mentioned, the distillation here is done in pots, of which the distillery currently has five. One of the stills is used to make Junípero gin, one is a tiny little thing that's used for test gin distillation, and the other three are for whiskey production. The two smaller whiskey stills are both made by the German still manufacturer Arnold Holstein. The smaller of them is as old as the distillery, with a strangely phallic head that was built by a local coppersmith.

"It seemed like, at the time, if you wanted a small whiskey still, you were on your own," says Bruce. "So we had to drag together all the pieces to get what we wanted." Bruce used to run first (wash) distillations in this still until he had collected enough low wines to fill the still, then run a spirits

TOP The bizarre coils at Hotaling are in fact the condensers for the stills, which feature a tube encased within another tube that has cool water running through it.

ABOVE Never forget your roots. This old nautical clock speaks of a time when Old Potrero and Anchor were two sides of the same coin.

LEFT Potrero Hill has been linked with artists since the 60s. It's also where they shot the car chase scene in *Bullitt*.

distillation. The phallic still is now in a period of semi-retirement, which leaves the larger Holstein still to run spirits distillation. The first distillation is now done in a much bigger still made by Forsyths in Scotland.

Warehousing is not located in San Francisco. Bruce complains that it's one of the big problems with an urban distillery—space is expensive. So barrels are filled in San Francisco then trucked to warehousing in Napa County. Once the whiskey has reached maturity, the barrels are transported back to San Francisco again for blending and bottling. In total the distillery is holding around 1,000 barrels.

Nearly all of them are 53-gallon American oak casks, but there are a handful of sherry, port, and wine barrels in stock too. The American oak barrels are sourced from Independent Stave in the state of Missouri and are made from 24-month air-dried timber. The barrels are both toasted and charred.

"We tried really light chars and really heavy ones to see what the different effect was on the spirit and what flavors were extracted," Bruce tells me.

This particular barrel recipe has stood for over 20 years, which is interesting given that some new distilleries would have you believe they are pioneering research in to barrel charring and toasting. In fact, much of that pioneering work was being done by Anchor and Independent Stave. "We learned off each other," says Bruce. "Nobody had ever asked them for a whiskey barrel designed with flavor in mind. Everyone at that time just wanted the cheapest possible whiskey barrel."

In 2010, Fritz Maytag sold Anchor Brewing & Distillers to the Griffin group, which comprised two former Skyy vodka executives, Tony Folio and Keith Gregor, alongside London wine merchants Berry Bros. & Rudd. Then, in 2017, the brewing side of the company was sold to the Japanese brewery Sapporo. The Anchor Distillery wasn't included in the sale, but the Anchor name and the physical location were. As a result, Anchor Distilling morphed into Hotaling & Co.

Leaving Hotaling, I feel a little like Luke Skywalker leaving Dagobah after his training with Yoda. Bruce is an original master of the craft-distilling world, a true sage of this side of the industry who has not only witnessed the rise of small distilleries but in no short measure, shaped it too. I think it's people like Bruce who are best placed to offer a sensible, dispassionate opinion on where the industry is heading and what pitfalls may be ahead. And yet there he is, all alone in his basement distillery, not posting pictures on Instagram or planning his next seminar. Just going about his business in the same considered manner that he always has.

OLD POTRERO STRAIGHT RYE (45% ABV)

Soft and herbal on the nose, with gentle baking spices and a little lavender. It's much bigger in the taste: heavily structured, with dark fruits and a little tobacco. The finish turns herbal again, with fresh sage and eucalyptus.

OLD POTRERO 18TH CENTURY (51.2% ABV)

There's a nice yeasty note to this whiskey that really speaks of the brewing heritage. This is accompanied by toasted cereal aromas, honey, and some dried fruit notes. The taste is like rye blended with malted barley: peppered and dark but accompanied with malty, cereal notes.

OLD POTRERO STOUT CASK FINISH (55% ABV)

Subtle coffee aromas pair well with the fruit and nut rye notes. It has amazing texture, feeling grippy and hard. The coffee becomes a gentle bittersweet chocolate backdrop in the taste of this whiskey, but those malty, spicy, fruity, delicious rye flavors are still front and center.

ROAD TRIP PLAYLIST

"Hotel California" – The Eagles

"San Francisco" – Scott McKenzie

"Into the Mystic" – Van Morrison

BOILERMAKER

I bottle Anchor Steam beer
50 ml/⅔ oz Old Potrero Straight Rye

Chill the beer, pour the shot. Sip alternately, or shoot the whiskey then sip the beer. It's your call.

For a whiskey that relies so heavily on local beer for its manufacture, it feels only right to feature a whiskey drink that couldn't exist without beer too. The boilermaker is a staple drink of some of the world's most famous cocktail bars and some of its most infamous dive bars. It's a leveling drink that doesn't discriminate against class, gender, or race, and that's because it's entirely customizable to the setting, time of day, company you're keeping and the mood. Bottle of Miller High Life and a shot of JD? Fine. Smoked porter from some obscure Scandinavian craft brewery and a glass of the latest release of William Laure Weller? That's okay too. In many ways, the boilermaker isn't a drink, but an entire category of drink. And there's something in this category for everyone, assuming you like beer and whiskey.

If you're still doubtful as to the cocktail credentials of this fantastic beverage, know this: the drink featured in the 1932 book, *The Art of Mixing* (by James Wiley and Helene Griffith), albeit under the guise of "Block and Fall" (i.e. walk a block, fall, walk a block, fall etc.) Another name it goes by which I am very fond of is "beer and a bump."

According to the Oxford English Dictionary, the term "boilermaker" was first defined (as a steam locomotive engineer) almost 100 years previously, in 1834. However, there is one tall tale that suggests the cocktail predates our greased-up railway worker. This is a story that I'm disinclined to believe, since it

originates from my home county in the UK and I'm aware that many storytellers from those parts are guilty of a certain amount of romanticization. Either way, the following tale is itself factually correct, but whether it has any connection to the boilermaker drink is open for debate.

It's Christmas Eve, 1801, and we're in Camborne, Cornwall. The town's blacksmith, Richard Trevithick has just finished engineering an early steam engine and plans to test it by driving it up Camborne hill. The engine, known as the "Puffing Devil," is a success and the event is now regarded as the first-ever example of steam locomotive transport. The engine comes to a halt outside the local pub and much celebration ensues, right on through until morning, with beer and whisky chasers being the choice beverage for the evening, matched with roast goose.

Sadly, the story ends in disaster as the engine was parked up and the boiler allowed to burn dry, resulting in fire and the total destruction of the engine. A powerful reminder of the potential pitfalls of enjoying one too many boilermakers! Regardless, the story became one of Cornwall's best-loved drinking songs, Camborne Hill.

Disregarding the questionable validity of this story, I can't imagine a better way to celebrate the burning down of a steam engine than by chasing an Anchor Steam beer with a burning shot of Old Potrero Rye.

ST. GEORGE

BY GEORGE!

"I should never have switched from Scotch to Martinis."

ACTOR HUMPHREY BOGART (1899–1957), ON HIS DEATHBED

The American Distilling Institute (ADI) lists four requirements that need to be met for a spirit to be classed as "Certified Craft Distilled."

First, the spirit must be distilled on a still at a registered Distilled Spirit Plant (the distillery) and the label needs to inform you of which one it is; second, no more than 25% of the distillery can be owned by a beverage company that are themselves not "craft;" the third stipulation is that annual sales must not exceed 100,000 proof gallons (spirit at 50% alcohol or 100 proof); and lastly, the production must be "hands-on," which is defined by the ADI as "produced to reflect the vision of their principal distillers using any combination of traditional or innovative techniques including fermenting, distilling, re-distilling, blending, infusing, or warehousing."

All of these conditions are geared towards the revival and preservation of traditional American distilling that we covered thoroughly in the earlier parts of this book. That's why so many of the craft distilleries that we see today push some sort of historical agenda with their product.

One that doesn't push a historical agenda, perhaps because its history is long enough that it needn't bother, is St. George in Oakland, dubbed by some as the OG "craft distillery."

St. George is located inside an old aircraft hangar on the old Alameda Naval Air Station, on the east shore of San Francisco Bay. The land it sits on was artificially filled in to the west edge of Alameda island

in the 1920s to create an airport and harbor. Originally designed for civilian use, the US government took control of the airport in 1936, and it was transformed into a military base that served as a launch site for the first air attacks on the Japanese mainland following Pearl Harbor.

A 65,000-square foot aircraft hangar might not seem like the most obvious location for a distillery, but it seems to work quite well for St. George, both in terms of functionality and aesthetics. It was constructed in 1941 and still has its original redwood timber roof. The spectacle of seeing casks racked alongside copper stills in such a vast open space is not one to be underestimated. Few distilleries have encapsulated the whiskey-making process in a single room, such as this, but the benefits are undeniable.

Jörg Rupf built the original St. George distillery about a mile away in 1982 and began making eau de vie (a colorless fruit brandy) from pears, raspberries, cherries, and even kiwi fruit on a single, 65-gallon Holstein pot still. Today, the distillery makes dozens of products from fruit brandies to absinthe, gin, and liqueurs. Last year they went through over 200 tons of pears just for their pear brandy. Their award-winning fruit brandies remain the backbone of the operation—it's how St. George established itself and continues to be a key part of its seasonal production schedule.

"There's nowhere to hide when you're making un-aged fruit brandies," says Dave Smith, Head Distiller.

RIGHT If you're after the best views of San Francisco, you really need to head to Alameda!

"So my job has always been to preserve the qualities of the fruit as much as possible in the final spirit."

And it's this careful and considerate approach to ingredients that has allowed the entire St. George portfolio to shine with unparalleled quality. The attention to detail here, particularly in respect to the quality, seasonality, and terroir of the base material, is on an entirely different level to any other distillery I have seen in North America, from the clarity of the Douglas fir and bay laurel botanicals used to make their gin, or the raw, natural ripeness of their apple brandy that is almost indistinguishable from the aroma of a freshly cut apple.

The story of whiskey started here 23 years ago, when Lance Winters joined St. George as employee number two. Lance's transition to booze making was a natural one—he was formerly a nuclear technician on the *USS Enterprise* (which coincidentally has Alameda Naval base as its home port). Lance was an experienced home brewer and dabbled with some (off the record) distillation too. He heard about Jörg through the reputation of his spirits, so approached him with a bottle of his homemade whiskey, which had been matured using wood chips. Jörg described the whiskey as "inoffensive" and hired Lance on the spot. (It turns out that "inoffensive" is high praise from Jörg.)

Lance would later describe Jörg in a Mr. Miyagi fashion, as he, the Daniel LaRusso character in this analogy, would turn up to work each day full of excitement about some ingredient they could try, like peat-smoked barley or sherry casks. Jörg would then sit Lance down and gently shatter his dreams by asking him "What does peat smoked barley have to do with us?" Or "what relevance do sherry casks have to an eau de vie producer in California?"

As a result of this, Lance learned to fall in love with the art of distillation itself. And over the years Jörg and Lance refined this art, mastering each ingredient as it arrived at the distillery, and learning how to extract the best from it through still management.

When Jörg retired in 2010, Lance took over the running of St. George.

When you think about the decades of experience that St. George has accumulated making fruit spirits, it's exciting to imagine what might be achieved when the same considerate philosophy is applied to whiskey making. Well, we needn't imagine. We can taste instead, and I can tell you that the results are remarkable.

Consistent with the theme of the last few distilleries on our journey, St. George's standard Single Malt whiskey is made from a blend of malted barleys, all of different roast levels: crystal malt, amber malt, chocolate malt, and black patent malt. They also use a small portion of malt that has been smoked over beech wood and alder wood. The exact recipe for this mash bill is divulged on a "If I told you I'd have to kill you" basis, but the raw spirit off the still indicates to me that there's only a subtle use of the darker cereals.

We taste two different fractions from the still, one from an earlier cut and one from later on in the distillation. Both have a chocolatey note to them, but the latter is reminiscent of bittersweet chocolate

while the earlier is a brighter, sweeter, milk chocolate. There's a subtle smoke note there too and Dave tells us that "the smoked malt gives a much sweeter style of smoke compared to peat-smoked barley."

The current distillery comprises five main stills used for production, with a couple of R&D stills in the lab. The production stills included the two original 250-liter Holstein stills, a 500-liter Holstein still that came later, then two 1,500-liter still pots which were introduced when the other equipment was maxed out. The larger stills are used for absinthe and gin while the smaller ones tend to stick with whiskey and eau de vie.

Whiskey season here is dictated by the seasonality of the other fruits and herbs that St. George distills. When there are no apples, pears, jalapeños etc. around, production immediately shifts to making whiskey and filling barrels.

True to the eau de vie style, most of the spirits made here (including whiskey) are distilled on a single pass with a conservative use of plates in the head of the still. "We do everything within our power to strip away as little as possible of the character of the product. We could make a higher

strength spirit with more purity, but we tend to employ a lighter touch," says Dave.

Like Copperworks, the brewing side of things is mostly outsourced to local breweries, including Sierra Nevada and the brewery in the hangar next-door, Faction. So when the tanker truck turns up with 6,000 gallons, there's a race on to distill the beer as quickly as possible. This takes days rather than hours, however, so as the beer sits in the beer-well, it slowly begins to change over time. Dave and the team must take this subtle shift into consideration when it comes to distillation, ensuring that they are capturing the same qualities from the beer on day three as they are on day one. The middle cut of the whiskey comes through at around 60 to 70% ABV.

Because St. George makes so many products that are barrel-aged, they are left with a lot of casks that have been seasoned with interesting things like fruit brandies, gins, Slivovitz (plum brandy), and agricole rums. The ability to utilize these barrels for their single malt program gives the distillery an incredible palate of flavors to draw from when blending. And when they can't find a barrel with the right seasoning, they'll just make a product and put it in

TOP LEFT Here's what happens when you install a distillery in an aircraft hangar (it looks totally awesome.)

TOP RIGHT Not a nuclear bomb but a barrel-aged cocktail containing whiskey and vermouth made at St. George.

MIDDLE LEFT Dave serves us up a sample of Baller Whiskey, directly from one of their seasoned umeshu casks.

LEFT Simply a work of art inside and out.

ABOVE A great name for whiskey that has been sourced, although they did buy it legally, as far as I know.

there. This happened a few years ago when Lance wanted to use port barrels but couldn't find any that were of the right quality. So he made a port called "Crusty Old Bastardo," with the main intention of putting whiskey in the barrels he used for it.

"It's easy to be distracted by the effects of oak when you're maturing spirits," says Dave, "but we view the wood as a frame for the beautiful picture we're making, not a part of the art itself."

So there are very few new oak casks at St. George; most of the inventory is actually French and American oak on its second or third fill. These barrels have already given over much of the "oaky" flavor that we might associate with a new bourbon barrel. Dave reckons a barrel loses around 50% of its remaining potency on each subsequent fill.

Wandering among the racks of barrels, Dave shows us some French oak wine casks which he managed to acquire through his brother who works at a winery.

"We at St. George are not afforded the privilege of buying these barrels directly," he says with no short measure of awe in his tone. "The oak is air-dried for 60 months and only 50 of them are made by the master cooper every year."

St. George is ramping up whiskey production so the total number of barrels in the distillery is a constantly increasing number. Dave estimates there are around 1,500 in the spring of 2019.

Given that this is an American craft distillery, the most straightforward first port of call would naturally be bourbon whiskey. And rightly so, St. George bottles a bourbon called "Breaking & Entering." But as the name cryptically suggests, this is not their own stuff and in fact a blend of individually sourced barrels from distilleries in Kentucky. That whiskey was discontinued in 2014 and more recently replaced with an American whiskey comprising a blend of Tennessee rye, Tennessee bourbon, Kentucky bourbon, and St. George's own single malt. The age ranges from two years to 13 years.

Baller Single Malt is one of the most exciting releases from St. George, as it's a Japanese-inspired whiskey intended for use in highballs (hence the name).

Launched in 2015, it's made from a blend of two-row pale malt and Munich malt, aged for 3–4 years in ex-bourbon and French oak casks, then finished for 6–12 months in umehsu casks. As with Lance's port cask experiments, this is yet another occasion where St. George has gone the extra distance and made a product from scratch just so they can season a barrel with it. Their umeshu is a liqueur made by steeping ume fruit (in this case, Californian ume fruit, a species of plum) in sochu, a rice-based spirit (which they also make), along with organic rock sugar. This result is a kind of plum/apricot flavored liquor.

So let's just go over that again: Dave and Lance made a sochu, so that they could make an umeshu, so that they could put it in a barrel, so that it could influence the malt whiskey they were planning to mature in that barrel, so that it could influence a wider blend of malt whiskeys.

Woah.

The Baller bottle is also a work of art, with the label depicting a samurai version of Saint George standing on a barrel of whiskey and a dragon. The whole idea for this whiskey came after a highball-fuelled dinner at Oakland's Ramen Shop, which set into motion the development of a mixable but mightily aromatic whiskey.

Managing all of this stock and remembering where things are must be a challenge in itself, especially when production is being ramped up to meet demand for their whiskeys. "It's a process of making sure we have more stocks than we need each year," says Dave. "If we want to bottle 3,000 cases of Baller in 2019, we need to have 5,000 cases worth of spirit so that we can be genuine blenders and pick only the spirit that will work best."

Anything that isn't deemed ready for the Baller blend will be left to mature longer and at some point contribute to another expression in the future. One example of where it might appear is St. George Single Malt, which in its last release contained whiskeys ranging from four years old to 19 years old. This expression is released in "Lot" numbers that correspond to the year of bottling. So this is yet another expression of seasonality, wherein each year the spirit may have changed subtly. "It should be like meeting and old friend with new stories to tell," says Dave. "I want you to smell the spirit and think 'ah yeah, that's what I remember,' but hopefully discover something new and exciting in there too… I'm getting goosebumps just talking about it!"

St. George Single Malt regularly features on the lists of America's best malt whiskey, so imagine the excitement when they announced that they would be releasing 30th Anniversary and then 35th Anniversary bottles in 2012 and 2017 respectively. These whiskeys both contained whiskey matured in barrels that were used to mature some of St. George's first ever pear brandy back in the early 1980s. Limited to only a few hundred bottles, you could expect to pay way in excess of $1,500 dollars a piece.

The general mood at this distillery is one of curiosity and control. No stone is left unturned, and if something can be tinkered with it will be—or perhaps it's better to say that it already has been? There is a sense of wisdom and relaxed confidence here that can only have come about through years of trial and error combined with a natural talent for knowing when something tastes good. We've been to a lot of distilleries and it would be unprofessional for me to pick a favorite, but if I had to…

BREAKING & ENTERING (43% ABV)

Creamy toffee and plenty of milk chocolate on the nose, like a box of novelty chocolates you might receive at Christmas. The festive theme continues on the palate, with Christmas pudding spices, a touch of brandy, and sweet vanilla custard. The end is orange peels and cinnamon spice.

BALLER (47% ABV)

The aroma here is intensely fragrant with very little cask character and more in the way of stone fruits and orange blossom. On the palate , it's brilliantly balanced with a kind of weird, gentle intensity… The structure is crisp and elegant right through to the finish where apricot makes an appearance.

SINGLE MALT LOT 17 (43% ABV)

Clarity is the first thing that stands out here. Fragrant stone fruit is layered elegantly over honey and cherry blossom. You can identify each aroma quite clearly, forming a balanced concert of aromatic delight. Honeydew melon and peach come through on the palate, which then delivers subtle oak notes and a tingling spice.

SINGLE MALT LOT 18 (43% ABV)

This whiskey has a more cereal, nutty aroma than Lot 17, seemingly supported by more toasted cask character. The taste is nutty and savory, but then shifts into a pronounced winey note, with grape juice and botrytis style (noble rot) concentration.

RYE 2 YEAR OLD (55% ABV)

The nose is delicate with pineapple, nougat, and a good waft of grapefruit peel. It smells like whiskey punch and is crisp and beautifully structured on the palate. Like the tastiest splinters in your gums, there's fruit, herbs, florals, and wood spice to accompany just a little pain. A beauty.

SINGLE MALT 35TH ANNIVERSARY BOTTLE (47.3% ABV)

An initial wave of plum and pecan is darkened by date and muscovado sugar, but then softens to honeydew melon and pear on repeat visits. A third visit brings about cinnamon- spiced creme brûlée. On the palate, there's a fungal and strangely umami/mushroom note. The barrel kicks back in the finish, with smoked peach and toast.

ROAD TRIP PLAYLIST

"(Sittin' on) The Dock of the Bay" — Otis Redding

"Ventura Highway" — America

"California Dreamin'" — The Mamas and the Papas

THE DERBY

30 ml/1 oz St. George Breaking & Entering
15 ml/½ oz lime juice
10 ml/2 teaspoons sweet vermouth
10 ml/2 teaspoons Grand Marnier

Shake all of the ingredients with cubed ice and double-strain into a coupe glass.
Garnish with a mint leaf.

There are at least half a dozen cocktail recipes that I know of that bear the name Derby, The Derby, or Brown Derby, reminding us that drinking and horse racing are never far from one another. One of my favorites is the Brown Derby, which was actually created for a Los Angeles restaurant chain with the same name. It's a blend of bourbon, pink grapefruit juice, and maple syrup, shaken and served straight up.

Another Derby cocktail, called The Derby, appeared in Trader Vic's 1972 *Bartender's Guide (Revised)*. Being one of the founders of the tiki movement, Vic was better known for his rum-based cocktails, but spirits such as gin and whiskey did occasionally feature on his menus and in his books.

Victor "Trader Vic" Bergeron was in fact a San Francisco native who opened a restaurant called Hinky Dinks in Oakland in 1934. The 30-capacity venue was inspired by Vic's trips to Havana, Cuba where he met the legendary cantinero (bartender) Constante at the equally legendary El Floridita cocktail bar. As such, it was Cuban sandwiches and daiquiris on the menu at Hinky Dinks.

LOST SPIRITS

MAKING UP FOR LOST TIME

*"I wish to live to 150 years old, but the day I die, I wish it to be with
a cigarette in one hand and a glass of whiskey in the other."*

AVA GARDNER (1922–90), ACTRESS

For the penultimate distillery on our trip we're in Los Angeles, visiting one of the more cutting-edge distilleries in the nation. Lost Spirits was founded by Bryan Davis and Joanne Haruta in 2010. It's located in Los Angeles' Arts District, close to downtown.

Lost Spirits is a distillery that has received a fair amount of attention in recent years, brought about by incredible claims, a self-assured founder, and a Willy Wonka-inspired distillery experience. The innovation that they're most widely acknowledged for, though, is their efforts to manipulate the maturation of whiskey. While there is undoubtedly a romance to waiting for whiskey to mature in barrels, as well as a sense of merit afforded to those who are patient enough to wait years for a spirit to evolve, it's a bloody pain, really, and from a financial point of view, a huge burden.

So it should come as no surprise to learn that distillers have been trying to speed up aging processes for at least a century. Shortly after Prohibition, the Publicker Commercial Alcohol Distillery in Philadelphia began selling whiskey. The game of aging whiskey quickly was even more competitive than usual, since there were no aged stocks left to market at the time of repeal. Most distilleries were content to bottle young product and throw their hands in the air apologetically. But not Publicker.

Publicker was founded in 1913 by Harry Publicker. The distillery became very successful selling alcohol products to the US government in World War I. So

when Prohibition came around the distillery kept on making industrial alcohol—up to the tune of 12 million gallons in the early 1920s. Federal regulations enacted at the time limited the total production of industrial alcohol to 70.5 million gallons, of which Publicker produced a whopping 17%. After Prohibition ended, Harry Publicker's son-in-law, Si Neuman, solicited the help of a chemist by the name of Dr. Carl Haner. Haner claimed he could age whiskey "artificially" overnight. This feat was achieved by shaking the barrels violently and blasting them with a heat. Publicker adverts from the time read, "Don't fill your stomach from a misty old keg."

When *Fortune* reported on the distillery in 1993, their conclusion was that artificially aged whiskey would only be drunk by "cabbies and cooks," though they were quick to applaud the fact that Dr. Haner had avoided killing himself thus far. In their final summary they concluded as follows: "Maybe Mr. Neuman's whiskey will revolutionize the industry. Or maybe Si Neuman is crazy." Which begs the question, is Bryan Davis crazy?

We arrive via the 101, at which point we're hit with the news that Lost Spirits had a fire shortly before our arrival. So a tour was off the cards. The cause of the fire was officially pointed at a smartphone, but given the range of proprietary equipment that this distillery houses, my intuitions would have pointed a finger towards some of that kit instead!

We head out for lunch and settle in at a bar in the Los Feliz neighborhood, and order a couple of glasses of single malt whiskey made by the LA-based Stark Spirits. While we enjoy our drinks, I manage to catch up with Bryan on the phone. He's understandably quite busy, what with the fire and all that, but that doesn't do too much to diminish the obvious excitement he has for what Lost Spirits are up to.

Bryan came out of college with an art degree in one hand and spare time in the other. So he did what any normal person would do and started making absinthe. When it turned out to be quite nice, he again did what any normal person would do and moved to Spain to start his own absinthe brand: Obsello. Unfortunately Obsello went bust, and Bryan returned to California. "One thing it taught me," he says, "is that I wanted to stay in the alcohol industry."

So in 2010, Bryan joined forces with Joanne Haruta, and set about turning an abandoned artichoke farm in Castroville, Monterey County, California, into a distillery. Much experimentation ensued, most of it down to a lack of funds. The budget for the entire project was $80,000, which didn't leave enough money to buy a still. "Everyone was buying Christian Carl stills and making similar products anyway," says Bryan. "Making our own stills forced us to think about the kind of product we wanted to make."

So Bryan did his research, becoming fixated on a forgotten style of bourbon-still he read about in an old *New York Times* article. The still was basically a large wooden barrel with a copper head and steam coil inside—a wooden still if you will. I should add at this point that wooden stills are not completely unheard of; there are a couple of very famous ones at the Diamond rum distillery in Guyana, and a handful of new distilleries are using them too.

"The idea was that as the still heats up it pulls some of the flavor out of the wood," says Bryan. "Once I knew that I wanted to make one I just needed to work out how many BTUs of power was needed to heat it and what would be the optimum proportions for the head and neck of the still."

So Bryan and Joanne bought a load of sheet copper and built tiny working stills of varying shapes and sizes that could be tested on a domestic stove. These experiments were intended to break down all of the variables in the distillation process and work out the most efficient shape. During testing, Bryan carefully calculated how much energy was going into each still and which shape had the best physical properties and temperature gradation. "I ended up making—I don't remember how many—but at least ten miniature pot stills," he says.

The result of all this crackpot investigation was a 2,000-liter wooden pot still with a copper head. It was quite possibly the first of its kind in California, and almost certainly the largest of its kind. The wooden base was an old vat from a vineyard in the Napa Valley. "I thought about coopering it myself," says Bryan, "but then I thought better of it."

The problem with opening a distillery on an abandoned artichoke farm in Monterey is—as it transpires—getting enough electricity onto the property, since without electricity he had no way of cooling his stills. The solution he came up with is the sort of remedy that could only have been thought of by a Californian—build a swimming pool. Constructing a swimming pool above the still house allowed Bryan to pump the cool pool water through a condenser, then cycle it back into the pool, which gets heated as a by-product.

The problem with using pool water to cool copper components, though, is that the chlorine in the water corrodes the copper. This reaction is accelerated when the chlorinated water is heated, which is of course is exactly what a condenser does. So while you're splashing around in your massive hot tub, drinking cocktails made from the still you're using to heat it, your distillation equipment is actually, quietly, falling to pieces. You can probably guess what happened next.

But before the distillery was destroyed by hot pool water, Bryan and Joanne did some pretty cool stuff. Their chief product at that time was single malt whiskey. Bryan was fascinated by peat and the terroir that it could bring to a whiskey. So he set about sourcing peat from all over North America: the Florida Everglades; a Saskatoon berry bog near

Winnipeg in Canada; cranberry bogs in New York; and an island off the Sacramento delta in California.

"They all have different kinds of decomposed vegetation," says Bryan. "Some have sedge moss, others have Sphagnum moss, some have both. The peat we got from Edmonton in Canada was made from decomposed pine needles and pine cones, and you can really smell that when it burns."

The dream was to build a malting floor and kiln to burn all this peat and make their own peated malt. Unfortunately, they were unable to get a permit, so instead took to smoking malted barley that they bought in from Washington. These early experiments culminated with the release of Umami, Ouroboros, and Seascape II single malt whiskeys, each made from a base of malted barley that had been smoked with peat from different locations.

Umami had another weird production component to it, which resulted in what Bryan calls "our most interesting whiskey." There's no real way to skirt around this, so I'll cut to the chase: they fermented the barley mash with sea water.

"The sea was so close by and we wanted to capture some of that flavor in the whiskey," says Bryan. "I just drove down there in my truck and pumped a load of it into a container."

Bryan says that the saltwater not only changes the biology of the yeast, but also introduces bacteria that feed off the sugars and introduce new flavors to the beer. Of course, the salt doesn't distill over, but some aromatic components reminiscent of the ocean do find their way over, sodium acetate being one example.

While all this was going on, Bryan and Joanne were spending quite a lot of time investigating the maturation process of spirits. Bryan wanted to mature his single malts in American oak barrels that had previously been seasoned with rum. But he didn't want to wait a year or two for the rum to strip out flavor. So he began looking at ways of speeding up maturation, exploring what happens inside a cask when liquor goes in there and developing strategies to speed those processes up.

It's an accepted fact that many of the extractive effects of maturation can be sped up by increasing surface area. In practice, this means using smaller casks, adding wood chips, or agitating the barrels (which increases the surface area of the spirit). Other processes are much harder to speed up, such as esterification—the chemical chain of events that produce fruity aromas. Under normal maturation conditions, esterification occurs when alcohol reacts with organic acids that are released during the slow degradation of the oak. An example of this would be ethyl lactate, which is made when lactic acid in the wood reacts with ethanol, and it's responsible for some of the creamy, coconut aromas in mature spirits. Bryan noted that esterification itself is not a slow process, and that the challenge was in fact to speed up the breakdown of the lignin in the wood.

This became the motivation and the obsession for three years. Then, in 2014, shortly after the distillery in Monterey had been destroyed, Bryan was at an American Distilling Institute conference where he was due to deliver a seminar on the subject of peat terroir. This event followed a publishing a paper on the topic of rapid maturation with a senior faculty member at UC Davis. At the last minute he changed his mind, and instead delivered a full report on his findings on the subject of catalyzing esterification. It was met with mixed responses, with many who attended believing that it was a late April Fool's joke (the conference was on May 1st).

Although Bryan's claims attracted some criticism, it also garnered a fair bit of positive attention from venture capitalists based in Silicon Valley. After all, a spirits company that can genuinely recreate the affects of 10 years maturation in 10 days would have a competitive advantage worth billions. So Bryan and Joanne did what any sensible people would do and took the money.

A year later, in 2015, Bryan introduced the world to what he calls Lost Spirit's "THEA (Targeted Hyper-Esterification Aging) One Reactor," a space-age, truck-sized piece of equipment that is designed to accelerate maturing of spirits from years down to days. The exact workings of this machine are protected by patent, but Bryan described the basic principles to me .

"The wood is blasted with a super-high intensity light," he says, "which has a similar effect on the wood to when wood decking becomes cracked over many years of exposure to light."

"So, like a laser?" I ask. "Yeah, it's a bit like a laser, except you blow the whole thing up."

The trick here, apparently, is to keep temperature under control. Once all that electromagnetic energy hits the spirit/wood, things heat up quickly and are at risk of exploding. So the temperature is kept in the window of 140°F and 170°F for a period of 12 hours for up to 14 days. "We didn't replicate the traditional aging process; we hacked it," he says. "There's a distinct difference here."

Bryan claims the THEA One Reactor can create the same effects of 20 years maturation in under a week. He was quick to prove this, by sending samples to a lab to be analyzed against spirits that were genuinely decades old. The results came back and Bryan was content that his young spirit could indeed be passed off as being much older. "If you were going to use the forensic data in a court case—unless you knew what we were up to, you'd say it was 20 years old."

Lost Spirits has a purpose-built distillery in LA's Arts District, filled with cutting-edge equipment (including a autonomous master distiller called TESSA) and a team of 45 lab technicians, chemists, engineers, botanists, and salespeople. The distillery features "tasting rooms," which are accessible only by ticket, and where brand-specific experiences are designed to transport you to a different time or place.

"Each product has its own universe," says Bryan. For example, at "Whisky Island," you take an actual boat that floats on the distillery's condenser cooling water to get to a special library room. There's even a carousel. The whole thing is intended to be not just a novel place to enjoy a few drinks, but an all-encompassing, reality-shifting experience that is representative of the brand—like you're drinking from both inside and outside of the bottle.

The focus in recent years has shifted more towards hyper-aged rums, but Lost Spirits is still bottling one whiskey expression and working on a few others. Their "Abomination" bottlings are made from a base of heavily peated single malt whiskey that Lost Spirits import from Scotland. Once they get their hands on the liquid—which by this point is probably feeling rather lost—they mix it "with the profane 21st century sciences that Lost Spirits is famous for." In layman's terms, that means finishing the whiskey with toasted Riesling barrel oak, and heavily charred Riesling barrel oak in the THEA reactor. Ludicrous liquids deserve ludicrous names, and thus far the distillery has released two versions of Abomination: "Crying of the Puma" and "Sayers of the Law." Their website proudly states that Abomination is "arguably the most cutting-edge spirit on the market today."

Cutting-edge it might be, but it's all for nothing if you can't get a taste of the stuff. Bryan and Joanne were unfortunately not very forthcoming when it came down to tasting their spirits but luckily we managed to track down a bottle in a bar in Los Feliz. See below for my tasting notes.

We leave LA feeling a little lost ourselves and more than a little conflicted around what Lost Spirits is all about. In a way, it's regrettable that the avant-garde distillery experience is housed under the same roof as the modernist tech that Bryan has developed. One of those elements is clearly intended for its Vaudeville, Instagram-able absurdness, which instinctively calls into question the legitimacy of the other—is it all smoke and mirrors? To that end, Lost Spirits has received no shortage of criticism from other distillers for their work on rapid maturation, and it feels like defensive scar tissue has formed in response. Part of the problem here is that they can't afford to divulge too much about how their technology works because it's theirs and it's potentially extremely valuable. But in this era of informed consumers, transparency is key, lest you be labeled as a snake oil salesman.

I feel that innovation in whiskey should always be commended. Bryan and his team undoubtedly possess a dogged determination to push the envelope in this field and aid in the transition of spirits into the 21st century. Whether Lost Spirits is capable of actually doing this is still uncertain, but what is perhaps more important is how the whiskey receives these changes. In an industry this old we must be careful about how new techniques are positioned so as not to diminish the work of others, in both the past and the present.

ABOMINATION—SAYERS OF THE LAW (54% ABV)

This is a hard-hitting peat monster on the nose, with plenty of smoldering smoke accompanied by barbecued apricots and burnt citrus peels. There's a slight hot rubber note to it too, which is actually quite pleasant. The taste is rich and concentrated, with hot smoke alongside cracked cocoa, pepper, and fruity espresso coffee.

ROAD TRIP PLAYLIST

"California" – Phantom Planet

"Good Vibrations" – The Beach Boys

"Route 66" – Chuck Berry

ABOMINABLE SNOWMAN-HATTAN

50 ml/1⅔ oz Lost Spirits Abomination—Sayers of the Law
10 ml/2 teaspoons gomme
I Oaked Vermouth Ice Sphere (see below)

Add all of the ingredients to a rocks glass and stir for at least a minute.

For my first cocktail book, I wrote a recipe for a drink called "Insta-aged Rob Roy," which was made by vacuum-distilling a bottle of whiskey to separate the taste and aroma components. The clear, boozy, aromatic distillate was mixed with vermouth and bitters to form a cocktail, while the dark, woody residue was frozen into ice cubes. The idea was that you drop the wood-flavored ice cube into your drink and the cocktail slowly "ages" in the glass. As interesting as the results were, it wasn't a very easy cocktail to put together.

So the recipe here is a version of the original that incorporates the same themes (along with Lost Spirits' pursuit of maturation character over short periods of time, particularly in respect to wood used to age Riesling wine), but it does so in a simpler and more accessible manner.

The premise is an Old Fashioned-style cocktail that transforms into a Manhattan through the slow melting of vermouth-flavored ice. There are a few brands of Riesling-based vermouth available now, but my preference is towards Belsazar Dr. Loosen Riesling edition. To get the added "age" effect, I take oak barbecue chips and toast them in a hot oven for 30 minutes, then infuse 100 g/3½ oz of chips into 75 cl/25 oz of vermouth for a week (or longer if you prefer). The vermouth is then best cut 50:50 with water and frozen into ice spheres.

EPILOGUE: ENDLESS WEST

THE BEGINNING OF ENDLESSNESS

*"Great spirits have always encountered violent opposition
from mediocre minds."*

ALBERT EINSTEIN (1879–1955), THEORETICAL PHYSICIST

Four hundred years ago, when our story began, the technology used to make whiskey was not fully understood by those that wielded it. Brewers and distillers were still ignorant to things like molecules, cells, etc. Thermometers didn't exist and neither did apparatuses for measuring alcoholic strength——in fact even the concept of an alcohol/water mixture wasn't understood. As such, the distillation technology easily surpassed the understanding of the people that had designed it, and its design was based not on scientific principle, but on centuries of empirical findings. Trial and error.

Then science started to catch up.

Robert Hooke discovered the cell in 1665, Gabriel Fahrenheit invented the first alcohol-based thermometer in 1709, oxygen was discovered in the 1770s, the branch of science known as thermodynamics (essential in the understanding of combustion, evaporation, and, well, distillation) was invented in the 1840s, and terms like ester and ketone were introduced by Leopold Gmelin in 1843.

By the early 20th century, we humans had a pretty good understanding of what was going on in our mash cookers, fermenters, and stills. We even had a basic understanding of maturation and the effects of oak on a spirit.

Knowing how things work is one thing, but knowing when things have worked well (and why) is another. As our taste and appreciation of good spirits developed, we became better at drawing links between cause and effect. We became better still makers and even better spirit makers. We scrutinized and further refined production methods to meet our needs. But the equipment we used to achieve all of this has remained, for the most part, unchanged over four centuries.

Which brings us to the present day. We find ourselves in a time where the marriage of technology and understanding has switched places. In even the most modern distilleries, at absolutely every level of production, our insight to the goings-on exceeds the potential of the equipment that we use. There are no unknowns in spirits production today, only goals that are made difficult to achieve by the rudimentary nature of the tools that we use. We can steer the direction of how a spirit develops and crudely shape its character as it matures, and we can check back on how we did afterwards by using hi-tech lab equipment to analyze samples. But what we cannot do is design and make a spirit in accordance with a specific molecular outcome. Until now.

For the final distillery on the tour, we retrace our route in to LA, returning to San Francisco.

It's rather fitting, given that our journey started in Richmond, Virginia, that it should end in San Francisco. Despite being nearly 3,000 miles apart, these two cities are separated by just 0.1 degree of latitude (around 10 miles). San Francisco is the natural endpoint from a chronological standpoint, too. After all, Virginia was the site of the United States' earliest colonial history, and the San Francisco Bay Area is the area of the US where the future is made.

Silicon Valley is, of course, home to some of the world's biggest technology companies, as well as thousands of startup companies vying for a slice of the venture capital pie. The area got its name from the silicon-based microchips that were birthed here, but as computers have seeped further into our day-to-day lives, many of the greatest successes of the past few years have been lifestyle brands like Uber, Netflix, and Airbnb. These, however, are still tech companies in the traditional sense—you still need a computer, smartphone, or television to use their services—but they represent a fundamental shift in commercial activity, as Silicon Valley startups set their sights on industries that one wouldn't traditionally associate with processors and coding.

As we arrive back in San Francisco, we stop at a Mexican restaurant called School Night, situated just off 3rd Street. The menu is delivered, and as we quickly scan past the fish tacos and pork empanadas, we find what we're looking for at the bottom "Impossible Meatballs."

The "meat" in these meat-free meatballs is manufactured by Impossible Foods, which is a Silicon Valley startup, backed by the likes of Google and Bill Gates. Their product looks like minced beef, tastes like minced beef and even sizzles and leeches juice like minced beef when fried on a griddle, but is in fact made from a unique mixture of water, plant proteins, and coconut oil, plus a bunch of other stuff. It's sustainable, ethical, and delicious—it's difficult to find fault in Impossible Foods.

With our bellies full and our consciences clear, we walk two blocks south, to the headquarters of another edible startup, Endless West. The task that these guys have set themselves sounds, on paper, to be just as impossible as fabricating meat from potatoes and fermented soy root: they're making whiskey, one molecule at a time.

2325 3rd Street is a large and somewhat labyrinthine building, but the Endless West team only inhabits a small segment of a single floor. They don't need much space. As we weave through the corridors I'm running the whole concept of 3D-printed whiskey through my head.

It's one thing to simulate the taste and texture of a burger with clever seasoning and binding agents, but to fabricate the subtle nuances of a sherry cask or the gentle honeyed fruitiness of a mature malt spirit? What about the "marriage" of flavors that can only take place over years of resting? Surely some things can only be produced over time and with patience?

We're greeted by Alec Lee, CEO and co-founder of Endless West. He's young, slim, wears a button-down shirt to work and he basically looks and sounds absolutely nothing like a distiller. But then, Endless West doesn't look like a distillery, and it doesn't smell like one either (which is normally the first thing you notice). There's no aroma of cereals mashing, no fermentation funk, none of that sensation of spirit vapor hanging in the air, and no comforting smell of cut oak or barrel char either.

Instead of stills and barrels, there are rows of computer screens, large, beige-colored pieces of analytical equipment, and a dozen or so clever-looking people interacting here and there. There are glass-fronted chambers with thick rubber gloves attached—the kind you'd imagine would be used to assemble a nuclear warhead. Some of the instruments are spinning very fast and others are vibrating. One of them seems to be magically stirring a solution using magnets.

Alec founded Endless West alongside Mardonn Chua and Josh Decolongon. Alec and Mardonn both have a background in chemistry and Josh is a qualified sommelier. The premise for the business came about after Mardonn visited a vineyard in Napa valley and encountered a bottle of the legendary Chateau Montelena 1973. Furious that he couldn't afford to buy a bottle (at $10,000) he began to consider what it was about the wine that made it so endearing.

"Peel away the story and the subjectivity of the wine," Marddon says, "and you're left with the taste and flavor. I began to realize that there's really nothing about taste and flavor that we can't engineer."

Alec takes us on a short tour through the workspace, explaining their research and development process and the methods they employ to make spirits. "The first stage of our process is basically mapping. We're trying to build digital taste and digital aroma profiles of spirits to understand their molecular structure," he tells me.

One of the R&D technicians, Taylor, is operating a machine that looks like an office copier (but likely costs a couple of orders of magnitude more) that analyzes all of the molecules in a liquid sample and creates a graph that displays the number of occurrences. Samples are placed in small vials, which get picked up by a thin needle that forces the liquid through a small column at extremely high pressure. A special matrix separates the molecules and spits out its findings onto the computer screen. Alec likens it to sorting through a bag of multicolored marbles of varying sizes: at first glance it's a total mess, but if you empty the bag and arrange the marbles in groups you get to understand the composition of the bag. The machine is called a liquid chromatography mass spectrometer (LC-MS) and its purpose is to assess the molecules that give whiskey (or any liquid) its taste and mouthfeel, but not aroma. That's the job of the (nearby) gas chromatography mass spectrometer (GC-MS), which also accepts vials of liquid but vaporizes them, then analyzes the gas using a "digital nose" made from a special polymer.

GC-MS is not uncommon in larger distilleries, and even small distilleries will sometimes send samples away to laboratories for analysis as a way of checking aromatic consistency over time. Combining GC-MS and LC-MS together is what provides the technicians at Endless West with a complete picture of the molecules that make a spirit taste, smell, and feel a certain way.

Not all of the molecules that these machines detect are equal in their importance however, and not all are relevant to whiskey. A molecule that contributes a musky aroma, for example, may be present in large quantities but remain under the threshold of detection by the human nose. On the other hand, a sample could contain only traces of a sulphurous (eggy) or phenolic (smoky) molecule but be quite noticeable in the whiskey.

By analyzing a broad range of samples, Alec and his team are able to create a kind of road map of whiskey that defines style on a molecular level.

"We're taking dozens of products off the shelf and finding out what makes them prototypically themselves. What makes a peated Scotch a peated Scotch? How does that compare to a Japanese whisky?" Alec asks.

These are questions that most of us ponder every time we sip on a whiskey, and especially ones that have well-defined or extreme flavors. We are, in a sense, running the same computations that Endless West are every time we sip and ponder. The difference here is that these styles can be quantified rather than imagined in purely subjective terms.

With the mapping done, next comes what Alec calls "the hard part".

"Our goal isn't really copying things, it's making new things that have never existed before. We have the opportunity to make the kind of whiskey that we like, or a kind of whiskey that we have identified that consumers like but that might currently be missing."

The process is rather like going to the DIY store to get a can of paint mixed, where a combination of base ingredients are mixed together to form a cohesive, balanced product. Endless West use neutral corn spirit and water as their canvas, before applying over 100 different (they're pretty secretive about exactly how many) taste and aroma molecules to build the composition. All of the ingredients they use are extracted from plants and tend to be in extremely concentrated form. Sometimes even a single drop in an entire bottle of whiskey may be overkill. We're talking parts per million and even parts per billion scale.

Alec has some examples of compounds that are found in whiskey (and that Endless West use to make theirs) for us to smell. The first is cis-3-Methyl-4-octanolide, also known as "whisky lactone" because it's a very important part of the aroma of many whiskeys. To me it smells most strongly of coconut; Alec tells me that he smells fig. Other people get a slight celery note from it. Next we smell a liquid that is less inviting—it reminds me a little of vomit and cheese. Alec immediately asks us to smell another vial, which has a similar smelling liquid in it but with more pleasant fruity notes of pineapple and grapes.

"The first sample is butyric acid and the second sample is ethyl butanoate. They share the same basic molecular structure, the first is the acid version and the second is when that acid reacts with ethanol to create an ester."

What Alec is showing us is the reactions that take place during fermentation and maturation that develop flavor in whiskey. We've seen whiskey makers like Leopold Bros. and Kings County deploying complex strategies to develop these flavors in their products, because they know they will result in a great-smelling or tasting whiskey.

Alec just buys them in bulk.

By this point I'm getting more than a little excited. Putting to one side the… ethics… of making whiskey this way, just imagine the opportunities this technology offers with respect to creating ancient bottles from the past over and over again. I mean, this could be as revolutionary to spirits as the printing press was to books!

But I'm getting carried away. Surely there are factors at play in bottles that simply cannot be replicated without time and marriage of flavors?

Alec doesn't think so.

"If when you say 'marriage' you mean some kind of supernatural relationship between the molecules in the spirit, no—we cannot do that. But if when you say marriage you mean you need to have the right proportion of the molecules that give the spirit the impression of harmony and deliciousness, then yes—we can do that." Alec tells me.

If had all of this power at my disposal I'm not sure I would even know where to start: a pre-Prohibition rye perhaps, or a high-ester bourbon? Endless West actually considered this themselves for quite a time, looking to the sherry-cask single malts of Scotland like Glenmorangie and Macallan, then throwing elegant whiskeys from Japan into the mix. The whole time, they were assessing which flavors they liked and then, for want of a better term, putting them under the microscope to find out which flavors they were tasting.

All in all, the development process took a little over a year, resulting in the launch of their first product, Glyph, in May 2018. I found the spirit to be lighter and more fragrant than I had anticipated (I'm not sure what I expected, but maybe something with more maturation character), but this is by design. It certainly tastes and smells like whiskey and I'd challenge anyone to pick it out in a blind tasting. The style is perhaps best described as a Scottish Lowland blend, or perhaps an Irish whiskey—light, accessible, and aromatic.

If I were in charge I might have launched with a show stopping extra-aged wine cask expression (like one of Balcones' malts or a W. L. Weller) to get everyone's attention, then followed up with a killer mass-market product like Glyph.

Glyph's packaging is as "craft" as they come. With Art Deco typography and bold colors, it wouldn't look out of place on a liquor shelf or, indeed, in a whiskey book. In my mind, Glyph is a legitimate craft product; the only difference is that Endless West's specific craft is science.

The plan is to release more Glyph products, but Endless West are not restricting themselves to whiskey. Eric is confident that his team can further refine their processes so that they can scan, design, and build spirits far quicker in the future. We're talking perhaps even in a matter of days or hours. We're talking about liquids that are tailored for flavor—perhaps even tailored to the tastes of the individual drinker, like a cocktail with hundreds of ingredients. Besides the obvious flavor-making advantages that this tech offers, there's also the advantage of being able to make the spirit anywhere in the world. If, for example, you were looking to make a product for an audience in somewhere like India, where import duty on spirits is 150%, it wouldn't be beyond the bounds of possibility to establish a facility there that manufactures whiskey made to taste like bourbon, rye, or Scotch that can be sold there at a competitive price.

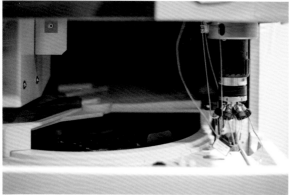

TOP LEFT This is the room where they mix together the components that make up Glyph. Not a barrel in sight.
ABOVE A liquid chromatography mass spectrometer (LC-MS), which is basically a digital tongue. Endless West tests the same liquid dozens of times to get a clear understanding of what makes it taste the way it does.

TOP RIGHT Making spirits at Endless West is a lot like making cocktails. The inspiration is established, then they amass the components needed to achieve it.
ABOVE Glyph is like the ultimate mashup between mixology and whiskey making, where many ingredients are unified to make a whole.

Is it a whiskey though? No, not at the moment. But I would be very surprised not to see more start ups like Endless West. One day we may need to discuss more seriously whether a product that is chemically identical to a whiskey, but hasn't been made through the linear processes that we associate with whiskey today, should also be classed a whiskey.

GLYPH (43% ABV)

The initial aroma is quite grassy, with notes of honey, citrus, and ginger. The texture is reasonably light, but it's lively with some forest fruits, just the right amount of vanilla, and perhaps just a wisp of smoke. The finish drops off quickly and cleanly.

ROAD TRIP PLAYLIST

"I've Been Everywhere" – Johnny Cash

"Home" – Edward Sharpe and the Magnetic Zeros

"Home for a Rest" – Spirit of the West

FOLLOWING PAGES It looks, smells and tastes like whiskey. From a molecular point of view it is indistinguishable from whiskey. Shouldn't it be called "whiskey" then?

INDEX

ABOUT THE AUTHOR

Tristan Stephenson is an award-winning bar operator, bartender, barista, chef, some-time journalist, and the bestselling author of *The Curious Bartender* series of drinks books. With Thomas Aske, he is a co-founder of Fluid Movement, the globally renowned drinks consultancy and, as such, is half the brains behind the drinks programs at some of the world's top drinking and eating destinations.

After launching his career working in various Cornish kitchens, Tristan was given the opportunity to design cocktails and run bar operations at chef Jamie Oliver's Fifteen restaurant in Cornwall in 2007. He went from there to work for the world's biggest premium drinks company, Diageo, and on to co-found Fluid Movement in 2009. Fluid Movement then opened their first two bars in London—Purl, in 2010, and then the Worship Street Whistling Shop in 2011. Worship Street Whistling Shop was named by *Time Out* as "London's Best New Bar" in 2011 and was placed in the "World's Fifty Best Bars" for three consecutive years. Tristan was himself awarded UK Bartender of the Year in 2012 and in the same year he was included in the *London Evening Standard*'s list of the "Top 1000 most influential Londoners."

In 2014 Fluid Movement opened their next venue. Surfside, a steak and lobster restaurant on Polzeath beach, this time back in Tristan's native Cornwall. It was awarded the No. 1 Position in *The Sunday Times*'s "Best alfresco dining spots in the UK 2015." Tristan served as head chef there for the first summer and continues to manage the food and beverage menu.

In 2016 Fluid Movement opened three more London bars, all at the same Shoreditch site—The Devil's Darling, Sack, and most significantly, Black Rock (a bar dedicated to whiskey), which has won *Time Out*'s "UK's Best Specialist Bar" for the past three years, 2017–2019. The original basement space has since expanded to also include the first-floor Black Rock Tavern, styled after the izakayas of Japan, and offering whiskey highballs, draught beers, and a curated collection of whiskies from around the world. Further Black Rock sites will be opening across the UK—starting with Bristol in the Summer of 2019.

Tristan's writing debut, *The Curious Bartender Volume I: The Artistry & Alchemy of Creating the Perfect Cocktail* was published in 2013 and shortlisted for the prestigious André Simon Award. His second book, *The Curious Bartender: An Odyssey of Malt, Bourbon & Rye Whiskies* hit the bookshelves in 2014. In 2015 he published *The Curious Barista's Guide to Coffee*, and in 2016 his fourth book, in what was by now an established series, *The Curious Bartender's Gin Palace*, was again shortlisted for the André Simon. His fifth book *The Curious Bartender's Rum Revolution* arrived in 2017 and his sixth, *The Curious Bartender Volume 2: The New Testament*, an eagerly anticipated follow-up to the original bestselling *Curious Bartender Volume 1*, was met with great enthusiasm by his worldwide fanbase upon publication in 2018.

Tristan's other commercial enterprises include his drinks brand Aske-Stephenson which manufactures and sells pre-bottled cocktails in flavors as diverse as Peanut Butter and Jam Old-fashioned and Flat White Russian. He has also launched an on-line whisky subscription service, whisky-me.com, offering top-quality single malt whiskies for home delivery. In addition, in March 2017 Tristan joined the supermarket chain Lidl UK as a consultant on their highly-regarded own-brand spirits range.

Tristan lives in Cornwall and is husband to Laura and father to two small children. In his very limited spare time he runs, rides a Triumph motorcycle, takes photos, designs websites, bakes stuff, cooks a lot, reads avidly, attempts various DIY tasks beyond his level of ability, and collects whiskey and books.

ACKNOWLEDGMENTS

The last time I wrote a whiskey book, I got a lot more than I bargained for, so this time I thought that I was prepared for what was coming. But it absolutely wasn't the case, and what ensued was easily the most ambitious, frustrating, grueling, wonderful project of my life so far.

But needless to say, a book such as this is more than the work of a single individual.

Obviously, there are hundreds of people working in the whiskey industry that helped to make this happen, by allowing us to tour, taste, talk, and take pictures at their distilleries, but mostly for being okay about the inflexibility of our travel schedule. Many of their names feature in the book, but for every one distiller/blender/owner there are usually two or three behind-the-sceners that made all the arrangements and ensured things run smoothly... you guys have my thanks.

Thanks to my co-pilots Addie and Matt. Neither of you hold a driver's license and both of you drank greedily at every distillery we visited, and for this you have both my enduring respect and eternal contempt. We're definitely getting a driver next time.

Thanks to Sarianne for once again providing styling for the cocktail shots, a job that she has approached with vigor for over 200 *Curious Bartender* photos.

Huge thanks to the team at RPS: David, Cindy, Julia, Leslie, Christina, Patricia, and Paul. I realise I don't make things easy for myself, so thanks for going easy on me!

And once again thanks to Nathan—for being a great editor and for providing words of encouragement during the "dark times."

Finally, thanks to my family for allowing me to go gallivanting around the US for weeks on end under the questionable pretence of "work." Then for allowing me to lock myself in a room for months on end, removing any doubt at all that it is indeed work, and very hard work at that.

PICTURE CREDITS

All photography by Addie Chinn apart from: Pages 8–9 prospective56/istock; pages 85–88 courtesy of WhistlePig Whiskey; page 95 Glenn van der Knijff/Getty Images; page 98a Steven Greaves/ Getty Images; page 98b Education Images/Universal Images Group /Getty Images; pages 100–101 M Swiet Productions/Getty Images; pages 119 & 121 courtesy of Heaven Hill; pages 132–133 Matthew Hastings; page 149 Daniel Dempster Photography/Alamy Stock Photo; page 190 Tabitha Booth for Old Forester; page 193 Davel5957/Getty Images; page 194a Andrew Hyslop for Old Forester; page 212 Renato Pessanha/ Getty Images; pages 218–219 Tony Sweet/Getty Images; pages 228–229 Matthew Hastings; page 250r Matthew Hastings; page 267 HawaiiBlue/Getty Images; pages 302 & 306 courtesy of Rossville Union; page 307 Drew Angerer/Getty Images; page 318 Corbis via Getty Images; page 322l Chicago History Museum/Getty Images; page 322r courtesy FEW Spirits; pages 376–377 Kris Turner for Glyph; Endpapers THEPALMER/Getty Images.